STUBBORN HOPE

'STUBBORN HOPE,

Religion, Politics, and Revolution
in Central America

PHILLIP BERRYMAN

ORBIS BOOKS

Maryknoll, New York 10545

THE NEW PRESS

New York

Published jointly by The New Press, 450 West 41st St., New York, NY 10036 and Orbis Books, Maryknoll, NY 10545

The Catholic Foreign Mission Society of America (Maryknoll) recruits and trains people for overseas missionary service. Through Orbis Books, Maryknoll aims to foster the international dialogue that is essential to mission. The books published, however, reflect the opinions of their authors and are not meant to represent the official position of the society.

Established in 1990 as a major alternative to the large, commercial publishing houses, The New Press is the first full-scale nonprofit American book publisher outside of the university presses. The Press is operated editorially in the public interest, rather than for private gain; it is committed to publishing in innovative ways works of educational, cultural, and community value that, despite their intellectual merits, might not normally be "commercially" viable. The New Press's editorial offices are located at the City University of New York.

Printed in the United States of America

94 95 96 97   9 8 7 6 5 4 3 2 1

Library of Congress Cataloging-in-Publication Data

Berryman, Phillip.
   Stubborn hope : religion, politics, and revolution in Central
America / Phillip Berryman.
      p.   cm.
   Includes bibliographical references and index.
   ISBN 0-88344-962-5
   1. Christians—Central America—Political activity.   2. Church and
social problems—Central America—History—20th century.   3. Central
America—Politics and government—1979-   4. Social conflict—Central
America—History—20th century.   I. Title.
BR620.B48   1994
277.28′0828—dc20   94-2253

The New Press/ISBN 1-56584-136-0

Orbis/ISBN 0-88344-962-5

CONTENTS

ABBREVIATIONS AND ACRONYMS

ANDES	National Association of Educators of El Salvador
ANEP	National Association of Private Enterprise
ARENA	National Republican Alliance
BPR	Revolutionary People's Bloc
CACIF	Coordinating Committee of Associations of Agriculture, Trade, Industry, and Finance
CACM	Central American Common Market
CBN	Christian Broadcasting Network
CELAM	Latin American Bishops Conference
CELEP	Latin American Evangelical Center for Pastoral Studies
CEPA	Center for Rural Education and Development
CEPAD	Evangelical Committee for Aid and Development
CERJ	Council of Ethnic Communities Runujel Junam ["We are all equal"]
CIA	Central Intelligence Agency
CIEDEG	Conference of Evangelical Churches of Guatemala
CIEETS	Interchurch Center for Theological Study
CISPES	Committee in Solidarity with the People of El Salvador
CNP	National Pastoral Center
CNR	National Coordinating Committee for Repopulation
CONAMUS	National Coordination of Salvadoran Women
CONAVIGUA	National Coordinating Committee of Guatemalan Widows
CONFER	Conference of Religious
CONFREGUA	Conference of Religious of Guatemala
COPEN	Committee of Evangelical Pastors of Nicaragua
COPROSA	Archdiocesan Commission for Social Development
CPR	Communities of Population in Resistance
CRIPDES	Christian Committee for the Displaced of El Salvador
CRISPAZ	Christians for Peace
CUC	Committee for Peasant Unity
CUSG	Guatemalan Confederation of Labor Unity
DEA	Drug Enforcement Agency
ECA	*Estudios Centroamericanos*

EGP	Poor People's Guerrilla Army
ERP	Revolutionary People's Army
FAR	Rebel Armed Forces
FARN	Armed Forces of National Resistance
FDCR	Democratic Front Against Repression
FDN	Nicaraguan Democratic Front
FDR	Revolutionary Democratic Front
FECCAS	Federation of Christian Peasants of El Salvador
FENASTRAS	National Federation of Salvadoran Workers
FMLN	Farabundo Martí National Liberation Front
FPL	Popular Liberation Forces
FSLN	Sandinista National Liberation Front
FUNDAPI	Foundation for Aid to the Indian People
GAM	Mutual Support Group
IDHUCA	Human Rights Institute of the UCA
IFCO	Intercommunity Foundation for Community Organization
IHCA	Central American Historical Institute
IMF	International Monetary Fund
IRD	Institute for Religion and Democracy
MLN	National Liberation Movement
MNR	National Revolutionary Movement
MPTL	Movement for Bread, Work, and Land
NISGUA	Network in Solidarity with the People of Guatemala
OAS	Organization of American States
ORDEN	Democratic Nationalist Organization
ORPA	Revolutionary People in Arms Organization
PBI	Peace Brigades International
PCN	Party of National Conciliation
PCS	Salvadoran Communist Party
PRI	Institutional Revolutionary Party
PRODEMCA	Friends of the Democratic Center in Central America
PT	Workers Party
RN	National Resistance
SERPAJ	Peace and Justice Service
SINE	Integral System for Evangelization
SIU	Special Investigative Unit
UASP	Union of Labor and Popular Action
UCA	Central American University
UNHCR	United Nations High Commission on Refugees
UNO	National Opposition Union
UNSITRAGUA	Labor Unity of Workers of Guatemala
UNTS	National Union of Salvadoran Labor
UPD	Democratic Popular Unity
URNG	Guatemalan National Revolutionary Unity
WOLA	Washington Office on Latin America

STUBBORN HOPE

INTRODUCTION

San Salvador, 1:00 A.M., November 16, 1989. About thirty uniformed troops of the Salvadoran armed forces approach one entrance of the UCA (Central American University) run by the Jesuits. This is a military action in response to a guerrilla offensive now in its fourth day—although the guerrillas entered the poor barrios on the north of town, not here in this middle-class area on the south.

Breaking open the gate the troops come to a Jesuit residence and begin banging on the doors and windows in the back. One group goes into the Pastoral Center and starts to burn documents. When Father Segundo Montes finally comes down and opens the door, a soldier nicknamed "Satanás" ("Satan") pulls him into the garden. One by one Fathers Ignacio Ellacuría, Ignacio Martín-Baró, Juan Ramón Moreno, and Amando López are ushered at gunpoint into the garden; all but Martín-Baró are wearing pajamas. Originally from Spain, all have spent decades in El Salvador and Central America. As they are ordered to lie face down, Martín-Baró shouts, "This is an injustice! This is an abomination!"

Two nights before the commander of this operation, Lt. Jose Espinoza Guerra, was here directing a search of the premises. Now he says to Satanás, "What are you waiting for?" Satanás then turns to another soldier. "Fast, fast; do it fast!" With an AK-47 and an M-16 the two shoot the priests in their heads and bodies as they lie on the ground. Elsewhere on the premises a sergeant shoots Julia Elba Ramos, the cook, and Celina Ramos, her daughter, who have taken refuge in the house thinking that during the offensive it will be safer than their own. They are still alive, clutching each other, when another soldier comes by to finish them off. Father Joaquín López y López, a seventy-year-old Salvadoran Jesuit, appears in a hallway and is shot down as he pleads for his life. Before leaving, the soldiers stage a fake firefight and paint a message, "The FMLN Executed the Opposition Spies. Victory or Death. FMLN."

After the operation, Lt. Espinoza, who attended the Externado San Jose, a Jesuit high school where Segundo Montes had taught, expresses misgivings to his superior, Col. Alfredo Benavides, who ordered the operation. "Be calm, don't worry," says Benavides. "You have my support. Trust me." The night before, during a long meeting to discuss how to respond to the guerrilla offensive, military commanders had decided to increase the use of air power and artillery in the capital and to kill leftist leaders. At the

1

conclusion of their meeting the officers prayed holding hands. Virtually everyone involved in what the military might regard as opposition — union leaders, left politicians, human rights activists, and many church and humanitarian aid workers — were in hiding, but these Jesuits, who had suffered threats and bomb attacks for over ten years, decided they did not need to seek cover.

Soon the efforts of the military — and for a time the U.S. embassy — to blame the killings on the FMLN (Farabundo Martí National Liberation Front) guerrillas unravel as eyewitnesses to the operation come forward and information seeps out from within the military ranks. The murders become a major problem for U.S. policymakers: How can they justify helping a military that has received almost a billion dollars in aid and ten years of U.S. tutelage and yet is capable of murdering respected priests and professors?

In a sense, this book is an effort to explain what those killings were about. Catholic and Protestant church people and institutions have been major actors in recent conflicts in Central America. In addition to these Jesuits, approximately two dozen other priests have been murdered in Guatemala and El Salvador, along with several sisters, most notably the four U.S. church women who were raped and murdered in El Salvador in December 1980. In Nicaragua priests served in the Sandinista government, while Archbishop Obando was the leading opposition figure. In 1982–83, as Guatemala's "born-again" president Efraín Rios Montt was presiding over a brutal counterinsurgency campaign, journalists wrote of a "religious war" between conservative evangelicals and Catholics who took inspiration from liberation theology. In the United States church people were a major force in the broad movement of opposition to the Reagan administration's Central America policy, while televangelists raised funds to aid the U.S.-sponsored contras against the "godless" Sandinistas.

This book deals with events and issues starting with a unique moment, the overthrow of the Somoza dictatorship in July 1979, which seemed to promise the possibility of a new kind of society not only in Nicaragua but in El Salvador and possibly Guatemala as well.

There are two parts to the book. After an introductory discussion (Chapter One), the public story of church involvement in revolution and counterrevolution in Nicaragua, El Salvador, and Guatemala is presented (Chapters Two–Four). The focus then shifts to the remarkable growth of evangelical churches in recent years (Chapter Five), various forms of solidarity with the poor (Chapter Six), and clashing understandings of Christian faith (Chapter Seven). Finally I attempt to assess the significance of this experience for Central Americans and ourselves (Chapter Eight).

One day in Guatemala during that brief season when revolutionary change seemed on the horizon I had a kind of flash: When the change comes here an Indian—maybe an Indian woman—will sit on the junta. What made the intuition radical was the fact that in this half-Indian nation no Indians hold positions of power in the government, the army, the courts—or in business. An Indian woman in a high government position would indeed be a "world turned upside down." I had felt the terror of Brazil and Chile under military rule; I had known labor and church leaders murdered and "disappeared" in Guatemala; I had seen infants die of dysentery because public health measures were not a priority; I had known a generation of priests, sisters, pastors, and lay people who had struggled for change. Now suddenly it just might be happening.

At that point many people of religious faith wagered their lives on a dream for a qualitatively different kind of society. This book tells what happened to them and to that dream. Much of what is important and deepest in religion is of course beyond the scope of this work. I have in mind that sense of ultimacy, the deep personal relationship of the believer to the ultimate, the mystical sense of wonder and awe that even nonmystics occasionally experience, the sense of groundedness and purpose that words can express only haltingly and indirectly. Much of what is said here may be quite secondary to religion in that sense. Yet to the extent people have been willing to die for a faith-based vision of a more just society, their struggles are not really foreign to what is deepest in religion.

A word of explanation and some acknowledgments and expressions of gratitude are in order. André Schiffrin and Wendy Wolf, then at Pantheon Books, first accepted my proposal for a book of this nature in late 1988. In 1989 and 1990 I carried out the immediate research in Central America, and then wrote the basic text in the fall of 1990 as a fellow at the Helen Kellogg Institute for International Studies at the University of Notre Dame. Pantheon honored our contract after the change in management in early 1990, but the extremely long delays after I submitted the manuscript in February 1991 indicated that the new staff was not really interested in publishing it. Finally in mid-1993 Pantheon Books released me from our contract, and The New Press and Orbis Books agreed to co-publish it. Although the book reflects that pivotal period when peace processes were beginning to take hold, I have taken into account more recent events in the editing and rewriting process.

Among the many who helped during the research phase are Ken and Rhoda Mahler, Gene Palumbo, and Tom Quigley. I wish to thank the staff at the Kellogg Institute and others at the University of Notre Dame for providing a pleasant and supportive environment while I was writing. The following have read the manuscript or portions of it and offered helpful corrections and advice: Bruce Calder, Michael Fleet, Dan Levine, Eleanor and Bob Ledogar, John McFadden, Dennis Smith, and David Stoll.

CHAPTER 1

WAGER OF FAITH

"Opico, Quetzaltepeque, Ciudad Arce, Chalatenango, Dulce Nombre de María, La Palma, Cojutepeque, Ciudad Delgado . . . " Monsignor Ricardo Urioste was reading off a list of towns in rural El Salvador that I had handed him. "In all of them the pastor tried to make the gospel and Catholic teaching alive," he said. As the Latin American bishops had taught at Puebla (1979), the aim of the gospel is that human beings forge history. Urioste then mentioned sisters and priests who had worked in these regions: Some were exiled, some dead, some still working in El Salvador. Prior to the Jesuit murders, ten priests and Archbishop Oscar Romero had been murdered. Sensitized by the gospel, they had fully committed themselves. "Around here the sin that is still not forgiven"—we were talking in mid-1990—"is to have approached this man and this woman and said, 'You are God's children, you are citizens, you have rights, you can get organized. God's word invites you to do so.' " Those who refused to forgive this "sin" were implicitly the Salvadoran oligarchy and military.

Urioste's words get at the heart of how a generation of church people have entered the conflictive history of Central America. They have wagered their lives for an ideal of both faith in God and justice for all human beings. Understanding the complex series of events in each country from 1979 to the present requires some prior consideration of the nature of religion in Central America and the experience of church renewal as the regional crisis unfolded.

A Church Both Strong and Weak

The nature of religion and religious practice in Central America is rooted in the historic role of Catholicism. To what extent did the Spanish and Portuguese bring the Christian faith to Latin America and to what extent did they provide a religious legitimation for a colonial enterprise? To what extent did the people really accept the version of Christianity brought and to what extent did they adapt its externals while continuing to practice their native religions under the new guise?

In fact the religion brought from Spain was not simply the reformed Catholicism emerging from the Council of Trent (1545–63) as the Catholic church tightened its discipline in response to the critique of the Protestant Reformation. Spanish popular Catholicism—the rich medieval cosmos of saints, angels and demons—came as well. Colonial Catholicism accordingly had two poles: official Catholicism, centered on sacramental practice, particularly Sunday Mass and frequent confession and a clear-cut set of ethical demands, and popular Catholicism, focused more on intercession of the Virgin Mary and the saints. In principle, the violation of the norms of official Catholicism, such as missing Sunday Mass, was a mortal sin, and those who died in the state of sin were punished in hell. Only a relatively small percentage of people truly internalized and practiced this form of religion. From the standpoint of the church's official representatives, the ordinary people were "ignorant" of their faith and inclined to superstitious practices.

Another way to view the matter, however, is to recognize that the rich religious life of ordinary people, especially the Indians, had another center of gravity: It was not centered around the sacramental practice of the official church but around a series of prayers, devotions, and beliefs, especially the intercession of many saints and the Virgin Mary; the object of prayer was not so much the fate of one's soul in eternity but more immediate needs such as health or a good crop. The priests and those more assiduous in the sacramental practice of the official church viewed popular belief and practice as at best a deficient form of true Catholicism. This attitude was even accentuated in the years immediately after Vatican Council II (1962–65), when increasingly secularized priests and sisters felt uncomfortable with popular Catholicism.

In recent years, theologians and pastoral workers have taken a more positive or benign view of popular Catholicism, and now regard it as a genuine expression of popular culture and indeed as a valid form of Catholicism. The Brazilian theologian, Leonardo Boff, rather than defend traditional Catholicism against Protestant accusations that Catholicism is a "syncretism" of Christianity and pre-Columbian beliefs and practices, has argued enthusiastically that Roman Catholicism is inherently "syncretist."

During the public conflict in Nicaragua between priests and others committed to the Sandinista revolution and those church forces aligned around Cardinal Miguel Obando y Bravo, many Nicaraguan Catholics were not vehemently committed to either side. Their faith had been transmitted primarily through family and culture, not through bishops and priests.

It was by no means easy for official representatives to enter into dialogue with popular Catholicism. For example, thousands of people in Managua participate each year in the ten-day celebration of the feast of Santo Domingo. The celebration commemorates the finding of the dark statue to which miraculous powers are attributed. On one occasion a Dominican priest was seeking to explain something of the real St. Dominic, the thirteenth-century saint and founder of his own order. A man who had been drinking spoke up. "Excuse me, Father, but Santo Domingo came from right here in the hills of Managua. He's one of ours—they found him in a tree trunk." To the priest a saint is a person whose heroic virtue has been recognized by the church; to the man who objected the "saint" meant the revered image present here and now that drew thousands of people like him out to celebrate.

Likewise the conventional notion of the institutional power of the Catholic church also needs to be qualified by some observations on the history of church-state relations and their consequences. The many colonial churches still standing attest to the institutional strength of the Catholic church from the seventeenth to the early nineteenth centuries. The strongest institutions, however, were the religious orders—Franciscans, Dominicans, Jesuits, Mercedarians, and others—which remained rooted in Spain. Little was done to develop a national clergy.

Some of the clergy participated in the movement for independence (1810–23) but many of the bishops were on the side of the crown and were obliged to leave. In Guatemala, for example, the archbishop was expelled and the new government, dominated by anticlerical liberals, passed a series of laws to limit church power. A conservative reaction in the late 1830s led to the dictatorship of Rafael Carrera, during which the church regained some of its power. In the 1880s the liberals again took power with the dictator Justo Rufino Barrios, who as part of an effort at modernization again passed anticlerical laws.

The upshot was that in Guatemala the church was institutionally weakened for decades. In 1940, for example, there was only one priest for every thirty thousand inhabitants. (By comparison, in the United States the ratio has been around one priest for every one thousand Catholics.) Moreover, most priests were in cities and large towns: In the heavily Indian department of Huehuetenango there were two priests for 176,000 people. Historian Bruce Calder notes that the very conservatives who were allied politically with the church did not allow their sons to become diocesan priests, whom they regarded as poor and ignorant. Those few who might become priests entered religious orders, went to Europe, and generally did not return to Guatemala. From Independence until 1944 new foreign clergy could not enter Guatemala. For a time in the nineteenth century there was no seminary. By the 1940s the church was a shell of its former self: Neither the upper classes who were its primary clientele, nor the masses with whom it had only sporadic contact could do much for the Catholic church as an institution. In El Salvador and Nicaragua independence and subsequent political conflicts had a similar effect.

In the past decade Protestants have come of age in Central America, a fact well symbolized in January 1991 when Jorge Serrano Elías became first elected Protestant head of state in Central America. Although the most rapid expansion has taken place since the 1960s, today's Protestants can trace their roots back over a century. In the mid-nineteenth century the Moravian church was established on Nicaragua's Atlantic coast, while that area was still under British domination. In response to an invitation from President Barrios, Presbyterian missionaries arrived in Guatemala in 1882. Although occasional bible salesmen passed through the region, the first wave of missions dates from the early years of the twentieth century with the arrival of the interdenominational Central American Mission (with strong ties to Dallas Theological Seminary), the Nazarenes, Baptists, and others. They brought a Protestantism that stood in conscious conservative reaction to theological liberalism, which was then influential in Europe and North America. As fundamentalists they believed in the inerrancy of the Scriptures, as codified in their particular set of doctrinal propositions. Although they were opposed to the "social doctrine," some churches established hospitals and schools. They made few inroads into these countries and often encountered hostility and violence.

The second wave of missions, dating from the 1930s and typified by the Assemblies of God and the Church of God, could trace their origins to the wave of pentecostal Protestantism that began in the early years of the century in Los Angeles and elsewhere. While these churches were also fundamentalist, their concern was not so much to be enlightened by Scripture texts or preaching as to enter into intense prayer and worship. However, as late as 1960, after decades of missionary effort, Protestants were only about 2 percent or 3 percent of the population in each country and showed few signs of the expansion about to take place. In keeping with their small numbers, Protestants played no role on the public stage. The rapid growth of evangelicals began in the 1960s and 1970s, but was noticed outside Protestant circles only in the 1980s.

Crisis Rooted in History

In 1980 a Salvadoran opposition representative whom a U.S. solidarity group had invited to provide a brief update on recent events in his country began with a forty-five-minute historical exposition with emphasis on the nineteenth century. His approach typifies Central American conviction that the recent conflicts can only be understood as the outgrowth of a historical process.

With little to offer the world economy, Central America remained a backwater after Independence (1810–23) until production of coffee for export began in Costa Rica in the 1840s. In the 1870s liberal governments in Guatemala and El Salvador enacted legislation making the communal lands of Indians and of religious orders illegal in order to "free" these lands for coffee cultivation and export. The ideological justification for the action was that both religious orders and Indians were seen as obstacles to "progress"; the enlightened Liberals and their associates were thus enabled to seize land legally and accumulate the basis for oligarchical wealth. At the turn of the century, newly formed banana companies began operations in the region.

Dominating the early years of the century were the coffee growers and dictatorial governments congenial to them. In Nicaragua, the United States sent marines against the Liberal dictator José Santos Zelaya in 1909 and then occupied Nicaragua almost uninterruptedly from 1912 until 1933. When the United States attempted to impose an electoral formula in the 1920s it found itself fighting a guerrilla war with Augusto César Sandino, who made peace only after U.S. troops left. He was then murdered by Anastasio Somoza García, whom the United States had groomed and installed to head the National Guard. Thus the Somoza dictatorship was the lasting legacy of a U.S. intervention.

Plummeting coffee prices in the Great Depression led to widespread unemployment and desperation. In El Salvador an attempted uprising led by Farabundo Martí and Indian religious leaders was quickly put down. Following orders from Maximiliano Hernández Martínez, troops continued to slaughter an estimated thirty thousand peasants. Dictators ruled into the 1940s in all countries but Costa Rica. In 1944 largely civilian revolts overthrew Hernández Martínez in El Salvador and the dictator Jorge Ubico in Guatemala. A CIA-organized overthrow of the government of Jacobo Arbenz in 1954 ended Guatemala's decade of elected civilian government and attempts at reform, and the country returned to the control of the military and oligarchy.

Economically, the period from the 1940s to the 1970s was an era of modernization and growth, but of a distorted development that sowed the seeds of the crisis. The coffee elites now expanded into sugar, cotton, and beef. These all required large tracts of land, which was thus unavailable to the expanding rural population. These new products required little permanent labor. They were also an ecological time bomb, since cotton growers used increasing quantities of pesticides, and forest was felled for cattle.

The other thrust of modernization was the industrial development associated with the Central American Common Market (CACM). Into the 1950s there was little incentive to industrialize for the tiny market of consumers in each country. The formation of the CACM enabled firms to market throughout the region. The new light industries did not generate enough jobs for the thousands fleeing from the countryside to the city, and the import–substitution strategy eventually reached its limits as it had elsewhere in Latin America.

The 1960s were also the heyday of "development" efforts of all kinds, in the spirit of the Alliance for Progress. Indeed development of a sort took place: From the 1950s into the 1970s the region as a whole enjoyed a remarkable 6 percent annual growth in gross domestic product. Although schooling and health care expanded, the new wealth generated went largely to landholders and business groups. The situation of many people worsened, especially the growing numbers of the landless poor. Thus the very development model that produced growth brought little improvement to the lives of many people.

Land tensions were at the root of the 1969 war between Honduras and El Salvador—misleadingly called the "Soccer War." For decades Salvadorans had migrated to Honduras to farm. When the Honduran military government began to expel Salvadorans, the Salvadoran elites reacted. Tensions were heightened and the Salvadoran military launched an attack. Several thousand peasants were killed before the OAS (Organization of American States) could stop the fighting. One result was a weakening of the CACM since the Honduran government would not allow Salvadoran goods into the country, and they could get to Nicaragua and Costa Rica only by ferry across the Gulf of Fonseca.

Although this book deals with the three conflictive countries of the region, it may be useful to consider briefly why prerevolutionary conditions did not develop in Costa Rica and Honduras, which have a great deal in common with their neighbors in their histories and the nature of their economies. In Costa Rica coffee cultivation was not monopolized by a single large class but was spread more evenly than was the case in Guatemala and El Salvador, thus allowing small and medium producers to share the bonanza. Moreover, after the 1948 civil war, the country not only abolished its army, replacing it with a police force, but the government committed itself to a series of welfare state policies, and to playing an active role in maintaining employment. Over the years most Costa Ricans have felt that their economic and political system works reasonably well—especially in comparison with what they observe in other countries. Even during the 1980s when their welfare state model was in crisis and the society became more polarized, conflicts generally remained nonviolent.

Economic indicators consistently place Honduras at the bottom of Central America in production, per capita output, and so forth. Nevertheless, Honduran underdevelopment may paradoxically explain the relative lack of violent conflict. The country did not become a major coffee exporter, and the banana companies ran self-enclosed enclaves on the northern coast that had little direct impact on people in the traditional center of the country. Consequently, there was no real Honduran agroexport oligarchy until the mid-twentieth century. Moreover, large amounts of undeveloped land offered a partial escape valve for at least some peasants. Finally, although the Honduran military committed isolated acts of violence, their violence did not reach the level of systematic killing that became the rule in Guatemala, El Salvador, and Somoza-ruled Nicaragua.

Pastoral Work as Liberation

In mid-1990 as Juanita, a scrawny peasant woman catechist in Ciudad Segundo Montes, a refugee resettlement area named after one of the murdered Jesuits, described her church work over a period of twenty years, I was struck by the fact that she spoke of "Medellín," referring to the meeting of Latin American bishops in that city in 1968. Normally one would not expect peasants to be aware of bishops' meetings, let alone regard them as important for their lives.

The Medellín conference, held at the highwater mark of the 1960s, expressed the concerns and criticisms of a new generation of priests and sisters on the front lines of the church's pastoral work, who had begun to look more critically at the situation of the church, largely as a result of the new spirit of openness deriving from the worldwide meeting of bishops at Vatican II (1962–65).

Shortly before the Medellín meeting the theologian Gustavo Gutiérrez, addressing a group of priests in the seaport town of Chimbote, Peru, outlined a "theology of liberation." Gutiérrez and other theologians were raising new questions prompted by their pastoral experience: What does Christian love mean in a class society? How should the mission of the church be defined? What does Jesus' saying "Blessed are the poor" mean today?

For centuries, "God's will" had seemed to be that the world remain as it is; now suddenly, "God's will" was reinterpreted to mean that people should work together in community and solidarity for a more just world. More than a set of theological ideas to be debated and refined, this new approach to theology provided the rationale for a new generation of pastoral workers. Thus, more than twenty years later "Medellín" was a meaningful term for "Juanita" not so much for the text—which she may or may not have read—but for this new kind of pastoral initiative by the Catholic church.

To give some sense of how this worked in practice, I would like to refer to the work of a pastoral team operating in Guatemala during the 1970s. This team was made up of six priests, seven sisters, and five lay people working together in four parishes. This itself was a departure from the traditional single priest circuit riding his rural parish. The area was that of Izabal, a flat well-watered valley on the way toward Guatemala's narrow opening to the Atlantic coast between Belize and Honduras.

A good deal of the evaluation of the team's experience prepared some years later is devoted to a description of Izabal, starting from its geography and especially the realities of land tenure (previous history of United Fruit, more recently its use for cattle ranching) as well as observations on the level of government services, political tendencies, and so forth. This procedure reflects the "observe-judge-act" methodology that was by then second nature to many Catholic church workers, as they sought to situate their activity within the overall situation of the people. This was a sharp departure from the notion that pastoral work is essentially a round of Masses, baptisms, and other ritual duties, varying little from one situation to another.

The team described its priority as "forming leaders who could be true agents of evangelization" and they characterized their aim as "liberating evangelization."

Through meetings in the communities themselves, and longer courses in centers set up for that purpose, the team trained hundreds of leaders. Some were "delegates of the Word," that is, lay people trained and authorized to lead worship in the absence of a priest, while others were health promoters, leaders of women's groups, or leaders of discussion circles connected to radio schools.

Ongoing Christian communities existed at the village level. Outwardly they might resemble evangelical groups that also met for Bible reading and worship. The key difference was that these groups viewed Christianity as a mission to work for the betterment of people's conditions, even if that took the form of organizing and struggle.

The author of the report described the aim of the team's pastoral work as "forming an indigenous church, with Christian communities celebrating and living their faith, committed to the liberation of their people." In order to reach that goal, the team proposed to "train leaders to stimulate the faith of these communities and guide the liberation process." This work was in turn divided into three areas: evangelization and catechesis, social commitment, and celebration of the faith. What is clearest about this formulation is that church and community work are related to one another: Faith is expressed in actions as concrete as building new houses or experimenting with new agricultural techniques or becoming involved in peasant organization; everyday life is integrated into worship services or preparation for the sacraments. The church's official ritual actions and the people's traditional piety are brought together.

In all their programs the team sought to start from the situation of the people both as individuals and community and to relate their analysis of local conditions to what was happening throughout Guatemala. In keeping with their professed aim of liberation, the team sought to avoid encouraging dependence. Growth of individuals was aimed at enabling them to become "protagonists" in the ongoing history of their country. The aim was to form a diversified and shared leadership, reversing the traditional caudillo (boss or strongman) model, which is often operative even at the village level. Coordination and ongoing evaluation were built into the process.

The team did not claim to be pastoral technicians but hoped to draw on "the wisdom of the people." Although they sought to be creative, they were willing to use existing materials, especially those developed in Honduras, where there was a longer tradition of work with rural lay Christian leaders. The people were to be part of the planning. This description is presented here as an example of what such pastoral teams sought to do. Whether the lay participants in Izabal might have a different understanding of their work is another matter.

After working for almost a decade the team could claim some modest but real success as measured in more than five hundred leaders, many with years of training, and a network of local communities, operating with only occasional contact with the parish team. However, the local landholders and military authorities came to regard them as subversives. Indeed the repression that intensified in 1980 (Chapter Four) forced most of the team and many lay leaders to flee.

Elsewhere in Guatemala others were taking similar approaches. Arriving in the 1940s and 1950s, Maryknoll priests and sisters had spread to towns throughout Huehuetenango. Besides organizing catechetics and worship, they provided health services and training as well as agricultural development projects. Belgian priests and sisters on the Pacific coast, and Sacred Heart priests from Spain in Quiché worked as teams like the group in Izabal. The dioceses of Quetzaltenango and the Verapaces were organized along similar lines. In Nicaragua, American Capuchins on the Atlantic coast and many parishes in the diocese of Estelí led the way with new pastoral approaches, especially the formation of "Christian base communities," small lay-led groups for Bible discussion, prayer, and local action. In contrast to Nicaragua and Guatemala, where about 80 percent of the clergy was foreign, in El Salvador native-born priests were prominent in renewal efforts.

Even some Catholic schools whose normal clientele was the urban middle and upper classes that could afford tuition made serious efforts at renewal. Sisters teaching at the Colegio Belga in Guatemala City organized "Operation Uspantán," a program in which students spent the summer working in catechesis and development projects in Indian villages, under the guidance of the sisters who worked there. A proof that the program led to further commitment is the fact that the school counts seven of its graduates as "martyrs" in the 1980s.

Catholic priests and sisters working with the poor in Latin America enjoy a unique situation. They are from outside the culture of the poor—by nationality, birth, and upbringing, or at least through incorporation into the clergy or a religious order—and yet they can live alongside the poor and share their lives in a way that politicians or professional people cannot. To baptize a child who is dying of an easily preventable disease is heart-wrenching; to do so repeatedly is radicalizing. It was such experiences that led those who at first worked in simple education and consciousness-raising—to encourage the simple sense of equal dignity in God's children, as Urioste put it—to become more committed and to come to the point where they were willing to wager their lives for the sake of a more just society. Throughout the process, moreover, they did not believe they were moving from the religious to the political, but rather following out the consequences inherent in their faith.

Nevertheless, some priests and sisters remained steadfastly traditional, resisting the developments ushered in by Vatican II and Medellín. The largest group of pastoral agents were neither traditionalists nor "liberationists" but were perhaps best described as "modernizers": They fully accepted the vernacular liturgy, increasing emphasis on the Bible, a less rigid understanding of morality, and new forms of spirituality and apostolic work, but they did not see commitment to struggling with the poor for a more just society as central to the Christian faith. Those for whom liberation was a primary ideal — who will be central to this book — were always a minority, albeit an important minority.

Cycles of Struggle: Guatemala, El Salvador, Nicaragua

It remains for us to outline the major events in each country that set the stage for the post-1979 conflicts. Guatemalans invariably point to the 1954 CIA-sponsored and organized overthrow of a democratically elected reform government as the key event in modern Guatemalan history. In 1944 a largely nonviolent mass movement overthrew the dictatorship of Jorge Ubico (1931–44). Presidents Juan Jose Arévalo (1945–50), and Jacobo Arbenz (1950–54) undertook programs of capitalist modernization. The United States became alarmed at the presence of some communists in the Arbenz government and even more at the land reform program, under which the government had expropriated the properties of United Fruit Company (offering to pay for the properties the sum the company had declared them to be worth for tax purposes). The Eisenhower administration began to organize a small army — a foretaste of the contras of three decades later — and to carry out covert operations, such as undermining Arbenz's support among his own army. The Catholic church cooperated in the person of Archbishop Mariano Rossell y Rossell, who wrote a pastoral letter against communism (which the CIA airdropped over Indian villages) and led massive processions with the Black Christ of Esquipulas in various parts of Guatemala — yet another striking parallel with the role of Cardinal Obando in Nicaragua in the 1980s.

The overthrow itself was simple: A small group of troops came across the Honduran border; CIA-piloted planes strafed the capital; and Arbenz's officers refused to fight. Col. Carlos Castillo Armas was flown into Guatemala City on a U.S. embassy plane. The upshot was that the military and the landholding oligarchy once more took control of the country. An estimated 250 activists were executed and others lost their jobs. Lists from CIA intelligence were used in these operations. Lands were returned to their owners.

The guerrilla movement of the 1960s was initiated by army officers indignant over the government's cooperation with the CIA in preparing the Bay of Pigs attack on Cuba. It then went through a complex history of factional strife and efforts to ignite an insurgency. The guerrillas' rural forces were defeated by a campaign in 1966–68 at the cost of several thousand civilian lives, even though they never numbered more than three hundred combatants. After Col. Carlos Arana, who had directed the counterinsurgency campaign, was elected president in late 1970, repression was directed against union leaders, students, and others identified with left opposition in Guatemala City. Throughout the 1970s political violence—death squads, torture, disappearances—was a political tool used primarily by the military itself, as well as by right-wing groups operating independently.

In 1967 three Maryknoll missionaries, Arthur and Thomas Melville and Sister Miriam Peter, were in contact with one faction of the guerrillas. While they were still preparing to become actively involved, however, they were detected and forced to leave the country. The "Melville case" put the military and oligarchy on guard against church-based "subversives" for years.

Operating mainly around the eastern town of Zacapa, the guerrillas of the 1960s had little contact with the Indians who live primarily in the western highlands and make up half or more of the population. Unlike native peoples elsewhere in Latin America (the Amazon, for example), Guatemalan Indians are not marginal to the economy; they have supplied the labor for export crops since colonial times. Nevertheless, they are scarcely represented in public life. Few Indian faces appear in daily papers, and even fewer on television. After the 1960s the Guatemalan left debated the "Indian question," that is, the relationship between class and ethnic oppression.

New guerrilla organizations emerged in the 1970s. At the core of each were surviving remnants of the 1960s guerrillas. In 1972 a small group went to the roadless area between the Quiché highlands and the colonization area of the Ixcán and spent two or three years largely learning how to survive and relate to the local peasant population. This group took the name of the EGP (Poor People's Guerrilla Army) and developed a strategy that relied heavily on "popular organizations" both for purposes of mass mobilization and as recruiting grounds. ORPA (Revolutionary People in Arms Organization) took a more narrowly military approach.

Both the EGP and ORPA successfully incorporated Indians from the highlands into their organizations. Differences in strategy between the EGP and ORPA were similar to differences between groups in El Salvador (see below). The FAR (Rebel Armed Forces) had some contacts with labor unions and operated in the sparsely populated lowlands colonization area of the Peten. One faction of the Communist party also had an armed group. Until 1979 guerrilla activities were limited to occasional propaganda actions and a few kidnappings for ransom.

The 1976 earthquake that devastated poor areas of Guatemala City and large areas in the highlands gave rise to a new cycle of activism spearheaded initially by labor unions, which formed a new united front around a conflict involving Coca-Cola workers. The unions were joined by more activist student organizations, and then in 1978 by CUC (Committee for Peasant Unity) and shantytown organizations. Popular militancy increased in response to repression. Massive demonstrations protested the murders of a labor lawyer (Mario Lopez Larrave) and two student leaders (Robin

Garcia and Efraín Leonel Caballeros) in 1977. In November of that year a group of Indian miners from Ixtahuacán near the Mexican border defied army threats and marched over three hundred kilometers to Guatemala City to dramatize their strike. They were cheered by an estimated one hundred thousand people as they entered. In September 1978 when bus fares were raised from five to ten cents (that is, a 100 percent increase in the transportation bill for families) spontaneous demonstrations broke out and the capital was paralyzed for several days.

In May 1978 the army reported that thirty-four Indians had been killed after they attacked an army garrison in the town of Panzós. Only after a couple of days did the true version begin to emerge: Over a hundred Indians had been shot down by the army and local landholders when they had assembled in front of the mayor's office to discuss a land dispute. This massacre—by no means the first in Guatemala's history—was a foretaste of what was to become routine practice in the early 1980s.

Word of the Panzos massacre reached a meeting of the newly formed Justice and Peace Committee, an unofficial group of church people, which had gathered at a Catholic girls' school. The group made a statement and was represented in the protest march that took place some days later. Church workers in the diocese of Cobán were the first to provide accurate information on the massacre, and one sister, Sor Alonso Queralt, was deported in retaliation.

Systematic repression increased with the accession of General Romeo Lucas García to the presidency in August 1978. The murders in broad daylight of two respected moderate left politicians, Alberto Fuentes Mohr and Manuel Colóm Argueta, in January and March 1979 indicated how ruthlessly the army was willing to act. In February 1979, labor unions, student organizations, and other popular organizations formed the FDCR (Democratic Front against Repression). An FDCR delegation traveled for several weeks through Europe and North America to draw attention to the wave of repression.

With some exceptions, such as a 1976 pastoral letter, the Guatemalan bishops had made few public statements about repression. Its dominant figure was Cardinal Mario Casariego, who rarely met face to face with priests and sisters doing pastoral work but breakfasted regularly with government and military figures. Unofficial groups such as the Justice and Peace Committee, and the ecumenical magazine *Diálogo* sought to raise a voice in defense of the victims.

The guerrilla groups began to act more audaciously. On the morning of January 20, 1979, the EGP occupied Nebaj, a town in the heart of Quiché. Enrique Brol, a coffee grower, was killed trying to resist. During the next several months the EGP carried out numerous similar propaganda actions in Quiché. ORPA was also carrying out actions, largely on the Pacific coastal plain. The increasing tempo of attacks was no doubt fueled by news from neighboring countries.

The origins of the present cycle of struggle in El Salvador and of church involvement in it can be traced back to the aftermath of the 1969 war with Honduras. Since the end of the Hernández Martínez dictatorship (1931–1944), the country had been ruled by a succession of military officers who inevitably won elections. These governments oversaw some modernization of the economy and of the political system, which permitted, for example, the emergence of the Christian Democrat party, whose leader, Jose Napoleon Duarte, had served three terms as mayor of San Salvador (1964–70).

In the 1972 election the Christian Democrats formed a coalition around the presidential candidacy of Duarte, but they were thwarted by a fraudulent vote count. One faction of the armed forces rose up to demand that the true results be respected but was defeated. Many concluded that elections could not be the vehicle for meaningful change. During the 1960s, as USAID, the Peace Corps, Christian Democrat-related organizations, and others were encouraging reformist development projects in the countryside, the armed forces—also with U.S. aid—were setting up ORDEN (Democratic Nationalist Organization), a village-level paramilitary network.

It was in this context that new left organizations emerged. The Salvadoran Communist Party (PCS), which had led a largely underground existence from 1930, faithfully followed Moscow's orientation and rejected guerrilla struggle in favor of legal activity within unions and a small political party. Impatient with this line, Salvador Cayetano Carpio, a longtime PCS militant, broke with the party to form what was to become the FPL (Popular Liberation Forces) around 1970. At about the same time, a group of more middle-class young people, many of them disillusioned Christian Democrats, formed what became the ERP (Revolutionary People's Army).

Both of these groups were going against the current in Latin America, since guerrilla struggle was on the wane following the 1967 defeat of Ernesto "Che" Guevara in Bolivia. In their early stages these organizations remained shadowy, and were known primarily for a small number of kidnappings. The FPL in particular emphasized political work in the countryside, while the ERP was more militaristic. Internal ERP conflicts came to the fore in 1975 when its best-known member, the poet Roque Dalton, was "executed"; that action led to a breakaway group that took the name RN (National Resistance).

The first stirrings of new movements in the Catholic church were observable around this time. During his long tenure (1939–77), Archbishop Luís Chávez y González devoted particular attention to the formation of a Salvadoran clergy, establishing a seminary and sending promising young priests to study in Europe. Consequently a number of Salvadoran priests were ready to undertake the new kind of pastoral work sketched out at the Medellín conference. Because of his base community work in Suchitoto, Father "Chencho" (Jose Inocencio) Alas was kidnapped in early 1970; it was probably only due to Chávez's vigorous protests and the spontaneous response of peasants who lit candles in churches that his life was spared.

His captors left him drugged in his underwear on a mountaintop.

It was at this time that the UCA began to take a public role. Like other Catholic universities, the UCA had been established in 1966 as an alternative to the national university, which middle- and upper-class Salvadorans saw as too leftist and academically deficient. Around 1969 a group of faculty led by Father Ignacio Ellacuría began to raise questions about the role of the university. They concluded that in a country like El Salvador, a university should not simply train young professionals, but rather should be a center of scholarship and criticism aimed at helping the poor majority achieve justice. An early product of their work was a book detailing the events of 1972, including an analysis of the failed rebellion within the military.

After the mid-1970s village-level organizing efforts became nationally linked. For example, the impending displacement of peasants by the Cerron Grande dam project spurred efforts to form a national front of popular organizations. Repression only seemed to increase people's determination.

In November 1974 members of a Christian base community in San Vicente seized some unused land with hopes of planting crops on it. When government forces attacked, six people were killed and others "disappeared." In July 1975 a demonstration of university students protesting another mass killing in the countryside was attacked, leaving at least twenty dead. A group of priests and sisters in a closed retreat on the outskirts of the capital hurried back to town and opened the cathedral for mourners and protesters. During the week-long cathedral occupation, various factions of the left engaged in heated discussion but did not overcome their rivalries. Out of that occupation emerged the BPR(Revolutionary People's Bloc), which for several years was the largest coalition of popular organizations.

A timid agrarian reform law proposed by the government in 1975 was rejected by the oligarchy as communist and by most of the left as a U.S.-sponsored ploy to undercut growing militancy. The UCA, led by Ellacuría, while admitting its flaws, supported the law as a step toward the kind of change needed. The military caved in to the private sector in 1976, and General Humberto Romero, the officer around whom the oligarchy had rallied, became the official candidate for president, running against a reform coalition whose presidential candidate was a retired army officer.

The campaign took place in an atmosphere of increasing polarization. In a confrontation with militant peasants of FECCAS (Federation of Christian Peasants of El Salvador), Eduardo Orellana, a landholder, was killed. Although how he died remained unclear—he may have been shot accidentally by his brother—the upper classes made Orellana a martyr. FECCAS became proof that church people were involved in subversion. Several priests were arrested, beaten, or expelled from the country.

Feeling unequal to the challenge, Archbishop Chávez resigned and was replaced by Bishop Oscar Romero in a hasty ceremony on February 22. At that moment the opposition was holding a vigil in a public plaza to protest the fraudulent voting results from the February 20 election. Early on the morning of February 28 troops attacked, again killing dozens. The next morning Romero suspended his first clergy meeting, suggesting that all the priests return home and be ready to shelter those needing protection.

On March 12, Rutilio Grande, a Jesuit and pastor of the parish in Aguilares, north of San Salvador, was shot to death along with an old man and a young boy as he was driving to say Mass on a Saturday afternoon. In May the military made a sweep through the area of Aguilares and then entered the town, where they turned the church into their barracks. The priests were expelled and not replaced. Alfonso Navarro, a young priest in the capital, was also murdered. In June, the White Warriors Union, perhaps the first public death squad, threatened to kill the Jesuits one by one unless they left El Salvador. (These events are presented—with considerable cinematic license—in the 1989 film, *Romero*.)

The guerrilla organizations were also committing acts of violence, in particular the kidnapping and murder of Roberto Poma, the head of the Salvadoran tourist agency, and Mauricio Borgonovo, the foreign minister. Indeed, the killing of the priests seems to have been intended as an "eye for eye" response to these killings, although neither of them were members of guerrilla organizations.

The archdiocesan print shop was bombed as were UCA offices. Flyers with the words, "Be a patriot! Kill a Priest!" circulated.

In the eyes of the military and the landholders church people, and especially Jesuits, were largely to blame for the growing militancy of what they spoke of as peasant "hordes." The germ of truth in this accusation was that there was in fact a network of priests, primarily Salvadorans, who met informally to share information and pastoral experiences. Unlike priest groups that had sprung up in several Latin American countries in the late 1960s, this group did not issue manifestos and did not even have a name, although it was sometimes called *la Nacional* or the "Thirty."

As is generally the case, women did much of the day-to-day pastoral work of the church, but their story was less well known. After the expulsion of priests from Aguilares, for example, two sisters continued to coordinate pastoral work there. In the capital Sister Silvia Arriola, who began as a traditional teaching sister, gradually became involved in barrio work. She wished to live in a poor neighborhood while still remaining in her religious community, but eventually she had to leave the congregation. She and other sisters formed a new community, renewing their vows in the presence of Archbishop Romero and members of a base community. By the end of the decade Silvia Arriola was working closely with left and guerrilla organizations.

From 1977 to 1979 the level of confrontation continued to increase. During Holy Week of 1978 conflict broke out between the leftist FECCAS and the paramilitary ORDEN in San Pedro Perulapán. The government and the Salvadoran press blamed FECCAS, but investigation by church people showed that all those killed were members of FECCAS and that about sixty-eight people had "disappeared." It was at this time that church documentation of human rights began. In the countryside peasants were continually being arrested and frequently "disappearing."

Popular organizations were spreading in San Salvador, especially among students and workers. Despite labor legislation that made most union activities illegal, strikes and more militant actions increased. To the end of his life Archbishop Romero defended the legitimacy of the mass organizations, while also criticizing their excesses and occasional violence. These groups organized marches, and frequently occupied churches, embassies, and other buildings. On May 8, 1979, a large number of reporters and camera crews were on hand as government troops opened fire on a demonstration as it was reaching the cathedral, killing at least twenty-five. Later that month a similar slaughter took place outside the Venezuelan embassy. Several more priests were murdered: Ernesto Barrera (November 1978), Octavio Ortiz, who was killed along with four youths at a retreat center (January 1979), Rafael Palacios (June 1979), and Alirio Macías (August 1979). Barrera was subsequently revealed to have been a member of the FPL.

The story of the overthrow of the Somoza dictatorship needs no retelling here. Rather I will highlight a few aspects that had a bearing on the ensuing ten years of attempted revolutionary transformation in Nicaragua.

In the late 1970s only the oldest among Nicaraguans could recall any form of government but rule by the Somoza family dynasty. The dictatorship affected every aspect of Nicaraguan life. Somoza was, as it were, an uninvited guest at every social gathering. Yet despite the long history of corruption and repression, most Nicaraguans accepted the regime as a fact of life. Indeed—and this is often overlooked—the regimes in El Salvador and especially Guatemala used political murder far more freely than Somoza, but not being personal dictatorships they did not provoke the same degree of international indignation.

In the decades after the murder of Sandino, groups of Nicaraguans periodically rose in opposition. Inspired by Cuba, in the early 1960s some Nicaraguans tried to initiate armed insurrection but all attempts failed. In 1969-71 there were numerous strikes and other actions, including occupation of the cathedral and the Catholic university. Church people, especially the incipient base communities in Managua, were involved in these struggles. When Somoza callously profiteered from the international aid that flowed to Nicaragua after the December 1972 earthquake, he alienated much of the business community.

The Sandinistas can trace their origins to the struggles of the early 1960s but their early history was largely one of defeats. Their first major successful public action was the kidnapping of a group of Somoza relatives and cronies in December 1974, forcing Somoza to agree to release some prisoners and pay a ransom. Archbishop Miguel Obando y Bravo served as mediator on that occasion. In response the National Guard unleashed a counterinsurgency campaign in the north whose main victims were hundreds of peasants. The Capuchin priests of the area documented a list of 350 of these, and some months later the bishops denounced the fact. In the meantime the Somoza regime was becoming a major test case for the Carter administration's human rights policy.

The gunning down in January 1978 of Pedro Joaquín Chamorro, editor of the opposition newspaper *La Prensa*, led to spontaneous demonstrations with tens of thousands of people in the streets. For the next year and a half the Somoza regime's problems increased. In August 1978 the Sandinistas boldly occupied the National Palace, holding hundreds of congressional deputies and government employees hostage until Somoza agreed to release prisoners and pay a ransom (again with the mediation of Obando). In September there were several uprisings in major towns, which Somoza could suppress only after about two weeks and at the cost of many civilian lives and the massive increase in Sandinista ranks. The U.S. embassy, the business and political elites, and the Catholic hierarchy agreed on one aim: to end the dictatorship without allowing the Sandinistas to triumph. Somoza's stubbornness frustrated that aim. By early 1979 the Carter administration had pulled back and its Nicaraguan allies had little choice but to work with the Sandinistas.

Church people and agencies were playing significant roles in the struggle. Fathers Fernando Cardenal and Miguel D'Escoto were members of "the Twelve," a group of prominent respected Nicaraguans, who had been the first to openly call for moving beyond the dictatorship and had said that the Sandinistas should be included in the resolution of the crisis. Father Gaspar García Laviana had joined the guerrillas in late 1977 and fell in combat a year later. Parishes often served as informal centers where censored news could be made known. As the likelihood of a final confrontation increased, church institutions stockpiled foods and medicines and made contingency plans. CEPAD (Evangelical Committee for Aid and Development), representing Protestant churches, began to take a position of moderate but clear opposition to the dictatorship in 1978 and it also readied for a showdown.

At the end of May 1979 the Sandinistas announced a final offensive. Within days, the Catholic bishops issued a document listing the traditional conditions for a "just insurrection," and in effect endorsed this insurrection. In major cities and towns, the people erected barricades, sheltered and aided combatants, and largely isolated the National Guard to their barracks. Most of the victims, almost all from the poor, were killed by bombing, shelling, and sometimes by outright murder. The Somoza regime became increasingly isolated diplomatically. Finally on July 17, Somoza and his closest followers flew to Florida. In negotiations the Sandinistas had agreed to share the government with others, including a remnant of the National Guard; that agreement fell apart, however, when Somoza's appointed interim president, Francisco Urcuyo, announced that he intended to serve out his term. The National Guard collapsed and the Sandinistas entered Managua triumphantly on July 19.

For twenty years—ever since Fidel Castro's similar march into Havana in 1959—Latin Americans had dreamed of revolution. After many attempts had been crushed, a revolutionary movement had taken power in tiny Nicaragua. Revolutionary hopes were high in El Salvador and Guatemala as well. Among the novel features of this new situation was the significant participation of church people in all three countries.

CHAPTER 2

NICARAGUA

Vicissitudes of Revolution

In July 1990 the Sandinistas were still struggling to come to grips with their surprise electoral defeat five months previously. When I began an interview with Father Miguel D'Escoto, who had served as foreign minister for a decade, with a general question about the church and the revolution, he shifted the question. The issue was not the revolution, he said, but the failure of the church—specifically the bishops—to oppose a war waged against Nicaragua "by the greatest power in the world," a war that had indeed been condemned by the World Court. The church was up to its ears in the blood of the people.

A few hours later, Pablo Antonio Cuadra, a respected poet and essayist, longtime staff writer and editor at *La Prensa*, and a militant lay Catholic, claimed that the Sandinistas had seized control of a popular revolution and had then imposed tyranny. When I mentioned the war he impatiently dismissed it and claimed that most Nicaraguans did not experience it. "The war wasn't here" in the central provinces, he insisted, "but off on the border." The Sandinistas had started the war, first with the Indians and then with the peasants. Reagan intervened only later and did the Sandinistas a favor by allowing them to portray themselves as David against Goliath. They should have taken advantage of Pope John Paul II's 1983 visit to have him mediate the conflict and return to democracy.

That two men who otherwise had much in common could express such diametrically opposed views says a great deal about the previous decade of conflict in Nicaragua.

In mid-1979 Nicaraguans felt relief at the end of a war that had cost perhaps thirty thousand lives and exhilaration at the possibility of building a new kind of society. The initial steps of the new government were consensus-backed measures such as the confiscation of all the Somoza properties and emergency efforts to restore basic government services. Normality returned only slowly; for weeks former guerrilla fighters were taking joyrides in the Mercedes-Benzes of Somoza and his cronies.

Even during this early "honeymoon" of less than a year the underlying tensions could be discerned; indeed they grew directly out of the anti-Somoza struggle. Had thirty thousand people died in the struggle simply to replace a family dictatorship with a smoothly functioning and honest system of electoral politics? Or was that struggle aimed at social revolution, at making fundamental structural changes in society, especially in the economy? Who had overthrown Somoza? "The people" with the Sandinistas at their head, or a diverse coalition of forces, and particularly business people and traditional political parties? Were the Sandinistas, as they claimed, the vanguard of a popular revolution, and did they have a mandate from the bulk of the population to carry out a revolution?

Even in the euphoria of the first days, the Sandinistas assumed that they would face opposition. History—from the Soviet Union to Mexico to Chile—offered numerous examples of U.S.-organized efforts to overthrow revolutionary or even nationalistic reform governments. Hence in setting up a security apparatus the Sandinistas took guidance from Cuba, which at that point had twenty years' experience in combatting counterrevolution from abroad and from within.

The churches were facing an unprecedented opportunity. The Mexican revolution had been anticlerical in its origins, while the Cuban revolution, to which this new revolution was inevitably compared, had turned against the Catholic church, which served as a refuge for those resentful of the revolution or actively conspiring against it. The Sandinistas were eager to work with the church and appointed four priests to major government positions.

On July 31 the Nicaraguan Catholic bishops issued a letter that foreshadowed many of their later characteristic themes. Written when most other Nicaraguans were still celebrating, this document seems to reflect their instinctive reactions. They pointed to "anguish and fear during this time of transition," and spoke of "serious confusion" over both ideology and the way the new state was to be organized.

At a moment when government officials were striving primarily to bring order out of the chaos left by Somoza, they were demanding respect for human rights, speedy legal processes, and freedom of expression. The church, they said, had to "remain free . . . vis-à-vis any system." In warning that "raising consciousness does not mean imposing something foreign," they no doubt expressed a fear that the Sandinistas were about to import a Cuban model of government and economy.

Ernesto Cardenal, poet and priest, and now minister of culture, chided the bishops for expressing such fears rather than the people's exhilaration. CONFER (Conference of Religious), the umbrella organization of religious orders, expressed similar sentiments.

In November the bishops produced a document so different from their initial expression of misgivings that one might wonder if it had been ghostwritten by a liberation theologian. They showed sensitivity to Sandinista terminology (referring, for example, to the revolution as the "process"), spoke positively of initial government measures, and even had good words to say about socialism. Much of the letter was a reiteration of the biblical themes centered around the poor and Jesus. For example, they stated that the revolution demanded a conversion: Some people would have to live more austerely for the sake of others.

A close reading of this widely reprinted letter reveals that its endorsement of the revolution was abundantly qualified. The bishops drew a distinction between genuine participatory socialism and a "spurious" variety which they characterized as arbitrary power that demands blind obedience and violates human rights. Even if class struggle was a reality there was no justification for deliberately stirring up class hatred. While recognizing that the Sandinista Front had earned a name in history by heading up the forces that had led to the overthrow of Somoza, they insisted that various other forces had been involved and no one should now hinder their participation. Pro-Sandinista Christians would later say the bishops had backtracked or had not really meant what they said; the bishops and their partisans saw no such contradiction.

Five hundred Protestant pastors on retreat, representing a significant proportion of the churches, also made a statement thanking God for the victory, and noted that their churches had played a "political, military, moral and spiritual" role in the struggle. Although they did not provide a lengthy theological rationale for their position, they urged people to be involved in "Christian witness and service" in efforts at "literacy, health and liberating education." They had particular recommendations for the Atlantic coast region, where Protestants were a majority in most communities. The retreat itself had been organized by CEPAD, an umbrella organization of most Protestant churches, which was already preparing to expand its development work with help from European and North American churches.

Sandinista officials liked to summarize the aims of their government under three headings: a mixed economy, political pluralism, and a non-aligned foreign policy. Their foes soon came to believe that these terms were intentionally deceitful. For proof they later pointed to the "72 Hour Document," so called because it emerged from a three-day meeting of top Sandinista leaders behind closed doors in September 1979.

The U.S. State Department, for example, later published it with the subtitle, "The Sandinista Blueprint for Constructing Communism in Nicaragua." With regard to the churches, both Catholic and Protestant, the document says that

we should strengthen relations on a diplomatic level, maintaining, generally, a careful policy which seeks to neutralize as much as possible conservative positions and to strengthen our ties with the priests sympathetic to the revolution, while at the same time we are stimulating the revolutionary sectors of the church.

The words can be read as implying a purely instrumental and manipulative approach to the church. Such an interpretation assumes that the Sandinista Front used one vocabulary for public consumption while elaborating its true agenda in secret councils and then implementing it with iron discipline. An attentive reading of the whole document suggests another, more plausible reading. Having emerged from a long and mainly clandestine struggle against the dictatorship, the Sandinistas now see themselves in a new situation. The battle to bring about revolution is not over, but rather it has shifted to economic, political, and diplomatic terrain. Their task is not only to win the support of the majority of the people but to organize and mobilize them, and in their analysis, the Sandinistas accordingly distinguish among allies, adversaries, and those who can be won over.

According to the document, the Protestant church in Nicaragua "is generally formed by North American religious sects," and hence toward it "we should adopt a restrictive policy, conduct an intelligence operation on them, and, if they are caught, arrange for their immediate expulsion." That assessment reflects a rather doctrinaire attitude common on the Latin American left. The larger Protestant churches had been in Nicaragua for decades and evangelical pastors were virtually all Nicaraguans, in contrast to Catholic priests, 80 percent of whom were foreign.

Anticipating that the honeymoon would end sooner or later, small groups of Christians began to prepare the groundwork for dealing with the ideological struggles that would inevitably affect the churches. Two already existing programs—CEPA (Center for Rural Education and Development), a center for training peasant leadership, and IHCA (Central American Historical Institute)—were joined by a new ecumenical agency, the Centro Antonio Valdivieso, named after a sixteenth-century Nicaraguan bishop who had been murdered for his defense of Indians. These think tanks took up new tasks of training leaders, holding seminars, gathering and maintaining documentation, and publishing. Heading the Centro Valdivieso was Father Uriel Molina, a Franciscan biblical scholar, who had pioneered base community pastoral work in his parish and had gotten to know major Sandinista leaders in the days of dangerous clandestine struggle.

Participants in an IHCA-organized conference held at the Jesuit university in September 1979 felt that Nicaraguan Christians were about to write a new chapter in liberation theology. In one panel Juan Hernández Pico, a Jesuit, pointed toward the great issue confronting all revolutions: "the relationship between party and masses, between vanguard and people." On the cover of the published version of the proceedings of this conference was an image the participants would come to regret: a line-drawing of a crucified Christ, head hung, arms outstretched, and behind as though arising out of him, a Che Guevara look-alike, arms upraised, one holding a rifle. Another more popularizing booklet shows a young guerrilla holding an automatic rifle and about to throw a molotov cocktail—upon closer inspection, a rosary can be seen around his neck. Similarly, when the French Protestant theologian Georges Casalis in a sermon said that he regarded Comandante Tomás Borge as the greatest example of love in Nicaragua—referring to a frequently repeated story of Borge's public action of forgiving a Guardia Nacional member who had tortured him—his hosts were made very uncomfortable at the impact of such a statement on ordinary churchgoers. Looking back on this initial euphoric period three years later, the IHCA team admitted that during this period of writings, "seminars, pamphlets, and posters," some church people, often newly arrived, became hyperrevolutionary in a fashion that was out of tune with the real situation of most Nicaraguans.

Between March and August 1980 classrooms emptied as tens of thousands of students went to the countryside and to poor neighborhoods in the Literacy Crusade, which was to be the last great expression of national unity. The bishops encouraged participation in the crusade, and more than three hundred priests, sisters, and brothers were involved, often as midlevel supervisors. CEPAD also encouraged local congregations to make their churches available for the campaign.

First Clashes

As the initial emergency period passed, questions about the basic direction of the country surfaced more clearly. Business groups feared that the Sandinistas ultimately intended to set up a Cuba-style state-run economy and one-party government instead of a Western market economy and pluralistic political party system. The government's economic plan for 1980 spoke of following the "logic of the majority": The implication was that economic policies should be evaluated on their impact rather than on a criterion of ownership. With the Somoza lands and properties already in hand, further broad nationalization was unnecessary. To the private sector the Sandinistas in effect proposed a deal: Maintain production, pay taxes, and obey labor laws, and your enterprise, no matter how large, will not be expropriated. Such an assurance did not satisfy business people and landholders, however, since the major economic institutions, such as banks and export operations, were in the hands of the state. They suspected that the Sandinistas, who spoke of moving toward a "Sandinista economy," were only biding their time until the opportune moment for expropriation.

For the Sandinistas the political problem was how to reconcile political pluralism with their own role as vanguard of a revolution that had merely begun with the overthrow of the dictatorship. Formally, the executive branch of the government was headed by a five-person junta, which included Violeta Barrios de Chamorro (the widow of Pedro Joaquín Chamorro, the editor of *La Prensa*, whose 1978 murder on the order of a

Somoza crony touched off the first massive rebellion against the dictatorship) and Alfonso Robelo (a businessman prominent in the civilian opposition to Somoza). Everyone knew, however, that ultimately all important decisions were being made by the Sandinista party. From a revolutionary standpoint, the essence of democracy (which etymologically means that power is invested in the people) was certainly not to be found in elections and assemblies, but in the organization of the poor majority.

Suspicions turned into open conflict in April 1980, when the Sandinistas announced that the State Council was to be expanded. This quasi-legislature was made up of representatives not of territories but of sectors (labor, peasants, business, and so forth). In choosing to augment the body from thirty-three to forty-seven delegates, the Sandinistas argued that they were simply responding to the rapid expansion of popular organizations. That move, however, also gave them a majority, and hence non-Sandinistas saw it as a violation of agreements made shortly before Somoza's fall. What the Sandinistas presented as a step toward greater democracy their adversaries saw as a move toward one-party control. Over this issue businessman Alfonso Robelo resigned from the junta as did Violeta de Chamorro, ostensibly for reasons of health.

When less than a month later the bishops ordered the priests in the government (Foreign Minister Miguel D'Escoto; Minister of Culture Ernesto Cardenal; director of the literacy campaign, Fernando Cardenal; and Vice-Minister of Social Welfare Edgar Parrales) to resign their posts, they were in effect breaking with the Sandinistas in lockstep with the anti-Somoza bourgeoisie. These priests—who seemed to embody the Sandinista slogan, "Between Christianity and revolution, there is no contradiction"—rejected what they saw as the bishops' political reasons and refused to step down. A year later, in mid-1981, the bishops again ordered the priests to resign. This time they offered a number of arguments, for example, that the priest cannot be a "figure of unity" if he is identified with a particular political group. The Vatican, which apparently wanted to avoid a reenactment of the Cuban revolution that had turned against the Catholic church, did not intervene but returned the matter to the bishops. The result was an interim settlement: While remaining in public office, the priests would not exercise their ministry either publicly or privately or use their priesthood to support state or party positions, and they would remain in communion with the bishops.

During this period, church people often described their position as one of "critical support," not for the Sandinista party as such but for the "revolutionary process." Thus, in March 1981 an informal group of about fifty mainly middle-class "Christians for the Revolution" issued a document that raised a number of critical issues, such as the growing bureaucratization of the government (twenty-one ministries, some in competition with each other), the need for the FSLN (Sandinista National Liberation Front) to learn from the poor, the danger of the mass organizations going into excesses, and so forth. This document was used in discussion groups and then at a conference held at the UCA, which was run by the Jesuits. Generally, however, criticism was conveyed privately.

It also became clear that many of the most active leaders and members of Christian base communities were so absorbed in working for the revolution that they had little time or energy for church activities. With clergy and sisters themselves often engaged in activities that were not directly pastoral, Catholics committed to the revolution could do little further outreach.

By mid-1980 religion had become a topic of constant public controversy. Some Christians were offended at billboards proclaiming "Sandino yesterday, Sandino today, Sandino forever!" which seemed to equate him to Christ. Similarly, Comandante Tomás Borge told a rally how archaeologists had gone looking for Sandino's supposed burial place only to find it empty: "Sandino had arisen!" It did not require subtle hermeneutics to interpret billboards proclaiming "Only one Lord!" as a response to Sandinista pretensions.

Indeed anti-Sandinista critics gravitated to religious themes. *La Prensa* endlessly argued that Marxism — materialistic, atheistic, fomenting hatred — was incompatible with Christianity. Humberto Belli wrote articles describing Marxist tactics for dividing the church and undermining belief. His sister, Giaconda Belli, a highly regarded poet, had asked whether if he came today, Christ would be writing in *La Prensa* or organizing workers and peasants. Her brother retorted that he would probably surprise everyone, even going to the jails to be with Somocistas. When a visiting Brazilian Dominican brother, Frei Betto, said that Christians should work out a synthesis between the "dialectical rationality of history and the life of faith" and be more concerned for the people as a whole than for the church, *La Prensa* editorialist Roberto Cardenal huffily replied that God had erred in sending Christ: "He should have sent Marx and Lenin." Christians who supported the revolution also wrote opinion pieces. Researchers later counted 6,500 items dealing with religion in the three daily papers during the first three and a half years of the revolution.

In issuing their "Official Statement on Religion" (October 1980) the Sandinistas sought to reply once and for all to those who accused them of trying to use religion in order to ultimately do away with it. They recalled the role played by Christians in the anti-Somoza struggle (mentioning Archbishop Miguel Obando y Bravo by name), and said that Christians had been fully involved in the revolution in an unprecedented manner; hence new possibilities were opening up in Nicaragua and elsewhere. They went on to outline their own position, stressing their commitment to freedom of religion. The Sandinistas were thus breaking with classical Marxist theory. Out of their own experience they were convinced that religion need not be a "mechanism of alienation," whatever "some writers" (presumably starting with Karl Marx) might have said. Likewise they were departing from the practice of all Marxist parties in power: Religious belief and practice were not hindrances to belonging to the Sandinista party.

Either not appreciating this novelty or choosing to disregard it, the Catholic bishops replied with a rambling statement filled with allusion and innuendo. Far from being liberated, Nicaragua had fallen into the clutches of a new pharaoh; the Sandinistas were using religion and dividing the church, especially with revolutionary Christians and priests; atheistic propaganda and "new invasions" (apparently Cuban health workers and teachers) were a danger. This exchange marked the definitive outbreak of hostilities between the hierarchy and the Sandinistas.

Traditional popular religiosity became an object of controversy. Near the town of Cuapa in Juigalpa, a peasant named Bernardo Martínez began to have visions of the Virgin Mary in 1980. Her message was rather like that given at Lourdes (France) in the nineteenth century and Fatima (Portugal) in 1917. Something of a cult grew up, although even sympathetic people did not see whatever Martínez saw. The message was a simple one of praying and loving one another; indeed, an Italian priest who knew him observed that some people were trying to have Martínez embellish his message with a more political comment. The priest said Martínez's message was in fact quite compatible with the revolution.

In late 1981 a "sweating Virgin" stirred Managua. From morning until midnight people flocked to a house where a statue seemed to be exuding liquid. *La Prensa* reported that preliminary investigation by a chemical laboratory had concluded that the liquid was indeed similar to human perspiration. Archbishop Obando visited the site. *El Nuevo Diario* claimed to expose the secret: The plaster statue was being soaked in water and then frozen; when it thawed the absorbed water slowly exuded like "perspiration."

From the outset the Sandinistas had reservations about Archbishop Miguel Obando y Bravo. He had indeed opposed Somoza from 1970 onward, and had played key roles in negotiating crises created by Sandinista hostage-taking actions in 1974 and 1978. At the moment of Somoza's fall, however, he had been in Venezuela negotiating a transitional government in which the Sandinistas would have only a partial role. In early 1980 religious ceremonies over which he presided began to look like a display of the church's power (similar to events organized by the Cuban bishops twenty years before). While lamenting the political involvement of some priests, Obando freely commented on matters such as Cuban influence in Nicaragua and the size of the Sandinista army.

In response to what they saw as his use of his office for political purposes, the Sandinistas suspended the television transmission of Obando's Sunday Mass. They were willing to allow the Mass to be televised over the state-controlled network if the celebrant, including Obando, rotated. The bishops rejected that proposal as an unacceptable limitation of the church's freedom.

Church people committed to the revolution accused the bishops of pursuing a deliberate policy of personnel transfer. By 1982 fourteen priests and twenty-two sisters had been removed from their parishes or had had their official authorization from the bishops suspended. Prorevolutionary Christians sometimes organized protest actions, such as occupations of churches, in response.

La Prensa was now calling militant Sandinistas "mobs." One such "mob" threw stones at the bishop of Juigalpa, Pablo Antonio Vega, as he was leaving a church, and a few weeks later another "mob" destroyed the windows and tires of Archbishop Obando's jeep. The so-called mobs were generally the Sandinista mass organizations, particularly the Sandinista Youth, who no doubt believed they were defending the revolution. At a time when the revolution's enemies, the Reagan administration and the incipient contras, were real but somewhat remote, defending the revolution tended to take the form of harassing business groups and church figures who were near at hand. What the Sandinistas may have seen as a "mobilizing" of the people to express their just anger, their foes saw as "mobs" and "thugs" deployed by the comandantes. Anti-Sandinista groups could also engage in mob-like behavior.

This initial polarization within Nicaragua took place during the final year of the Carter administration, which had accepted the anti-Somoza struggle albeit belatedly. With the election of Ronald Reagan to the presidency the Sandinistas assumed that they had to be prepared for a direct U.S. attack. Although the new administration initially devoted primary attention to El Salvador, where the FMLN had just formally begun its guerrilla war, its rhetoric and actions, such as suspending all aid to Nicaragua, were a foretaste of what was to come. In August 1981 U.S. Assistant Secretary for Inter-American Affairs Thomas Enders arrived in Managua to present to the Nicaraguan government what may have been an offer of accommodation with the Reagan administration but was likewise an ultimatum. His 6'8" stature drove home his words to Daniel Ortega and Miguel D'Escoto: "You can forget defending yourselves because we are one hundred times bigger than you are."

Contra Complications

Armed opposition to the revolution began shortly after Somoza's National Guard disbanded in July 1979. During the five-month literacy campaign in 1980, for example, nine young people were murdered. By mid-1980 various actors—a Honduran general, a U.S. general, CIA agents—were involved in developing a guerrilla force, and training camps were operating in Florida. By September a contra radio station was broadcasting from Honduras. Although the contra war did not become a major issue in the United States until mid-1982, Nicaraguans were aware of these activities, which only confirmed Sandinista convictions about U.S. imperialism.

While the Reagan administration's public actions were aimed more at El Salvador, the CIA was quietly working with the incipient counterrevolutionary organization.

Tensions between the Sandinistas and the Miskito Indians and other ethnic groups on the Atlantic coast were ripe for exploiting. Although this area was part of Nicaraguan territory, it had always been isolated from the Pacific coast—indeed the first dirt road from west to east was only completed in the late 1970s. Since the eighteenth century when the British had armed and anointed a Miskito "king," the people on the Atlantic coast had scarcely seen themselves as Nicaraguans. The Sandinistas were seen as one more group of "Spaniards" who could not be trusted. Sandinista officials and troops sent to the Atlantic coast naively assumed that the people of the coast should be ready to embrace their revolutionary program, and reacted when they met resistance.

In February 1981 thirty-three Miskito leaders were arrested. All were released except Steadman Fagoth, whom the government accused of plotting subversion. Four Miskitos and four Sandinista soldiers were killed shortly afterward as troops tried to make another arrest. In an effort to make peace, the government released Fagoth under the condition that he accept a scholarship abroad. Instead he joined the contra movement in Honduras, and many Miskitos followed him.

In late 1981, as U.S. and Honduran troops engaged in large-scale maneuvers, the Sandinistas detected what they saw as a plot to create disturbances (code-named "Red Christmas"). In December 1981 and January 1982 about sixty Nicaraguans were killed in cross-border attacks. Fearing an increase of attacks along the Coco River (which divides Nicaragua and Honduras), the government ordered an evacuation of all the villages in the area and sent in troops to enforce it, often destroying whole villages to prevent them from being used by the contras. Troops also arrested some local leaders and expelled three U.S. sisters and two priests. About ten thousand people accepted the transfer and resettlement but six thousand to ten thousand others fled to Honduras. Years later the Sandinistas themselves admitted this transfer was a "mistake" and that indeed their policies with the Miskitos and other peoples of the Atlantic coast were misguided. It was by no means, however, the "genocide" it was pronounced by representatives of the Reagan administration, which had just approved $19 million for covert war against Nicaragua.

The bishops' conference issued a statement, which while recognizing the right of the state to take measures for self-defense, criticized this action on human rights grounds and expressed solidarity with the Miskitos and other peoples of the Atlantic coast. Sharply rebuking the bishops for immediately making a public statement rather than using established communication channels, the junta called the bishops' statement political rather than pastoral and noted that both the contra radio and the U.S. embassy had used language very similar to that of the bishops. A former priest from the

United States who had worked on the Atlantic coast for twenty-five years commented that the bishops had been silent for many years while people suffered from Somoza on the Atlantic coast; they had said nothing while some two hundred Nicaraguans had been killed near the border since July 1980; none of the bishops had attended a Mass for Maura Clarke, one of the U.S. church women raped and murdered in El Salvador, who had spent more than ten years working on the Atlantic coast and elsewhere in Nicaragua; yet some of them had attended and preached at the funeral of Jorge Salazar, a businessman who had been killed while engaged in counterrevolutionary gun running. At the very least, the bishops seemed to be selective in their concern for human rights.

Most Miskito Indians were not Catholic but belonged to the Moravian church, which had been established by missionaries on the Atlantic coast in the nineteenth century. Moravian pastors Norman Bent and Fernando Colomer were held in prison in Managua for five days and then prohibited from returning to the coast. On a trip to Washington, Bishop John Wilson said Christians were faced with a choice: "either we stay in the revolution or out of it. As a bishop of the Moravian church, I think I should be in — to try to see what I can do for my people."

Pope John Paul II, who had maintained a prudent distance during the early period of the revolution, now stepped into this confrontation with a letter in June 1982 exhorting Nicaraguan Catholics to maintain their unity around their bishops. To that unity the pope opposed the "popular church" which, he said, saw itself in opposition to an institutional church. (This term, coined in Brazil in the mid-1970s, was not intended to refer to a separate organization, but to the new forms of expression of the church taking place in popular milieus as a result of new pastoral initiatives, particularly base communities. It could be used polemically, however, to imply that some were seeking to form their own church, whose criteria would be political and ideological.) The pope went so far as to say that "the most insidious dangers and the most deadly attacks are not those that come from without — these can only strengthen it in its mission and its work — but rather those that come from within." Although his warning was ostensibly an internal church affair, the government's interpretation was that the pope was urging Nicaraguan Catholics to rally around the bishops' ever clearer political opposition. Sandinista officials initially prohibited its publication, thereby endowing the letter with a samizdat quality. Although the letter was published in *La Prensa* in August, the controversy reinforced the feeling of some Catholics that theirs was a persecuted church.

Religious conflicts continued to break out during 1982. In August Sandinista militants occupied about thirty small churches of the Mormons, Seventh Day Adventists, and Jehovah's Witnesses, prompted by suspicions that the CIA was working through them. While some pastors may have cooperated with the contras, this action was the product of misinformation and frustration. Its main result was to alienate members of these churches, whose natural instinct was simply to shun any political involvement what-soever. CEPAD stepped in to negotiate, and the churches were returned to their congregations.

In August Father Bismarck Carballo, press spokesman for the archdio-cese, was photographed naked as he ran from a house at midday. According to the Sandinista media, he had been caught in a tryst by a jealous husband; cameras and reporters only happened to be present because they were covering a nearby demonstration. Carballo's own version was that upon arrival to lunch with a woman parishioner he had been forced to undress at gunpoint and that the whole incident was staged. The official version stretched credulity; at the very least, Carballo seems to have been entrapped, perhaps seduced. He resolutely insisted that he was entirely innocent.

The incident unleashed confrontation. *La Prensa* portrayed him as "another suffering Christ," and Catholics loyal to the bishops were bused in from the countryside to take part in a "Mass of reparation," leading to angry confrontations with Sandinista organizations. A few days later anti-Sandinista young people occupied Catholic schools. In Masaya, snipers inside a Salesian school fired upon a demonstration, killing one young San-dinista supporter and wounding others. A Salesian priest was expelled for his involvement in the incident. The government took over the school, which was returned only after negotiations with the Salesians.

While government foes believed Sandinista mobs were being sent against them, Sandinista supporters believed it was only the discipline of the San-dinista mass organizations that prevented them from venting their anger even more freely. Self-serving as this sounds, it may contain an element of truth, insofar as the religious targets were near at hand and easier to reach than the contra army in Honduras and their paymasters in the Reagan administration.

Events in San Francisco del Norte may help explain this anger. Located near a triangular piece of land jutting into Honduras, this town of eight hundred people was a logical target for the contras to make a first attempt to hold territory. On July 20, a man named Salvador Cruz, who claimed to be a Jehovah's Witness, came through the village preaching door-to-door and talking with people. He stopped to help some villagers who were dig-ging a bomb shelter. Townspeople later suspected that he had been exam-ining the town's defense arrangements, and inquiring about the location of political and army leaders. Shortly after dawn on July 24, more than a hundred contras began mortaring the town. About twenty-five young militia members—there was no regular army detachment—fired back from a hill with automatic rifles until their ammunition ran out. The contras then took the hill and slaughtered the youths, slitting their throats, cutting some of them to pieces, beating one to death, and parading another around the town, jabbing him with bayonets and ordering him to repeat their slogans. The killing of a local government representative brought the number of their victims to fifteen. Along the adobe walls of the town they put up posters proclaiming, "For God and Patriotism." As they left town they took eight young men back to their camp in Honduras. Sandinista leaders, including Daniel Ortega and Tomás Borge, visited the site and attended the funeral, along with ambassadors from several countries.

The pattern of contra activity was to attack civilians, often slaughtering them brutally, and sometimes taking away captives. Development projects were favorite targets. In the issue of their bulletin in which they took credit for the San Francisco del Norte attack, the FDN (Nicaraguan Democratic Front) praised Archbishop Obando for being "ever more identified with the struggle for the liberation of Nicaragua." In October they tortured, mutilated, and murdered a Catholic lay leader and his four sons, carving the words "With God, without Communism" on the chests of two of them. Throughout the war, the contras constantly invoked religion.

For Catholics the abduction and murder of Felipe and Mary Barreda became a symbol of contra viciousness. During the 1960s and 1970s this middle-class couple had been enthusiastic participants in church renewal programs. During the anti-Somoza struggle they had sometimes provided the Sandinistas with a "safe house" in Estelí. One of their sons was a political prisoner under Somoza. After the 1979 victory, Mary Barreda was elected to the city council in Estelí and both intensified their work on behalf of poor people.

In late 1982 they responded to a Sandinista call for volunteer coffee pickers even though they were in their early fifties and were not in robust health. On December 28 their brigade was attacked and they along with several others were captured, blindfolded, and led to the border. A witness who later escaped described how they were bleeding, covered with mud, and that Mary was kept naked. They were taken to Honduras where a contra commander code-named "Suicida" unsuccessfully tried to videotape the Barredas making some remark sympathetic to the contras that could be used for propaganda purposes. The Barredas were kicked and pistol-whipped and finally killed with shots to the head.

Such contra attacks elicited no response from the Catholic bishops. They did, however, issue a document on education, insisting on the right and duty of parents to provide a Catholic education for their children and criticizing educational reforms then underway.

John Paul II Confronted (or Insulted?)

Expectation was high from the moment it was announced that Pope John Paul II was going to visit Central America in March 1983. Study groups met, booklets were published, statements were prepared. Although the Sandinistas claimed to have spent $3 million and used two months' supply of gasoline on the visit, their miscalculations began at the airport. In what was perhaps an unscheduled action, the pope moved down the reception line greeting people, and he came face to face with Ernesto Cardenal. Dressed in his customary rough embroidered blouse, the priest and poet smiled, doffed his beret, and kneeled to kiss the pope's ring. Wagging his finger, the pope told Cardenal that he must normalize his situation. None of the other priests in the government were at the ceremony; D'Escoto, for example, had arranged to be on a diplomatic mission. President Daniel Ortega devoted much of his welcoming speech to a lengthy quote from a 1912 letter of Bishop Simeón Pereira y Castellón of Leon to Cardinal Gibbons of Baltimore condemning the U.S. occupation of Nicaragua at that time. The quote was lost on journalists who described Ortega's speech as a "harangue."

Helicoptered to Leon, the pope addressed a mainly rural group in a large open field. There he said little of relevance to the largely peasant crowd but gave a prepared speech on education, which could be taken as a challenge to the curriculum change then being implemented. Back in Managua the pope held closed-door meetings with representatives of political groups of both the government and the opposition. He then had a half-hour meeting with government officials, and was taken to the papal nunciature to meet with the bishops.

In the Plaza of the Revolution an estimated six hundred thousand to seven hundred thousand people had been waiting in temperatures near 100°. Different sympathies were evident: Some held banners praising Archbishop Romero of El Salvador, while a priest led cries of "Long live Archbishop Obando!" The Sandinista-controlled sound system played the Nicaraguan folk mass. About an hour before sundown the plaza began to cool slightly, and the pope arrived at the platform. In welcoming the pope, Obando told a story about an Italian prisoner and Pope John XXIII (1958–63) – the point seemed to be that just as meeting the pope had "freed" the prisoner, the present encounter would help liberate Nicaraguans from their Sandinista prison.

In his homily the pope made little direct reference to what was happening in Nicaragua. His harsh remarks about the popular church and "parallel magisteria" (that is, those who would claim a teaching authority in opposition to that of the official church) prompted some applause. The second half of the sermon dealt with church unity, which the pope understood to mean support for the bishops. Not far from the papal platform were fifty women dressed in black – "Mothers of Heroes and Martyrs." As the pope spoke they began to murmur and then to chant slogans that were picked up by others: "We want peace." When the pope departed from his text to say, "The first to want peace is the church," some hoped he was about to address their concerns, especially the war. A large funeral for seventeen young people killed by the contras had been held in this same plaza the previous day. However, the pope only shouted an annoyed *"Silencio!"* – almost the equivalent of "Shut up!" As the murmuring and shouting continued, he shouted back twice more. The disturbance continued even after the sermon. Government and Sandinista party officials seemed caught aback, but ended up raising clenched fists and shouting "People's Power!" along with the crowd. The petitionary prayers mentioned "those in prison" (a hint at former members of Somoza's Guard) but not contra victims. The pope left the podium still visibly annoyed. As the papal entourage departed, reporters and TV crews rushed news of the clash around the world.

The Vatican called the events a "premeditated political provocation." What the Sandinistas stood to gain from such an outcome is hard to imagine. Some pro-Sandinista commentators implied that the shouting for peace was an entirely spontaneous outcry of people who were indignant over contra attacks and were pleading for a word of consolation. At this point shouting political slogans was an integral part of Nicaraguan culture, and could easily be set in motion. It seems unlikely, however, that such chanting would begin spontaneously. Perhaps Sandinista militants hoped to elicit from the pope some sign of sympathy for the victims of violence.

While Obando claimed that of the six hundred thousand people in the plaza, five hundred thousand were devoted to the pope, a priest who had concelebrated the Mass said it was very difficult to calculate how many people were on either side. Obando commented that only those who are in communion with the bishops and the pope constitute the Catholic church. "If any group is not in this line, it is not part of the institution; it is a sect."

Perhaps he and others believed revolutionary church people were a small clique that could be isolated. Data, insofar as they exist, do not support that position. A 1982–83 survey taken of 220 priests (60 percent of the total in the country) found that 46 percent supported the revolution and 54 percent were opposed. On the basis of studies done in 1983–85, Philip Williams made the following estimates of clergy stances toward the revolution:

Direct or active collaboration	15–20%
Passive collaboration	20%
Passive opposition	40–45%
Active opposition	20%

If these estimates are to be believed, a clear majority of the clergy could be classified as in some sense anti-Sandinista, but most priests (60–65%) sought to avoid the extremes of active opposition or "critical support." The papal visit strengthened the resolve of anti-Sandinista sectors of the Catholic church, and in that sense furthered polarization rather than unity.

Responses to War

Throughout 1983 the contra war, which had begun with sporadic attacks from Honduras, increased in intensity. By May Daniel Ortega told the State

Council that five hundred Nicaraguans had lost their lives and $58 million in damage had been done during the first four months of the year. On October 18, for example, 250 or 300 contras attacked the village of Pantasma in the morning, after most of the men had gone to the fields. The contras shelled with mortars, rockets, and grenades for two hours, and then entered the village. They killed forty-six people, mainly civilians, and destroyed buildings and installations.

The Sandinistas faced three distinct armies: one operating out of Honduras, initially led primarily by former Somoza National Guardsmen; another made up of Miskito Indians on the Atlantic coast; and a third group operating out of Costa Rica, whose leading figure was the flamboyant ex-Sandinista, Eden Pastora. All three received CIA money and other assistance from the United States. Only slowly did the Sandinistas begin to distinguish the Indians, who had deep roots in their own communities, from the other groups.

While battling the contras, the Sandinistas had to face a potential war with the United States, which was building up its military capacity in Honduras, Panama, and elsewhere, and staging unending military exercises. In a major speech to Congress on April 27, 1983, President Reagan defined Nicaragua as a security threat to the United States. Although he expressly said, "We do not seek its overthrow," he also said that it should not be protected "from the anger of its own people." He had likewise asserted that El Salvador was closer to Texas than Texas to Washington, and that Central America was the "fourth border" of the United States. Liberals in the United States criticized such rhetoric as disproportionate to U.S. interests in Central America; they did not defend Nicaragua's right to self-determination.

Alarmed by the possibility of a Vietnam-style war in Central America, the governments of Mexico, Colombia, Venezuela, and Panama (the "Contadora Group," named after the Panamanian island where they had met) drew up peace proposals in the form of draft treaties to limit the size of armies and arsenals in the region and prohibit cross-border support for insurgencies. While professing support, the Reagan administration undermined such proposals. In mid-1983 the administration also assembled the bipartisan "Kissinger Commission" whose January 1984 report simultaneously spoke of development, the Marxist threat, and the need for the United States to "prevail" in Central America in order to preserve its worldwide "credibility."

Pressed by reporters about the contra war during a visit to Rome, Archbishop Obando said it was difficult to know whether the United States was supporting aggression from Honduras since "We know only what the Sandinistas say through their official media. . . . It is very hard to judge when all the information comes from one side." At this time the contra war had been daily fare in the international media for a year and had been a *Newsweek* cover story. Obando could have received information from the Christian communities of the town of Jalapa, near the border, which had written a public letter speaking of the "murder and kidnapping of delegates of the Word, teachers, technical advisors, young people, children and entire families." In June forty priests and sisters and many lay leaders from around the country had gone to Jalapa to celebrate Mass in solidarity with the people of the town.

Although the Sandinistas had been continually expanding and upgrading the army, the brunt of the contra war was initially borne by local civilian defense groups. In September 1983 the government formally proposed a draft law requiring registration by men and women and a compulsory two years of active service by males aged seventeen to twenty-five. In a public statement the bishops acknowledged the "classic concept" of a state's right to self-defense, but then distinguished it from a "revolutionary" concept that identified state, party, and people. Such an "absolute dictatorship of one political party" calls into question the "legitimacy of its institutions, including the army." Forcing citizens to become members of an army when they do not agree with the party's ideology is a violation of the human rights of free thought and free association. "Consequently, no one can be obliged to take up arms to defend a particular ideology with which he or she does not agree, nor to fulfill obligatory military service to benefit a political party." Those who took a stance of conscientious objection should not be punished. The bishops were not envisioning the situation of Catholics led to pacifism by their reading of the gospel, nor were they defending "selective conscientious objection," that is, a refusal to serve in this particular war on the basis of just war principles (such as the U.S. Catholic bishops admitted late in the Indochina war).

In response, a group of lay Catholics noted that this "open call to desertion, to massive disobedience and to rebellion" was not based on any biblical text, church document, or historical precedent. Some bishops were trying to make the church "an anti-Sandinista and anti-national party." The FSLN was "a genuine movement of national liberation that has restored the dignity and identity of the whole nation," making the state and army what they should be: instruments at the service of the people. What totalitarian state would allow even bishops to publicly call it illegitimate and call for desertion at a moment when it was in danger? they asked rhetorically.

Opposition to obligatory military service became one of the bishops' standard themes for the rest of the decade. At an October 9 procession organized by Obando, people passed out flyers that read, "I am a conscientious objector—Thou shalt not kill." Among those taking part was U.S. ambassador Anthony Quainton, bible in hand. When members of base communities showed up carrying signs critical of the procession, they were attacked.

Opposition to military service was an issue among non-Catholics as well but was handled differently. The Sandinistas were concerned that evangelical churches might be used to undermine the obligation to military service. In practice Protestant pastors were exempted from military service if they so desired. Over time the Sandinistas also came to respect the principled opposition to military service of Seventh Day Adventists. CEPAD quietly engaged in dialogue with the government in particular cases and on the principle of conscientious objection on religious grounds.

The U.S. invasion of Grenada in late October 1983 reconfirmed the sense that an invasion of Nicaragua was not only possible, but was becoming increasingly probable. A veritable war psychosis took hold of many people in Nicaragua. The leaders of the Baptist Convention in Nicaragua sent a letter noting recent attacks along the border, in ports and even at the airport. A CIA-organized attack on fuel storage tanks at Corinto had endangered the whole population of the town, including three hundred Baptists. They encouraged local congregations to be ready to allow their churches and church properties to be used as centers for refugees or medical treatment. Members should be involved in local health committees, firefighting groups, popular organizations, and the militias, and they should not be prevented from enlisting in the military in accordance with the draft laws. People should use scarce goods conscientiously and believers should be conspicuous for their discipline and efficiency.

At the end of October, when Sandinista authorities detected plans by nine priests to have youth groups occupy churches and several other buildings to protest the draft law and demand that the government dialogue with the contras, they took the matter to the papal nuncio and the bishops. Some of the accused were jailed temporarily. Mass organizations surrounded the church of Father Silvio Fonseca. A demonstration prevented Bishop Bosco Vivas from officiating at a confirmation ceremony. Confrontations between priests and popular organizations took place in some other barrios that same Sunday.

In response, the archdiocese declared November 2 (traditional "Day of the Dead," [All Souls Day], when people visit family graves at cemeteries) a day of mourning, fasting, and prayer in Managua and forbade Mass in any of the sixty parishes of the archdiocese. The Vatican newspaper, *L'Osservatore Romano*, commented that the disturbances added "another case of provocation and religious intolerance," to what had happened to the pope and the "ongoing humiliations" of Catholics, and spoke approvingly of the closing of churches.

Two Spanish priests who taught at the Salesian high school in Masaya were deported from the country for promoting resistance to the new draft law and for publishing a booklet advocating dialogue with the contras.

In December the Sandinista government announced that Bishop Salvador Schlaefer had been killed while a contra unit was kidnapping a group of Miskito Indians. To the government's embarrassment, Schlaefer showed up in Honduras, where he said he had not been kidnapped, but had freely chosen to accompany a group of Indians as they fled to Honduras from a government refugee camp.

"Reconciliation" Call Widens Gap

As defense expenditures began to consume about half the government budget, it became clear that the Sandinistas would have to scale back their original ambitious development schemes. They now began to talk of moving toward a "survival economy," although there was a considerable lag between the birth of the notion and actual steps taken. Despite their claim to be serving the majority, in practice the Sandinistas had maintained a longstanding bias toward Managua (for example, through food pricing policies that favored urban consumers at the cost of peasants who produced corn and beans). Now recognizing that the contras were making inroads in rural areas where the programs of the revolution had brought few tangible benefits, they began to pay attention to the peasants' real demands (for example, land in individual plots rather than cooperatives or other communal formulas).

The battle over legitimacy continued throughout 1984, especially in the national electoral campaign and the election itself. The Sandinistas scorned "bourgeois democracy" as a mask for elite rule, which they contrasted with the kind of popular empowerment embodied in education, health care, cooperatives, and so forth. They assumed that they could win an election against any of the traditional parties, which most Nicaraguans would view as defending business and upper-class interests. Had they implemented a winner-take-all system of representation by district, the Sandinistas would probably have gained an overwhelming majority in the assembly. They opted instead for a parliamentary proportional model that would give the opposition a presence that reflected its strength among the population. The election was thus something of a plebiscite that would serve to institutionalize the revolution and provide international legitimacy. The opposition coalition, the Coordinadora Democrática (Democratic Coordinating Body), chose as its candidate Arturo Cruz, who had served the Sandinista government as head of the central bank and as ambassador to Washington. He could thus represent those who believed that the revolution had been betrayed or lost its way. To many Nicaraguans, however, he was a distant figure who had spent most of the previous fifteen years outside the country. Even after Cruz had been nominated, the coalition refused to accept the electoral procedures.

In March the bishops made a brief statement on elections, insisting particularly that people should not be compelled to vote against their conscience. When reporters noted that the position was similar to one the bishops had made in 1974, supporting the opposition's refusal to participate in Somoza-run elections, Obando said that they had repeated the principles because, like the commandments, they did not change, no matter what the context.

On Easter Sunday the bishops issued a pastoral letter on reconciliation. Although the overall tone was rather abstract and doctrinal, at one point the bishops called for a dialogue among all Nicaraguans, "inside or outside the country, without any discrimination on the grounds of ideology, class or partisan position." They further asserted that "those Nicaraguans who have taken up arms against the government, should take part in such a dialogue. Otherwise, there is no way of settling things, and our people, especially the poorest, will continue suffering and dying."

The Ministry of the Interior had placed a prior note in the newspapers saying that publication was being permitted even though the letter contained "violations of our country's laws and positions of open confrontation with the revolution." Progovernment papers dug up and published photos of the bishops with Somoza and letters from them thanking him for favors. Christians sympathetic to the revolution criticized the media for this smear campaign, but they also challenged the bishops' position. The Dominican priests and sisters said that the bishops were ignoring that the United States was imposing the war on Nicaragua. The bishops had in fact stated that "Foreign powers are taking advantage of our situation in order to foment economic exploitation and ideological exploitation." That oblique reference may have enabled the bishops to feel that they were being evenhanded, but it was not at all satisfactory to those who were afflicted by daily attacks, and the blatant Reagan administration's championing of its "covert" war. It was quite unjust, said the Dominicans, not to mention any of the revolution's accomplishments. It was utterly false and scandalous to ask for dialogue with the "mercenaries" who were killing, robbing, kidnapping, torturing, pillaging, and raping, sometimes in the name of an alleged Christian faith. In a similar letter, the Jesuits included a compact catalogue of the revolution's faults and shortcomings. A group of religious superiors representing many orders called for greater pluralism, consultation, and dialogue within the church.

In June the Sandinistas accused Father Amado Peña, a Managua pastor, of trafficking in arms and explosives. As evidence the Sandinistas produced a video in which Peña was heard to speak at some length and in vulgar language about having people – apparently top Sandinista leaders – killed in order to spread panic. Another video showed him delivering a piece of luggage that turned out to be filled with explosives. Interior Minister Tomás Borge had called Obando and suggested that Peña seek asylum in the papal nunciature in order to avoid having him arrested. Peña himself said he had been framed and the bishops believed him. At the very least, the video was evidence of a highly organized surveillance system.

When Peña celebrated Mass on June 21, Sandinista militants surrounded his church, climbed up on the roof, burned tires, and roughed up parishioners. The bishops announced and organized a silent march in support of

Peña. For three days in a row the Voice of America reported that the "first anti-Sandinista demonstration in five years" was going to be held. The Interior Ministry warned that the march would be illegal and that Obando would be responsible for the consequences. Fifteen or twenty priests took part in the march along with two or three hundred other people, including numerous foreign journalists. The government canceled the residency visas of ten priests—all of them close to Obando—who thus had to leave the country. President Ortega announced that Peña would be tried for war crimes. After being under house arrest in a seminary for almost a year—and designated a "prisoner of conscience" by Amnesty International—Peña was "pardoned" by President Ortega.

After months of vacillation over election procedures, Arturo Cruz met with Comandante Bayardo Arce in Rio de Janeiro. The agreement they concluded foundered when Cruz insisted he needed a few days to consult with the Coordinadora leadership. Several other opposition parties remained in the election. The Sandinistas received 67 percent of the vote while the opposition, the right and a minuscule left, divided the rest. The election was a kind of plebiscite, and at this point, when economic conditions were worsening but had not become desperate, and when opposition groups seemed to operate in concert with the United States, most Nicaraguans either supported the Sandinistas or passively accepted them. Had Cruz remained in the race, he probably would have been defeated by a lesser but still decisive margin.

In March 1985 the major contra leaders sent a letter to the Sandinista government proposing a national dialogue to be moderated by the church between the "totalitarian tendency," as they called the newly elected government, and the "democratic tendency," presently divided into armed organizations and civic organizations. The bishops pointed to their own call for dialogue of the previous year, and indicated a willingness to mediate as long as both sides agreed. Shortly afterwards the Reagan administration proposed a peace plan for Nicaragua, urging a dialogue mediated by the bishops. In a Holy Thursday sermon being broadcast, the papal nuncio mentioned Reagan's plan and said that no peace initiative should be dismissed.

Managua and Rome

The issue of the priests who remained in the Sandinista government had been a continual irritant to the bishops and the Vatican. Fernando Cardenal, now the minister of education, had been urged to resign his post repeatedly by his Jesuit superiors in Central America and even in Rome. They made it clear that although they admired him and his work, they were transmitting orders from the pope. In late 1984 Cardenal was faced, he said, with the "final alternative of either abandoning my commitment to the Nicaraguan revolution or being expelled from the Society of Jesus." In a widely circulated "Letter to my Friends," he explained that he held an objection in conscience "to the pressures of the ecclesiastical authorities." He sincerely believed he would be committing a "serious sin" if he abandoned his priestly option for the poor in the revolution. "I cannot conceive of a God who asks me to abandon my commitment to the people."

Reiterating a more or less standard defense of the revolution, Cardenal insisted that he did not feel he could abandon it at the very moment when it was most under attack. The basis of Rome's order was neither theology nor the gospel, but a political stance by the bishops, and the Holy See seemed to be viewing Nicaragua in the light of Eastern Europe. The Vatican's political stance toward Nicaragua was like that of President Reagan. The aim of forcing him to withdraw was "to delegitimize the revolutionary process." The revolution was by no means antireligious, as its critics contended, and his presence within it enabled him to bear witness to the faith. On a personal level, what was most painful was the fact that the Jesuit family to which he had devoted thirty-two years was expelling him.

Action soon followed on the three other priests in the government, although with variations. For well over a year Edgard Parrales had been asking unsuccessfully for a dispensation from the priesthood for personal reasons. The Maryknoll Fathers refused to expel Miguel D'Escoto since such an action would be used to legitimize an unjust U.S. policy. Since leaving the Trappists, Ernesto Cardenal had been a diocesan priest. Both D'Escoto and Cardenal received ultimatums directly from the Vatican. From the Vatican's viewpoint, the issue was settled by February 1985: They could no longer function as priests in the government. In practice, however, the priests' change of status made little difference in the eyes of most Nicaraguans, and they continued their lives as before. Maryknoll still regarded D'Escoto as a member, and Fernando Cardenal continued to live with his Jesuit confreres in Managua.

Archbishop Miguel Obando y Bravo was among a group of bishops made cardinals by John Paul II in April 1985. President Ortega called it "an honor for all Nicaraguans" and the entire investiture ceremony in Rome was broadcast over state television. Although in itself Obando's cardinalate was simply an ecclesiastical honor entailing no power (except to vote in papal elections), it had political implications. The selection of Obando was read as a Vatican seal of approval on his anti-Sandinista stance. As if to confirm this reading, on his return journey, Obando stopped in Miami to celebrate Mass for members of the Nicaraguan community there. Photos of Adolfo Calero, Eden Pastora, and other contra leaders at the Mass appeared in Nicaraguan papers. For several months after his return, Obando traveled throughout Nicaragua on dozens of highly publicized visits. These ostensibly religious occasions demonstrated Obando's ability to bring out crowds.

Cardinal Obando and his supporters felt they were prophetically confronting an all-powerful state, and regarded revolutionary Christians as opportunists who enjoyed access to state power and received generous funding from Europe and North America. Sandinista sympathizers were just as convinced that Nicaragua was David confronting the bully Goliath.

In frustration Miguel D'Escoto took a leave of absence from his post as foreign minister in July and began a water-only fast "for peace, in defense of life and against U.S.-sponsored terrorism." Years of studying Gandhi and other pacifists had convinced D'Escoto of the power of nonviolence. It was time, he thought, to open a new — "theological" — front in a struggle that was military, diplomatic, economic, and legal. He held his fast at the church of the Dominican priests in the lower middle-class Monseñor Lescano neighborhood in Managua. Others joined him at the church, and thousands were said to have responded to his request for a national day of fasting.

Official church representatives did not respond directly to the fast, but by repeating scriptural passages from Isaiah and Matthew on fasting, *Radio Católica* subtly implied that the foreign minister's was a hypocritical action. *La Prensa* ridiculed the fast as a diet for the corpulent D'Escoto. A statement by the bishops questioned the right of those other than the hierarchy to organize religious activities.

Some came from afar to express solidarity, including Bishop Sergio Mendez Arceo, the retired bishop of Cuernavaca, Mexico, Adolfo Perez Esquivel, the human rights activist and recipient of the 1980 Nobel Peace Prize and coordinator of SERPAJ (Peace and Justice Service, a network of Latin American human rights organizations), and Bishop Pedro Casaldáliga of São Felix do Araguaia, a rural diocese in the center of Brazil. Casaldáliga had long been an activist on behalf of Indians and poor peasants, as well as a champion of new pastoral approaches. The Nicaraguan bishops objected to Casaldáliga's unauthorized trespassing on their territory. The day after his arrival Casaldáliga celebrated funeral masses for eight women killed by the contras as they were carrying food to their children who were on combat duty and for a group of thirty soldiers killed in battle. For the next several weeks Casaldáliga crisscrossed Nicaragua in visits less triumphal than Obando's, encouraging groups of church people involved in the revolution. D'Escoto and others spoke of this period as a "gospel insurrection," in which they could deepen their faith.

The year 1985 marked both the high point of contra advance and a decisive Sandinista counteroffensive. In March contra forces were able to make attacks even in La Trinidad, just off the Panamerican highway in the center of the country. By the end of the year, however, their largest forces had been driven back to Honduras or to more remote parts of Nicaragua. Nevertheless, for several more years they continued to attack targets and kill civilians. Moreover, a direct attack by the United States remained a possibility until the Reagan administration became embroiled in the Iran-contra scandal in late 1986.

During this period the government took a number of measures against

Obando, whom they regarded as the leading figure of the Sandinista opposition. As "Cardinal of Peace" he was continuing to make pastoral visits that looked like political rallies and were regularly advertised by the FDN radio station in Honduras. In October the government seized the whole printing of a new archdiocesan bulletin, *Iglesia*, on the grounds that its director, Monsignor Carballo, had refused to submit to government regulations and prior censorship. The government also moved to take over COPROSA (Archdiocesan Commission for Social Development), an archdiocesan agency that was engaged in a series of activities in health, housing, and so forth, and announced its intention to conduct an audit. Some of the activities of this office, partly funded by USAID, seemed quite political, such as supporting efforts to reunite the fractured Conservative Democratic party. At least one of the groups funded, the Union of Women for Peace and Democracy, appeared to be a phantom organization. Then in January 1986 the government closed *Radio Católica* for failing to carry the president's year-end message (as all radio stations were obliged to do). The Sandinistas claimed that this refusal came after approximately fifty previous violations.

However legitimate these wartime actions might have seemed to many Nicaraguans, elsewhere they were largely regarded as human rights violations. Americas Watch protested the actions against *Iglesia*, COPROSA, and *Radio Católica* and called on the government to reverse its decisions. Bishop Bosco Vivas claimed that in October and November about two hundred church activists, including fourteen priests, had been arrested for short periods, usually no more than two hours. These people were fingerprinted and photographed and warned against violating state security. Several evangelical pastors were also arrested around this time; some were held for a few days and harassed. Some were accused of having had contacts with U.S. embassy personnel.

Throughout the first half of 1986 the Reagan administration was making strenuous efforts to convince the U.S. Congress to provide a $100 million aid package for the contras, an amount considerably larger than previous requests. In this context, Cardinal Obando went to Washington where his portrayal of the Catholic church as "persecuted" looked like at least an indirect form of lobbying. He unsuccessfully sought to convince the general secretaries of the United Nations and the OAS that they should intervene to halt religious persecution in Nicaragua.

In this atmosphere Miguel D'Escoto undertook another variant of his "gospel insurrection." From Jalapa, the town near the Honduran border that had been the site of some of the earliest contra attacks, he and one hundred believers set out on a Way of the Cross that would cover three hundred kilometers in two weeks. Although only seventy people went the whole route — including Gregorio Martínez, who had fought in Sandino's army and who had lost eight of his twelve grandchildren to the contras — many joined at various points along the way. At the head of the procession went a group of war victims in wheelchairs. Local communities hosted and fed the marchers. D'Escoto's rhetoric continually escalated: The bishops "have gone to Washington and Miami, and here among their people they have said nothing [about the war]. . . . We have to pray for our bishops . . . [so that each] may speak as he must speak, independent of whether it pleases Obando and whether the Holy Father understands it or not."

Surprisingly, when the procession reached Estelí, Bishop López blessed and prayed with the marchers. Farther on fifty evangelicals who had come 250 kilometers from Nueva Guinea joined the group. Entering Managua at dusk on a Friday, fifty thousand people came to the ruins of the Managua cathedral. Seventy-two priests (20 percent of the total in the country) joined in the ceremony. D'Escoto called on Obando to repent, and "in the name of God" ordered him to stop saying Mass "because the sacrifice celebrated by one who is in complicity with the assassination of his people is a sacrilegious sacrifice and profoundly offends the faith of our people."

Less dramatic instances of the issues that pitted the "two Miguels" against one another could be found throughout the Catholic church. One of the bitterest complaints of revolutionary Christians was the de facto policy of refusing to provide a church burial for fallen Sandinista soldiers and victims of contra attacks. Journalist Penny Lernoux recounted going to an appointment with Obando and finding the way blocked by a procession of people who had walked or come in wheelchairs to ask Obando to pray for peace. A Spanish Christian brother told her that if you did not know the words to hymns written to honor Obando, "you're automatically considered his enemy." This brother, who was likewise critical of the revolution, said that it was very difficult to pursue and state the truth, because one who did so would be attacked by both sides.

Lernoux observed that with inflation headed toward 200 percent most people were primarily concerned with survival. A truck driver said it was impossible to support a family on his wage of $20 a month. Exports were declining, and war expenses, including subsidies to war victims and the families of the 13,930 killed so far, were rising. The early dreams of the revolution were ending. The tragedy, said a European diplomat, was that "we will never know what might have been."

The revolution's grassroots programs were working where there was a prior history of community organizing, as in Estelí, but elsewhere, where people were not used to independent initiative, it was much more difficult. The war was reinforcing the natural militaristic tendencies of the Sandinistas. The contra war, said a Sandinista official, was creating "a pyramid . . . in which the bottom is composed of a mass of women and children and the top of technocrats and military people formed in the army tradition." This was the top-down model common in Latin America, "only in this case it is leftist, not rightist."

Lernoux also registered complaints over the existence of a dollar store in Managua, where foreigners and high-ranking officials could buy luxury goods unavailable to ordinary people. Although no doubt defensible on policy grounds—it could soak up dollars that might otherwise go to the black market—that store remained a symbol of privilege. It may also have cushioned some high officials from truly experiencing the plight of the poor majority whom they wished to serve.

Some revolutionary pastoral workers were also looking critically at their own work. Internal church affairs were draining much energy. María López Vigil, a lay theologian, observed that something was seriously wrong when people had more to say about their archbishop than about Jesus Christ, and she urged church people to put their energies into developing the kind of theology needed in Nicaragua's revolutionary situation. Pointing out that the Centro Valdivieso had been forced to spend two months battling an effort to transfer Father Uriel Molina, its director, a Nicaraguan lay theologian said, "That's why there never seems to be time to work with the grassroots groups." A Sandinista official also said both sides spent too much time in petty squabbles, and that if church people could have done more to promote "a genuinely popular voice at the grassroots level that would have been an antidote to militarism." Others said the base communities could have done more to foster dialogue, and that more attention should be given to train lay pastoral workers who could have a multiplier effect. Such self-criticism tended to be forgotten in the heat of controversy, however.

In an April 1986 pastoral letter the bishops reiterated the theme of reconciliation, obviously meaning dialogue with the contras; however, they also condemned "any form of aid, whatever its source, which leads to the destruction, pain and death of our families or to hatred and division between Nicaraguans." This bland statement, which seemed to include contra aid, may have been a response to longstanding criticisms that the bishops had been onesided in their criticism. However, in a commentary in the *Washington Post*, Obando spoke of the continuous violation of human rights, and said that the church would not oppose contra aid because such a stand would be "manipulated" by the Sandinistas. Speaking to the U.S. government-sponsored PRODEMCA (Friends of the Democratic Center in Central America) in June, Bishop Pablo Antonio Vega of Juigalpa said, "armed struggle is a human right. What remedy is left to a people that is repressed not only politically but militarily?" President Reagan, making his final public appeal for the $100 million, quoted Vega and said, "Reverend Father, we have listened to you, because we in the United States believe, like you, that even the most humble peasant has a right to be free."

For years, Vega, who was now the president of the bishops' conference, had voiced the most uncontrolled criticisms of the Sandinistas. He frequently described Nicaragua as "caught between two great power blocs." Shortly before the 1984 election, when U.S. visitors had asked him about U.S. interference he insisted that all imperialism, including ideological imperialism, was evil. How could he compare the aid of Cuban doctors with the recent killing of six children by the contras in Nueva Segovia? "To kill the soul is worse than to kill the body says the Lord," he replied, "and here we have an ideology that starts from the perspective that the other is my enemy, and therefore a bomb placed in the soul is worse." Pressed on whether this was worse than murdering children, Vega insisted, "The submission of people means the death of the soul." One of the exasperated Americans could not resist responding, "With all respect, Bishop Vega, I think that the six murdered children, were they alive, would not agree with you." Vega, it may be noted, was not uniformly anti-Sandinista. At the 1985 inauguration of President Ortega he was warm toward Fidel Castro, and contrary to the practice of his fellow bishops, he later celebrated a Christmas Mass for Sandinista combatants returning from military service.

On a March 1986 trip to Washington, Vega appeared at the right-wing Heritage Foundation together with contra leaders or representatives Adolfo Calero, Arturo Cruz, and Enrique Bermúdez. There he was quoted as saying that the Sandinistas had killed three priests—who turned out to be three lay leaders who had been killed in the immediate aftermath of the fall of Somoza before the government had assumed full control.

The Nicaraguan government interpreted the June 25, 1986 vote by the U.S. Congress to approve $100 million in contra aid as a declaration of war. *La Prensa* was closed the next day. Thirty hours later the World Court decision against the United States for mining Nicaraguan ports and sponsoring the contra war confirmed the government's sense of righteousness. As Monsignor Bismarck Carballo attempted to board a plane in Miami to return to Nicaragua after a tour through Europe and the United States in which he had made numerous statements against the Nicaraguan government, he was told he could not return. A State Department spokesman immediately defended him.

Then, on July 2, Vega held a two-hour press conference. He said he could not criticize the $100 million contra aid package, when billions were being given from the other side. He also said that it was the Sandinista army's ideological aggression and snatching children and imposing ideas on them, that was driving people to take up arms. He took issue with the World Court's decision, stating that it should look not only at the rights of governments but the "rights of man." The Sandinistas might have been well advised to overlook these remarks, but feelings were intensified when on that same day a contra land mine killed thirty-two peasants in a civilian vehicle.

On July 4 government troops took Vega to the Honduran border, sent him across, and suspended indefinitely his right to live in Nicaragua. In its official statement, the government accused Vega of "criminal labor" and of being an accomplice in the suffering and death of thousands. He no longer deserved to be a Nicaraguan; his place was rather "alongside Reagan and the mercenary bands, murderers of children."

Contrary to what might be expected, the Vatican did not react vigorously to Vega's expulsion. Indeed, when he went to Rome, Vega received a cool reception—perhaps curial authorities were becoming more familiar with the bishop's penchant for extravagant expression. Nor did Rome delay in sending the new nuncio, Paolo Giglio. In his first public statement, he said that it was the church's mission to "make good citizens, to teach our Catholics to love their country," which entailed "opening one's heart to work and one's conscience to follow the commands of God and country." Elsewhere such conventional pieties would attract no notice, but in Nicaragua they were a signal that the Vatican was intent on reversing the confrontation that had been taking place since 1980 and especially since the pope's 1983 visit.

The Vatican apparently had concluded that since the contras were largely defeated as a military force, only a U.S. invasion would unseat the Sandinistas, and that it ill behooved the church to be doing advance work for such an eventuality. Latin American sensitivities were being offended by the onesided and pro-U.S. positions of some of the bishops. Moreover, the Nicaraguan bishops had been silent on the contra war, which the U.S. Catholic bishops had condemned as "illegal and immoral." One sign that the Vatican was seeking rapprochement was the private audience the pope had given Vice-President Sergio Ramírez two weeks before Vega's expulsion.

President Ortega approached the nuncio and asked him to facilitate a face-to-face meeting with the cardinal. The meeting took place at the nunciature in the hills above Managua. The president then went on to meet with the bishops as a whole, and the hierarchy and the government each appointed a commission for dealing with points of conflict. The two sides clashed over how to proceed: The government wished to establish a general framework for government-church relations, while the bishops wanted to proceed immediately to a long list of issues, such as the reopening of *Radio Católica*. After the initial statement of positions the dialogue did not advance.

Proof of a changing climate could nonetheless be found in the Eucharistic Congress held in November. The government provided lodging and transportation for invited guests. President Ortega met with Mother Teresa and welcomed her proposal to send four sisters to the eastern market section, a request that had previously been refused because that area was conflictive and largely opposed to the government. Reflecting a more moderate tone, neither the pope's message nor the bishops' preaching referred to the church as persecuted.

Despite several more meetings, the government-hierarchy talks languished during the first half of 1987—the period when the Iran-contra scandal was unfolding in the United States, and what would become the Central America Peace Plan was beginning to take shape. News reports that Cardinal Obando was passing information gained in the church-state meetings to opposition parties further complicated matters since the two sides had agreed to keep the discussions confidential. Matters were further complicated with *Newsweek*'s revelations that Obando had apparently received $125,000 from Lt. Col. Oliver North through a Cayman Islands contra bank account. Obando called the report lies; it is possible that he was unaware of the source of the money.

At this time the Virgin of Cuapa made a bizarre reappearance. Auxiliary Bishop Bosco Vivas announced that Bernardo Martínez had seen her again, now under the title of the Virgin of Victories. She asked, among other things, that bad books, those that denied God or taught sin, be destroyed. The bishop himself had lit a bonfire of Marxist books. From Honduras the contra radio station said that the Virgin's message was: "Suffering people of Nicaragua, you will soon receive a new life, full of joy." Meanwhile Bishop Vega, speaking on a contra radio station, said a dialogue with Marxists is like "those homosexual marriages they're talking about these days." It is sterile because it fails to acknowledge the need for the union between matter and spirit. He was also quoted as calling the contras the "new Christs" who would liberate Nicaragua from communism.

In July in Matiguas, Matagalpa, a mine blew up a truck killing Brother Tomás Zavaleta, a Salvadoran Franciscan, and seriously injuring a priest and a lay worker in the parish. "What is Cardinal Obando going to say now?" asked Daniel Ortega after visiting the morgue. In a sermon Obando retorted that in a situation in which "information is so manipulated" only God knew who was responsible.

"Only God knows how much money he is receiving from the CIA," was Ortega's angry rejoinder.

Winding Path toward Peace

"The world changed with Esquipulas II," later observed María López Vigil, referring to the Central America Peace Plan signed August 7, 1987, by all the presidents of the region. After years of peace efforts by other Latin American countries, which had been frustrated repeatedly by the Reagan administration, the five presidents, taking up an initiative begun by President Oscar Arias of Costa Rica more than a year earlier, had asserted that they were in charge of the destinies of their countries. Major elements of the plan included an amnesty for irregular forces (contras and the Salvadoran and Guatemalan guerrillas), a call for a ceasefire, a commitment to pluralistic, participatory democracy, and the end of aid to irregular forces and their use of the territory of other countries. If the peace plan were implemented the contras would be denied aid from the United States and sanctuary in Honduras. The Nicaraguan government was obligated to allow civil liberties and to move toward reconciliation.

Unlike neighboring countries, Nicaragua moved quickly to implement the plan. Soon after the signing, President Ortega met with the political parties and the bishops' conference and requested that they each nominate three possible candidates for the National Reconciliation Commission mandated by the peace plan. He also held a long private meeting with Obando — just days after their angry exchange. From among the three bishops proposed, the government chose Obando. As the "distinguished citizen" it chose Gustavo Parajón, a physician and Baptist minister who was president of CEPAD. Completing the commission were Vice-President Sergio Ramírez for the government and Mauricio Diaz, general secretary of the Popular Social Christian party, for the opposition political parties. At the inauguration of the commission, Ortega announced that Vega and two expelled priests could return to the country.

Surprised by the peace plan, Reagan administration officials called it "seriously flawed," and in general sought to blunt its effect, especially provisions entailing the demobilization of the contras. At a press conference the State Department criticized the Reconciliation Commission, calling Parajón "pro-Sandinista" and asserting that Obando was the only independent member.

Protestants welcomed Parajón's appointment as a recognition of their role in the country. From a biblical standpoint, said Parajón, reconciliation meant that "all of us have sinned, have committed errors, but we are going to put the past aside in a change of attitude and work together for the welfare of the Nicaraguan people." The "obstinacy" of certain groups who were unwilling to work together, whether in the government or in the opposition, was an obstacle to peace, but the most serious obstacle was the Reagan administration, which "besides funding the continuing slaughter of our people, feeds some of the opposition parties, encouraging them to thwart cooperation with the Sandinista government and movement toward peace." The church, he said, as ambassador of Christ with a vocation to peacemaking, had a great challenge and opportunity. "Evangelicals are a minority, but a significant one, and if pastors and churches throughout the country would envision this role as called for in Romans 13 and the Beatitudes, we could make a difference."

During an ecumenical worship service at Parajón's First Baptist Church, Vice-President Sergio Ramírez announced that *La Prensa*, which had been closed since the U.S. Congress had approved the $100 million in contra aid, could reopen without any restrictions or censorship. *Radio Católica* could also reopen and the government would provide hard currency for buying needed parts. The political parties began a National Dialogue, and the Democratic Coordinating Committee organized a protest march in Masaya.

Within weeks about three hundred local reconciliation committees chosen by the local community were set up throughout the war zones. Many of their members were church people. For example, on the twenty commissions in Las Segovias there were twenty evangelical pastors and eleven priests, and on the fifty-eight commissions in Boaco and Chontales, there were fifty-five catechists, forty deacons and delegates of the word, twenty-three evangelical pastors, eleven priests, and five sisters.

A contentious issue was that of what kind of amnesty should be given to the four thousand "political prisoners," half of whom were former National Guardsmen and half contra members or supporters. Calling for a complete amnesty were the Catholic bishops and the right, but family members of those killed by the Guard or the contras would have difficulty accepting such a decision. At one point the Mothers of Heroes and Martyrs, a Sandinista-formed organization, clashed in Managua with the January 22 Movement of Mothers of Political Prisoners, which was backed by the U.S. embassy and the Social Christian party. At a retreat in September, Parajón conferred with 120 Protestant pastors on the issue. Their conclusion was that for the well-being of Nicaragua there should be a "total, general, and gradual" amnesty and that the churches should "develop a ministry of accompaniment and consolation" for those who had lost their children.

Despite the general atmosphere in favor of peace the contra war itself hardly relented. Father Enrique Blandón of Waslala and Seventh Day Adventist pastor Gustavo Adolfo Tiffer, both members of the local amnesty commission, were kidnapped by the contras and held for eleven days. Their release came after orders "from Washington," in response to international pressure. In one month 395 contras and 215 government soldiers were killed in combat.

This new context affected the ongoing life of the churches. Yiye Avila, a Puerto Rican faith healer known throughout Latin America, carried out a three-week tour of Nicaragua. Present at Avila's final appearance in Managua, President Ortega called the peace accords "a true miracle," and suggested that they were the result of prayers for peace offered by Avila and others. Laying hands on Ortega and praying for him, Avila called on the sixty thousand people present to pray for their leaders, "because they are placed there by Christ."

In November President Ortega asked the cardinal to be an intermediary with the contras. A few days later both of them were in Washington to talk to U.S. Speaker of the House Jim Wright. The contras rejected Ortega's ceasefire proposal. There followed meetings in the Dominican Republic, Costa Rica, and Guatemala. At this point Obando presented an agenda for future talks, making four demands of the government and only one of the contras. The government judged that Obando was not acting impartially but in favor of the contras, and reduced his role to that of observer.

For a brief moment in March 1988 peace seemed imminent. At Sapoá near the Costa Rican border representatives of the contras and the government met for the first time on Nicaraguan soil. Having just been routed by a Sandinista offensive, the contras signed a ceasefire, agreeing to enter special zones where they would lay down their arms. They were to receive only humanitarian assistance through neutral organizations. This fragile agreement was undermined by the U.S. Congress, which passed a new contra aid package, and by the more hardline contra leaders who by June were making demands that the Sandinistas would certainly reject so as to justify their own withdrawal from the negotiation process.

In late May the Mexican newspaper *El Día* outlined what it called a CIA plan for destabilizing Nicaragua. Money was to be funneled to opposition groups, which were to be encouraged to act in such a way that the Sandinistas would respond with repression and thus ignite further disturbances. Included in the "Melton Plan" (after the new U.S. ambassador, Richard Melton) was a role for the Catholic hierarchy, which was to issue a pastoral letter highlighting issues such as the draft, the mass media, family breakdown, corruption, and so forth.

As if on cue, the bishops issued a pastoral letter in late June that dealt with many of the suggested themes. They pointed to serious economic deterioration, aggravated by military spending and bureaucratic waste; they criticized not only the materialistic and atheistic content of education, but the decline in educational standards; they condemned trial marriages and the increase of divorce and abortion. Politically they noted a sense of disillusionment: Political dialogue, amnesty, democratization, and progress toward a ceasefire had come to a halt, the bishops said.

The Sandinistas observed Melton and embassy staff engaging in what looked like organizing and unifying the opposition groups. The most serious incident came in the town of Nandaime, where on July 10 Sandinista police broke up a large opposition rally. Accounts of how the violence began and who was responsible vary. At least two embassy staff people were present and were photographed with clenched fists raised. The next day Melton and several embassy staff people were expelled; the Reagan administration retaliated by expelling the Nicaraguan ambassador Carlos Tunnermann and an equivalent number of the embassy staff. Whether there was a clear "Melton Plan" can be disputed. However, Undersecretary of State Elliott Abrams confirmed to Congress that the National Endowment for Democracy had channeled $2 million to the Nicaraguan opposition (*La Prensa*, business, labor, and human rights groups) and two priests, (Federico Argüello and Bismarck Carballo). House Speaker Jim Wright also confirmed CIA destabilizing actions.

Toward the end of the year Cardinal Obando found himself in something of a financial scandal. He admitted that he had accepted some vehicles and electrical transformers from USAID funds. The Nicaraguan congress had prohibited the reception of any money from the U.S. government, because it was still sending contra aid. The ostensible reason for the vehicles was to monitor the peace process—which the bishops themselves had described as stalled. Further information indicated that for his five-person office he was receiving $30,000 a month—an extraordinary sum at a time when professional salaries in Nicaragua might be a couple of hundred dollars a month. Newspapers reported a total of $2 million for just a month's functioning. A U.S. government audit found that Obando was paying $9,000 a month each to his Nicaraguan consultants in the United States.

The economic crisis was affecting most Nicaraguans even more than the war. Inflation in 1987 was 1347 percent, while official salary scales rose only 865 percent. A drought destroyed 75 percent of the bean crop, 45 percent of the sorghum, and 25 percent of the corn. In February 1988 eight thousand members of opposition unions marched to protest government policy. That same month the government sought to halt inflation by a complete change of currency, new exchange rates, government restructuring, and large-scale layoffs. Further austerity measures followed in June. Just when the economy was showing some signs of improvement, Hurricane Joan devastated Nicaragua. Although loss of life was minimized, tens of thousands of people in eastern Nicaragua lost their homes. Once again inflation soared, reaching an estimated 36,000 percent in 1988.

Meeting in El Salvador in February 1989 the Central American presidents presented a plan (Esquipulas IV) to demobilize and relocate the contras within ninety days in order to advance the stalled peace process. The Nicaraguan government then announced elections to take place on February 25, 1990. The new Bush administration and Congress undermined the peace plan with a $66 million "humanitarian" aid package to keep the contras intact until after the election. Thus the contra war continued, although at a lower level. Between January and May there were some 881 actions, with about 50 civilians killed and about 175 wounded or kidnapped, as well as hundreds of military casualties on both sides.

The economy continued to roll downhill. In 1988 imports ($802 million) exceeded exports ($223 million) by almost four to one; the negative trade balance was almost one-third of the gross domestic product. In an effort to contain the hyperinflation that had returned despite the currency change, the government laid off thousands of workers and carried out several severe devaluations.

Such was the context of the February 1990 election, which, like that of 1984, was something of a plebiscite. The UNO (National Opposition Union) coalition (composed of from a dozen to over twenty opposition parties, depending on when the count was taken) was quite divided and only settled on Violeta Chamorro as candidate after considerable squabbling. Rather than outline a program, UNO focused on a few themes. It played on people's fears that a Sandinista government would bring six more years of war and economic deterioration. In particular UNO advocated the end of the draft and the dissolution of the present army. Underlying the opposition's appeal, although not clearly formulated, was the population's growing sense that tiny Nicaragua could not defy the United States. The opposition implied that not only would Chamorro end the war but that she would bring Nicaragua the dollars it needed. Francisco Mayorga, the UNO's chief economist, claimed he could start economic recovery in one hundred days. Frail in health and not a powerful speaker, Chamorro, always in long white dresses, projected a motherly concern rather than mastery of the issues. Although she was ridiculed when she said that she consulted with her murdered husband and with God, the claims seem not to have lost too many votes.

With the aid of U.S. political campaign consultants, Sandinista campaign rhetoric proved equally vacuous, with slogans like, "We win, and move ahead!," "Everything will be better," "Yes to peace, no to the contras." Obviously their hope was that having won an election certified by thousands of international observers, the Sandinistas finally would be able to achieve an accommodation with the United States, and would then be able to shift priorities back to development.

Both campaigns eagerly appealed to religious motivation. In their major pastoral letter on the elections, the bishops focused primarily on encouraging people to vote. However, in mentioning their special concern for youth, they seemed to be referring to the draft, which they had criticized since 1983 and which Chamorro promised to abolish.

Ortega cultivated both Catholic and Protestant church people. In January, he met with about two thousand evangelical pastors and church leaders at the expansive and modern Olaf Palme Convention Center. Dozens of evangelicals approached the microphones to make requests, such as the inclusion of a Protestant minister in his inauguration ceremony. More than two dozen evangelical pastors were candidates on the Sandinista ticket.

Chamorro made little effort to court the evangelical vote, although she sent representatives to the conference of the Assemblies of God. Through *La Prensa*, the UNO campaign could take advantage of the affinity between Obando's positions and their own. At her closing rally, she promised to have a new cathedral built to replace the one destroyed in the 1972 earthquake.

At his final rally, Daniel Ortega invoked a passage from 1 Kings 3:5–12, which Father Antonio Castro had just shown him. In a dream God asks Solomon what he desires; he requests wisdom so he can judge the people and distinguish right from wrong. Standing before four hundred thousand people and confident of his reelection, Ortega prayed, "Lord, give me the wisdom to govern, give me the wisdom to be just, give me the wisdom to forgive."

Shortly before the election, the president released more than one thousand former Guardsmen and contra prisoners at Obando's request. The Sandinistas then pasted up thousands of small posters of the two with the legend: "Many years of peace and reconciliation are coming to Nicaragua — Ortega and Obando." On the eve of the election *La Prensa* carried a full-page photo of Obando blessing Chamorro and Virgilio Godoy, her running mate. The next morning's *Barricada* ran another photo of the cardinal and the president, with biographical sketches emphasizing the parallels in their lives.

Journalists, the U.S. government, the Sandinistas, and UNO had all been following the polls, most of which showed the Sandinistas with an approximately 10 percent lead over UNO. The relative size of the Sandinista and

UNO final rallies confirmed these impressions. Initial results favoring UNO were discounted, but as the night went on, Sandinista disbelief turned into stunned chagrin. At dawn a chastened Daniel Ortega made his concession speech.

There were no large victory rallies for the new president—UNO had made no plans for victory. Traffic in the streets of Managua was light and people seemed stunned with what their vote had wrought. An American Jesuit later said he found "surprise, shock and grief" among base community members he served. A woman whose three sons had served in the Sandinista army "went into a deep depression, not eating for several days; after a few hours of hospital treatment, she returned home and gradually recovered from what she called 'an attack of nerves.' " Some likened the experience to what they had felt when they had lost children in the anti-Somoza struggle or the contra war.

Like the 1979 revolution itself, the election prompted diverse interpretations. UNO partisans regarded it as a total repudiation of the Sandinistas; the Sandinistas asserted that Nicaraguans had voted to end the war and reverse economic decline. Several months later, María López Vigil observed that if war brings out heroism, ultimately people's concern for survival comes to the fore. She further observed that the "burden of war . . . and the economic crisis have been borne unequally. . . . Since 1983 or 1985 the people have had to eat promises."

Within days the contours of the new political situation were developing. Cesar Jerez, the Jesuit rector of the UCA in Managua, summed up the situation crisply: "One side has to realize it lost, and the other has to realize that it cannot govern without the cooperation of those who lost." Violeta Chamorro and her circle of close advisors, especially her son-in-law, Antonio Lacayo, opted to seek an accommodation with the Sandinistas. To try to govern in defiance of such a large and well-organized political force would assure further strife and violence. Although some Sandinistas might have been tempted to annul the elections on the grounds that the results reflected years of unjust pressure from the United States, they realized that their only realistic option was to accept the result and to become an opposition party. With their mass organizations they could be a powerful force and "govern from below," in Daniel Ortega's perhaps ill-chosen expression.

Thousands of Sandinista cadres who had spent a decade working for the revolution now found themselves unexpectedly facing an uncertain future. Many began an anxious search for nongovernmental organizations in which they could continue to work in development. In its final days the Sandinista government passed measures legalizing ownership of land and houses in order to prevent a mass reversion of property. Although most of the beneficiaries were small landholders, what attracted attention was the fact that leading Sandinistas acquired confiscated properties for a negligible cash price. From their viewpoint they were simply legalizing their ownership after a decade of selfless devotion to the revolution, but their foes called it looting.

Looking Back, Looking Forward

It was not easy for Sandinista partisans to admit that UNO had indeed won the election. They believed that many people had voted for UNO hoping to send the Sandinistas a message of discontent, scarcely imagining that they might be defeated. Five months after the election Cesar Jerez said there were still some people "including priests and sisters who are not really convinced that the Sandinistas lost the election." In mid-1990, when I tried to elicit critical reflection on the decade of revolution from church people, they tended to veer off in other directions.

The Sandinistas themselves seemed more willing to engage in public self-criticism. In a series of long articles Luis Carrión, one of the nine top-ranking comandantes, drew up a balance sheet of the past and suggested issues for a party congress scheduled to take place some months in the future. The Sandinista "historic program" had largely been carried out; the great task now facing the organization was to become democratic. He drew up an extensive catalogue of mistakes: The FSLN had turned into an instrument for mobilizing the people for a revolutionary program that may not have enjoyed majority support; the revolution had been disproportionately urban and the contras had become a genuinely peasant movement; the party had become bureaucratic and out of touch; its leaders enjoyed privileges and corruption had crept in. Other issues he mentioned included mistaken marketing policies, conflicts with the Catholic hierarchy, and ignorance and mistreatment of people on the Atlantic coast. Speaking in Britain some months later, Tomás Borge frankly admitted that the Sandinistas had become arrogant and triumphalistic; they had recruited by force rather than persuasion. "We put too much emphasis on the state and took people away from their land"; the result was "scarcity and rationing, the forced sales of agricultural produce, and crimes committed by our soldiers and officers against the people in the war zones. ... We were taught a lesson and it brought us back down to earth." When I noted the new level of Sandinista self-criticism, Jerez chuckled and invoked a somewhat archaic Catholic terminology: "The Sandinistas are always ready to confess their sins. The question is whether they really have a firm purpose of amendment."

By hindsight, the revolution seems to have foundered not in the 1990 election, but when the Sandinistas opted — seemingly with no other choice — to divert resources away from development into defending the revolution (which in practice was identified with their own regime). The extension of schooling and health care, advances in land reform, and the availability of credit to small farmers had improved people's lot in the early 1980s, but from mid-decade onward living standards began to decline, especially in the hyperinflation of 1987 and 1988. Sandinista officials, development workers, and many in the churches, who drove vehicles and had access to dollars, were sheltered from the worst effects of the economic decline.

In claiming that the "people" were the "subject" of the revolution, the Sandinistas ran a danger of reifying those very people. When a 1988 poll showed that only 29 percent of the population identified themselves as Sandinistas, they took comfort in the fact that all other parties were under 10 percent. Only later did some reflect that a highly organized minority should not assume that it represented the majority, even if its policies were intended to benefit the poor. Moreover a considerable part of the Sandinista constituency belonged to the middle class.

Something similar could be observed among prorevolutionary Christians. Those working with base communities admitted that only a small number of people participated, but they believed that these communities were articulating the faith of much larger numbers of Christians. By viewing Nicaragua through the eyes of these small committed groups, they had largely lost contact with masses of people who no longer believed that a Sandinista government could improve their lot.

At the inauguration of President Chamorro on April 25, no one seemed happier than Cardinal Obando, who turned his invocation into a twenty-five-minute speech, seemingly making himself as prominent as Chamorro and Ortega. A central assertion in his address was that the "soul of Nicaragua" was Christian—by which he apparently meant Roman Catholic—and that the new government had to return the country to its "cultural identity." The implication was that for a decade the Sandinistas had been imposing an alien and un-Christian culture, through schools "without God and morality," for example.

President Chamorro warmly praised Obando. With a passing reference to those who had died in the war, she said "more honor still is due to those who have understood that reconciliation is more beautiful than victory," and went on to express gratitude "to the highest spiritual authority, his Eminence Cardinal Miguel Obando y Bravo, our Archbishop, tireless in his struggle for reconciliation and mediator and witness of the peace agreements." Both president and cardinal seemed insensitive to the approximately 15 percent of Nicaraguans who were Protestant.

In the church in La Paz Centro along the highway from Managua to Leon the pastor had a commemorative plaque installed near the altar: "So that future generations may know: when our country was wandering in the gloom of sadness, hunger, war, tears, pain and death, the people raised their pained weeping eyes, and there they encountered the sweet and serene gaze of our Mother of Perpetual Help (the Victorious One) and the next day the radiant sun of peace was shining. April 25, 1990, Rev. Enrique Martínez Gamboa, pastor." Like him many clergy spoke as though the country had been delivered from years of captivity. They blamed the Sandinistas for ills ranging from declining standards in public schools to atheism to teenage pregnancy. At the same time, church representatives began to speak of the tasks of Christians to build God's kingdom in a language they had never used during the Sandinista years.

A pressing task for the new administration was demilitarization: disarming the contras and reducing the size of the army as well as separating it from the Sandinista party. In addition the contras had to be resettled. To mark the end of the war, on June 9 at El Almendro, Obando celebrated Mass for contra troops, still holding weapons. The event ended with cries to the Virgin Mary. Later that month top contra leaders turned over their weapons to a UN peacekeeping force, again before both president and cardinal. Commander "Ruben" praised Obando who had "always offered a helping hand and gave us advice. ... When the road ahead seemed darkest, there was Cardinal Obando lighting the way and encouraging us to continue to struggle." Such praise only confirmed the Sandinista conviction that Obando had been thoroughly involved in the political struggle.

The Sandinistas pledged to defend certain "conquests" of the revolution that they regarded as irreversible. The many Sandinista supporters in the government were determined to resist any wholesale firings. Within weeks government employees went on strike and forced concessions. In July Sandinista unions again brought the country to a halt for ten days and forced the government to a settlement assuring a measure of job security and union participation in economic decisions.

Almost immediately the UNO split into two tendencies. Chamorro and those around her took a moderate line of accommodation with the Sandinistas. Indeed the UNO government retained many midlevel specialists from the previous government. Most of the party politicians in UNO, including Vice-President Virgilio Godoy, quickly took a harsher line. Soon they were charging that the unelected advisors around President Chamorro were failing to carry out the mandate of the voters. The U.S. embassy and the Bush administration also read the election as a complete repudiation of the Sandinista period. In their public positions, Obando and the bishops tended to sound "Godoyista." For example, in an August 1990 letter they said that it would be a "sin against justice ... to prevent those elected by the people from governing or to make arrangements or pacts which would disregard or change the popular will." CEPAD advocated a moderate line and called for greater "flexibility" on all sides.

On May 16, less than a month after her inauguration, President Chamorro went to Obando's office to publicly announce the "good news": "We are going to rebuild the cathedral." In 1989 Cardinal Bernard Law of Boston had put Obando in contact with Tom Monaghan, the founder of the Domino's Pizza chain, an active Catholic who avidly supported a number of conservative religious organizations and coalitions. Monaghan hired architects and got the project underway. Chamorro and Monaghan each pledged $100,000 to the project and Monaghan agreed to lead a pledge drive to raise $3 million. La Prensa proposed that the cathedral should follow the traditional Latin American pattern in which the "house of God [stands] alongside the house of government or National Palace, with a great plaza as the heart of the city." The city hall would be the part of this "new civil and religious center of the city." Many Protestant leaders were concerned over this identification of Catholicism with Nicaraguan nationality, although Bartolomé Matamoros, the head of the Assemblies of God, the largest single non-Catholic denomination, publicly welcomed the project. The notion of spending $3 million on a church building in an economically devastated nation was dismaying to some, but there was no evidence that most of the poor themselves were opposed. Moreover, the Sandinistas had also accepted monuments such as the Olaf Palme Convention Center, built with European money.

Not only did Chamorro surround herself with active Catholics; a number of those in prominent posts were members of a charismatic Catholic movement called Ciudad de Dios (City of God), which had been formed in 1978 by a group of upper middle-class charismatics in Managua who were searching for a deeper spiritual life. They came into contact, and formed a close association with Sword of the Spirit, an Ann Arbor-based cult-like group. One of its characteristic practices is "shepherding discipleship," whereby an individual submits himself or herself to the direction of another member, in effect surrendering personal judgment to that person. Ciudad de Dios members in the Chamorro government included the ministers of education, health, and construction, and four vice or deputy ministers. Carlos Mántica, the leader of Ciudad de Dios, was chosen head of the international Sword of the Spirit and thus found himself commuting between Managua and Ann Arbor.

In his invocation at the inauguration, Obando had made it clear that he believed Nicaraguan education needed to be changed. Sofonías Cisneros, the education minister, now said that the aim was to inculcate the values of a "modern, Western citizen," on the basis of a "Christian vision of man, which promotes ... Western values ... brotherhood, charity, love, reconciliation." Cisneros, who had been a president of the parents' association of private (mainly Catholic) schools, opened some meetings by having staff members hold hands and recite the Lord's Prayer.

Existing textbooks had been criticized on numerous grounds ranging from their Sandinista slant to sex education. Within months hundreds of thousands of textbooks had been sold for pulp and replaced by more traditional books. Once again the "intrepid" Columbus "discovered" the Americas, while the decimation of the native peoples was ignored; church symbols, such as crosses and first communion dresses reappeared; children read traditional tales in which masters beat servants, and read sentences such as "The girl is white, tall, and pretty," in a country in which the elites are notably taller and lighter-skinned than most of the inhabitants. Overseeing the curriculum change was the vice-minister of education, Humberto Belli, also a prominent Ciudad de Dios member. He had spent most of the

1980s writing and speaking against the Sandinistas in the United States. In January 1991 he became minister of education.

Further strikes in October and November 1990 issued in a basic understanding: The Sandinistas accepted the basic thrust of the government's free market economic agenda, and the Chamorro government agreed to forego massive layoffs. However, Chamorro soon faced a movement from discontented ex-contras in the countryside, who blocked a one-hundred-mile section of road leading to the east, took over buildings, and set up barricades. Supporting them were a number of UNO mayors and Bishop Pablo Antonio Vega who, having returned from exile, was something of a chaplain to the most rightist sectors of UNO.

The former contras complained that the government had not fulfilled its agreements and had forgotten them. "We were abandoned by our chiefs, never given our land, and left to be harassed by the army," said one. "We all fought in the resistance for years, and what did it get us?" Rising to oppose the "recontras" as they were called, were "recompas," a reconstituted Sandinista militia. Both sides felt their grievances were being ignored and that they were acting in self-defense. Over the course of time some recontras and recompas even joined forces against the existing order. Although the combatants had little public support from a war-weary public, such periodic conflicts indicated that the needs of Nicaragua's poor majority were not being addressed.

CHAPTER 3

EL SALVADOR

God's Patience Exhausted

On October 15, 1979, a group of Salvadoran officers seized the government, exiled President Humberto Romero and about fifty high-ranking officers, and proclaimed their intention of carrying out wide-ranging reforms. They were alarmed at the growing left militancy that was making the country increasingly ungovernable and had seen the remnants of Somoza's National Guard fleeing in disarray. The left, split into several factions, generally regarded the coup as an imperialist-inspired effort to blunt their move toward insurrection, and challenged the new government with strikes and demonstrations.

On October 7 two officers had visited Archbishop Oscar Romero at night to alert him to the impending coup. On October 10 priests and lay advisors urged him to be careful not to overcommit the church, and they listed certain requirements for a new government: It would have to purge the army, intend to carry out deep structural change, and allow the people to participate and express their points of view in a true democratic opening. These issues, it should be noted, were still being debated more than a decade later at the close of a civil war with massive U.S. involvement. In a short radio address the day after the coup Romero pointed to the need for change and counseled patience. When Col. Jaime Abdul Gutiérrez and Col. Adolfo Majano called on him that day, he insisted that the new government had to prove itself with deeds.

Two of the three civilians on the five-man junta were from the UCA: Roman Mayorga, the rector, and Guillermo Ungo, a professor who had been Duarte's running mate in the 1972 election. About a half-dozen UCA professors accepted cabinet-level or high administrative positions in the government.

On the very day after the coup, government forces attacked five factories occupied by mass organizations, killing eighteen people and arresting seventy-eight. A funeral organized by a leftist popular organization a week after the coup was attacked near the church in Soyapango, and at least three people were killed. Meeting that night with the relatives of the 176 people who had "disappeared" in recent years, Romero issued a challenge to the new government: If these people were in jail, they should be released or properly brought to trial; if they were dead, their family members should be notified. Failure to do so would prove that the government did not really have control over the armed forces and security forces.

Despite the military junta's declared reformist intentions, the level of official violence continued to climb. According to church human rights agencies, 281 people were killed in December. On January 3 the major civilian figures in the government resigned, despite last minute mediation efforts by the archbishop. The Christian Democrat party agreed to organize a new government.

Meanwhile, the left guerrilla organizations began to overcome their long-standing divisions. On January 22 the Revolutionary Coordinating Body of Mass Organizations held what may have been the largest political march in Salvadoran history. As it reached downtown, snipers shot at the demonstrators, killing 21 and wounding about 120.

Although a curfew was in effect and violators could be shot on sight, death squads operating with impunity were killing hundreds of people a month. Roberto D'Aubuisson, the ex-major who had emerged as the charismatic leader of the far right, appeared on television denouncing a number of people as communists. One of them, Mario Zamora, the attorney general and brother of the prominent young Christian Democrat leader, Rubén Zamora, was gunned down in his house days afterward.

In early March 1980, desperate to rescue its reform credentials, the government announced a land reform. Declaring a state of siege, the military moved out into the countryside, ostensibly to take over the large properties destined for the land reform. This action provoked the first flows of what would soon be a flood of refugees fleeing from the countryside into San Salvador or over the Honduran border.

In his Sunday sermons, broadcast by radio throughout the country, Archbishop Romero first preached for some time on the biblical texts of the day, and then reported and commented on events and developments in the country. He welcomed the fact that the mass organizations were coming together. In a letter in February he appealed to President Jimmy Carter's religious sentiments and concern for human rights and urged that military aid not be sent to El Salvador and that the United States not use its power to determine El Salvador's fate.

On Sunday, March 23, Romero ended his sermon by directly addressing the army, the National Guard, and the police. He reminded the troops that the many people being killed were their brothers and sisters, and that God's command "Thou shalt not kill" must prevail over orders from human beings. "No soldier is obliged to obey an order against God's law." He was in effect urging soldiers to disobey superiors who ordered them to kill civilians. To thunderous applause he concluded, "I implore you, I beg you, I order you in the name of God: Stop the repression!"

The next day as he was saying Mass in the chapel of the Catholic hospital where he lived, a red Volkswagen pulled up and parked. A passenger in the back seat took aim through the open door and fired one shot that hit Romero in the heart. Evidence indicates that the murder was planned and arranged by former Major D'Aubuisson and military and nonmilitary members of his circle.

Had they so desired, the mass organizations might have channeled anger over Romero's murder into a popular uprising like that which followed the 1978 murder of *La Prensa* editor Pedro Joaquin Chamorro in Nicaragua. Believing that the crime was intended to provoke a premature insurrection and thereby justify a mass slaughter, they used their discipline to impose restraint. The outdoor funeral held at midday the following Sunday was interrupted by bombs and gunfire, and about twenty-six people were killed, most of them crushed as the crowd sought to flee.

Romero's murder demonstrated how far the dominant group in the military and its civilian allies were willing to go and the impunity they enjoyed. It was a calculated move to hush "the voice of the voiceless" and to curtail some church activities. To replace Romero the Vatican appointed his auxiliary, Bishop Arturo Rivera y Damas, but maintained him in an interim status until 1983. Rivera had been a member of the generally conservative Salesian order, and had been trained in canon law. In the 1970s, before the emergence of Romero, he had been regarded as the most open Salvadoran bishop but his mind-set and temperament were different from Romero's. In contrast to Romero's enthusiasm for popular organizations, Rivera assumed a mediating position.

In April 1980 the FDR (Revolutionary Democratic Front) was formed; it was headed by several of the civilians who had withdrawn from the government at the beginning of the year. The UCA team led by Ellacuría devoted the March–April issue of its important journal *ECA* (*Estudios Centroamericanos*) to a lengthy analysis of proposals by the popular organizations—apparently with the hope that the more legitimacy the impending uprising enjoyed, the more the violence would be reduced to a minimum.

Business groups and the armed forces were meanwhile arguing for the need to impose order. The Carter administration continued to insist that the government of El Salvador was centrist and should be supported against the extremes of right and left. Romero's murder only momentarily delayed congressional approval of an aid package, including the military aid the archbishop had warned against. In May D'Aubuisson was caught redhanded in a coup attempt. When the head of the junta, Col. Majano, had him jailed, however, the high command voted overwhelmingly to have him released and demoted Majano.

An *ECA* editorialist, presumably Ellacuría, observed that the number of victims of repression could reach ten thousand before the end of the year—

a forecast that proved chillingly accurate. On May 14 National Guard troops and members of the paramilitary group ORDEN killed from three hundred to six hundred civilians as they were trying to cross the Sumpul River near the hamlet of la Arada and flee into Honduras. Although guerrillas were operating in the border area this action was directed at civilians. A young woman named Vicki later described how she saw troops throw a baby into the air and shoot at it. While hiding in a ravine she watched a mother put a ball of cloth into her baby's mouth to keep it from crying and revealing the location of the group. The baby choked to death. When the people tried to cross the river they were shot at by both Salvadoran and Honduran troops. Vicki saw her father hit by bullets; the two children he was carrying were drowned in the current. When she was rescued by Honduran fishermen farther downstream, the little girl she was carrying had died from bullet wounds. This "Sumpul River massacre" was made known by priests and other church workers in Honduras.

Throughout 1980 there were dozens of attacks on church workers and institutions. Churches and convents were machine gunned, sometimes during services; offices were searched; bombs were set off, especially in the offices of the archdiocesan radio station; lay activists were picked up, tortured, and murdered; and death threats became routine. A number of church sites had been turned into refugee camps, especially the large yard of the seminary complex where the archdiocesan offices were also located.

Many priests had to go into a semi-underground existence, and others fled the country. Rogelio Ponceele, the Belgian priest who had worked in the area of Zacamil on the northern edge of San Salvador for almost a decade, after prayer and reflection decided to go to Morazán in eastern El Salvador to be with the guerrillas, but not as a combatant.

As troops surrounded the Externado San Jose, the Jesuit high school, on November 28, twenty armed men entered and abducted six major FDR leaders, including the organization's president, Enrique Alvarez Córdova, a wealthy dairyman and former minister of agriculture, and Juan Chacón, the leader of the Revolutionary People's Bloc. Their mangled bodies were found the next day.

On the night of December 2, Dorothy Kazel, an Ursuline sister, and Jean Donovan, a lay volunteer and co-worker, met Maryknoll sisters Ita Ford and Maura Clarke at the airport. The four were friends, and were doing similar pastoral work—Clarke and Ford in the mountains of Chalatenango in the north, and Kazel and Donovan in La Libertad on the coast. National Guardsmen were observing them at the airport. The sisters' van was allowed to pass through a checkpoint where other vehicles were being detained. At another checkpoint Guardsmen in civilian clothes questioned them, then ordered them back into their van; they drove them about fifteen miles on a dirt road where the women were sexually assaulted, and then shot under the orders of the sergeant who explained to his men that the women were "subversives."

In the United States, the raped and murdered nuns immediately became a symbol of what was happening in El Salvador, and an obstacle for policymakers who sought to portray U.S. policy as that of supporting a centrist government. The Carter administration initially cut off all aid, but then restored economic aid within days, when the government promised to investigate the murders. Salvadoran National Guard officers covered up the involvement of higher officers.

This crime evidenced the fanatical conviction of the military—who made few distinctions among active involvement with the guerrillas, support for popular organizing, and aiding the victims of army violence—that church people were to blame for popular discontent and organizing. Socorro Jurídico, the church legal aid office, had tabulated 180 acts of violence against pastoral workers and lay activists between January and early October: murders, arrests, violent searches, bombings, and shooting at church buildings. Moreover right-wing military and civilians in Central America who had fired guns into the air to celebrate Ronald Reagan's electoral victory now anticipated an administration in Washington that would share their worldview.

Theologian Jon Sobrino expressed the feelings of others when he said that "God's patience must be exhausted" and that this new martyrdom, coming on the heels of an endless procession of people killed for their faith, must mean that liberation was near. These women had embodied a very profound kind of equality, equality in suffering and hope. In contrast to other forms of the U.S. military, diplomatic, and economic omnipresence in El Salvador, these women brought the best the United States had to offer: "faith in Jesus instead of faith in the almighty dollar; a thirst for justice instead of a lust for exploitation. . . . Christ lies dead here among us. He is Maura, Ita, Dorothy and Jean. But he is risen too, in these same four women, and he keeps the hope of liberation alive." Despite the mourning "our last word must be: Thank you. In Maura, Ita, Dorothy, and Jean, God has visited El Salvador."

On January 10 the FMLN, only recently united, launched what it called a "final" offensive. Throughout 1980 many had assumed that the impending insurrection would be short: A protracted guerrilla war would be impossible in a country as densely populated as El Salvador, which has no real jungles or large forests. They may also have been influenced by the recent example of Nicaragua, where the Sandinista final offensive had lasted less than eight weeks. The most spectacular success was in Santa Ana where troops rebelled and burned the army garrison. A number of military installations around the country and even in the capital were attacked. Rogelio Ponceele spoke over the newly established Radio Venceremos defending the legitimacy of the FMLN's cause, which he categorized as self-defense.

Killed along with several dozen other people in the army's counterattack in Santa Ana was Sister Silvia Arriola who in late 1980 had gone from San Salvador to be with the guerrillas. An organizer who had worked with her later commented that in the mid-1970s she "never would have supported armed struggle; she was very much against it, and insisted, 'We can't create a new society if we don't change ourselves.' " He said her example was typical of what happens with priests and sisters. "First, they are committed to the poor. Then the army comes to the community where they are working and seizes or kills a couple people. They then need to link up with others in order not to be isolated," and so they join an organization. One of Silvia Arriola's legacies, he said, was that the people who had worked around her have striven not only for overall change in their country but for change within themselves, and that they reflect in their own lives her particular kind of gentleness.

The general insurrection the left had expected did not materialize; the death squads had already broken urban networks and intimidated the population. The Carter administration immediately moved to renew military aid. Although the offensive had failed to spark a general insurrection, it was not a failure. Over the next few months the FMLN took control of a number of areas in the countryside, especially toward the Honduran border.

Commenting in his Sunday sermon, Archbishop Rivera stated that the insurrection did not have the backing of the church and that most people did not support either side. Reviewing the traditional ethical conditions for a just revolution, Rivera said only the first could be established, that is, that those holding power were responsible for grave abuses. The other conditions were not fulfilled: Peaceful means for resolving the conflict had not been exhausted; there was no assurance that a socialist regime would be better than the existing one; and there was no reasonable hope of victory.

Early in the Reagan administration, Rivera sought to open the way toward negotiations. After meeting with Pope John Paul II and heads of state in several European countries, he went to Washington where he met with Vice-President Bush and other Reagan administration figures, but they ignored his plea. Rivera's position, as outlined to journalists in Washington, was that no military solution was possible, and that there had to be a dialogue. He was opposed to military aid from the United States but also condemned Cuba and Nicaragua for sending arms. When asked why his position was more moderate than his predecessor's he said, "I am not questioning the stance taken by Archbishop Romero, but making clear how I see the situation today."

Since the first few months of 1980, thousands of Salvadorans had fled to the Honduran side of the border. At first they were taken in by Honduran families in border towns like La Virtud, and received food and other help from Caritas, the Catholic aid agency. In March 1981 the UNHCR (United Nations High Commission on Refugees) decided to set up a refugee camp. Most of the refugees had personal experience of violence at the hands of Salvadoran troops. They were not entirely safe on the Honduran side, since Salvadoran troops made occasional forays into the area, abducting refugees. Honduran troops were hostile as well. Both armies viewed the refugees as guerrilla supporters, if not guerrillas themselves.

Human rights groups drew up a tally of 11,727 civilians murdered from January to November 1981; 4,563 had been killed in "massacres," that is, killings of twenty people or more.

In December 1981 the FMLN warned the people of the area of Mozote in Morazán that a military invasion was imminent. Perhaps because they were largely evangelicals and had shown no sympathy for the FMLN, the residents were confident that they had nothing to fear from the army. On December 11 the U.S.-trained Atlacatl Brigade rounded up the people, separated the men, women, and children, and executed them. The number of people killed in Mozote and the surrounding villages numbered over seven hundred. When reporters Raymond Bonner (*New York Times*) and Alma Guillermoprieto (*Washington Post*) wrote stories based on an on-site visit, U.S. embassy officials claimed that there was no evidence of a massacre and impugned their qualifications.

In a joint declaration in August 1981, Mexico and France called for a political settlement in El Salvador. By calling the FMLN-FDR a "representative political force," they were in effect legitimizing it. Within El Salvador the army prohibited the circulation of the document. At the instigation of Venezuela, whose Christian Democrat government was aiding the Salvadoran junta, most Latin American governments (Argentina, Bolivia, Chile, Colombia, Guatemala, Honduras, Paraguay, Dominican Republic, Ecuador, Peru, and Venezuela) immediately accused Mexico and France of intervening in El Salvador's affairs. The bishops' conference of El Salvador also condemned it as an intervention. While they acknowledged that the FMLN and FDR had the support of some people, the bishops stated it was losing that support and was now sowing terror among the people, and damaging the economy in order to create conditions for taking power and imposing a Marxist-Leninist dictatorship. Rivera himself, however, said that if the statement forced Salvadorans to rethink their situation, to reassess the damage being caused by the war, and to seek "more rational, civilized and Christian ways of resolving the conflict, I do not see why we should rend our garments." He warned that consultations taking place among the armies of Guatemala, Honduras, and El Salvador might further internationalize the conflict.

Rivera also denounced continuing violence and threats against church people, such as a dynamite explosion set off in a school run by Passionist sisters, personal attacks against him for his observations on the Mexican-French declaration, and hate sheets with titles like "Down with Marxist Jesuits!" and "Down with Progressive Priests!" He likewise criticized the guerrillas for actions such as the destruction of the Puente de Oro, a major bridge in the heart of the country.

War Becomes Routine

Despite their determination to "draw the line" in El Salvador and "send a message to Moscow," Reagan administration officials stumbled for several months. Statements by administration officials that the murdered church women were "activists" (Jeane Kirkpatrick) or that they might have been running a roadblock (Secretary of State Alexander Haig) aroused indignation and forced hasty clarifications. A CIA-prepared white paper claiming to prove massive arms shipments from the Soviet Union to the FMLN produced skepticism and derision.

By mid-1981, however, the administration began to achieve some coherence. In his first major speech after confirmation, Secretary of State for Hemispheric Affairs Thomas Enders outlined the U.S. position on El Salvador: The country should solve its problems through democratic elections, and the United States would provide military and economic aid as long as necessary. More important, however, was the unpublicized work of General Fred Woerner, who arrived in San Salvador in September with a seven-man military assistance strategy team. They spent two months in the Salvadoran Defense Ministry working with a counterpart team to analyze their political objectives, the threats they faced, and their military objectives, concepts, and capabilities. The whole purpose was to force the Salvadoran military to focus on its long-term problems and to think through its strategy, intelligence gathering, manpower needs, and logistics — or as journalist Roy Gutman later put it, to "develop a national plan for El Salvador and to have an end product that looked as if the United States had played no role in the drafting." The United States began to intensify its training of the Salvadoran military at Fort Benning, Georgia, and Fort Bragg, North Carolina.

The March 1982 election was intended to begin the return to democracy by electing a constituent assembly whose task would be to draw up a new constitution. Contesting the elections were the Christian Democrats and ARENA (National Republican Alliance), a party newly formed by Roberto D'Aubuisson. Investigative journalists later discovered that ARENA's founders were consciously seeking to imitate their enemies, the "communists," by setting up a three-part structure: an armed group (death squads), a political party, and a fundraising apparatus. Their objective was to wrest back control over the political process that they had lost through the 1979 coup and deepening U.S. involvement. The left refused to participate in the election and thus the Reagan administration could accuse it of wanting to "shoot its way into power," conveniently ignoring the fact that death squads and government forces were killing hundreds of civilians a month with impunity.

About two months before the vote, the Salvadoran bishops issued a statement welcoming the election which, they said, would permit the country to pass from a situation of de facto government to government by law. They further reminded Catholics of their "obligation in conscience to go to vote." The *Letter to the Churches*, which the UCA had begun to publish as a means of communication among base communities and others in the church, raised serious questions about this statement, pointing out that the bishops said nothing about conditions for elections, such as freedom of expression or an end to repression. The bishops also failed to acknowledge the possibility that people could express their will by refusing to vote. The author concluded that this statement was "political and partisan" as had been earlier statements, and noted that the United States was very eager to use the bishops' letter—telexing it to embassies in Europe and broadcasting it over the Voice of America—while continually ignoring the position of Archbishop Rivera, who stressed that elections were only one element in a solution.

Having assumed that the Christian Democrats would win a majority and thus provide a "centrist" government, U.S. officials discovered to their chagrin that ARENA and other conservative parties held a majority in the assembly and would probably make D'Aubuisson president. U.S. ambassador Deane Hinton impressed upon the military that such an outcome was unacceptable. Alvaro Magaña, a banker who had played no role in politics, was accordingly designated to be president.

A few weeks after the election, an *ECA* editorial became news by asserting that the election results had been inflated. The argument was that the number of votes registered, almost a million and a half, could not have been processed given the number of polling places and the amount of time each vote would take. The UCA team concluded that the numbers had been inflated across the board, preserving the proportions of each party, but presenting to the world the spectacle of a large vote for democracy. The editorial also criticized the left's "terrorist" actions surrounding the election. The author (presumably Jesuit social psychologist Ignacio Martín-Baró) suggested that the FDR-FMLN had around "a half million people either organized or in sympathy," while those opposed to them would have "around three hundred thousand"—presumably meaning people seriously committed. Given a fair chance the left might be able to appeal to the large group of the undecided, but it should not assume that it had the support of the bulk of the population; indeed the left should be aware that it was not communicating well with that majority. In any case, the elections would not resolve El Salvador's basic problems, and the fate of the country should not be resolved by Washington. As the war, which had already cost thirty thousand lives, went on, negotiation would become more attractive at some point. These arguments exemplified the stance of the group of Jesuits and others at the UCA.

Repression and war were taking their toll on church people. In the archdiocese of San Salvador it was estimated that 40 percent of rural parishes had no resident priest, and the number of priests and religious had declined by 35 percent. Many base communities were being "dismantled," according to an analyst in *ECA*.

The country was now divided into areas under government control, areas under guerrilla control, and areas in dispute. A few more priests and sisters went to live in guerrilla areas. Father Rutilio Sánchez, who had fled the country after many parishioners had been killed and a military hit squad had come looking for him, returned to Chalatenango in 1982 and worked to commission catechists in each community. Feeling that she could no longer work in San Salvador, a "Sister Rosa" worked to set up schools within what she and others assumed to be the beginning of a new revolutionary order.

Archbishop Rivera acknowledged that the people living in guerrilla-held territory had a right to pastoral care. It would not be logical to allow for military chaplains, and to prohibit priests from associating with the guerrillas, provided they did not bear arms. Not all the bishops were so tolerant. Bishop Pedro Aparicio of San Vicente, after meeting with President Magaña and the army high command, told journalists that "at least thirty" priests had joined the guerrillas. Two years previously he had suspended ten priests of his diocese, that is, prohibited them from exercising their priesthood. Now he specifically mentioned David Rodríguez, Bernardo Boulang, and the UCA Jesuit Ignacio Ellacuría. From France Boulang replied, accusing Aparicio of calumny; he added, however, that he thought it was better to accompany guerrilla combatants, than to go around as a military vicar and colonel in a murderous army, or to betray and turn over fellow priests or catechists.

In July 1982 the bishops' conference exhorted the government and the guerrillas to engage in a sincere dialogue. The next month Pope John Paul II sent the bishops a letter telling them that one of the most important aspects of their mission was to work for reconciliation. He also noted that the conflict was rooted in social injustice. This exchange helped legitimize the notion of "dialogue," which the Salvadoran military and right wing saw as a code word for negotiations and therefore as tantamount to treason.

In October 1982 Archbishop Rivera delivered to the Magaña government a proposal for dialogue from the FMLN-FDR. Throughout the decade Rivera was to serve as a courier many times—most often to the government from the FMLN, which made almost all peace overtures.

On the eve of his departure for Central America in March 1983, Pope John Paul II made Rivera's appointment as archbishop of San Salvador permanent, thus giving papal approval to his efforts at peacemaking and denunciation of human rights violations.

Expectations for the pope's visit were varied. Conservative editorialists hoped that he would enforce discipline on those priests, including Archbishop Rivera, who went too far in their homilies, "mixing politics with Christ." The two crucial questions were what stance the pope would take toward Archbishop Romero—whose memory was still both revered and reviled—and what he might say about dialogue between the government and the insurgency. During the preparatory stage a poster of Romero and John Paul II together became an object of controversy. The UCA had printed twenty thousand copies of the photo in poster and postcard form, but Bishop Gregorio Rosa Chavez ordered the posters withdrawn, reportedly after two ARENA women complained to the papal nuncio; many of the posters, however, were already in circulation. The Vatican itself sent its own signal on March 2 when *L'Osservatore Romano*, its official newspaper, ran a very positive article recounting Romero's life and work and calling him a "martyr and prophet."

The day before the visit the FMLN halted traffic along a thirty-kilometer section of the road north toward Chalatenango and Honduras. Over Radio Venceremos two priests, Rogelio Ponceele and Miguel Ventura, addressed the pope, saying that the people hoped he would communicate understanding and hope like Archbishop Romero.

The normal conditions of the state of siege seemed to be suspended during the papal visit. Members of base communities went to the streets carrying placards and singing songs of moderate social protest. Some of the young people singing and playing were arrested. Conservative groups passed out anticommunist propaganda. On his way to the main gathering, the pope made an unofficial side trip to the cathedral and Romero's tomb. Fearing a spontaneous rally, the government had posted troops to keep people away, and thus only a handful of journalists observed the visit. He went to the altar of the Virgin where he prayed in silence and then he went to the opposite side where he knelt in front of Romero's tomb, covered his hands, and prayed in silence. He then stood up and prayed the Lord's Prayer in Latin, and proceeded to the main altar where he said he had prayed for Romero "who gave his life for his faithful."

An estimated quarter of a million people were waiting at the parking lot of Metrocentro, a shopping center serving the middle and upper classes, where the pope delivered a homily on the topic of peace and reconciliation. Speaking of the evil in human hearts and social structures, which leads to war and the spiral of hatred, he exclaimed, "So many homes destroyed! So many refugees, exiles and displaced people! So many orphans. So many noble, innocent lives cruelly and brutally cut off." He then mentioned the lives of priests and sisters and "a zealous and venerated pastor, the archbishop of this flock, Oscar Arnulfo Romero, who tried, like his other brothers in the episcopacy, to bring about an end to violence and reestablish peace." These words prompted prolonged applause and chanting of slogans. The pope urged "that his memory always be respected and that no ideological interest seek to take advantage of his sacrifice as a pastor committed to his flock." He was obviously at great pains to make certain that his endorsement of Romero not be construed as a criticism of the other bishops—who opposed Romero, and had not even attended his large public funeral.

During the next few minutes the pope three or four times used the word "dialogue" when virtually no one outside the church would use the word publicly. However, he qualified his use of the term with references to Marxists, in effect questioning their sincerity. With such people dialogue becomes "difficult and sterile." The gospel calls to conversion: The rich —

"unconcerned, unjust, self-satisfied in their goods—can and must change, as must those who make use of terrorism, or who harbor hatred." The pope said he was not urging the kind of peace that would ignore problems, but a true peace for all. "No one should be excluded from dialogue for peace," he said.

Bishop Rosa Chávez, who had been in charge of the papal reception, said that during his lunch with the bishops the pope expressed disappointment with the FMLN, although he hoped that the FDR (its civilian allies), might be more open to dialogue. Rosa Chávez speculated that the pope might have been affected by the treatment he had just received in Nicaragua, two days before coming to El Salvador.

Vatican and papal action was clearly an endorsement of Rivera's overall approach as opposed to the progovernment and promilitary sentiments of most of the other bishops. Whatever they thought of the content of his addresses, grassroots Catholic church workers later looked back on his visit as a moment when they were able to overcome fear and demoralization and look toward the future with greater confidence.

In an extensive and generally positive survey of John Paul II's "ethico-political message" based on all his addresses in Central America, Ignacio Ellacuría noted that the pope had failed to use one term essential for understanding the recent history of El Salvador: repression. The use of repression to preserve the existing unjust order antedated guerrilla violence; it was one of the key elements of the current situation; and it could justly be called "state terrorism," a term used even by the OAS. Furthermore, although the pope had referred to outside intervention, he had not been specific, particularly with regard to El Salvador, where the United States had given "hundreds of millions of dollars for war and repression." The level of intervention by communist countries did not even approach that of the United States.

Since the late 1970s the churches, both Catholic and Protestant, had been working with the victims of repression. Because of repression within El Salvador, some aid was channeled through groups working outside the country, primarily in Mexico City. People fleeing army violence tended to seek the protection of the Catholic church, and the agencies of the Lutheran, Episcopal, and Baptist churches; those who were fleeing the guerrillas or the general situation of war might gravitate to programs run by the government or conservative evangelical churches and agencies.

The first large refugee flows had been caused by the militarization accompanying the land reform of March 1980. Hundreds of people, mainly women and children, were living in makeshift shelters in the large seminary yard when Romero was murdered. Over time the number of church-run refugee camps grew to twenty-three. They were often surrounded by armed troops. Refugees would not venture beyond the barbed wire fences because many had no identification papers and could easily be abducted and killed.

Archbishop Rivera firmly defended the legitimacy of church work with refugees, even when some people working for the Social Secretariat of the archdiocese were accused of being part of an ERP cell and when the police said that mass organizations sympathetic to the guerrillas were present in archdiocesan refugee sites. In a sermon he noted that the first refugees had appeared as far back as 1979 and that many people were fleeing simply because they were accused of aiding the guerrillas. He said it was "natural" that those who did not agree with the present regime should seek shelter from the archdiocese and that having lost their identification papers they were afraid to leave the refugee camps. The church's stance was simply that of the Good Samaritan. He also declared that the army had taken food that the church agency Caritas had set aside for 1,500 poor people, and arbitrarily handed it out in a single day to whomever they saw fit. "The way to do away with the refugee camps . . . is not by accusing the people of being guerrillas . . . but stopping once and for all the repression that exists out in the villages and in the cities."

Formalizing already existing cooperation, in 1982 the Lutheran church, the Emmanuel Baptist church, the Episcopal church program Credo, and the Catholic church established an organization called Diaconia, in order to coordinate their efforts and rationalize aid to needy groups. Diaconia did not itself administer the programs, which were run by the churches, but was a conduit to funding sources in Europe and North America.

Humanitarian programs and pastoral work continued to operate in an environment of hostility and repression. On March 13, 1983, a week after the pope's visit, Marianela García, head of the Salvadoran Human Rights Commission, was killed along with thirty civilians near Suchitoto as she was attempting to gather evidence on alleged use of napalm and white phosphorus by government troops.

Salvadoran troops continued to commit massive human rights violations. Whereas the typical actions during the 1979–82 period had been death squad killings, now civilians were increasingly being killed in air attacks or mortar shelling. In order to obtain congressional approval for military aid, the Reagan administration had to certify that the Salvadoran government was improving in its observance of human rights. Since the numbers of civilian deaths were declining from the high point of 1981, when perhaps 12,000 people had been killed, it was indeed possible to claim improvement, even though official forces were still killing, torturing, raping, and causing "disappearances" on a massive scale. Areyeh Neier of Americas Watch said that for the administration to make such a certification was like claiming that a mass murderer who killed twenty people last year and ten people this year was "improving." The first serious expression of displeasure from the Reagan administration occurred in late 1983 when Vice-President Bush arrived in San Salvador bearing the names of nine officers judged to be the worst human rights offenders. They were not brought to justice, however, but simply transferred from positions of troop command.

In June 1983 the army high command announced a National Plan for

Security and Development, aimed at both dislodging the guerrillas from their areas and reasserting control through development programs such as reopening schools, building roads, establishing health programs, distributing food, and training local civilian defense forces. Loosely modeled on similar efforts in Vietnam and drawing on counterinsurgency theory, this program was to begin in two of the country's fourteen provinces. Within months it became clear that the guerrillas were skillful at evading troops during clean-up operations, and in some instances, U.S.-funded projects moved ahead with the approval of local FMLN commanders.

Conflicts within the revolutionary organizations became apparent at this point. In April 1983 Melida Anaya Montes, a leading figure in the FPL, was brutally stabbed to death by partisans of the organization's founder and head, Salvador Cayetano Carpio, in Nicaragua. Within days, Carpio committed suicide. Within the left these events took some of the glow off the almost mythic image of the guerrilla leadership.

In areas where it had control—where in fact the national government did not function—the FMLN was establishing its own local government structures, especially in Chalatenango, Guazapa, and San Vicente. Elected bodies, called "Popular Peoples Powers," took charge of community life, including production decisions. ANDES (National Association of Educators of El Salvador), the national teachers' union, was active in literacy programs. A volunteer later described working in some twenty-four communities situated in the eastern part of Chalatenango. A number of "internationalists" trained thirty-six local people to be teachers and also developed a basic workbook for teaching literacy. Disruption from air attacks and military sweeps eventually made their work almost impossible.

Letter to the Churches (April 1983) gave a glimpse of pastoral work on the run. Very early one February morning, a community fleeing the army gathered under the trees at the bottom of a deep ravine to baptize two-month-old Sonia, whose mother had been killed by a bomb three days before. Jose, a seminarian, explained the significance of baptism, drawing a contrast between the pomp often observed in the church and the poverty of Jesus. The people then discussed the symbolism of water, like the river that had given them life during the past three days. Father Rutilio Sánchez said that just as they had shared whatever food and drink they had, in baptizing this girl they were making her a member of their community. She would suffer and struggle and win her freedom along with her community. He also said that "in a liberated community all of us are the child's godparents."

An American layman later described his presence in Chalatenango as a matter of "remaining faithful, not abandoning people even though the official church to a large degree had abandoned them," insofar as it accepted the government that was bombing them and sending the army against them. It meant "remaining present and active in a liberating process that is much larger and deeper than military struggle."

President — and Nation — Prisoners of War?

In early 1984 José Napoleón Duarte and Roberto D'Aubuisson faced off as presidential candidates. The Reagan administration hoped to further legitimize the regime, and, assuming a Christian Democrat victory, to advance the reforms begun in 1980, undercut the appeal of the left, and end U.S. public and congressional doubts about policy in El Salvador. Despite D'Aubuisson's earlier ties with prominent U.S. conservatives such as Sen. Jesse Helms, by now it had become convenient for the Reagan administration to highlight the contrast between the Christian Democrats and ARENA; hence the election was portrayed as a contest between a hero of democracy and a dangerous gangster.

From within El Salvador, however, matters looked different. UCA analysts noted that the "center right" Christian Democrats and the "rightist" ARENA shared an anticommunist ideology and the aim of destroying the FMLN; they differed only over their degree of vehemence and preferred means. The "center right" hoped a strong civilian government could control the army and security forces, curb the death squads, instill respect for human rights, strengthen the judicial system, and promote a kind of development that would reach the masses. For its part, the "right" hoped to be able to gain a monopoly hold over political power, end the guerrilla threat by whatever means necessary, and annul the 1980 reforms, thus restoring traditional oligarchical control over the economy. There was "little distinction in practice" between the two sides.

The real alternative — not on the ballot — was the "left" program of the FMLN. Making another of its periodic peace proposals, the FMLN in February issued a twenty-point document, which, as summarized by the UCA writers, called for a direct share, but not a monopoly, in power; far-reaching reforms in agriculture, finance, and trade; a mixed economy, in which private enterprise would have a place but not abusive privileges; political pluralism; and the restructuring of the army and security forces to remove those responsible for human rights violations; and a merger of the present army with the FMLN. These positions, commented the authors, represented considerable change from the FMLN's initial position in 1980 but seemed "irreconcilable with those of the right and only slightly less so with those of the center-right." Although the presidential candidates and the United States ignored or made light of this proposal, Auxiliary Bishop Gregorio Rosa Chávez welcomed it and said it might permit a new move toward dialogue.

In a statement in the name of the bishops' conference, Archbishop Rivera called elections the "formalization" of democracy, which required respect for people's lives, participation in public life without fear, and the right to organize. "We believe in elections, but they are not the only way to achieve peace."

In Duarte's favor were his long political career and the reputation of the Christian Democrat party for honesty and commitment to development. Its constituency was made up of workers and peasants, and especially those who had benefited from the land reform programs. In order to get the backing of labor and peasant groups for the election, Duarte signed what was called a "social pact" with their representative organization, the UPD (Democratic Popular Unity), a U.S.-funded organization designed expressly as an alternative to the more radical mass organizations. The AFL-CIO helped channel over a half-million dollars of CIA funds to enable the Duarte campaign to hire campaign organizers. D'Aubuisson had a fiery, charismatic style, a slick campaign largely designed by U.S. political consultants, the traditional mobilizing ability of landholders, and undoubtedly a degree of intimidation. Duarte's clear but not overwhelming victory (54% to 46%) seemed to signal that the Reagan policy was working. With one visit to Washington, Duarte coaxed an additional $70 million in additional aid for El Salvador. More important, human rights violations ceased to be of major concern to the U.S. Congress for several years.

The new government also served to mute criticism from the Catholic church. Most Latin American bishops have an affinity for the ideology of Christian Democracy, which in fact claims to take inspiration from Catholic social teaching. Duarte and Rivera were contemporaries and had much in common. Rivera regarded the newly elected government as legitimate.

Expectations of Duarte, nourished by his campaign appeal, revolved around three issues: peace, ending human rights violations, and economic recovery. What remained ambiguous was how they were related to each other. Was peace itself, including some concessions on all sides, a condition for economic recovery? Or was peace to be defined as victory over the FMLN—thus subordinating economic policies and human rights to an overall counterinsurgency strategy? Could Duarte have fulfilled his campaign promises, or was he from the outset trapped by his dependence on the Reagan administration? Constrained by an ARENA-dominated legislature, he did not attempt significant economic initiatives during his first year in office.

U.S. involvement in El Salvador inevitably deepened. The 1984 military aid of $243.5 million was equal to the total of the previous three years. With that aid the Salvadoran military shifted to a new strategy aimed at halting the FMLN's ability to mass large forces. Included in the strategy were more small patrols, expanded civic actions and psychological warfare, and an increased ability to attack from the air through bombardment and helicopter assault. As death squad-style killings declined, the numbers of civilians killed by air and artillery attack increased, although these were harder for human rights monitors based in San Salvador to document.

This period saw a resurgence of both popular organizing and a new public presence of Christian groups. For example, in February 1984 the Christian community of Zacamil in northern San Salvador gathered at a

Catholic school to celebrate fifteen years of pastoral work. Posters on the wall honored three of the community's many "martyrs," Father Octavio Ortiz, Sister Silvia Arriola, and Alfonso Acevedo. Among the one thousand people attending were representatives of twenty-eight communities, numerous priests and sisters, and Archbishop Rivera. At the offertory a commentator explained the symbolism of the various items presented: sandals (messengers announcing the good news), chains (to be broken in the liberation of the poor), candle, bible, red flowers (community flourishing and spilling its own blood), food, medicine and money (collected for the needy), a large wooden cross, a photograph of a dawn, a poster of Romero, and a book bearing the names of martyrs of the preceding fifteen years. Each symbol was greeted with applause. At the ceremony a sister and a married couple made or renewed their vows. After the Mass, those attending were given a small wooden cross on a string to be worn around the neck. Participants lingered afterwards over sandwiches and cold drinks, singing and conversing. The event indicated that people were beginning to shed their fear. Two days later a newspaper called it a fiesta by subversives and for the sake of subversion, and attacked Rivera and other church officials.

Then on March 24, 1984, the fourth anniversary of Archbishop Romero's murder, about three hundred women of CoMadres (Committee of Mothers and Family Members of the Disappeared, Murdered, and Political Prisoners) marched from Sagrado Corazon Church toward the cathedral. Although few bystanders joined them, some cheered from the sidewalks. The presence of an estimated one thousand journalists who were in the country to cover the election, which was to take place in a few days, obviously afforded some protection. As they marched, they called for justice, denounced the electoral "farce," and accused D'Aubuisson of murdering Romero. Upon their arrival at the cathedral, they took part in a Mass. This was an unofficial celebration of the anniversary of Romero's death. The previous day Archbishop Rivera had spoken against the extremes of trying to silence Romero or to use him as a "political banner."

This march was the first significant street demonstration since mid-1980. Despite the violence of the "dirty war" that had been directed primarily at the mass organizations, some activists had remained in the country and had quietly begun to organize again. On May 1 workers in groups began to gather in the Parque Cuscatlán, despite the state of siege. At that moment a factory was surrounded by troops, and inside the union leaders were saying they would leave only under the protection of the International Red Cross. Soon three thousand workers were gathered in front of the cathedral, where Father Miguel Cavada addressed them. "Christ was a worker who gave his life for the poor," shouted a woman. "In San Salvador there are many Christs. ... May our Christs be resurrected, may they come back alive." Others shouted, "Long live the working class!"

The resurgence of organizing took numerous forms. From cautious beginnings in 1983, a new labor movement gradually began to take shape.

One study indicated that between July and mid-October 1984, workers carried out thirty-four strikes and eighty-eight other actions. The new wave of organizing was strongest in the public sector. On November 5, 1984, three thousand members of ANDES, the teachers' union, public sector workers, members of the Human Rights Commission, and organizations representing prisoners and the disappeared marched, shouting "Bullets no, beans yes." The government accused them of being used by the FMLN-FDR. In May 1985 hundreds of workers from the water works went on strike to protest the firing of labor union members. At one point in mid-1985 around forty thousand workers were on strike. A July 1984 assembly of people displaced by the war led to the formation of CRIPDES (Christian Committee for the Displaced of El Salvador). This organization also soon took to the streets, organizing a march in August. The refugees began to emerge from a state of dependency in which others served as their advocates and were demanding that their rights be respected. Even political prisoners formed an organization in the Mariona prison; in April 1984 women prisoners organized a hunger strike.

Speaking before the United Nations General Assembly in October 1984, Duarte invited the FMLN-FDR to meet with him at La Palma, a mountain town near the Honduran border. Press accounts portrayed this move as a bold challenge to the guerrillas, ignoring the fact that the FMLN had made numerous previous proposals. The announcement caught the Reagan administration off guard. Indeed, Duarte himself perhaps had no clear idea what he intended beyond rescuing his already waning credibility. When their initial proposal that President Belisario Betancur of Colombia facilitate the dialogue was rejected, the FMLN-FDR insisted that the Catholic church be involved. Duarte at first maintained that there was no such need, but when Archbishop Rivera raised questions about what the procedure should be, the need for the presence of third parties became clear. Bishop Rosa Chávez also became involved in delivering messages between the two sides. In addition to Rivera, several Salvadoran bishops and the papal nuncio were present at La Palma, along with hundreds of Salvadorans and numerous journalists.

For the first time representatives of the warring parties met on Salvadoran soil. The positions of the two sides, however, were irreconcilable. The conditions that the Salvadoran military and the Reagan administration proposed to the FMLN were tantamount to surrender; for its part the FMLN pressed for a transition process, sometimes called "power sharing," in which the army would be purged and repression ended. Elections could take place only as part of a more comprehensive process.

The atmosphere at a second meeting held at Ayagualo a few weeks later was considerably chillier. Col. Domingo Monterrosa, a legendary army commander, and several other officers had died in a helicopter crash caused by a clever guerrilla sabotage that once more revealed the army's underlying ineptitude despite massive U.S. assistance. Pressure from business representatives had also hardened Duarte.

In June 1985 a bomb in a cafe in the Zona Rosa district killed four U.S. marines and eleven other people, both U.S. citizens and Salvadorans. Whether it was the work of the FMLN itself or a guerrilla faction operating independently, it was seen as a terrorist action. While condemning this attack, Rivera said it was just as truly terrorism as certain acts of the army, "such as bombing, destroying crops, and burning people's huts." He also noted that the Zona Rosa was notorious for drug use and sexual license, which made it a symbol of the "indifference and unconcern" of many people toward the tragedy bleeding away at El Salvador. Right-wing groups predictably attacked Rivera but others applauded. A university researcher said Rivera had touched a taboo, the moral breakdown of the dominant class; a union leader said he was only reminding the rich of what the popular classes knew all too well.

In the March 1985 legislative and mayoral election the Christian Democrats did surprisingly well, capturing thirty-four of the sixty seats in the legislature and over 75 percent of the municipalities. With the election behind him, Duarte sought to implement an orthodox austerity and stabilization program as urged by Washington and the IMF (International Monetary Fund), including the usual measures of keeping wages and salaries down, curtailing social spending, and devaluing the currency—all measures that would harm the popular sectors with which he had made a "social pact" prior to his own election. A new round of strikes, once more mainly by public sector employees, was met by repression. In June official forces raided five hospitals and twenty clinics to end a four-week occupation by workers.

In August 1985 the Salvadoran bishops' conference issued a pastoral letter on reconciliation and peace. While the overall tone was somewhat doctrinal, in one passage they expressly delegitimized the FMLN. They contrasted "a constitutional government," the result of "a democratic process, endorsed by a massive turnout at the polls in four elections in a row," to "the FMLN/FDR which claims to represent the people but cannot clearly prove it, and which moreover makes use of violence and sabotage as an essential weapon in its struggle." The bishops also implied that the guerrillas were not sincerely seeking peace.

In a carefully worded reply, the FMLN-FDR distinguished the doctrinal from the political aspects of the letter and went on to point out a number of shortcomings. The bishops overlooked the role of the Reagan administration in the conflict, and also ignored the causes of the war as well as the terrorism used by government forces. The FMLN-FDR also made a number of quite specific complaints about the way Bishop Rosa Chávez had failed to carry out his own responsibilities as an intermediary in the dialogues and subsequently.

On the afternoon of September 10, 1985, Inés Guadalupe Duarte, the president's daughter, and a friend were kidnapped on their way to university classes. Church representatives played an important role in the negotiations that led to her release and had important political repercussions. The FMLN did not immediately claim to have kidnapped Ms. Duarte, and throughout the negotiations, it claimed to be acting on behalf of a Pedro Pablo Castillo guerrilla unit. In recent months, however, the FMLN had abducted several dozen mayors in rural areas that they regarded as under their control or over which they were asserting control.

The FMLN presented the government with two separate sets of negotiations: Duarte's daughter would be released in exchange for thirty-four political prisoners, and the kidnapped mayors would be released if ninety-six war wounded were allowed to leave the country and twenty-nine labor union members were released from jail.

The negotiations paralyzed Duarte's government for forty days. Although the Reagan administration expressed its opposition to any deals with terrorists, Duarte would not risk losing his daughter — and the United States at this point was unwilling to lose Duarte. After first contacting the FDR and the Socialist International, the government sought the help of the church, and specifically Archbishop Rivera and Ignacio Ellacuría, the rector of the UCA. They and a representative of the Socialist International were summoned to Guazapa, the volcano near San Salvador that had been both a guerrilla stronghold and a constant area of attack. Some days later after complex negotiations, Ms. Duarte and her friend were exchanged for twenty-two political prisoners, while twenty-five mayors were exchanged for one hundred one injured people. The FMLN's demands that the government account for nine of the "disappeared" (of a list of five thousand in its possession) and release the labor leaders were not met.

Although Rivera's presence was essential for the negotiations, when the complex negotiations threatened to break down, it was Ellacuría who skillfully proposed alternatives and deserved a good deal of the credit for the eventual solution. An *ECA* writer commented that for the first time direct dialogue had led to an important agreement between the government and the FMLN and that it had gone into effect immediately. Despite the negative attitude of the United States, most democratic governments welcomed the agreement.

Duarte's effectiveness was plainly diminished. After ignoring the plight of the mayors, he had suspended all other matters to rescue his daughter. To their chagrin, the armed forces had been forced to recognize that they needed Duarte for U.S. support, but his submission to the United States undermined his credibility.

When he went to Guazapa, Rivera also visited the local civilian villages of Ojos de Agua (Chalatenango) and Aguacayo (Guazapa). These were his first visits to FMLN-controlled areas. Priests had not been there for years and some Catholics felt abandoned. During a mass Rogelio Ponceele, the Belgian priest who had now been working in Morazán for almost five years, told Rivera that many people had to live underground or were compelled to flee like wild animals. Rivera also heard accounts of women being raped and murdered, children being burned, people being forced out of their hiding places with gas, bodies being hacked to pieces with machetes. All buildings in the area had been destroyed, including the church. At the Mass someone read a document listing all the attacks by the military since 1980. Acknowledging the temptation to hatred or revenge, Ponceele nevertheless gave voice to the people's sentiments of forgiveness and love. The people implored Rivera to defend them and to send them church workers. He replied that having seen with his own eyes, he could now appreciate what they were enduring.

In early 1986 the UCA team published a collection of analytical articles summarizing the situation of the country. Having poured $2 billion into El Salvador the United States was operating as a kind of "super-government." The country's formal rulers were simply managers, "running a political and military program that they had little or no role in shaping, and that was not designed to address El Salvador's national interests. . . . In the old days, the armed forces ran the country for the benefit of the oligarchy; now the Christian Democratic party runs the country for the benefit of the Reagan Administration." Although the dependence of the United States on Duarte gave him some power vis-à-vis the right and the military, his own dependence on the United States vitiated his reformist intentions. The United States designed his economic policies and he had no room to negotiate any agreement that would entail concessions to the FMLN.

The nature of the war was shifting as U.S. military aid increased and the Salvadoran armed forces were expanded (from 12,000 in 1980 to over 50,000 by mid-decade); the armed forces began to engage in more aggressive small patrol tactics. Inevitably, the role of the military in society grew, absorbing a larger proportion of the budget. Local military commanders overshadowed civilian authorities. Changes in the area of human rights included directives on rules of conduct for aerial bombing, instructions on arrest procedures, the dismantling of the Treasury Police intelligence unit (once a center for death squads), strengthening of the judicial system, the establishment of some commissions to investigate death squad killings, and a decline of human rights abuses. Nevertheless, much of this remained on paper as civilians continued to be bombed and death squads continued to carry out their operations. The Duarte government could not account for the four thousand or more "disappeared" prior to 1984, as it had not been able to do so for the nine requested by the FMLN during the kidnapping negotiations.

In analyzing the FMLN, Ellacuría began by noting their affinity with the Christian Democrats: Both appealed to the poor as their constituency, and indeed the FDR was largely made up of disaffected Christian Democrats. Nevertheless, because of its alliance with the United States and the army, the Christian Democrat government was indeed the target and enemy of the FMLN. He went on to conclude that the prospects for negotiation were bleak, insofar as the FMLN saw ending U.S. intervention as an objective of negotiations, and Washington regarded its counterinsurgency as non-negotiable. Although war was destroying the country, neither side was willing to cede. The government was dreaming that after defeating the FMLN it would receive a Marshall Plan type of aid. The FMLN had not given much thought to economic recovery or sources of aid. Both sides wanted power.

Ellacuría modestly urged a "humanization" of the war, including a halt to "all forms of terrorism," full respect for civilians and their property, and humane treatment of the wounded and war prisoners. The FMLN could halt sabotage that hurt the population economically, while the government could guarantee political space for the mass movement to make its real weight felt through popular organizations—labor unions, cooperatives, and so forth. This would pave the way for a far-reaching process of democratization and mass participation, far outstripping the "limited ritual of elections." Convinced that Duarte would be unable to make changes, the authors predicted—accurately, as it turned out—that if Duarte concluded his term, he would have to turn over power to the right. The report's title, "Duarte: Prisoner of War?" might have been applied to the nation itself.

Contrary to his constituency and ideology, Duarte proposed an essentially orthodox austerity plan as urged by Washington and the IMF: Hold down wages and salaries, reduce social spending, and devalue the currency in order to stimulate exports, lower imports, and improve the balance of payments. In January 1986 he announced a "package" of measures including price hikes for gasoline, the prohibition of some luxury imports, minor wage increases, and some price controls (which proved unworkable). These measures spurred the formation of a new labor coalition, the UNTS (National Union of Salvadoran Labor), which included some organizations once supportive of Duarte. On May 1 the UNTS organized a march of eighty thousand people, the largest demonstration since 1980.

Opening Space for Reconciliation

In late 1985 and early 1986 government troops launched "Operation Phoenix" in a major effort to dislodge the guerrillas from the Guazapa volcano region.

The bombs could be heard in San Salvador, and thus served as a reminder of a war that was only a distant rumor to some residents of the capital. As was generally the case, the guerrillas were able to evade the army attacks but civilians were killed or had to flee. A woman later described how she had hidden with other people during the air attack and then the ground operation, without food and suffering from malaria. She had already lost her first child and now a child died in childbirth because the midwife was unable to provide adequate treatment.

Rivera himself witnessed A-37 attacks against civilians in the village of Guarjila, Chalatenango, on a pastoral visit there in December. He later commented that this area now had only a few hundred occupants whereas there had once been 10,000. Similarly, the population of Guazapa had declined from 15,000 to about 2,000 just before Operation Phoenix.

Nevertheless, it was at this very time that with the aid of church and humanitarian organizations, the thousands of refugees who had spent years in camps began organized efforts to return to their land. A human rights observer later noted that the civilians who fled Operation Phoenix into refugee camps were among those who spearheaded this drive to return. Thus, a military operation aimed at asserting government control over Guazapa may have propelled people to assert their human right to live on the soil from which they had been driven.

The first organized movement took place in early January 1986 in the municipality of Tenancingo, about thirty kilometers northeast of San Salvador. The area had come under attack starting in mid-1983. After the armed forces bombed the area in September in what they regarded as a preemptive strike, killing an unknown number of civilians, virtually all residents had fled. Forming a committee in 1984, some of the more financially secure residents asked Archbishop Rivera to involve the poorer residents in a resettlement project. After negotiating an agreement with both the military and the FMLN not to establish a military base in the town, Rivera in June 1985 secured the collaboration of an experienced Salvadoran development agency to help the project.

The ambitious aim of church workers was that the Tenancingo project not only resolve one community's problems, but that it provide an example of how the conflict itself could be reversed and offer a model of a new kind of development, a microcosm of a new El Salvador. During the latter months of 1985 the area was prepared; the armed forces, the government, the FMLN, the U.S. embassy, the International Red Cross, and numerous development agencies were involved in negotiations.

In January 1986 fifty-six families (187 people) returned to Tenancingo. After an initial emergency period, the emphasis was on reactivating the local economy through agriculture and small trade as well as through public works projects, which provided some cash income ($1.60 a day). The project was designed to help even the poorer become self-sufficient and avoid the previous patterns of land rent and money lending.

The Tenancingo project eventually disappointed the enthusiasm of its original proponents. The townspeople themselves were largely ignored in the planning, and such paternalism undermined the project. Reneging on its promises, the army ended up occupying the area. The community's new structures did not have legal status and hence the old structures ultimately prevailed.

Nevertheless, this project was the first step in what would soon become a large movement of people to their places of origin. At a National Forum of the Displaced held in May 1986 the CNR (National Coordinating Committee for Repopulation) was set up and in June twenty-six families returned to San Jose las Flores, Chalatenango, in the heart of a conflictive district. Soon the town grew to over five hundred people. The following month six hundred peasants returned to El Barillo, on the slopes of the Guazapa volcano, just six months after being driven out by Operation Phoenix. Soon other repopulations were taking place in dozens of communities. Refugee camps occupied for years began to empty.

The criteria established by church agencies for resettlement were later outlined by Archbishop Rivera. All those who wanted to return to their places of origin should be able to do so, with no discrimination for ideological reasons. There should be a serious reconstruction plan. The parish priest should be involved because he would know the people and could help work for the reconciliation of opposing groups. Finally, Rivera said that the aim was "not to prolong the war but to open a space for people to come together again and for reconciliation in order to repair the torn social fabric."

Throughout 1986 numerous peace initiatives were attempted but none led to concrete results. In February former President Jimmy Carter had contacts with both the government and the FMLN. In March President Duarte proposed a peace plan for Central America that was similar in some respects to what Guatemalan President Cerezo and Costa Rican President Oscar Arias would later propose. The FMLN rejected the offer on the grounds that it was really intended as propaganda for the Reagan administration, insofar as it sought to put pressure on the Sandinista government by making a false symmetry with El Salvador. In May and June, Rivera met with FMLN-FDR leaders in both Panama and Mexico City, serving in effect as a courier between the two sides. Bishop Rosa Chávez observed that a July set of proposals from the insurgents was more moderate than previous stances. After new exchanges mediated by Rivera the stage was set for a dialogue in Sesori, San Miguel, in eastern El Salvador, but the left would not attend because the armed forces had refused to demilitarize the area around the site. In a bit of showmanship, Duarte nevertheless went to Sesori on the designated day, with high government officials and diplomats, including U.S. Ambassador Edwin Corr, and Bishop Marco René Revelo, the head of the Salvadoran bishops' conference.

Late in the morning of October 10, an earthquake (registering 6.4 on the Richter scale) shook San Salvador. Nine older mainly public buildings were immediately destroyed and others had to be demolished; 890 people were listed as killed, 10,000 were injured, and 30,000 were left homeless, primarily renters in the older downtown areas. Owners of small businesses or shops lost their livelihood or were forced to seek a place to live on the outskirts of the city. The middle and upper classes were not affected.

Although it received offers of aid, including an emergency $126 million from the United States, the Duarte government was unable to respond quickly or efficiently. The churches, whom the government excluded from its administration of incoming aid, established their own operations. Within days the Catholic church was dispensing food to some 33,000 families. Archbishop Rivera interpreted the earthquake as a "call to conversion" making even more obvious the need to end the war. "The cry of nature that shook the earth . . . is an unexpected and overwhelming argument for ending this other earthquake [the war] once and for all."

Since the FMLN 1981 offensive, the war had taken place largely in the countryside. The earthquake accelerated the process already underway of bringing the struggle back to San Salvador. Like earlier earthquakes in Nicaragua (1972) and Guatemala (1976), this one highlighted existing political and economic problems. The Salvadoran economy was deteriorating as factories had been closing and unemployment increasing. Duarte had been favored momentarily by high coffee prices early in his term but now they had begun to fall.

The mainspring of the economy was not what El Salvador produced, particularly coffee and other exports, but U.S. aid. A study prepared for the U.S. Congress found that for fiscal 1987, the U.S. contribution to El Salvador's budget was greater than the revenues raised by the Salvadoran government. Never in the history of U.S. foreign aid had that happened. Even when emergency earthquake aid was subtracted, the proportion of U.S. aid in comparison to Salvadoran government revenue was quite similar to the proportion reached in South Vietnam at the height of the war.

A further unprecedented source of outside aid came in the form of remittances from Salvadorans abroad. Based on research he had conducted in the United States, Jesuit sociologist Segundo Montes calculated that Salvadorans there were sending an average of $113.60 a month to El Salvador. In a letter to President Reagan, Duarte himself estimated the amount sent to be somewhere between $350 million and $600 million a year and noted that it exceeded U.S. aid. He therefore urged the Reagan administration not to forcibly repatriate Salvadorans. Mentioning the cost of the war, destruction by guerrillas, and reductions in income from sugar, cotton, and coffee, he said that to "eliminate remittances from the United States would be yet another blow that seems counterproductive to our joint aims of denying Central America to Marxist-Leninist regimes." Duarte thus acknowledged the artificial nature of the Salvadoran economy.

In late 1986 and early 1987, his government proposed a set of economic measures, quickly dubbed the "war tax"; the implicit argument was that those whose interests were being defended should pay their proper share of the cost. In response, ANEP (National Association of Private Enterprise), the umbrella private sector organization, called for a business stoppage, which was nearly total in the capital and widespread in the provinces as well. For its part the FMLN had called for a transportation stoppage. In February 1987 the ARENA-dominated Supreme Court declared the "war tax" unconstitutional. A Western diplomat commented that since 1981 the rich had enjoyed "their shopping trips to Miami and weekends at their beach homes. They lived pretty well. Their children weren't going into the army. Now they're being asked to help pay for the war, and they're saying no."

Internal FMLN documents indicate that by late 1986 the guerrillas were planning to move toward an insurrection attempt. They were confident that they had successfully matched the armed forces' increasing capability (for example, they had attacked and heavily damaged U.S.-designed military bases). They also observed with satisfaction the resurgence of mass movements. In view of the deterioration of the Duarte government, they thought conditions might ripen by 1988. Nevertheless, their aim was not to take power but to force a negotiated settlement on acceptable terms.

In September 1987 the archdiocese of San Salvador held a week of study and reflection on social pastoral work, with almost 500 lay people participating, including 150 peasants from very conflictive areas such as Arcatao and San Jose las Flores in Chalatenango. They heard speakers and participated in workshops and were able to present their own situation in sociodramas. In one's own village one might encounter doubts or persecution; here "you feel so happy to see so many people who are working for God's reign, working and praying like you. And we're almost all poor with ragged pants or shirts. And you say to yourself: The church really does belong to us poor!"

Although people in the military and the right regarded Ignacio Ellacuría as deeply involved with the FMLN — indeed, as their "brains" — since the early 1980s he had maintained an independent position, both sympathetic to, and critical of, the left. He believed that a "third force" was emerging in El Salvador, although he did not intend the expression to signify a midpoint between the guerrillas and the army. A mid-1987 article, unsigned but clearly his, "The Question of the Masses," spelled out this idea. After considerable analysis of recent history, he pointed to the emergence of a new mass movement, one less radical than that of the late 1970s. The emerging organizations should be independent, and should be able to decide independently on their strategy and alliances. He criticized the tendency of left vanguard organizations to utilize popular organizations for their own political ends, sacrificing the people's more specific demands for longer-range political objectives. The Salvadoran left did not initially welcome this criticism.

Early international efforts at peace in Central America by Mexico and then the Contadora countries (Mexico, Venezuela, Colombia, and Panama, later augmented by the Support Group of Brazil, Argentina, Peru, and Uruguay) were primarily aimed at resolving the Nicaragua crisis. In 1986, when these efforts had been largely thwarted by the Reagan administration, Central American presidents began to make their own initiatives, leading to the Central America Peace Plan (Esquipulas II), which was signed by the five Central American presidents in Guatemala on August 7, 1987.

The crux of the new plan was its simultaneity: It applied to all five countries and addressed not only security concerns, such as the size of armies, but emphasized democratic mechanisms for resolving conflicts. The aim, it was said, was not to end conflicts, but to shift from armed to political struggle. The same set of commitments—to establish reconciliation commissions, to cease supporting subversion in neighboring countries, and so forth—was binding on all five countries, although particular circumstances would condition how the provisions were to be implemented in each.

Initially, the FMLN had serious reservations about the peace plan, which in effect regarded existing governments as legitimate and insurgent movements as illegitimate, thus ignoring the massive violation of human rights in Guatemala and El Salvador. Nevertheless, the insurgents soon saw the plan as an opportunity to renew dialogue with the government.

On October 5 and 6 FMLN-FDR representatives met with high-level government officials at the papal nunciature in San Salvador. Archbishop Rivera played a key role in the prior meetings held in Costa Rica and Guatemala to establish conditions for the meeting. Duarte himself headed the government delegation, which met with a team made up of FDR politicians and FMLN commanders. The talks, mediated by Rivera, highlighted the differences between the two sides, as the FMLN-FDR refused to simply discuss a ceasefire but insisted on considering the wider context of the war. Nevertheless, the resumption of public meetings after they had been suspended for almost three years was significant. The Christian Democrats attempted to call out their supporters to capitalize on the event, but they were overwhelmed by left mass organizations, which took advantage of their first opportunity to see guerrilla leaders in the capital and held a vigil outside the nunciature that looked like a street festival. Progovernment forces downplayed the meeting. ARENA said that it had created false expectations, and General Adolfo Blandón expressed the armed forces' concern over the demonstration in front of the nunciature and argued that no more peace talks should take place in the capital.

Church people had played prominent roles. Bishop Rosa Chávez, for example, accompanied the FMLN commanders from Chalatenango to the capital. Parishes held observances and the Confederation of Religious held a two-day prayer vigil. The bishops' conference as such, however, did not offer support to the Esquipulas II process.

Whatever possibilities of dialogue might be developing were cut short by the murder of Herbert Anaya, the president of the Human Rights Commission, on October 26. His own previous arrests and death threats, as well as numerous bombs, and the murder and harassment of other human rights workers all strongly suggested that government forces were responsible. Indeed a colleague had been arrested recently and under interrogation was told that Anaya was next to be killed. He was the seventh member of the Human Rights Commission to be killed in El Salvador.

The day after Anaya's murder, the legislature passed an amnesty law, ostensibly in order to fulfill the requirements of Esquipulas II. This was a cynical gesture, however, since it amounted to a self-pardon by the military for massive violations of human rights, including the massacres of the early 1980s. In a telegram to Duarte, Americas Watch called Anaya's murder, "a shocking reminder that death squad activity persists in El Salvador. We call on you to drop your plan for an amnesty for death squads and for members of the armed forces who have engaged in the murder of civilians." In response to Catholic church concerns, the amnesty law had excluded the killers of Archbishop Romero. One positive result of the law was the release of about five hundred political prisoners.

Although the FMLN-FDR broke off dialogue, left civilian politicians Rubén Zamora and Guillermo Ungo returned to El Salvador in mid-November to reestablish a political presence. This was perhaps the clearest sign that political space was being forced open inasmuch as two major representatives of those whom the army and right wing regarded as "terrorists" were now living openly in El Salvador. They joined with the small Social Democratic party to announce that they were establishing a political coalition called the Democratic Convergence.

For some time peasants who had taken refuge in Honduras had been filtering back into El Salvador. Refugees in the camps in Honduras began to discuss and plan their return. After both Salvadoran and UN authorities had stalled repeatedly, the refugees fixed October 10 for their return. Although on October 9 Duarte said they would not be allowed to enter El Salvador, they arose at 3 A.M. and in seventy buses they headed toward the border where they were forced to halt by Honduran troops and Salvadoran border officials. After a twelve-hour delay the refugees were permitted to reenter their country, but without the international group accompanying them for security. Meeting them from within El Salvador was a delegation of representatives from church and humanitarian agencies. As they reached their lands the people, disproportionately women and children, sought out the graves of their relatives and went digging through the rubble trying to recover their belongings.

Like the organized repopulations from within the country that began in early 1986, this repatriation was a defiant nonviolent assertion of people's right to live in and plant crops in what the military and government had once defined as "enemy" territory.

ARENA Triumphs — and Faces Reality

Duarte's presidency was beset with difficulties from the beginning. He was unable to make great progress toward peace; widespread human rights abuses continued even if the numbers of victims declined, and not a single military officer was brought to justice; business and popular organizations alike combatted Duarte's major economic proposals. For its part, the military regarded the civilian government as an ineffective partner in counterinsurgency.

Although Reagan administration officials claimed that the FMLN was being defeated and that the Salvadoran military had turned the corner in the war, four U.S. officers who studied the war were more skeptical. Acknowledging some successes, especially the rapid expansion and upgrading of the Salvadoran armed forces, they nevertheless observed that the military had become overly dependent on technology, particularly aircraft, and that the promotion system did not reward merit. Lacking the equivalent of noncommissioned officers, the armed forces were made up of a privileged officer elite and poorly motivated recruits. Civil defense units and civic action schemes had not been successful. The "jury is still out," they concluded.

Economic decline continued. Fifty percent of the population was unemployed or in the informal sector. Half the school age children were not in school, partly because one thousand schools had been closed by the war.

By late in Duarte's term serious allegations of corruption were being raised: government contracts awarded to phony companies, payroll padding, and resale of goods intended for relief. An investigation revealed that U.S.-funded jobs intended for those displaced by the war had been going instead to Christian Democrats, and that 30 percent of earthquake aid had also gone improperly to party members. Looking out for themselves like other politicians, Christian Democrats had lost their image of integrity.

ARENA, a party designed in 1982 to serve as a vehicle by which the traditional elites could retake political power, now saw its chance. The Reagan administration had been cultivating younger technocrats who professed a free market philosophy. These modernizing groups were said to be gaining ground in ARENA, as symbolized in the emergence of Alfredo Cristiani, the Georgetown graduate and businessman who became a major party representative after the legislative elections of 1985. Many observers remained convinced, however, that D'Aubuisson remained the real power broker within ARENA, and that the main role of Cristiani and others was to present a more acceptable public image, especially in the United States.

In the March 1988 elections, ARENA won three-quarters of the mayorships (178 to 79), defeating even Alejandro Duarte, the president's son, in San Salvador. Initial results in the legislature produced an apparent tie between ARENA on the one hand and the Christian Democrats and the PCN (Party of National Conciliation) on the other. The vote count for one seat was still in dispute. ARENA refused to accept the decision by the Supreme Electoral Council to adjudicate the seat to the Christian Democrats and took the case to the Supreme Court (which it controlled). The problem was "solved" when a PCN member defected to ARENA, perhaps with monetary inducement. During this same period, the Christian Democrat party split into rival factions, as one leader controlled the party machinery but another had more support from its constituency. From

March to June these disputes paralyzed the government, seemingly demonstrating the irrelevance of elections and the civilian government for addressing the country's underlying problems.

ECA commented that, contrary to appearances, the situation in El Salvador was neither a political crisis nor a power vacuum. What had come crashing to the ground was not democracy but a democratic facade; it was the building that had to be democratized, not the facade. Nevertheless, the FMLN should not be assumed to be democratic; given its militarism and its ideology it would have to change, and indeed demonstrate that it could contribute to resolving El Salvador's problems.

The anonymous author—probably Ellacuría—questioned whether Nicaragua could achieve rapid economic growth even without a war, and asked whether the FMLN had really sufficiently pondered the Nicaraguan experience; the left must come to a realistic sense of what was actually possible and what was impossible on the isthmus, taking into account the emerging new relationship between the superpowers. This latter observation, made more than a year before the dominos began to fall in Eastern Europe, was evidence of Ellacuría's way of pushing the left to rethink even firmly held convictions.

For its part, the FMLN in early 1988 was openly telling reporters of its plans for an insurrection. On the basis of their internal documents it can be inferred that the guerrillas envisioned a situation in which people in San Salvador and other cities would become increasingly discontent and willing to collaborate with organized groups. The guerrillas had been preparing urban commandos and other cadres. They hoped that their own attacks and spontaneous popular actions would stretch the armed forces very thin and indeed make the country ungovernable. Planning for insurrection did not necessarily mean that participation in peace efforts was insincere, but rather that the FMLN was pursuing a two-track policy.

Mass organizations continued to expand and proliferate. In addition to labor unions, there were groups representing refugees and the displaced, the unemployed, urban slumdwellers, and women. Some of these groups had church ties, at least in their origins. Perhaps the most radical was the MPTL (Movement for Bread, Work, and Land), which resembled a group formed in the final months of the anti-Somoza struggle. New women's groups began to emerge at mid-decade. CONAMUS (National Coordination of Salvadoran Women), formed in 1986, was a coalition that had provided a number of services including a weekly radio program. In September 1988 six hundred participants took part in the First Conference of Salvadoran Women.

Violence against labor and popular organizations increased. During the first four months of 1988, sixty-four labor union leaders were murdered, captured, or "disappeared." At the May 1 march, public telephones were destroyed and gas stations burned. In an interview, Humberto Centeno, a UNTS leader who had been arrested and was released only after intense international pressure, said that police had been in the march and he blamed them for the burnings. U.S. Ambassador Corr reflected the hardening tone toward popular organizations when he stated that "masked, lawless, violent vandals demonstrating as national university students, members of the UNTS, and guerrilla front groups," should be made to observe the law—by force if necessary. Tutela Legal pointed to rising rates of political murder during the first six months of 1988 by government forces (52%), death squads (225%), and the guerrillas (74%).

The rise in violence was commonly regarded as a foretaste of what would be unleashed when ARENA, which already controlled the legislature and most municipalities, gained the presidency and attempted to end the conflict once and for all, in accordance with its leaders' longstanding desire. Promotions and shifts in the military in June 1988 brought into power members of the 1966 graduating class from the military academy, who were believed to be hardliners and sympathetic to ARENA ideology.

The most important church initiative undertaken during this period was the National Debate. The underlying idea was similar to what the UCA team had been proposing for years, namely, that in addition to the parties most directly involved in the conflict (the two armies, the government, and political parties) civil society as a whole should be given an opportunity to make its contribution. Included in this understanding of civil society would be the major organized groups: business, labor, cooperatives, cultural groups, educational institutions, religious bodies, and so forth. The aim was to gather perspectives from as wide a sample of Salvadoran society as possible. Fearing—correctly, no doubt—that they would be in a minority, the major business groups refused to participate.

To avoid having the agenda set by a small committee, the organizers established a cumbersome procedure whereby the participating organizations were first polled about causes of the crisis in El Salvador and its possible solutions. These results were then tallied and put into proposition form. At a meeting held in early September 1988 representatives from sixty organizations (universities, labor unions, cooperatives, church groups, and popular organizations) voted on each of the propositions; 147 of these were approved by a majority of the organizations, often by 90 percent or more.

The assembly was almost unanimous in seeing the cause of the war in the failure of El Salvador's economic structures (both the traditional oligarchic structures and the free market structures imposed as a condition of U.S. support), the unbridled power of economic elites and the Salvadoran military, and U.S. involvement. The delegates did not blame the FMLN for the war, and they overwhelmingly advocated dialogue. While supportive of the Central America Peace Plan, they pointed to its limits. Seventy-nine percent of the organizations in the debate agreed that the solution for the country should be a "broad government"—an expression rather close to the FMLN's "government of broad participation." When given an opportunity, Salvadorans from a variety of perspectives had endorsed positions close to those of the left.

The delegates voted to establish a Permanent Commission of the National Debate. Disappointed by the boycott by the right and business groups and the apparently partisan nature of the results, Rivera distanced himself from the new organization. Lutheran Bishop Medardo Gómez and Baptist pastor Edgar Palacios assumed major roles as the Debate Commission continued to take initiatives for peace. In mid-November thousands of people—students, peasants, urban poor—participated in a commission-organized march in San Salvador. None wore masks, as participants from popular organizations often did in order to foil police photographers. When helicopters flew low to intimidate the crowd they waved back their white banners and the Salvadoran flag. The only songs sung were religious, and all participants recited the Lord's Prayer.

When Duarte was diagnosed as having cancer in late May 1988, he had already lost much power. A West European diplomat noted that already he was "almost completely forgotten. It is really very chilling."

With the Christian Democrats divided and discredited, the 1989 presidential campaign between the U.S.-educated businessman Alfredo Cristiani and Christian Democrat politician Fidel Chávez Mena was the final step toward an ARENA government. The campaign itself was lackluster but created apprehension over what an ARENA administration would bring. Many feared that Cristiani was simply a front for D'Aubuisson. One priest reported seeing D'Aubuisson tell a rally that after winning they would have to "take care of this archbishop, these Jesuits, these other priests and especially these foreigners who are ruining the minds of our children. And if the gringos want to help the communists and cut military aid, we didn't need military aid in 1932. If we had to kill 30,000 . . . in 1932, we'll kill 250,000 today." (Even if his memory was not entirely accurate—and he insisted that he had heard these words—it attests to the climate at that moment.)

At one point the FMLN upstaged the campaign with a startling offer delivered by Archbishop Rivera from Mexico City to the government: The FMLN would be willing to participate in elections under certain conditions, most notably that they be postponed from March until September. The timing—a day or two into the Bush presidency—could not be accidental. Duarte initially objected on constitutional grounds, but found himself backtracking when U.S. officials did not reject the proposal out of hand.

Archbishop Rivera urged that the proposal be taken seriously, and dismissed the constitutional argument. Bishop Rosa Chávez said simply that if peace required revising and changing the constitution, the needed changes should be made. Bishop Romeo Tovar, the president of the bishops' conference, organized a peace march in his own diocese of Zacatecoluca, with an estimated two hundred people participating, in which he spoke only of FMLN violence and ignored that of government forces. The

Diario de Hoy headline read "Rivera Becomes Messenger of Terrorism," while the paper congratulated Tovar for breaking nine years of silence on FMLN violence (ignoring Tutela Legal's practice of regularly reporting on FMLN violations of human rights).

Unable to appear indifferent to a peace proposal, all the political parties sent representatives to a meeting with the FMLN in Mexico. In the end the armed forces rejected the idea and the election was held on schedule. Alfredo Cristiani defeated the divided and discredited Christian Democrats with a comfortable margin of 54 percent.

As had been feared, ARENA's consolidation of political power coincided with rising violence and intimidation. Tutela Legal documented 153 cases of political arrests during the first eight months of the year — almost triple the previous rate. On July 17 troops opened fire at the National University. Numerous union leaders were arrested. Harassment of humanitarian aid organizations increased.

During the first few months of 1989 the FMLN murdered several rightwing or military figures. Partly in response to those murders, ARENA proposed a sweeping antiterrorist law, whose wording was so vague that it could have been used to apply severe penalties for labor activity, human rights work, humanitarian activity, or even talking to journalists. The obvious aim was to provide a quasi-legal basis for a massive crackdown. After intense opposition, ARENA backed away from the law but continued to look for a way to enact its provisions.

A climate of accusation surrounded many church workers. In March Vice-President-elect Merino accused Father David Sánchez of having been part of an urban commando group that set off a bomb against his house. At a ceremony in the UCA shortly afterward, Rivera spotted Sánchez in the audience and had him brought forward to sit near him in the sanctuary, prompting appreciative applause among those in the church. The armed forces publicly accused Tutela Legal of waging a campaign to undermine the country's reputation. The ARENA party newsletter and paid ads by the armed forces accused Jesuit Segundo Montes of defending FMLN terrorism. Col. Orlando Zepeda accused the UCA of having FMLN ties and said that the murder of the attorney general had been planned there. A bomb caused $100,000 in damages to the UCA print shop.

Ignacio Ellacuría now argued forcefully that circumstances were demanding renewed efforts at peace. He was particularly emphatic in noting that the FMLN, which had been in permanent consultation since May 1988, was undergoing major changes in its outlook. The organization had come to the realization that "in the present situation El Salvador will not tolerate a regime or government of a Marxist-Leninist type." He found evidence for their changed thinking in statements FMLN leaders made as a result of a diplomatic tour. During this same period Francisco Jovel, a comandante, told interviewers that the FMLN was not thinking of installing a socialist regime, even should there be a popular victory. Joaquin Villalobos said that the present context, including a "crisis of socialism," was calling into question many previous "certainties," and admitted that "the notion of one-party societies is doomed." The FMLN now accepted pluralism, and was judging policies not on the basis of their ideology but with a view to their possible contribution to resolving El Salvador's problems. Ellacuría saw a number of signs that ARENA had changed — but found little evidence that the armed forces were doing any rethinking.

Contrary to expectation, perhaps, but in accordance with Ellacuría's observations on changes in the world context, ARENA and the FMLN found themselves taking steps toward negotiation. Cristiani's initial overtures failed when individuals appointed to a dialogue commission refused to serve and the FMLN rejected the proposal. At their August 1989 meeting in Tela, Honduras, the Central American presidents focused specifically on El Salvador and urged the FMLN to dialogue with the government. In September the FMLN and government offered to meet on a regular basis for dialogue. However, at their meeting in Costa Rica in October, FMLN delegates concluded that the ARENA government was not serious. A series of attacks against unions and popular forces culminated in a bomb that destroyed the FENASTRAS (National Federation of Salvadoran Workers) labor headquarters and killed ten labor leaders, including "Febe" Elizabeth Vásquez. The FMLN leaders decided to set in motion the insurrection attempt they had been planning for two years or more.

On November 11 FMLN units descended into San Salvador from the volcano on the north of the city, fanned out into poor and lower middle-class barrios, and attacked the presidential palace, and garrisons of the National Guard, the National Police, and the army's First Infantry Brigade. The guerrillas also carried out major attacks in San Miguel and elsewhere in the countryside. The military's counterattack was primarily from helicopters and planes. Damage was heavy in the barrios, and many civilians were killed. In addition to attacking popular barrios the military made systematic sweeps of humanitarian and church agencies. Labor union leaders, political figures, and university professors stayed away from their homes and normal work sites.

The UCA Jesuits had decided not to go underground, reasoning that it would be irrational for the military to risk the international repercussions of direct violence against them. They also disregarded the repeated accusations against them on call-in shows broadcast over the government-monopolized airwaves. When troops searched their quarters on the night of November 13, claiming to be searching for weapons, Ellacuría invited them back the next day to search the whole campus.

At about 1:00 A.M. on November 16, about thirty uniformed troops entered the area, dragged the Jesuits out, and murdered them: Ignacio Ellacuría, Segundo Montes, Ignacio Martín-Baró, Juan Ramón Moreno, Amando López, and Joaquin Lopez y Lopez. Also murdered were their cook, Julia Elba Ramos, and her fifteen-year-old daughter, Celina, both of whom were spending the night at the Jesuit house because they regarded it as safer than their own.

Looking at the bodies, Archbishop Rivera said, "As if 70,000 are not enough for them." On the afternoon of the killing Rivera and archdiocesan staff workers heard voices over loudspeakers on military vehicles saying, "Ignacio Ellacuría and Martín-Baró are dead. We will continue killing communists. . . . We are the soldiers of the First Brigade."

During the month after the offensive about forty-nine church workers were arrested, and government forces carried out sixty-one searches of forty-seven church facilities. Military authorities were convinced that church and humanitarian agencies were serving the FMLN. On a television program various Protestant and Catholic church workers were accused by name. A news report called the church aid network Diaconia a "front for the FMLN." Government reports said Bishop Gómez was a member of the Salvadoran Communist party, Father Octavio Cruz was a member of the FPL, and Episcopal priest Pedro Morataya belonged to the FARN (Armed Forces of National Resistance). Twenty members and workers of an Episcopal parish in San Salvador were arrested. Lutheran Bishop Gómez was threatened and Episcopal priest Luís Serrano was arrested and jailed. Troops arrested Jennifer Casolo, an American who arranged tours for U.S. delegations. A video of troops unearthing weapons and ammunition from her yard was then broadcast repeatedly. Casolo, a pacifist, maintained she had no knowledge of how the weapons had gotten there. At one point the army shelled El Despertar refugee camp where about one hundred people were holed up.

On November 18 Attorney General Mauricio Eduardo Colorado wrote a public letter to Pope John Paul II stating that many Salvadorans blamed the "popular church" for the problems of the country, including the current offensive. He said that he therefore feared "for the lives of some bishops, who . . . have persisted in keeping alive this questionable ideology of the 'church of the poor.' " He was suggesting that certain unnamed bishops leave the country. Since the government-controlled radio network had been vilifying Rivera and Rosa Chávez, the blanks could be filled in.

During the offensive a catapult bomb launched toward the Salvadoran armed forces headquarters was assembled on the grounds of the Episcopal church. Americas Watch later called this "an unconscionable and inexcusable act by the FMLN," stating that church property should "be respected and not drawn into the conflict."

From hiding, Bishop Gómez wrote a letter to sister and brother churches elsewhere praising Ellacuría for his work and said the Jesuits had been merged with their slain fellow Salvadorans. He also asked for food and medicine and intervention "to protect the lives of leaders of political groups, people's organizations, humanitarian agencies, and churches," and asked the churches to keep praying. A Lutheran who had been arrested said his interrogators accused the bishop of being the intellectual author of the offensive. Gómez and Luís Serrano reluctantly flew out of the country in early December.

Although some young people joined the rebels, received brief training, and became combatants, there was no massive response to the invitation to insurrection. Many people sought to flee the conflict. The army ignored Rivera's plea for a three-hour ceasefire in order to evacuate the wounded. At one point when the rebels seemed to have withdrawn, they came down from the volcano again, this time entering the upper-class area of Escalón. When the military did not respond by bombing, its disregard for the lives and homes of the poor was made all the more transparent.

Moving toward Peace

When the FMLN had withdrawn into the countryside, Salvadorans began to assess the results of the November offensive. The need for a negotiated settlement was clear, although the process itself would entail numerous advances and retreats. Throughout this period, the "Jesuit case," like a basso ostinato, dramatized the need to end the impunity with which the military had acted.

Since the offensive had taken place in the capital itself, it was abundantly clear that the FMLN was still a military power and that the armed forces did not do well in combat despite hundreds of millions of dollars of U.S. aid and training. A diplomat noted that the right-wing civilians who had once taken a hard line would now recognize the imperative need to negotiate. The presidents of Central America — all business-oriented civilians — agreed that the region as a whole had to move toward demilitarization as a condition for economic reactivation. That sense of urgency increased with President Bush's proposal for a hemispheric free trade zone in June 1990.

The FMLN also had to ponder the fact that despite considerable cooperation in some neighborhoods, they had not triggered anything like a general uprising. Moreover, in the aftermath they had to digest the implications of changes in Eastern Europe, and the unexpected defeat of the Sandinistas in February 1990. Interviewed in Managua shortly after the election, an FMLN official said, "What is happening now is the breaking of all models, all of the dogmas. We're sailing on a choppy sea with many dangers and many opportunities." By May, Salvador Sanabria, a guerrilla spokesperson, said, "We don't see ourselves as a revolutionary Marxist movement anymore. There is no space anymore for a subsidized revolution like Cuba or Nicaragua." FMLN representatives now indicated that they were willing to compete in truly fair elections.

U.S. officials began to express exasperation with the Salvadoran military. "Trying to reform them is like squeezing a bag of water," said one. They complained of human rights violations, military incompetence, and corruption (contract kickbacks, illegal sale of jet fuel, and drug trafficking). President Cristiani, some members of the military, and U.S. officials were convinced that the military had to be reformed.

The most immediate problem, however, was how to deal with the Jesuit murders. The government and military implausibly continued to blame the FMLN. In a Sunday homily Rivera said that the murderers were "from the Armed Forces or close to them" and a Tutela Legal report issued less than two weeks after the killings provided indications that the military had been involved.

Lucía Barrera de Cerna, a housekeeper for the Jesuits, who had witnessed some of the events, gave her version to María Julia Hernández of Tutela Legal. Under the protection of the Spanish and French embassies, she and her family were flown to Miami in a French military aircraft, but U.S. officials, uninvited, insisted on accompanying Cerna. Upon arrival she was turned over to the FBI and held for four days of intensive questioning. On the second day a Salvadoran lieutenant joined the questioning. Under harassment, insults, and threats, she retracted her story. U.S. officials then leaked to the press that Cerna had lied and had not seen soldiers on the UCA campus. When Archbishop Rivera stated that she had been "aggressively and violently" interrogated in Miami, the State Department said he had been misinformed. The attorney general accused María Julia Hernández of a crime for removing two bullets from the scene of the crime, and said that the "strange attitude of the bishops" suggested that they sought "to block the investigation."

On December 20 a Salvadoran colonel told Erick Buckland, a U.S. military advisor, that Col. Benavides had been responsible for the killings. Ten days later Buckland told his superior who immediately rushed to Salvadoran military headquarters with the information. Summoned before the high command, the Salvadoran colonel denied what he had told Buckland.

The testimonies of Cerna and Buckland were now making it difficult to deny the direct responsibility of the military. An unrestricted investigation would probably implicate the high command itself, perhaps jeopardizing the U.S. aid on which the military was dependent.

Officially, the investigation of the crime was the responsibility of the Special Investigative Unit (SIU), which had been created in 1985 as part of a USAID program to improve the Salvadoran justice system. The SIU's sloppy and slow work, especially in the first days and weeks, gave the military time to limit the damage by covering up evidence. For example, the SIU delayed weeks before questioning Col. Benavides, and did not request the log books of the military academy from which the crime had been committed. These log books were burned before the judge handling the case could examine them.

Confronted by the U.S. embassy with Buckland's information, on January 5 the Salvadoran military appointed an Honor Commission made up of six high-ranking officers and two civilians. On the basis of its report, President Cristiani publicly charged Benavides, another officer, and seven enlisted men with the crime. How the names were obtained remained unclear. Church people, including the Jesuits, the left, and diplomats were convinced that Benavides was designated as a scapegoat to protect other military officers. Former Col. Sigifredo Ochoa, once notorious as a field commander and now an ARENA congressional deputy, told *Sixty Minutes* that Benavides had not acted alone and that the action had been planned beforehand. (The internationally appointed Truth Commission in its April 1993 report concluded that Col. René Emilio Ponce along with Gen. Juan Rafael Bustillo, Col. Juan Orlando Zepeda, Col. Inocente Orlando Montano, and Col. Francisco Elena Fuentes "ordered" Benavides "to have the priest Ignacio Ellacuría assassinated, leaving no witnesses" and that other officers knew of the killings and covered them up.)

In mid-January responsibility for the investigation shifted to Judge Ricardo Zamora in whose jurisdiction the case lay. Zamora was also in charge of the case of Archbishop Romero, on which no progress had been made for years. Under Salvadoran judicial procedure, it is the judge (rather than the prosecution and defense) who gathers evidence and testimony. During the first few months of investigation the military repeatedly impeded progress. Several of the soldiers who had earlier given "extrajudicial confessions" now said they had been blindfolded or threatened, and retracted their statements. Witnesses failed to answer summonses, nullified their testimony by ignoring legal requirements, and claimed not to have seen anything or to know anything relevant to the crime.

Throughout the early stages of the process the Salvadoran military and government perhaps felt they were getting mixed signals from the United States. For example, the *Sixty Minutes* reporter was astonished to find that Ambassador Walker had passed on to Col. Emilio Ponce a tape of one interview so that he could better prepare for his own interview. On the other hand, the embassy and the Bush administration expressed their displeasure at reports that Col. Benavides was living in luxury at military headquarters and had even been seen at a beach resort owned by the armed forces.

A congressional task force chaired by Rep. Joe Moakley (D.-Mass.) monitored the various steps of the case. An August report asserted that the Salvadoran Joint Command was "engaged in a conspiracy to obstruct justice," and cited "withheld evidence, destroyed evidence," and perjury. Some high-ranking military officers showed a new willingness to offer testimony. The Arms Control and Foreign Policy Caucus issued a report stating that fourteen of the fifteen top Salvadoran commanders had been responsible for serious human rights violations, particularly the killing of prisoners. Eleven of them had received U.S. training.

Despite the glare of publicity over the Jesuit case, human rights abuses and threats against church workers and popular organizations continued.

Father Francisco Estrada, who had been appointed to replace Ellacuría as head of the UCA, said he was sleeping in different houses, taking different routes to the UCA, and being cautious in his statements. In February he said a sergeant had asked a university employee where the "surviving priests" were living. Lutheran pastor Eliseo Rodríguez said he had stopped wearing clerical clothes and his children were ordered to tell phone callers that he was not at home. Rivera y Damas continued to receive threatening phone calls and accepted an offer from Cristiani to have an armed forces patrol stationed outside the archdiocesan offices.

In early February air force planes and helicopters bombed and strafed Corral de Piedra, a resettlement area in Chalatenango. Four children and one adult were killed and at least twenty were wounded. They had taken refuge in the only brick building in the area, a small room for grinding corn. Bishop Alas of Chalatenango made known the peasants' story, and the armed forces reversed its initial denial and admitted responsibility for the incident.

The Cristiani government's efforts to move ahead with its economic plan provoked labor militancy, even though labor unions were only slowly surfacing after the repression that followed the offensive. When the government announced its intention to lay off 11,000 public sector employees in order to battle budget deficits, unions called for demonstrations. Dismissed employees of the Ministry of Agriculture occupied a San Salvador parish in a hunger strike for a week and a half. Church officials agreed to make an appeal on their behalf. ARENA also announced that it was going to apply a free-market approach to the long paralyzed land reform. Contrary to the Christian Democrat emphasis on cooperatives, ARENA offered to sell land to individual farmers. Continuing militancy was evident on May Day when an estimated forty thousand marched, and in June when thousands of members of opposition political parties, unions, and human rights groups marched for peace.

Refugees continued to assert their right to reoccupy and freely work their lands. In the midst of the November offensive the first returnees from Colomoncagua, Honduras, had crossed the border to make their way to an abandoned village named Meanguera, which they renamed Ciudad Segundo Montes. This "city" was really a series of four settlements scattered along the paved highway from the town of Gotera heading north toward Perquin, which had been an FMLN stronghold for years. Using materials brought from Honduras, they set up a number of shops and businesses. They deliberately reached out to neighboring villages where people had not fled the violence. The army occasionally violated the neutrality it had initially pledged to respect.

Three weeks before the tenth anniversary of Romero's murder, Rivera announced that he was initiating the canonization process (official Catholic procedure for declaring an individual a saint) for Archbishop Romero. He thereby violated the normal Vatican practice of waiting decades, although he no doubt did so with Vatican approval. His action displeased upperclass Catholics and ARENA diehards. The observance began with a three-day program of both prayer and theological conferences. On the final day thousands of people gathered at the Parque Usulután with the Permanent Committee for the National Debate. Despite accusations and intimidating actions, the people marched to the cathedral where Bishop Gómez and Father Palacios had joined Archbishop Rivera at the altar. A helicopter hovered overhead.

Meanwhile the peace process slowly labored forward. In late January 1990, only weeks after the FMLN offensive, the two sides made the decisive step of agreeing to a UN role in the peacekeeping process. From this point onward, UN Secretary General Javier Pérez de Cuellar made the El Salvador conflict an important personal priority, and appointed the Peruvian, Alvaro de Soto, as his special envoy. A critical question was to what extent the United States would use its leverage with the military to press for a peace settlement.

In March the FMLN agreed to suspend economic sabotage. At a meeting in Caracas the two sides were separated by a wide gulf, the government demanding a ceasefire before considering other issues, and the FMLN wanting progress in other areas first. Their compromise was to set up an agenda for agreements to be reached under UN supervision. Talks moved to issues of substance during seven days in Oaxtepec, Mexico, in June. The issue of army reform was set on the agenda for the next meeting. Col. Mauricio Vargas, a member of the government commission, agreed that the army needed restructuring, but said the military would do so on its own terms.

The FMLN made detailed proposals for ending the "impunity" of the military, such as the dismissal of approximately two hundred officers responsible for human rights violations, the disbanding of particular units, and the subordination of the army to civilian control. In exchange the guerrillas would disband and reenter Salvadoran society as a political organization. Fearing a "Colombian-style democracy" (a reference to the hundreds of leftists murdered in recent years in Colombia when guerrillas reentered civilian life) the FMLN refused to accept a "forgive and forget" kind of law that would grant amnesty to all. In effect, they were demanding an effective way to assure that murder would no longer be a political tool. Bernard Aronson, who oversaw Latin America policy at the State Department, said the FMLN was making impossible demands. Nevertheless, the discussion put the word "impunity" into common political discourse in El Salvador.

Meeting in July under de Soto's mediation, the government and the FMLN signed a nineteen-point agreement allowing a UN verification commission. Since it was conditional on an FMLN ceasefire, it remained somewhat hypothetical. At this moment Bishop Rosa Chávez drew attention to the army's murder of a young mentally retarded man, calling it "particularly chilling." In the first half of the year the Human Rights Commission recorded 695 political murders, attributing 561 to the army, 87 to death squads, and 14 to the FMLN, as well as 92 "disappearances."

Throughout most of 1990 some members of the U.S. Congress sought to cut or diminish aid in order to pressure the Salvadoran military and government to pursue the Jesuit case, improve human rights observance, and engage in good faith negotiations. Rejecting the Bush administration's argument that an aid cut would send the wrong signal, Congress cut military aid for the next year (to $42.5 million). The effect was primarily political, since the military had no immediate need of equipment.

In November 1990 the FMLN launched another offensive, this time in the countryside, not with the illusion of taking power, but in order to demonstrate its continual military strength and to force the armed forces and government to negotiate seriously. Using surface-to-air missiles for the first time, the FMLN downed an A-37 Dragonfly. Pilots consequently flew much higher and more cautiously, and Salvadoran ground troops could no longer count on quick air support. In one instance two hundred soldiers of the U.S.-trained Atlacatl Battalion retreated ingloriously across the Honduran border.

Whatever political momentum the FMLN gained from these developments was soon dissipated when it was discovered that some of the missiles had come from Nicaragua. Sandinista officials hastily arrested four officers and twelve civilians. Then, in early January, a helicopter with three American military advisors aboard was shot down in FMLN-controlled territory. According to witnesses, one of them was killed in the crash and FMLN soldiers killed the other two. U.S. officials immediately called the killing an affront to human decency. The FMLN announced that two of its members had been taken into custody and offered to put them on trial before a jury made up of the FMLN and impartial observers. The Bush administration suggested that it might indict Joaquin Villalobos, with the hint that under the Anti-Terrorism Act, he could be seized, as the United States had seized General Noriega of Panama a year before.

In mid-January 1991, while the U.S. public was focused on the impending war with Iraq, the Bush administration restored the $42.5 million previously cut by Congress. The military took this move as a vote of confidence, while an analyst at the UCA said it was catastrophic for negotiations.

Less than a week after the aid was restored, fifteen people in the hamlet of El Zapote, six miles from San Salvador, were stabbed and shot to death. The ages of the victims ranged from fourteen to sixty-eight; eighteen children were left orphans. In his Sunday homily Archbishop Rivera said, "All of the evidence collected leads us to solely and exclusively indicate responsibility of members of the First Infantry Brigade"; he called the massacre "a crime committed with total impunity." When a government investigating commission blamed the crime on a feud between two families, Bishop Rosa Chávez said that the government "did not have the courage to accept the truth" and had chosen to lie. Rosa Chávez also accused the judge investigating the case of trying to coerce a witness into changing her story. He said the government was seeking to cover up the army's role so as not to jeopardize U.S. aid. Alluding to the seemingly stalled Jesuit case, he said the commission investigating the peasant massacre did not deserve any credibility, given the government's past record. In an ominous sign of the climate, a radio station reported getting calls from a death squad claiming that its members were standing by awaiting instructions to kill religious, political, and labor leaders.

Elections for congress and some mayors' seats provoked some disagreement among the left opposition and within guerrilla ranks over whether to participate. Some felt it served only to legitimize the ARENA government's economic plan, while others saw the election as an opportunity to gain further political space. After the election, ARENA no longer had a majority in congress, and the Democratic Convergence gained eight seats.

Shortly afterward, the FMLN made further peace efforts by proposing a ceasefire agreement and asking President Chamorro of Nicaragua to negotiate. The government balked at the terms, which would have amounted to acknowledging guerrilla control of some parts of El Salvador.

In April the FMLN and government representatives held their longest and most serious meeting thus far. After twenty-four days of discussion they agreed to a package of constitutional reforms and new legislation. Among issues discussed were restricting the role of the army, reforming the judicial system, and appointing a Truth Commission to determine what had happened in some of the most notorious human rights violations by both sides. The work was completed so that both the outgoing and newly elected national assemblies could vote on the constitutional reforms, thus speeding the process. Peace seemed to hover on the horizon.

A Mexican newspaper gave some insight into debates within the FMLN. An urban guerrilla leader spoke of a fierce debate between the high-ranking leaders who were negotiating in Mexico and middle-level cadres, some of whom still adhered "to the classical theory of class struggle" and dreamed "of entering the capital triumphantly as the Vietcong and the Sandinistas did." A further question was which FMLN leaders should come out from underground and enter the legal political struggle. Another debate was whether the FMLN should strive to take the reins of government electorally. If no government could truly resolve the country's problems the FMLN could only be discredited if it governed directly. When asked how the rank and file would accept a new political line, the guerrilla leader said that the challenge was to explain to combatants that "the objective of the revolutionary war was not to seize state power but to achieve social changes that would guarantee better living conditions for the entire population."

In June a UN team of 110 civilian, military, and police specialists arrived to begin to monitor human rights violations and the peace processes. Progovernment newspapers called the group an insult to El Salvador and accused the UN mediators of being procommunist. Leaflets from the Salvadoran Anti-Communist Front warned merchants in a commercial area not to serve them. At an elegant restaurant a well-dressed man began to berate Iqbal Riza, the Pakistani UN diplomat who headed the team, and ended by shouting, "We're going to kill all of you."

Meanwhile, the Jesuit case meandered toward trial. In January 1991 two of the prosecutors, Henry Campos and Sidney Blanco, resigned in protest, saying that the attorney general had prevented them from aggressively pursuing the investigation. In May they returned to the case as private prosecutors representing the victims' families and the Jesuits.

The jury trial finally held in late September 1991 differed markedly from procedures in the United States. The defendants, Col. Benavides, Lt. Espinoza, and six enlisted men, sat in a row across the courtroom. Their backs to the judge, they faced those present in the courtroom. To protect the jury members from retaliation, during the trial they were hidden behind a wood panel and were visible only to the judge and those arguing the case.

Sessions took place for three days from morning to midnight. The first day and a half was devoted to reading from the four thousand pages of evidence and testimony that Judge Zamora had gathered, beginning with the initial confessions of those accused. Then the representatives of the attorney general's office, the private prosecutors, and finally the defense presented their arguments, and were then allowed an hour for rebuttals. There was no cross-examining of either witnesses or defendants. The prosecution dwelled on the confessions of the soldiers and walked the jury through the grisly details of the murders. The defense appealed to their patriotism and said the honorable soldiers had suffered enough and should be returned to their loved ones. Throughout the procedure the defendants maintained a stoic impassivity. Members of the defendants' families held bibles and, at some moments, quietly prayed together.

Late on the third day the jury was given a list of eighty questions, each presenting an accusation against one of the defendants to be answered with a "yes" or "no." Somewhat astonishingly in the light of the defendants' graphic and detailed confessions, only Col. Benavides and Lt. Yusshy Mendoza were found guilty. The jury's logic seemed to be that Benavides bore the primary responsibility since he was the senior military commander in the zone the night of the crime. Bishop Rosa Chávez commented, "The church is not satisfied. . . . The decision is logical in that it puts the emphasis on the men with greatest responsibility and illogical in that people clearly involved in the action itself will be freed."

Commentators likewise emphasized both the significance and the limitations of the verdict. For the first time, an army officer had been found guilty of a human rights violation. (In 1984, after considerable pressure from the United States, five enlisted men had been found guilty of and sentenced for the murder of the U.S. church women. Despite considerable evidence that officers had been involved, none were accused.) Efforts to trace responsibility beyond Benavides had been systematically blocked. What prospect would there be for justice in other cases if intense U.S.

pressure had produced such meager results? A few days later a jury acquitted thirteen soldiers accused of murdering seven people in 1981. Perhaps in order to maintain the pressure, the Catholic church released an eighty-one-page report detailing the December 1981 Mozote massacre of 794 people by the army. Refugees returning from Honduras had initiated legal procedures, but church authorities said they were at a standstill.

Just two days before the trial the FMLN and the Cristiani government made a breakthrough in the peace process, signing what were called the "New York Accords." A sticking point had been how the armed forces could be reduced and the FMLN disarmed. A key part of the solution was the formation of a new police force in which former guerrillas would be accepted. Upon returning to El Salvador Cristiani sought to convince his own right wing, which believed the government had conceded too much. Surprisingly, Roberto D'Aubuisson, now suffering from terminal cancer, supported Cristiani's "conquest of peace." In a homily Bishop Rosa Chávez expressed the "almost universal conviction that we now have real possibility of burying violence."

The FMLN announced a ceasefire to begin November 16 — the second anniversary of the killing of the Jesuits. Negotiators raced against the clock to come to an agreement before Pérez de Cuellar's term as UN Secretary General expired on December 31. The agreement reached included a 50 percent reduction of the armed forces, and the removal of military officers whom an independent panel should determine to have been responsible for human rights abuses.

On January 15 the official ceremony marking the end to the war was celebrated with street parties in San Salvador. The large banner portrait of Farabundo Martí draped over the cathedral certainly did not signify a revolutionary victory but might symbolize a moment in which conflict need not mean bloodshed.

CHAPTER 4

GUATEMALA

Persecuted but Not Defeated

In January 1980 a group of several dozen Indians from the Quiché region came to Guatemala City to denounce the abuses of the army, which since 1975 had been abducting members of their communities as part of its counterinsurgency campaign. As early as 1976 representatives had come to make inquiries in government offices. Now they were demanding that a commission of respected nonpartisan observers go to Quiché to investigate their claims. For about two weeks they made the rounds of UN and OAS offices, embassies, and various government offices, including the congress. They also made a presentation to dozens of participants in the Justice and Peace Committee, an informal network of Protestants and Catholics.

One day they entered the Colegio Belga, a Catholic girls' school, where they knew some of the sisters who had worked in Quiché. The peasants came through denouncing what the military was doing and taking up a collection. Informed that the police were coming, one of the sisters led them out the back way. That night the minister of education, Col. Clementino Castillo, falsely declared that the peasants had been armed and that the sisters were linked to the guerrillas.

On January 31 a group of these people together with labor and university activists entered the embassy of Spain in an upper middle-class neighborhood. Still pressing for the formation of an investigatory commission, they took the ambassador and his staff as hostages, although they did not have firearms. Máximo Cajal, the Spanish ambassador, was familiar with the situation in Quiché through his visits to Spanish Sacred Heart priests there. As it happened, a former vice-president and a former foreign minister of Guatemala were meeting with him when the occupation began.

When several hundred police surrounded the embassy, Cajal and the two former officials warned them that to enter the embassy would be a violation of diplomatic immunity. Nevertheless, the police began to break into the building around 2 P.M., and around 3 P.M. made a concerted attack.

When a fire broke out the police would not allow firefighters to help the people trapped inside. A total of thirty-nine people — twenty-seven occupiers, ten embassy staff people, and the two Guatemalan dignitaries — burned to death. (One of them was an old man named Vicente Menchú, father of Rigoberta Menchú, who in 1992 was awarded the Nobel Peace Prize.) In the confusion of the attack, Ambassador Cajal managed to escape.

The incident proved very embarrassing to the Guatemalan government as it sought to justify what had happened. The one peasant who survived the fire under the pile of bodies, Gregorio Yujá, was kidnapped from his hospital bed, and his body was dumped the following day in front of the downtown campus of the university. Despite the clearly Indian names of the victims, the government insisted they were not peasants but university "terrorists." Just before the funeral procession on the following day, two university leaders were gunned down in full sight of hundreds of onlookers. As dozens of uniformed and plainclothes men stood menacingly with their weapons, thousands of people marched in the funeral procession, chanting, "The color of blood is never forgotten." Although Spain broke relations with Guatemala and many governments expressed indignation, the Guatemalan government defiantly admitted no error.

"This means war," was the feeling of left activists who were influenced by the half-year-old Sandinista government in Nicaragua and the insurrection that seemed imminent in El Salvador.

"They Will Kill Us All!"

CUC, a militant organization formed in 1977–78, had been preparing a campaign in the Pacific coast plantation area to raise wages — the legal minimum was then a little more than a dollar a day, with slight variations according to the crop picked. In February 1980 a strike begun on one plantation spread rapidly as workers spontaneously commandeered vehicles to spread the word. Thousands of workers gathered along the highway while troops stood menacingly nearby. After tense confrontation and the killing of some leaders, including a catechist, the government agreed to raise wages to $3.20 a day; in practice the new rate was often ignored, however.

On June 13 in the coastal area of Tiquisate, more than one hundred peasants were abducted by treasury police, who claimed to be looking for weapons. On June 21 armed men stopped traffic in Guatemala City and abducted twenty-seven union leaders, nine of whom were women (one pregnant), who were meeting within two blocks of two police stations and close to the presidential palace. In July armed men entered the university and began shooting at random, killing eight students and wounding twenty-five.

On July 28 about fifty EGP guerrillas attacked the army garrison in San Juan Cotzal, a town that together with Nebaj and Chajul forms the so-called Ixil triangle in Quiché. In the attack they killed sixteen soldiers and wounded eight. The guerrillas burned the archives of the town, symbolically destroying the legal basis of unjust land tenure. Ringing the church bells to convoke the people, they held a political rally and left by 7 A.M. An hour later helicopters arrived and began to drop bombs around the town. Soldiers went door to door picking up all males between the ages of twelve and sixty, gathering two hundred in the town square. Then, checking their names against a list, the troops drew aside sixty and shot them down one by one in full sight of the rest. The survivors were forced to dig mass graves for most of the victims, since the terrorized family members were unwilling to claim the bodies. The military commander who had come from Huehuetenango shouted, "The next time they kill one of my soldiers I'll kill all the men because all you people do is cause problems."

In August a large number of union leaders were abducted from Emaus, a church retreat center in the diocese of Escuintla. In October troops occupied the town of Santiago Atitlán and swept through looking for leaders of cooperatives, literacy programs, and basic Christian communities, as well as Protestant pastors, apparently in response to an occupation and rally held by ORPA guerrillas. The Guatemalan media offered only the army's version of these events.

In addition to mass killings and abductions, many Guatemalans were murdered or "disappeared" individually. A catechist came to the lectern in one church and after reading the text, "Blessed are the persecuted," went on to say, "In my village, we all feel persecuted these days. Never in the memory of even the oldest person in our village have things been so bad, or has life been so cheap." Mentioning the abduction of three people for no apparent reason, he said, "No one knows where they are. Our only consolation is that they are known by God, somewhere, alive or dead. Our faith is our strength, and if those young men are alive, their faith is also their strength. Let us pray, brothers and sisters, not only for them, but for all innocent victims of this persecution."

This overall pattern of repression, which the army justified as a response to guerrilla advances, provides a background for understanding the assault against church people. After an EGP attack in the town of Uspantán, Quiché, the army surrounded the parish compound where both priests and sisters lived and threw grenades into the patio. On another occasion they searched the premises; one night the area was machine-gunned. When the priests and sisters went to Santa Cruz to consult with other colleagues, the army took over the parish area for its own use.

Meanwhile church workers in the plantation area on the Pacific coast were also coming under attack. On May 1 Conrado de la Cruz, a Filipino priest, was abducted in Guatemala City along with Herlindo Cifuentes, a parish collaborator. Neither was ever seen again. Less than two weeks later, Walter Voordeckers, the Belgian pastor of the neighboring parish of Santa Lucia Cotzumalguapa, was gunned down while crossing the street from the parish house to the post office. Although neither had been a member of a guerrilla organization, de la Cruz had supported people's organizing efforts, and Voordeckers had a reputation for being outspoken in his sermons. Thirteen members of their Immaculate Heart of Mary congregation, priests and seminarians, Guatemalans and foreigners, soon left the country.

In Quiché on June 4, Spanish Sacred Heart Father José María Gran was being followed by helicopter as he was returning to Chajul. Somewhere along the way he and Domingo Bats, a lay assistant, were shot in the back. The army announced that two insurgents had been killed in combat. The Guatemalan bishops reacted with a strong statement on persecution. On July 10 two men shot and killed Father Faustino Villanueva in Joyabaj and rode off on a yellow motorcycle. The following day the killers were seen inquiring about another priest and about two sisters.

On Saturday, July 18, villagers detected an ambush being set for Bishop Juan Gerardi, along a road he would be traveling to say Mass. Since all church workers seemed to be in danger—the men on the yellow motorcycle continued to make inquiries—the bishop summoned all the pastoral workers and proposed that they leave the diocese since it was impossible to work there. "They will kill us all," he said.

Not without misgivings, the priests and sisters accepted the bishop's decision to leave the diocese. They hoped that this unusual action of withdrawing all church personnel—an action perhaps unprecedented in church history—would draw attention to Guatemala. In this respect they were disappointed, since the international media paid little attention.

Privately, some sisters and priests questioned the decision. "I never agreed with leaving Quiché," a sister later observed. "I thought it was our duty to remain there." She admitted, however, that some of the local people thought they themselves might be persecuted more if the priests and sisters remained. In a terse statement the bishops' conference expressed its solidarity with the bishop and church workers, called for a dialogue with authorities, and urged people to pray that the problem be resolved as quickly as possible. The somewhat neutral tone suggested that not all his brother bishops agreed with Gerardi.

In Rome Bishop Gerardi explained the situation to Pope John Paul II and Vatican officials. Writing to the Guatemalan bishops over three months later, the pope condemned human rights abuses and the death of priests in "obscure circumstances." He did not support the notion that church people had overstepped the bounds of their ministry into politics; on the other hand, the pope's letter did not indicate who was responsible and seemed more concerned about the church's inability to attend the people's religious needs than the slaughter of the population. Some concluded that the pope had not been pleased by the decision. As a priest later put it, the Roman authorities believed that a bishop should be like a captain willing to go down with his ship.

At a September rally in front of the National Palace, President Romeo Lucas threatened to expel from the country priests who did not limit themselves to "guiding souls." When Cardinal Casariego personally handed him the pope's letter, he was said to have blamed it on Gerardi. When Gerardi landed in November, the authorities halted him in the airport, and put him back on a plane. He then lived in exile in Costa Rica for about two years.

Several of the exiled priests from El Quiché went on speaking tours in Europe and North America. Their organization, the Guatemalan Church in Exile, began to issue statements with a strong revolutionary thrust. Rhetorically asking what alternatives the people had left, they answered, "clandestine struggle and people's struggle inside the country, and organized exile outside the country." They no doubt assumed that their time of exile would be relatively brief since a revolutionary change was around the corner.

Years later a priest said that the people "were pushed into political commitment." It was like a "pressure cooker." Observing events in Nicaragua and El Salvador people said, "We can't wait five more years; it will be one year or two at most." However, a sister was critical of the approach of church people. "We didn't look forward enough. None of us realized how far the persecution against the people would go. We didn't have a political vision. . . . We exaggerated the number of really conscious people."

In a July 1980 statement the EGP had acknowledged the role of Christians in consciousness-raising and organizing. The enemy's response of "indiscriminate, repressive violence" must be combatted. Christians had to recognize that when peaceful methods had been exhausted—and such had long been the case in Guatemala—"revolutionary violence is legitimate and just." Hence the doors of the EGP were open to catechists, priests, sisters, and church people whether Catholic or evangelical. "You cannot love your neighbor and not play a specific and serious role within the people's war, whether in guerrilla organizations or in the various militant mass organizations."

A sense of impending change was present in the meeting of over six hundred priests, sisters, and brothers at the mid-1980 meeting of CONFREGUA (Conference of Religious of Guatemala), the umbrella organization of religious orders. Behind the speaker's podium were large portraits of the five priests killed thus far. A joint statement referred to the people's struggle and the repression they were encountering. Being witnesses to the reign of God meant solidarity with the new alternative for Guatemala taking shape among the people. This sense that the present sufferings were the birth pangs of a new kind of society no doubt reflected the Central American context—this was the time of the literacy campaign in Nicaragua, and optimism still ran high.

Popular organizations were becoming more militant in language and actions. CUC encouraged strikes and sabotage as ways of compelling landholders to pay just wages, and called on people to use machetes and whatever weapons they might have for their self-defense in villages. "Let us not permit the army and landholders to instill fear in us." Such an exhortation did not entail joining the guerrillas, but it reflected the sense that the level of confrontation was steadily increasing.

In January 1981 four priests sought to reinitiate pastoral work in Quiché. Father Juan Alonso, a Spaniard of the Sacred Heart congregation, who had worked for years in both the Ixcán and Peten colonization areas, chose to live in the most conflictive area. On February 15, two days after being interrogated and insulted by the military, he was halted as he was motorcycling toward Cunén, tortured, and then shot three times in the head. Church workers from around the country attended the funeral in Quiché as a show of solidarity. Once more the diocese was closed, although one priest soon quietly returned and others occasionally arrived to celebrate Mass.

The language of revolutionary organizations, especially the EGP, remained confident and even triumphalistic through 1981. In its propaganda meetings with peasants, the EGP repeated a simple promise: "When we win, you will all have enough land." Guerrilla confidence was bolstered by the seeming disarray of the Lucas government, whose representatives seemed to be primarily concerned for their own enrichment.

In 1981 mass killings became a common practice of the army. In February three hundred troops attacked villages in the area of Chimaltenango with machine guns, grenade launchers, and helicopter fire; they killed about forty-five people and abducted about twenty-seven. In the same area in April, heavily armed men took two dozen peasants from another village, tortured them, and dumped their bodies. In July troops slaughtered at least 150 people in the hamlet of Coyá, San Miguel Acatán, Huehuetenango.

A sister described how the army in early 1981 came through the village of Nueva Catarina in Huehuetenango and killed everyone in their path, about nineteen or twenty women and children. Coming to another village a few days later, troops put the women and children in a school, and then took the men to the church where they killed them. A church worker later attributed the violence not only to a general policy of stopping insurgency by any means necessary, including destruction of whole villages, but to the freedom given to individual army captains to act as brutally as they wished with no fear that they would be held accountable. Such massacres were not completely random, but took place in areas where army intelligence had detected the presence of guerrilla members or sympathizers, or suspected their presence.

The left underestimated the army, particularly its intelligence capability. In mid-1981 army intelligence discovered and attacked a number of safe houses of both the EGP and ORPA in Guatemala City. Guerrilla militants had rented houses in upper middle-class neighborhoods, perhaps reasoning that they would be less suspect. Army intelligence may have detected them through methods borrowed from Argentine military officers (e.g., searching electric company records for suspiciously large bills that might indicate weapons manufacture). The fact that peasants arrived regularly at some houses also aroused suspicion. Information gathered in one raid often led to further raids.

In April 1981 about fifteen foreign development organizations received death threats. The director of one of these agencies used family connections to ask army officers whether the threat was serious and was assured it was. The agencies closed or severely curtailed operations. The military evidently wanted to reduce to a minimum the number of witnesses in the countryside. Such a motive partly explains the continued threats and violence against church workers.

The military was convinced that church people were directly involved with the guerrilla organizations. Indeed Donald McKenna, an Irish priest, joined the EGP, and a Mexican reporter found him in the mountains on the Ho Chi Minh Front in Huehuetenango. Although he was photographed with an automatic rifle on his shoulder, he described his role as that of a "chaplain in the army of the people." McKenna's case can hardly be described as typical, however. In contrast to the many church workers who had been radicalized over years of experience in Guatemala, McKenna, an IRA (Irish Republican Army) sympathizer from Belfast, seems to have arrived in Guatemala looking for the revolution that he had previously failed to find in Peru. In any case, he was soon seriously ill, and by early 1982 left the EGP. After hiding with a fellow priest for some months, he then left Guatemala.

This guerrilla priest no doubt fueled suspicions that many church people were also members. Police claimed that two of the people killed in a mid-1981 raid on a safe house were Jesuits; they were in fact lay volunteers Raoul Leger, a Canadian, and Angel Martínez, a Spaniard. The bishops stated that both had ceased working with the church some time previously.

Repression had the effect of dismantling work in other parts of the country. In Izabal, along the road to Guatemala's Caribbean port, grenades thrown into a convent forced sisters and priests to abandon parishes where they had been working for a decade and had trained more than five hundred local leaders. Then, in July 1981, Father Tulio Marcelo Maruzzo, an Italian Franciscan priest, was murdered along with a young parishioner.

The next victim was Father Stanley Rother, an Oklahoma priest who had worked in Santiago Atitlan since 1968. Rother was not involved with the left, and, indeed, had let it be known that he did not want CUC to use parish facilities. Yet he was later quoted as having said, "To shake the hand of an Indian is a political act." In mid-1980 Rother had written that he knew some "younger catechists are working with those that are preparing for a revolution." Rother had experienced the feeling of helplessness as he saw Diego Quic, one of his lay collaborators, being kidnapped; by January 1981 thirty parishioners had met the same fate. Under threat himself, he went to the United States, but decided to return for Holy Week of 1981. Rother had had much time to ponder what he would do if attacked. When three tall men in masks entered his house shortly after midnight on July

28, he fought back, and shouted "Kill me here!" Unable to abduct him they shot him three times.

In June, Luís Pellecer, a Jesuit who had worked widely with popular organizations, was abducted and presumed "disappeared." Three months later the government produced Pellecer at a press conference. In his opening statement, Pellecer said he had been a member of the EGP for seventeen months, but having repented, he had contacted a friend in the security forces to arrange a "self-abduction." He explained that church people were working with three basic "weapons": liberation theology, Marxist-Leninist analysis, and the "option for the poor." Describing his own work in El Salvador, Nicaragua, and Guatemala, he wove a web of subversive activity implicating several religious orders (both male and female), lay church leaders, CUC, other popular organizations, literacy programs, and European funding agencies (whose money for development or popular organizing was said to be helping the guerrillas). At the center of this web were the Jesuits and two former Jesuits who were now in the EGP. Repeatedly Pellecer emphasized his own repentance and desire to make amends by serving his country, still as a priest.

Pellecer remained under tight government control and was brought out for only a few press conferences and controlled contacts with church authorities. His speech was also mechanical and at times he lapsed back into his opening lines, "My name is Luís Eduardo Pellecer ..." Few believed the self-abduction story, and it was widely assumed that he had been brainwashed or psychologically manipulated.

The EGP issued a statement acknowledging that Pellecer had been a "collaborator" from June 1980 until the moment of his kidnapping, but insisted he had never been a "leader" or a "militant." The guerrillas noted that Pellecer's statement was aimed at justifying repression against church workers and activists. Much of Pellecer's testimony—names, organizations, relationships—was true. Some elements were untrue, however, and the whole presentation seemed to be Pellecer's experience as enhanced and scripted by army intelligence.

There followed a "sweep of all the people who had been working with him," as a sister recalled later. Popular organization activists had little time to speculate on what had happened to Pellecer: They could only assume that the army would be acting on information extracted from him, including many details he had not mentioned publicly. A priest close to these groups commented, "It was panic; everything started coming apart in October 1981." He said that the EGP leadership, feeling they were on their way toward victory, put increasing pressure on the various organizations of slumdwellers, workers, university students, and revolutionary Christians. In fact, these organizations were often "empty shells" and the revolutionaries had lost touch with the vast majority of the poor who were not organized. In the final months of 1981, many involved with popular organizing hurriedly fled Guatemala.

This priest then went into the mountains near Chimaltenango and was present during a major army assault against the village of Chupol. He hid in the fields for several days. Observing the EGP's actions close at hand he became increasingly disenchanted. He saw the EGP encourage the people to seize weapons from the army to use in the struggle and then take the weapons for themselves, leaving the people more exposed; he himself was given a single grenade made from a tomato can. When a major EGP commander was almost captured in a surprise army attack, the guerrillas hastily departed, leaving the local people to their own devices. After three weeks the EGP escorted the priest out of the region. He later realized that internal struggles were weakening the EGP. Only slowly, however, did he distance himself from the organization.

On January 6, 1982, Sister Victoria de la Roca was kidnapped from the Bethelemite convent in Esquipulas, the town to which thousands of Guatemalans and Central Americans make pilgrimages to pray to its "Black Christ." President Lucas said he did not know where she was, but had a great deal of proof of her involvement with the guerrillas. Her assignments came directly from Nicaragua. Lucas also claimed that a truck with 160 sticks of dynamite hidden in tamales had been found near the convent and asserted that the dynamite was to be used to blow up the city hall of Esquipulas. This city, it may be noted, was far from the areas of guerrilla activity. Moreover, Sister Victoria—who had indeed worked in Matagalpa, Nicaragua—had advanced cancer. The president's remarks suggest a very crude justification for government-organized abduction.

A Belgian priest and a Guatemalan priest kidnapped the following day were released in front of the papal nunciature after rapid action from the Belgian parliament and Bishop Charles Graham of San Antonio, Texas, who had pressured the Reagan administration to act. An American brother James Miller was not so fortunate. He was gunned down in Huehuetenango in February; possibly he was mistaken for another Christian brother who had irritated local military authorities by his defense of Indians.

"Born-Again" Ruler

By hindsight it became clear that in 1981 the army began to reassert control through its brutal but effective policies; at the time, however, matters were considerably more confused. In Huehuetenango, where the EGP commander was operating independently from the rest of the organization, the guerrillas seemed to move freely in the mountains, while the army was on the defensive in its garrisons in the towns. The guerrillas were confidently claiming that victory was near.

Some guerrilla actions alienated people. In burning buses and destroying bridges they intended to strike blows against the economically powerful, but they also hurt the poor, such as farmers whose small amounts of coffee were their only source of cash income. In one instance, guerrillas stopped a bus in the mountains of Huehuetenango and had the passengers take out their goods. A lame basket maker asked them why they were doing this if they were on the side of the poor. One of the guerrillas, perhaps a panicky new recruit, shot the man and told the rest not to touch his body. The story circulated and undermined the sympathy the EGP had been gaining.

In January 1982 the four guerrilla organizations announced the formation of a unified coalition, the URNG (Guatemalan National Revolutionary Unity). In its manifesto, the URNG described its aims as ending repression and domination by the wealthy, achieving equality between Indians and non-Indians, and forming a new government that would represent everyone and be nonaligned internationally. Business would be welcome in the new order to come. They explicitly stated that Christians would be one of the "pillars of the new society," since they had already proven their commitment. A group of exiles in Mexico City likewise formed a loosely knit civilian coalition and endorsed the URNG position. The message to Guatemalans was that an alternative was taking shape on the horizon.

Meanwhile Guatemalan voters went to the polls in March 1982 to choose between the army candidate, Gen. Aníbal Guevara, and three right-wing civilians. When Guevara was proclaimed the winner, the opposition parties banded together to protest what they saw as election fraud. The street demonstration they convoked was tear-gassed in full view of international media. Since the army was clearly determined to bring Guevara to the presidency, the Reagan administration, which had earlier sent retired Gen. Vernon Walters to try to persuade Lucas to allow for a civilian presidency, now began to speak favorably of Guevara.

On March 23 nine hundred troops surrounded the National Palace. Radio stations, which the army had taken over, issued a call for retired general Efraín Rios Montt. Reached by phone at the school run by the Iglesia del Verbo (Church of the Word), where he was an active member, Rios Montt went to the improvised headquarters of the coupmakers facing the National Palace. There they offered to make him head of the new government junta with two fellow officers. At around 4 P.M. Lucas surrendered and left the country.

In the army Rios Montt had served as director of the military academy, and had risen to become army chief of staff in 1972. At that point, however, he was sent to the Interamerican Defense School in Washington — apparently to "golden exile" as often happens as a result of military rivalries. In 1974 he accepted an invitation to run for president on the Christian Democrat ticket. Cheated of the presidency through electoral fraud, Rios Montt again went into exile, this time to Madrid, and returned in 1978. Invited to a Bible study group, he was drawn into the Verbo (Word) church, a missionary offshoot of the California-based Gospel Outreach, which had arrived in Guatemala in the wake of the 1976 earthquake. At the time of the coup, "Brother Efraín," as his fellow congregation members called him, was in charge of maintenance at the church. Some observers nonetheless believe that the coup plotters consulted with Rios Montt some days in advance.

"I am confident in God, my Lord and my King," said Rios Montt in battle fatigues on the night of the coup, "because He guides me, for only He gives and He takes away authority." Few listeners suspected that his own evangelical convictions would take on public importance. After all, his brother was the Roman Catholic bishop of Escuintla, Mario Rios Montt. It seemed reasonable to assume that one who had been a victim of election fraud would agree to head a transition government leading back toward civilian rule. Rios Montt, however, soon dispensed with the triumvirate formula and ruled in a highly personalistic fashion.

Some analysts believe the coup plotters represented a younger group of officers who were disgusted with the corruption and incompetence of the Lucas clique. Thus the coup affected not only the presidency, but the inner workings of the military, particularly the normal procedures of promotion by seniority.

For the next sixteen months, this born-again Christian became a controversial figure due to his self-assurance and often extravagant statements. Human rights activists accused him of wholesale massacre in the highlands, justified as a "holy war"; his supporters dismissed such charges as fabrications of the international left.

It is not easy to determine to what extent he was truly in charge of matters. The massacre and scorched earth policies certainly accelerated during his first few months in office, but they were already underway; Gen. Benedicto Lucas, the brother of the deposed president, was widely regarded as a major architect of those policies.

On March 31 a delegation of bishops met with the members of the triumvirate. They handed the new leaders a letter expressing the hope that a period of enormous human rights violations was ending. The bishops made references to returning to democracy, and urged structural changes. Their clearest demand, however, was that the church be allowed to carry out its mission, including humanitarian aid for the many victims of violence.

In another statement issued that same day they said "there are indications that more than one million Guatemalans have been forced to leave their homes and their small plots of land, losing their few possessions." One million people would be one-seventh of Guatemala, an astonishing assertion if true. Thousands had been left widows and orphans, many old people were destitute, and more than two hundred thousand had been forced to flee to other countries. The violence had destroyed more houses than the 1976 earthquake, said the bishops, making an appeal for a collection. As he often did, Cardinal Casariego made public declarations diminishing the impact of the statement. He implied that the coup had been sent by God, and that the military were good people. Lightheartedly he said, "If I had not been a priest, I would have been a soldier."

The Guatemalan Church in Exile said the bishops had already "legitimized the new usurpers of power." The bishops should be aware that the only solution was a victory by the people lest some day, perhaps soon, they would have to "beg for the place that should be theirs in the New Guatemalan Society." Their triumphalism reflected the attitude of much of the organized left, especially among exiles.

People in Guatemala City briefly had the feeling that Rios Montt was curbing official violence. The numbers of urban abductions dropped, the *judiciales* (plainclothes police responsible for much abduction, torture, and killing) were said to have been disbanded, former government officials were jailed, and the government even set up an office to investigate the fate of the "disappeared" — and received hundreds of complaints in just a few days. After a momentary lull, however, abductions resumed, the *judiciales* returned under another name, no military officers were brought to justice, and none of the "disappeared" were found.

Reflecting the Reagan administration's eagerness to play a greater role in Guatemala, U.S. Ambassador Frederic Chapin said, "The killings have stopped. The Guatemalan government has come out of the darkness and into the light." Assistant Secretary of State Elliott Abrams contrasted the new government with that of Lucas, which had waged a "war against the populace" — a war that the Reagan administration somehow overlooked while Lucas was in power.

Amnesty International reported that between January and November 1982 "some 3,000 people described by government representatives as 'subversives' and 'criminals' were either shot on the spot in political assassinations or seized and murdered later; at least 364 others seized in this period have not yet been accounted for." At San Francisco Nentón in Huehuetenango 350 people were massacred from July 16 to 19. On July 18, 200 people in Plan de Sánchez, Rabinal, Baja Verapaz were killed; in September the army burned over six dozen villagers in Agua Fria, Rabinal.

Jesuit anthropologist Ricardo Falla later made a detailed study of the pattern of massacre in the isolated Ixcán region. Army violence against the people dated back to an abduction of sixteen leaders from Xalbal in 1975. By the end of 1981 eighty-one people had been killed or "disappeared." Army actions became more systematic in 1982. The largest single action took place in Cuarto Pueblo, which the army surrounded on Sunday, March 14, as the people had gathered for market. A few fled as the army fired some shots; the rest were trapped in their houses or in the Protestant or Catholic chapels. Beginning on Sunday afternoon, army troops killed the people in groups. More than a hundred people were burned alive in the chapel of the Central American Church. By Wednesday all the people had been killed except a man who had been lying as though dead throughout the ordeal. He later said that the last voice he heard was that of a boy about fifteen crying "Ayyy papá, papá," and he thought that it might have been his own son. Falla compiled a list of 324 names of people killed at

Cuarto Pueblo, and a total of 692 killed or disappeared in the Ixcán from February to October 1982.

Anthropologist Robert Carmack later described how the army classified Guatemalan communities, identifying each with a colored pin: green for those free of subversion, which were kept under observation but generally left alone; red for those "in enemy hands," where no distinction was to be made between Indians and guerrillas; pink and yellow, where guerrilla presence was "thought to be more ambiguous." Here, according to an observer cited by Carmack, "terror and threats were used to force guerrilla sympathizers into submission, exposing and isolating the 'hard core' revolutionary cadre, who could be picked off clinically." Although such a pattern may have been discernible by hindsight, in the midst of the terror, "it all seemed very irrational," said a sister later. "There were more massacres in areas that had been more sympathetic [to the guerrillas] but it was by no means exclusive."

Tens of thousands of Indians fled to Mexico and some fled to Honduras. A large number of people, unwilling to leave Guatemala but unable to live in their villages, lived on the run in the mountains. Falla calculated that perhaps 25,000 lived on the run permanently and to these he added another 20,000 from Nebaj and Chajul who frequently had to leave their villages during army incursions. For years thereafter in several places in Guatemala such *poblaciones en resistencia* (communities in resistance) sought to avoid capitulating to the army. Some priests and sisters worked with these groups, obtaining resources for them and serving them pastorally.

Church workers could also serve the army. Evangelical missionaries Ray and Helen Elliott, who had spent almost three decades in Quiché as Bible translators, returned in mid-1982 to work with a project of International Love Lift (a Verbo church agency). On the basis of the tales of brutality and repression they heard from the people, they made recommendations to the army that David Stoll later summarized as follows: "(1) refrain from shooting unarmed civilians just because they were running away or digging holes to hide in; (2) start remunerating its forced labor crews, many of whom had no way to feed themselves or their families; (3) provide the refugees it had created with corn and blankets; and (4) provide its compulsory civil patrols with arms, instead of sending them out to fight guerrillas with machetes and hunting pieces." Within a few months these recommendations were largely implemented.

In Cotzal, a pastor of the Full Gospel Church of God named Nicolás, seeing the danger that the whole region would be wiped out by the army because of the guerrilla influence there, opted to take a leading role in the civilian patrols the army was beginning to set up. Due largely to his work, the army was able to reassert control over the area. The lesson, as Stoll puts it, was that the people "could survive the holocaust by cooperating with its perpetrators." In Salquil, a pastor of the same church became disenchanted with the EGP, which at one point had control of the area, but now could no longer defend them. Six members of his church had been killed by guerrillas, but twenty-nine had been killed by the army. On August 3, 1982, he led 237 evangelicals out of Salquil by night, to escape from the EGP, and accepted living in an army-established camp on the airstrip in Nebaj. This pastor and his people helped the army pioneer the strategic hamlets they later established throughout the highlands.

Falla observed that the evangelicals could temper the worst excesses of the army and serve as intermediaries between the army and the population. They were serving as agents of the army whose overall design was to reconcentrate people in population centers. In this situation of high conflict in an area in which many Catholics had become radicalized, identifying oneself with evangelicals offered a measure of protection. By 1983–84, 30 percent of the heads of household in Cotzal identified themselves as evangelical, and 44 percent of those in Salquil Grande did so in 1986.

Falla also analyzed the military's method. In the "bullets" phase, the army slaughtered rural villages and settlements, wholly, partially, or selectively. Some people turned themselves in; others fled in terror. In the abandoned villages the army burned houses and food supplies, and destroyed kitchen utensils and clothing, claiming that people had declared their own guilt by fleeing. The people on the run were then under attack and could not return to production. During this process the army was also looking for guerrilla combatants.

In the "beans" phase the army gave food, medical attention, and clothing to those who surrendered; they even did so with a certain friendliness, especially if foreign evangelicals were present. Those judged to be involved with the guerrillas were eliminated. Through a variety of means (radios, loudspeakers, airplanes, their own agents among the people) the army carried out a propaganda campaign showing its new face.

There is no evidence that Rios Montt saw any clash between the army's counterinsurgency methods and his own very public religious convictions. Early in his presidency Rios Montt asked that two elders in the Verbo church, Francisco Bianchi (who had accompanied him to meet with the young officers the day of the coup) and Alvaro Contreras, be freed from their church duties to serve as his advisors and by their presence to keep him honest. The president and his wife, María Teresa, also made it a practice to meet Monday nights with church leaders for prayer and Bible reading. Jorge Serrano Elías, a prominent evangelical of the Elim church, was made president of the State Council, an appointed legislative body. Critics accused Rios Montt of surrounding himself with evangelicals.

Rios Montt projected a heavy dosage of legalism and moralizing. In imposing a state of siege on July 1, he said the government could "kill legally"; it was better that people know that the government will kill those who violate the law than that twenty bodies appear mysteriously on the roadside. Press censorship was imposed; the only news permitted about the revolutionary movement was provided by government press offices. One of

Rios Montt's most noted innovations was that of the "special tribunals," clandestine military courts empowered to try suspected subversives who would have no lawyers and could be killed by firing squad if found guilty.

In August 1982 the army was issued a ten-point code of conduct, including such points as "1. I will not take so much as a pin from the population. 2. I will not flirt with or take liberties with local women," and other pledges not to harm crops, to pay for items received, to respect customs, graves, and churches, to refuse gifts, and not to abuse hospitality. In November, 450 higher government officials were gathered in the National Theater where they were required to take an oath, "I don't steal, I don't lie, I don't abuse," and then to have their subordinates take the same oath. Every Sunday evening Rios Montt gave televised informal talks to the nation focused largely on personal and family morality.

On May 28 the Catholic bishops issued a vigorous condemnation of violence, mentioning massacres, new orphans and widows, terror and hunger, abandoned fields, refugees, schools closing as teachers and students fled. "Never in the history of our nation have things gone so far." Calling what was happening "genocide," they said it was a great violation of the commandment, "Thou shalt not kill."

CONFREGUA made its own statement in early June condemning the massacres and reiterating the faith-based grounds for their opposition to them. They quoted the bishops' 1976 letter to the effect that the most humble, exploited, outcast, sick, and ignorant Guatemalan "is worth more than all the wealth of the country and that person's life is sacred." The religious declared their intention to aid people in need in accordance with Jesus' statement that whatever is done for the least is done for him. Sisters and priests were quietly aiding people fleeing the violence, especially Indians arriving in Guatemala City.

Most evangelical leaders dismissed the criticism of human rights organizations as unsubstantiated or exaggerated, or as leftist propaganda. However, a group of Protestants within Guatemala calling themselves the "Evangelical Confraternity" began a newsletter taking issue with Rios Montt. Calling his methods "anti-Christian" they objected to his use of personal religiosity to garner support for the government. They also accused him of wrapping political arguments in biblical language, and of taking advantage of the naivete of church leaders, for example, by inviting them to presidential breakfasts. Jesus' message must not be identified with any legal and political order, let alone with the present system whose injustice and inhumanity were ever more obvious.

In September 1982 James Boldenow, a U.S. missionary of the Christian Reformed church was abducted, threatened, and beaten. He was released when his captors realized that he was not in fact the Rev. James Dekker, whom they were seeking. Dekker's offense was apparently that of aiding a Guatemalan pastor whom the army regarded as a subversive. After both missionaries had left the country, Andrew Kuyvenhoven, a church official in the United States, chastised Rios Montt for what was happening in Guatemala: "We cringe when we think of the dishonor that is heaped on the name of Christ by whom we are saved. We beg you not merely to listen to us but to obey the Word of God: 'Learn to do good; seek justice, correct oppression; defend the fatherless, plead for the widow.' And if you do not wish to listen to this word, please do not mention the name of Jesus any more."

In 1982–83, while the Indians in the north fled to Mexico, others went to Guatemala City. As part of its "bullets and beans" counterinsurgency, the army controlled all aid for victims of war; any independent aid was regarded as intended for the guerrillas. A sister who had worked in Quiché explained, "When they arrived they might have the sisters' address. We would help them get a room, find their way around the capital and get something to eat until they could get by on their own." Although they explored the idea of opening a relief agency with other members of religious orders and with some bishops, they decided it would be impossible for the church to work openly with displaced people. An internal army document referred to church people working with the displaced as "subversive."

Another sister said, "The army sent *comisionados militares* [rural men, often former soldiers, who function as army informers] to spot displaced people. One year they 'disappeared' twelve of our people here in the capital. One they grabbed while he was selling gum on a corner; a woman was seized while crossing a bridge and they threw her body into the Trebol [major intersection where many buses stop] with her tongue cut out." An important part of helping people get settled was obtaining identification papers where possible.

Two events further dramatized the increasingly public role of religion: the one hundredth anniversary celebration of the arrival of Protestantism in Guatemala (November 1982) and Pope John Paul II's visit (March 1983). Indeed Protestants and Catholics scarcely concealed their effort to prove their influence by assembling the larger crowd.

After months of planning, Protestants came to the capital from all over the country, some camping out on empty lots and the dividers of major highways. On the final day columns of marchers converged from several parts of the city at the Parque Nacional, in front of National Palace, and then marched toward the Campo Marte, the army's parade ground near a major garrison.

Several hundred thousand gathered for a program of prayer, speeches, testimony, and sermons. On the podium was President Rios Montt with his whole cabinet together with Jorge Serrano Elías and other government figures. Rios Montt himself was among those who prayed publicly. The main invited preacher was the evangelist Luís Palau, who was well known from his years of radio broadcasting. Evaluating the whole event later, a Protestant theology professor characterized the atmosphere as one of joy and gratitude to God, and a hope that Rios Montt's presidency would facilitate conversion—and yet it was also "tremendous political propaganda" for Rios Montt and thus ultimately a mockery of the people.

This Protestant celebration only heightened Catholic determination to show that Guatemala was "an overwhelmingly Catholic nation," as the bishops put it in a document discussing Pope John Paul II's impending visit. They also noted the commitment of many priests, religious, and lay leaders, many of whom had been "faithful to the point of martyrdom."

Many groups issued statements or addressed public letters to the pope shortly before his arrival. A group of Protestants sent him a letter pointing out that under Rios Montt's rule, fifty pastors had disappeared, ten were in jail, thirty-five had been murdered, and others had fled the country. The URNG issued a statement and declared a five-day truce surrounding his visit.

Three days before the pope's arrival the government executed six men who had been condemned to death by the "special tribunals" despite appeals from the Vatican. Rios Montt claimed he was merely carrying out what the law mandated. Defense Minister Oscar Humberto Mejía Víctores criticized the Vatican for "interference in Guatemala's internal affairs," and the government also prohibited the media from publishing news of the Vatican's efforts. James Degolyer of the Verbo church defended the legitimacy of the executions by saying that the government was reestablishing the rule of law, and claiming that government forces had been trained to respect the judicial process.

For most Guatemalan Catholics, the pope's visit was a moment of celebration. Organized groups from every region of the country lined the sidewalks; marimba groups performed, and the road from the airport to the center of the capital was covered with *alfombras*, drawings and designs made out of colored wood chips and sawdust, similar to those prepared for Holy Week. After a visit to the cathedral the pope went to the same Campo Marte where the Protestants had celebrated their gathering three months before. There he addressed perhaps the largest crowd of his Central America trip.

After rooting his presentation in the Trinity, he spoke of various aspects of the church's work including that of condemning injustice, not in the name of any ideology but in the name of Jesus Christ. Because the human being is God's image and likeness, torture, abduction, or killing is a crime and a most serious offense against God. The pope's most outstanding moment in Guatemala occurred in Quetzaltenango, where Indians had gathered from around the highlands. In his address the pope praised Indian cultures, while maintaining the need for evangelization. Although he said the church would raise its voice to condemn human rights violations, the pope did not mention the huge numbers of refugees, nor did he hint at the army's culpability for massacres. The strongest line was an exhortation: "May no one ever again try to confuse evangelization with subversion, and may ministers of worship be allowed to exercise their mission safely and

without hindrance." However, he tempered his implied criticism by immediately adding, "And do not let yourselves be used by ideologies that incite
you to violence and death." He ended his address with a few words in
Quiché. More important than his words was his action of embracing Indians—"the best thing he did in Central America," said a priest later.

For many Catholics the pope's visit was "Christmas and Holy Week
together"—a moment of relief, of a feeling of coming out into the light,
that "we are persecuted, but not defeated," said a priest.

Rejecting the "Peace of the Graveyard"

The pope's visit helped spark a renewal for Catholics in Guatemala—
even those dismayed over what had happened in Nicaragua. A sister noted
the contrast between his deaf ear to the mothers of slain young people in
Nicaragua and his vain appeal on behalf of those scheduled for execution;
she attributed the difference to the Guatemalan bishops. In their adult
education work she and others used the pope's statements, which the bishops had organized into a study guide. "It was something you could take
hold of, to give the gospel principles without getting yourself killed."

Years of repression had taken their toll on the church. A report prepared
earlier for CELAM (Latin American Bishops Conference) said that the
number of priests had declined from 700 to around 450. (Official statistics
reflected a lesser but still significant decline from 723 [1978] to 652 [1981]—
the truth probably lies in between.) One diocese (probably Quiché) was
said to have only one priest while another had four. The conservative
authors asserted that in its effort to devote itself to the poor, the church
had ignored the rich, "who have felt abandoned and have even shown
contempt and hatred for the church." Violence still made Catholic pastoral
work in Quiché almost impossible. Some church buildings had been
destroyed, and other churches, schools, clinics, parish houses, and convents
were occupied by the army. In 1983 a small number of priests and sisters
returned to Quiché.

Taking John Paul II's visit as their starting point, the bishops in a June
1983 pastoral letter, "Confirmed in Faith," spoke with a new confidence,
reiterating some of the pope's main themes. They focused their reflection
on the Indians, the poor, and human dignity. The church cannot be indifferent when it sees Christ suffering in its children, and hence it must
become the voice of the weakest. Using the terms "massacres" and "disappearances" and referring to "unacceptable abuses of power on the part
of some authorities," they were implicitly pointing the finger at the army.
The bishops also objected to the special tribunals and they found the "gradual militarization of the country" even more objectionable insofar as it was
at the cost of health care, education, and other social needs. They criticized
the obligatory civil patrols which, they said, fell almost entirely on peasants
and Indians, forcing them to risk their lives. They went on to mention the

pillaging of the national treasury and capital flight, both of which were unquestionably sinful and offensive to God. Finally, they complained of aggressive attacks by many "Protestant sects."

When Defense Minister Oscar Mejía Víctores accused the bishops of collaborating with "subversion," Bishop Ramiro Pellecer, the acting archbishop, made no apologies. He said that if some priests had joined the guerrillas in the past, "that was natural given the circumstances in Guatemala at that time." Now, however, priests were working to renew the country. It was the military that was stepping out of its proper role since their leader was proselytizing from the government pulpit.

Cardinal Casariego, who for almost two decades had blunted efforts by his colleagues to take a more prophetic stance, was already ill when the bishops composed their letter, and he died on June 15. At his funeral the army gave him military honors and the army chief of staff, Gen. Héctor Mario López Fuentes, praised Casariego as the "spiritual guide" and confessor of many officers, and the "religious guide of the military institution with which he was always identified."

The president of the Episcopal Conference, Bishop Próspero Penados del Barrio of San Marcos who was soon to be appointed archbishop of Guatemala City, manifested a very different mentality and approach. Interviewed in mid-1983, he told of a place in his diocese where parishioners had been murdered and the priest had to flee due to threats. When the priest returned a half-year later, he and the bishop went to see a local military commander who said, "Bishop, we don't prohibit you from speaking, preaching the gospel, talking about the church; but follow the example of Protestant pastors who just talk about God." Penados said evangelicals were given a green light because they were not concerned about poverty or human rights, but only about God in an alienating way, "like a spiritual drug," tranquilizing or distracting people.

On August 6 military officers gathered in Guatemala City and planned a coup; as their new leader they chose the defense minister, Gen. Oscar Humberto Mejía Víctores (who on August 7 met with U.S. military officials on the aircraft carrier *Ranger*). On August 8 troops surrounded the National Palace and after an exchange of fire in which five soldiers were killed, Rios Montt found himself ushered out of office just as he had come in.

Exactly why Rios Montt was removed from power remains unclear. A popular explanation was religion: "the pope was Rios Montt's downfall," said one young man. Rios Montt's very public profession of evangelical Protestantism had offended many Guatemalans, including army officers who regarded themselves as very "Catholic." Curiously, on August 18, days after the coup, police went into dozens of Protestant churches in Guatemala City, intimidating worshipers and looking for information on pastors.

Religion by itself, however, could only be a minor factor. Rios Montt took a more activist role in both the government and army than the planners of the 1982 coup expected. His moralizing and his connections with the religious right in the United States were helpful for a time. Discussion of the "religious war" in Guatemala also diverted attention from the army's massacres in the highlands. Nevertheless, at some point—perhaps around the time of the papal visit—costs began to outweigh benefits.

Although he took some steps toward a return to civilian rule, Rios Montt apparently intended to rule for several years, while the economy was put in order. Personally he seems to have had contempt for democracy. Some saw his as a crony government, although he claimed that he had chosen qualified, honest people.

From the army's viewpoint, however, his most egregious offense was probably the violation of normal procedures of promotion by seniority. In making Defense Minister Oscar Mejía Víctores the new head of state, the army high command began a process of restoring normality both within its own institution and in society at large. With the tide turning against the guerrillas, they believed it was time to begin a calibrated return to electoral democracy with a civilian president.

One aspect of this agenda was the improvement of relations with the Catholic church. Matters got off to a poor start, however, in October when security forces opened fire on a group of religious and kidnapped and tortured Father Alfredo García. At a meeting with the bishops in Rome in early November, the pope referred to "long lists" of priests who had shed their blood or been kidnapped, and repeated his words in Guatemala to the effect that evangelization should not be confused with subversion and that church people should be able to work in safety.

Apparently in reply to news accounts of this visit, Mejía Víctores said that "soldiers have also died," and accused religious of working with leftist rebels. The following day, the bullet-ridden body of Father Augusto Ramírez Monasterio, a Franciscan who worked in Antigua, was found in an abandoned vehicle. In June he had been arrested by an army patrol in Chimaltenango while helping an insurgent obtain amnesty and he had subsequently been under intimidation and harassment. The Guatemalan bishops sent a telex from Rome, where they were meeting, condemning the murder of Ramírez Monasterio and demanding "that this execrable crime be promptly cleared up."

Although Vatican representatives are normally reserved and often do all in their power to prevent church-government conflicts, the papal nuncio, Oriano Quilici, now publicly blamed the security forces for attacks on the church and defended the legitimacy of the five hundred catechists who had been arrested or were missing. Thousands gathered in Antigua for the Ramírez funeral, which thus became a kind of demonstration. Toward the end of November the interior minister and a press official criticized the bishops' statements in Rome as "shameful, regrettable, and unpatriotic."

Interviewed by Americas Watch, a Catholic bishop in October had said the bishops did not trust Mejía Víctores' openness to them, saying that the military did not know how to listen. One hundred persons had been abducted or killed in this bishop's diocese in the first two months of Mejía's government and he had not even been able to have a meeting with the military to discuss the issue. He added that Caritas, the Catholic aid agency, had stopped functioning in Quiché because it refused to allow the military to distribute food. Nevertheless, when Penados formally took office as archbishop on January 9, 1984, Mejía Víctores and other government officials were present, signaling an intention on both sides to normalize relationships.

Under Mejía the army moved to consolidate its control over the countryside. Army spokespersons now boasted that nine hundred thousand men were incorporated into civilian patrols. Some locations were designated as "development poles" — although little development took place. In March 1984 the government announced the formation of a peace commission, but after two months Archbishop Penados withdrew in frustration.

Mejía called for elections to form a constituent assembly, whose task it would be to draw up a constitution in preparation for a return to civilian rule. In "To Build Peace," a pastoral letter issued about three weeks before the election, the bishops offered what they called an "objective, calm and impartial analysis" of the situation in Guatemala. At one point they listed the various kinds of violence such as abductions, "disappearances," massacres, and the uprooting of large groups of people. In describing how this violence came about, they made a firm defense of the legitimacy of the liberation process that had led communities to become organized and take initiatives, distinguishing this process from the "subversive violence" of the guerrillas. They went on to say that instead of welcoming the people's efforts toward orderly and peaceful change, and thereby isolating those who had taken up arms, the wealthy and powerful had unleashed an indiscriminate bloody repression against the people, leading some to conclude that their only alternative was to work with the subversive groups. Repressive violence by death squads, paramilitary groups, and the security forces brought about a spiral of violence. They strongly criticized the civil patrols and urgently asked that this requirement be changed or lifted.

Toward the end they said, "When public authority falls into a practice of crime, which unfortunately has happened and continues to happen in our country, it loses all its power and, in order to regain control, it can only call on the brute force of arms."

In April 1984 members of religious orders gathered for the Third Congress of CONFREGUA. The significance of the meeting lay not so much in its content — an overview of the context for pastoral work in Guatemala and discussions of church social doctrine — as in the fact that people were beginning to come together after years in which violence had made joint reflection and planning impossible. The number of portraits of martyrs had grown since the last meeting in 1980. A sister who attended later recalled, "We looked around and saw how few of us remained" — she meant those who worked with the poor and had a critical social conscience. Around this time some sisters began to take new initiatives in working in barrios in Guatemala City, while others were returning to Quiché.

Although the Constituent Assembly was assigned the task of preparing for a return to civilian government, what the army intended was to institutionalize its hold over Guatemalan society. Thus the assembly was compelled to approve all the laws and decrees enacted by the military since the 1982 coup. During this period the army began to set up what were called Interinstitutional Coordinating Bodies, that is, committees at the local, regional, and national levels, made up of representatives of major government agencies with military officers on each committee. Despite their stated purpose of coordination, in practice these committees assured a military presence at all levels of government. They withered away after 1986, but they had underscored the military's intention to continue intervening in all spheres of life.

Yet it was also at this time that new popular and human rights movements began to emerge. In 1984 a number of people who were continually encountering each other in morgues as they searched for "disappeared" family members began to discuss banding together. On June 4 Archbishop Penados celebrated a Mass for the disappeared in the cathedral, saying, "We do not want the peace of the graveyard." The following day the Mutual Support Group (GAM), made up mainly of women who had lost their spouses or children to government violence, was formed. Twenty-five people, all from the capital, attended the first meeting. Within a few months their number had grown to over two hundred.

On October 12 the GAM held an eighteen-mile march to downtown Guatemala City. They subsequently met with Mejía Víctores several times and also once occupied the Guatemalan congress. Similar to the Argentine *Madres de la Plaza de Mayo*, GAM dramatized the reality of Guatemalan violence in a new way. By early 1985, when the group was holding weekly vigils and banging pots and pans to protest government inaction on their demands, members and leaders began to receive anonymous death threats by telephone and in a veiled way from government officials. On March 30, 1985, Héctor Gómez Calito was abducted just after leaving a GAM meeting and his body was dumped on a highway. Another board member, Rosario Godoy de Cuevas, who gave the eulogy at his funeral, was found dead in a car at the bottom of a ravine with her two-year-old son and her brother. The government presented it as an accident; Archbishop Penados called it a triple murder. Although two of the GAM's six board members had been murdered and a third had fled for his life, the group soon held another march that swelled to over a thousand people when it reached downtown. After defiant speeches, the participants threw red carnations toward the national palace and ended the march outside the cathedral.

Labor unions also began to reassert themselves. The Coca-Cola union became a rallying point as it had during the 1970s when about eight Coca-Cola union workers had been murdered during a protracted struggle with the management. That conflict had been settled in 1980, when under international pressure and mediation, the company was sold to new owners. In February 1984 these owners claimed the company was approaching bankruptcy and attempted to close the plant. The workers then occupied the plant, and with solidarity from abroad and in Guatemala, they held out for a year until the dispute was settled.

Americas Watch titled its January 1984 report *Guatemala: A Nation of Prisoners*. The "prisoners" were the "700,000 or so members of the civil patrols obligated to perform uncompensated counterinsurgency services for the army who must inform on their neighbors or risk implication as guerrilla collaborators . . . the hundreds of thousands of displaced people . . . the tens of thousands of residents of resettlement camps undergoing 're-education' . . . the hundred thousand or so refugees who have fled to Mexico . . . the millions of Indians in the Guatemalan countryside who have relinquished hope for a better life as virtually all the institutions that stood between them and the state have been destroyed . . . the residents of the cities who silence themselves to avoid winding up as corpses on the street to be dragged off to the morgue by the firemen." A February 1985 Americas Watch report found little improvement. To cite but one gruesome example, in January 1985 the bodies of two men, both showing signs of torture, had been dropped from a helicopter onto a soccer stadium in Mazatenango.

A report prepared by two anthropologists, based on systematic visits and interviews in the highlands and on data from the Guatemalan government itself, concluded that 50,000 to 75,000 people had been killed or "disappeared" between 1978 and early 1985. The army admitted that 440 villages had been destroyed. The very fabric of society in much of the Indian highlands had been destroyed or was under assault.

The army seemed to have made a decision to avoid unnecessary clashes with the Catholic hierarchy: No priests were killed after Father Ramírez Monasterio in 1983. However, in June 1984 Sergio Alejandro Ortiz Toledo, a seminarian, was abducted and killed. Felipe Balán Tómas, a member of the Missionaries of Charity (founded by Mother Teresa) was also abducted in February 1985. The nuncio expressed his regret at the lack of respect for the church. An anonymous church source told a newspaper that relations with the government were such that now it was possible to learn when a priest or catechist was in danger. "We managed to get four out of the country this way."

Throughout 1985 there were signs of a growing economic crisis as inflation increased faster than wages. In September 1985 a proposed bus fare rate hike of 50 percent triggered spontaneous demonstrations and bus burnings; riot police chased angry crowds through the streets while helicopters rattled overhead. One thousand people, particularly high school students, were arrested. At night Guatemala was an occupied zone; said Jean-Marie Simon: "roving army vehicles mounted with machine guns and blinding lights stopped citizens at will, while in poorer neighborhoods boys burned tires on major streets, sometimes aided by their parents." In September army troops and tanks entered the university, ransacked offices, and caused a half-million dollars in damages before departing.

This was the context of the election that would return a civilian presidency. Mimicking Reagan techniques, the major candidates emphasized image over substance. There was no hint of the slaughter that had been regularly documented not only by human rights agencies, but also by the UN and the OAS.

Shortly before the election, the bishops issued a letter recognizing that a certain opening was taking place but cautioning that elections in themselves were at best only a first step. It was not enough to assure freedom at the moment of depositing one's ballot but rather a whole series of social, political, and economic conditions were required; unfortunately, these were not being created in Guatemala. The remainder of the letter alternated between cataloguing numerous problems and injustices and expressing hope that matters would change. In a section on criteria for voting, the bishops emphasized honesty in deeds as well as words. In the bishops' advice to "vote for the candidate whose party has a serious and Christian idea of man, whose dignity it is prepared to recognize and whose rights it will unceasingly defend," some read a subtle tilt toward the Christian Democrats, whose ideology was based on Catholic social teaching. Despite their strong reservations, the bishops wanted to believe that a new civilian government might bring change.

The presidency of Rios Montt had led some evangelicals to reconsider their long-held stance of shunning partisan politics. Jorge Serrano Elías, a member of the Elim church, who had served in the Council of State under Rios Montt, published an open letter to evangelicals. "God placed in my heart the conviction that I had a responsibility to play a role in the recovery of this country for the honor of his name and the good of the whole people." After finishing third, Serrano fixed his sights on the future.

The winner of the two-stage election was the Christian Democrat candidate, Vinicio Cerezo Arévalo, who was inaugurated in January 1986.

Civilian Government, Army Rule

Although foreign press accounts often associated the advent of the Cerezo government with the larger wave of "democracy" sweeping Latin America — hedging with some reference to violence — few Guatemalans expected dramatic change. The "dirty war" of the 1960s had been fiercest during the term of civilian President Julio César Méndez Montenegro (1966–70). Moreover, the army had not lost power and was not even "returning to the barracks" in any true sense. Just before leaving office the Mejía Víctores administration had enacted a number of decrees that preserved army interests, including an "amnesty" protecting the military from being prosecuted for human rights violations committed during the 1982–85 period.

In late 1985 one of the rare reform-minded officers told journalist Jean-Marie Simon that on his first day in office Cerezo should go out to the balcony of the National Palace and announce that he had been forced to make a pact with the military and then ask the people, " 'Should I break the pact? Should I fire so-and-so?' He would get 50,000 people in that square, shouting 'yes' in response. If he doesn't do this during his first two weeks in office, then he has lost." Such an unrealistic scenario highlighted Cerezo's impotence.

In some respects the situation resembled that of El Salvador: The Christian Democrats had come into government for the first time in the context of a guerrilla war. The primary difference was that in Guatemala the major architect of return to civilian rule was not the United States, but the Guatemalan military, which was more successful on its own than the Salvadoran military had been with massive U.S. aid. As a junior partner in the overall enterprise of running the country, the new civilian government was to handle development in the countryside, end Guatemala's international isolation, and attract new financing.

Early in his presidency Cerezo appealed for *concertación*. The notion, then current in Latin America, meant that the various organized forces in society, business, labor, and government should work in concert, through publicly made agreements if necessary. From the outset, however, the major business groups distrusted Cerezo despite his clear disavowal of reform intentions.

The Guatemalan economy had been declining for several years, although not as seriously as those of Nicaragua and El Salvador. The government saw its task as halting decline, restoring private sector confidence, increasing production, and creating jobs. This recovery was to be led by the private sector, without the ambitious social programs that one might expect from the first Christian Democrat government in Guatemalan history. The Cerezo government's modernization strategy assumed that the country should move beyond reliance on a few traditional exports (coffee, cotton, beef, bananas, sugar) to produce nontraditional exports, such as fruits and vegetables for the U.S. market, and should develop free trade zone manufacturing to take advantage of Guatemala's cheap labor.

By overcoming Guatemala's international pariah status, Cerezo managed to attract new aid from the United States, European governments, and international agencies. Although he did not seek to raise tax rates, which were said to be the lowest in the hemisphere, his administration's efforts to close loopholes alienated business and the right. The Cerezo government's most notable economic innovation was a decree earmarking 8 percent of the national budget to be administered by municipal governments. The most immediate effects were visible projects in municipal towns, such as paving main streets with interlocking concrete blocks.

Cerezo used his political skills to finesse rather than confront institutionalized violence. For example, the apparent disbanding of the Department of Technical Investigations (plainclothes detectives), who were responsible for many abductions, turned out to be a reshuffling and repackaging. Human rights violations continued at more or less the same pace as under Mejía Víctores. Although Cerezo had promised the Mutual Support Group that he would appoint a commission to look into what had happened to the "disappeared," he fended off their request for some time and then reneged in mid-1986. The group continued to pressure his government. In one very bold action, GAM members dressed in mourning black stepped into an army parade in September 1986.

Unable to deal effectively with Guatemala's major domestic problems, Cerezo put emphasis on international diplomacy. He continued the already established policy of "active neutrality" in Central American conflicts. At his invitation the Central American presidents met in Esquipulas in May 1986, where he proposed the formation of a Central American parliament. That meeting was a major step toward the 1987 Central American Peace Plan (Esquipulas II).

At noon on May 2, 1986, a group of peasants from the Pacific coast agroexport belt finished a four-day walk to Guatemala City attempting to meet with President Cerezo. Walking at their head was Father Andrés Girón, the pastor of the coastal parish of Tiquisate, who was daring to raise land tenure issues, which were obvious to all Guatemalans but which, like political violence, could not be discussed frankly in public.

Girón was familiar with political violence — his father had been killed for political reasons. Girón said that his commitment to nonviolence began when the Christian Brothers sent him to study in Memphis in the 1960s and he attended rallies of Martin Luther King, Jr., and marched alongside Coretta Scott King. After some years as a Christian Brother in Guatemala, he was ordained a priest in 1978 and worked in Huehuetenango. In 1981 he felt he had to flee and went to work in Oakland, California. Upon returning to Guatemala, he found it difficult to get an assignment until a priest suggested the parish of Tiquisate, where four sisters had been working since the 1980 murder of Father Conrado de la Cruz. In June 1984 Girón organized a march to the shrine of the "Black Christ" in Esquipulas (near the Honduran border). He regarded it as not only a pilgrimage, but a condemnation of government violence. That march led Girón to feel that "the Lord wanted me to serve him as a prophet."

Girón moved into the land issue when several thousand people were put out of work as the result of a landowner's decision not to plant cotton due to lower world market prices. He organized meetings and gathered seven thousand signatures, which he took to President Cerezo with a request that land be bought and provided for landless farmworkers. Having received no response, they decided to march to the capital. Girón heard veiled hints from government representatives ("We don't want more martyrs in Guatemala"). Raquel Blandón de Cerezo, the president's wife, and other government figures paid a late night visit to the marchers in an attempt to dissuade them from continuing. Girón deftly fended off their suggestions, and the marchers entered Guatemala City in a column more than a kilometer long, wearing straw hats and carrying hoes on their shoulders. Cerezo met them, promised to deal with their request for land, and provided government buses for their return.

Girón insisted that he was not calling for the government to confiscate land, but to initiate a process whereby rural workers and peasants would be enabled to buy land. However, it was unrealistic to expect that peasants could in fact buy the rich agroexport belt that was the heart of the economy. Within several months the Cerezo government had in fact obtained several properties that Girón and his group sought to manage in a new cooperative way, perhaps with the idea that they could serve as a demonstration of a new approach to agriculture. Some harbored a suspicion that Girón was in alliance with the Christian Democrats, or that he had his eye on political office.

In early 1988, spurred at least indirectly by Girón, the Guatemalan bishops issued a pastoral letter, "The Cry for Land." The strongest section was the initial analysis, which spelled out with statistics and emphatic language the extreme inequity of landholding and the consequences of poverty in the rural population. In the country 89.56 percent of the farms had but 16.53 percent of the land, while 2.25 percent had 64.52 percent. The second section was a kind of "theology of land," starting with Scripture and moving through Catholic social teaching. Some church people were disappointed that after having made a clearsighted diagnosis the bishops seemed to hold back when making their recommendations. Without mentioning land reform, they urged legislation to make available state and insufficiently cultivated private lands, and to provide measures for protecting peasants and refugees, more education, salary increases, and so forth. In short, while their diagnosis seemed to point toward thorough transformation of land tenure patterns, their recommendations were an assortment of piecemeal reform proposals, which even if implemented would scarcely resolve the problems the bishops had outlined in the first part of the letter.

Interviewed later, Bishop Juan Gerardi—who had made the decision to leave Quiché and had lived in exile—insisted on the need for "realism." Despite the shift to civilian rule, matters remained largely the same. The years of violence had left their mark, but he said that the efforts of the left had not borne fruit but had only left orphans. It was not up to the church to propose models, but it could suggest directions, methods, and measures to take. What good was a letter then? It had a "prophetic value," he said.

Right-wing polemicists attacked the letter in the newspapers, and received an acerbic reply from Bishop Rodolfo Quezada Toruño of Zacapa. Since one critic euphemistically referred to the poor as the "less favored," he made allusions to the "more favored." The diocese of Quetzaltenango prepared a popular version of the letter with simplified text and comic book style drawings illustrating each paragraph.

During the first two years of the Cerezo government, however, the bishops' conference avoided public criticism aimed at the military or government, perhaps feeling that the Christian Democrats should be given a chance to bring about change. Archbishop Penados made occasional critical statements. In 1987 the bishops began to reenter the public arena when they supported the positions of refugees in Mexico who refused return to Guatemala unless a number of conditions were met. Besides agreeing that the government had to assure the safety of the refugees, the bishops said that they should not be required to live in model villages or development poles but should be free to return to their homes. They were questioning whether the refugees' human rights could be assured.

When the government proposed a new set of taxes in September 1987, the major private sector umbrella organization CACIF (Coordinating Committee of Associations of Agriculture, Trade, Industry, and Finance), which had mistrusted Cerezo from the outset, declared a national stoppage. Archbishop Penados offered to mediate between Cerezo and the business groups. Although he may have intended to defuse a confrontation and potential major crisis, some wondered whether it was appropriate that an official representative of the church should be so quick to help resolve interelite conflicts.

Church workers now focused on slowly undertaking new initiatives after the disarray and demoralization caused by years of repression. Most dioceses held week-long pastoral renewal sessions. Over three hundred people participated in such a week held in Guatemala City. A common thread in such meetings was the need for coordinated pastoral planning and coordination, although in practice church workers differed widely in their visions, methods, and approaches. Church workers who had spent years in exile quietly returned and resumed their activity.

Groping Steps toward Peace

Addressing the Central American presidents who had gathered at Esquipulas in August 1987 to draft the Central America Peace Plan, Archbishop Penados said, "Peace is possible. It is within our reach. It can become something real in history." Although government and URNG representatives met face to face in Madrid in the immediate aftermath of Esquipulas, right-wing and army objections prevented any significant further steps toward peace for another year and a half.

An important factor was the cautious but steady reemergence of popular movements, made up largely of a new generation of leaders. In 1987 UNSI-TRAGUA (Labor Unity of Workers of Guatemala) formed an alliance with CUSG (Guatemalan Confederation of Labor Unity), a larger but less militant organization that had been founded in 1983. Unions and popular organizations took a further step toward unification with the formation of UASP (Union of Labor and Popular Action) which besides the two large labor federations included organizations of state workers, bank employees, and others. The CUC, a peasant organization, which had been virtually underground since the early 1980s, also joined UASP. In January 1988, fifty thousand protesters marched in front of the National Palace. When UASP threatened a general strike, the Cerezo government negotiated a "social pact" agreeing to maintain price controls over some basic goods, raise minimum salaries, create conditions for the return of exiles, and set up a government commission to investigate disappearances and other human rights violations. By midyear labor leaders said that the Cerezo government had failed to comply with its side of the agreement.

New groups emerged to defend human rights. The Quiché-based Council of Ethnic Communities (CERJ, acronym for "We are all equal" in Quiché) was organized to oppose forced participation in civil patrols, and was supported by GAM, UASP, and CUC. In 1988 indigenous women whose husbands had been killed or "disappeared" formed CONAVIGUA (National Coordinating Committee of Guatemalan Widows) to pressure the government for help with their own immediate survival and to assure the education of their children. Yet another force was that of the refugees in Mexico and those who had been displaced within Guatemala by violence.

Although organized labor was still very important, this new popular movement reflected a changing horizon. As elsewhere in Latin America, the proportion of the labor force in the informal economy was growing. The large number of unemployed and underemployed reduced the bargaining power of labor unions. At the same time, people's own need to survive motivated them to join these new types of organizations.

In some parts of the country, such as the Petén and in the mountains near Lake Atitlán, URNG attacks were effective militarily, if not politically, and its actions were more coordinated than in the past. After Esquipulas II, several guerrilla leaders donned business suits and made a diplomatic tour, visiting Latin American heads of state. The leader of ORPA, "Gaspar Ilóm," was revealed to be Rodrigo Asturias, son of the Nobel prize winning novelist Miguel Angel Asturias. (Gaspar Ilóm is the Indian protagonist of *Men of Maize*.)

The Guatemalan army continued to target the civilian population as much as the URNG. In an "end of the year offensive" lasting from September 1987 to March 1988 troops attacked areas of the Ixil triangle and lowland areas near the Mexican border. More than three thousand people were captured or turned themselves in and were relocated in new villages. The army claimed to have "rescued" people whom the guerrillas had forced to serve as "recruits, load-carriers, lookouts, or shields."

At an unusual meeting with top business representatives in August 1987, two colonels and two generals offered a glimpse into the military perspective in a presentation titled "Twenty-Seven Years of Struggle for Freedom." The very names of the steps of the five-year plan implemented since 1982 (Victory '82, Firmness '83, Institutional Reencounter '84, National Stability

'85, National Consolidation '86) indicated that they saw elections and civilian government as elements in a comprehensive counterinsurgency strategy. The final speaker, Gen. Héctor Gramajo, the minister of defense, claimed that the Guatemalan army had been successful in its aim of turning Clausewitz, "the philosopher of war," on his head, "when we say that in Guatemala, politics must be the continuation of war." Gramajo's call for collaboration by all, including the business sector, was understood as an implicit accusation that those who were benefiting most from the army's struggle were not doing their share, especially in paying taxes.

Gramajo was regarded as the representative of a pragmatic sector of the army that realized that the country's problems, including the insurgency, had to be addressed politically. The opposing hardline group, believed to be made up of officers closer to the guerrilla war, was said to be impatient with politics and to advocate greater repression. These were differences in degree, since Gramajo himself had been head of general headquarters during the 1983–85 period when many people "disappeared" after interrogation.

These divisions were behind three "failed coups" (May 1988, August 1988, and May 1989). During the August 1988 crisis helicopters hovered above the National Palace as Gramajo was summoned out of a cabinet meeting to go to a gathering of top officers who went so far as to telephone Vice-President Roberto Carpio to ask whether he would be willing to serve as president. Although these coup attempts were said to have failed, they all sent a message to the Cerezo government. On the very night of the May 1988 attempt, for example, Cerezo met with discontented representatives of CACIF.

Labor militancy continued to increase. During harvesttime in January 1989 the CUC called a strike on the Pacific coast to pressure for a raise in the minimum wage; at one point an estimated fifty thousand people on thirty farms had responded. In mid-1989 teachers held a national strike for almost three months and were joined by other public sector employees. In neither case, however, were the strikers' immediate demands met.

Political murder continued unabated. The Guatemalan Human Rights Commission documented 434 individual killings and 99 forced "disappearances" in 1988. The outcry over the massacre of twenty-two peasants in El Aguacate, near Chimaltenango in November 1988 could not be stilled. Few believed the army's attempt to blame the guerrillas, but no one in Guatemalan public life could directly accuse the army. As in the past, political violence was clearly meted out in varying dosages in accordance with an analysis of what was needed. In mid-1989 ten student leaders at the national university were killed and many university and labor leaders had to flee the country. Bombs were set off at the headquarters of the Mutual Support Group and Peace Brigades International.

In this context in March 1989 a peace process began to take shape in Guatemala. As in neighboring countries, the government had established a National Reconciliation Committee in compliance with the Central America Peace Plan. This commission, led by Bishop Rodolfo Quezada of Zacapa, proposed that the process begin with National Dialogue, which was to operate through a set of fifteen commissions; representatives from religious, civil, labor, and professional organizations and virtually all organized sectors of Guatemalan life were invited to send representatives. This rather cumbersome structure would provide a space for a dialogue that could then lead to negotiations to end the conflict. The process was hampered by the unwritten rules of discourse in Guatemalan society that prohibited accusing government forces of political violence.

Beginning at Pentecost (May 1988) an ecumenical group had been meeting regularly to discuss and pray over the peace process. In September 1988 several hundred Catholics and Protestants held a joint liturgy on the theme of true national reconciliation based on justice. Late in 1988 the Permanent Assembly of Christian Groups urged that the National Dialogue address the war in Guatemala, human rights, land tenure, justice for ethnic groups, the reasons for mass poverty, freedom of organization and expression, and the militarization of the country. Their proposals helped define and frame the issues. In this effort they worked in concert with the popular organizations and human rights groups. Members of church-related organizations became active participants on most of the fifteen National Dialogue commissions.

The National Dialogue process, which lasted throughout most of 1989, was hampered by the absence of the major protagonists: the army, the URNG, and the business sector as represented in CACIF. Despite its cumbersome process and the fact that its only apparent product was a series of fifteen documents, which could state the issues only with circumspection, the National Dialogue was a step toward peace. One measure of the impact of the dialogue were the threats and violence against some of its members. The May 1989 coup and increased repression at midyear were regarded as reactions by army hardliners to these halting steps toward peace.

Bishop Rodolfo Quezada of Zacapa played a key role. Acknowledging that the process was hampered by the absence of the main protagonists, he nevertheless insisted that the participants should take advantage of the available space and widen it. He welcomed the ecumenical groups working within the dialogue process and they supported him. Quezada thus helped legitimize groups whom army officers and the Guatemalan right wing regarded as "subversive."

On November 2, 1989, Diana Ortiz, an American Ursuline sister, was in the garden at a retreat house in Antigua when a man came from behind and put his hand on her shoulder, with a mock familiar address—roughly "Hi baby!" She recognized him as a man who had previously accosted her in Guatemala City. He and another man took her to Guatemala City, first on a public bus and then in a police car. They then drove her into what seemed to be a warehouse. She heard the echoing screams of a woman in a great deal of pain and men moaning.

After leaving her in a dark, cold room for several hours, her captors returned and explained the "rules of the game": They would ask questions and if they approved of her answer they would allow her to smoke; otherwise they would burn her back with a cigarette. In fact they burned her no matter what she said — over one hundred times — and they laughed when she reminded them she was an American citizen. They took off her shirt and began to abuse her sexually, continuing to ask her questions and compelling her to identify people in pictures whom she did not know. They also showed her pictures of herself on several occasions. They then raped her repeatedly, and abused her sexually in other ways. Finally she passed out. After she returned to consciousness, she was lowered into a pit filled with dead bodies and rats, which crawled over her.

Later she was raped again repeatedly. When a newcomer entered, her captors said, "Alejandro, come have some fun," but he cursed back in English and told them she was an American and that news of her disappearance was already on TV. He helped her put on her clothes and led her out to a jeep. The man explained that they had confused her with someone else. He also said that they had tried to prevent something like this from happening by sending her anonymous threats, but that she had not taken them seriously. Ortiz answered that she had remained in Guatemala because of her commitment to the people. Although the man spoke in Spanish she was certain he was an American. He said he was driving her to talk with a friend from the U.S. embassy who could help. When the car halted in traffic, Ortiz jumped out and ran into the neighborhood where she took refuge with a woman who was willing to let her into her house. She was then sheltered at the Maryknoll house and the papal nunciature until she could leave Guatemala. (A few weeks previously, Maryknoll Sister Patricia Denny had fled Guatemala after men came to her door and told her to leave or be killed. She had also received threatening phone calls in English.)

Defense Minister Gramajo dismissed Ortiz's injuries as the result of a fight with a lesbian lover. His remarks reflected not only a high degree of cynicism, but the state of surveillance in a country where the defense minister saw nothing unusual in making allegations on the personal life of a nun working in a remote mountain town. Traumatized by the experience for many months, in 1992 Ortiz returned to Guatemala to testify in court; she hoped that seeking justice in her own case might aid the human rights struggle in Guatemala.

In January 1990 Hector Oquelí, the deputy secretary general of the MNR (National Revolutionary Movement) party in El Salvador, was kidnapped along with Gilda Flores, a Guatemalan political party leader who was driving him to the airport. Their bodies were found on a roadside. In the weeks before the murders Guatemalan union leaders had warned that Salvadoran security agencies were roaming Guatemala City, perhaps looking for Salvadorans fleeing the repression that followed the November 1989 FMLN attack in San Salvador. The murders were apparently the work of Guatemalan and Salvadoran forces working together. In a March 1990 report called "Messengers of Death" Americas Watch detailed the pattern of killing and disappearance of university students, Indians, human rights workers, union members, and journalists.

In March 1990 U.S. ambassador Thomas Stroock was recalled for a week of consultation in Washington. A State Department spokesperson said Guatemala's democracy was being "challenged by acts of terrorism and human rights abuses perpetrated by extremists who seek to undermine the democratically elected civilian government." Shortly afterward the United States halted $16 million in health aid when an audit discovered that $2 million, a quarter of the funds already disbursed, could not be accounted for.

U.S. policy showed notable ambiguity if not hypocrisy, however. Reluctant to support the increasingly corrupt Cerezo government and fearing what might happen if the Christian Democrats won the next election, the United States increasingly turned to the military. The *New York Times* reported that U.S. agencies were making payments to Guatemalan officers for information on events in Guatemala and Central America, especially Nicaragua, as well as for their cooperation in combatting drug trafficking. By this time Guatemala was increasingly being used as a transshipment site for drugs and as a site for money laundering. Both the CIA and the DEA (Drug Enforcement Agency) were said to be giving money to high-ranking officers, to some extent in rivalry with one another. Thus despite a professed concern for human rights, the U.S. government was undercutting the civilian government and bolstering the military, which acted with its accustomed impunity.

The unexpected 1990 Sandinista defeat in Nicaragua drove home the point that the context of Central America and Guatemala was changing. As economic factors began to displace geopolitics in the post-Cold War era, thoughtful Guatemalans perceived that unless their country and the region could resolve their conflicts, they might find themselves increasingly ill-adapted to a world economy in which the value of tropical exports was ever diminishing.

Somewhat like their Salvadoran counterparts, the Guatemalan guerrillas were evolving and seeking to take into account the changing circumstances. Their once shadowy leaders, known only by their *nommes de guerre*, were becoming increasingly public. By mid-1989 right-wing newspapers printed lengthy interviews with them. Rodrigo Asturias of ORPA claimed that the URNG had 3,500 regular combatants and 1,000 to 1,500 irregulars. Military spokespersons tended to number the guerrillas at several hundred, while diplomats made an estimate of 2,000. While the guerrillas could inflict damage on the army, they could not evoke much support in the population.

Although Cerezo had played an important role in creating conditions for the Central American Peace Plan, his administration could do little to advance the peace process in Guatemala, given the army's insistence that the government could not engage in peace talks with the guerrillas until they laid down their arms. Hence the National Dialogue had been carried out in the absence of the two armed antagonists.

The peace process nevertheless inched forward. In March 1990 at a meeting arranged by the Norwegian Lutheran church, delegations from the National Reconciliation Committee headed by Bishop Quezada and from the URNG met at Oslo. They announced their decision to "begin a serious process to achieve peace" and both parties invited the United Nations to participate. The mechanism was to be a series of dialogues between the URNG and delegations representing various sectors of Guatemala: the political parties, business, the churches, and labor and popular organizations — not the government or the military in any formal sense.

This approach reflected the URNG's position that since the struggle affected all of Guatemalan society, all sectors should be involved. Upon return to Guatemala the commission described the process at the meeting as "long, tense and extremely delicate" and spoke well of the URNG. Cerezo welcomed the agreement but repeated his and the army's position that the rebels must lay down their arms and reenter the political process.

Two months later representatives of political parties and the URNG met at El Escorial, Spain, for five days of talks and agreed to work together toward a revision of the Guatemalan constitution. Bishop Quezada mediated the meeting and a UN official attended as an observer. The most dramatic moment occurred when Mario Sandoval Alarcón, the major leader of the ultraright MLN (National Liberation Movement), who for many years had been regarded as a godfather of death squad violence, tearfully embraced the guerrilla representatives. Bernard Aronson sent Bishop Quezada a note expressing U.S. support for the efforts of the commission and the URNG.

These talks were followed by others with business groups in Canada, church groups in Ecuador, and popular and labor groups in Mexico. The meetings were held in widely separated venues in order to give them international exposure and perhaps — in a world rapidly losing interest in Central America — further pressure toward peace. "Gaspar Ilóm" said, "Never before have all these different sectors of society met together. ... It has been a very dynamic rich interchange ... an invaluable experience." Although no government or military figures participated formally, Col. (ret.) Francisco Luís Gordillo, who represented opposition political parties, served as an indirect channel of communication. Throughout this process Bishop Quezada, sometimes aided by Bishop Gerardi, continued to serve as facilitator.

Evangelical President

The three coup attempts in 1988 and 1989 apparently convinced Cerezo that far from being able to broaden the scope of civilian power, he could at best survive to hand over presidential power to his successor. News reports pictured him frequently at the beach, and according to the *New York Times* he "seemed to give up on governing, preferring to spend his time yachting and partying." His critics said he was leading the country into corruption, patronage, debauchery, and lawlessness.

Disenchantment with the Cerezo government seemed to translate into disenchantment with democracy. The *New York Times* reported that "Civilian government exists largely in name. The armed forces build the roads, provide services in rural areas, and run the government television station." Edmund Mulet, a Guatemalan congressman critical of military abuses, claimed that people were saying, "if this is a democracy, let's go to a military government."

As he had chosen friends from school for many important posts, Cerezo now picked Alfonso Cabrera as his choice to run for the presidency in 1990, despite the fact that two of his brothers had been linked to drug traffic and that Cabrera used a private helicopter whose owner was regarded as the country's leading narcotics smuggler. In interviews Cerezo dismissed the scandals and plots surrounding him as "the music of democracy."

Voters were apathetic to the half-dozen candidates, all of them more or less right-wing. Newspaper publisher Jorge Carpio, who had had his eyes on the presidency for years, mounted the most extensive campaign. Somewhat astonishingly, at least to outside observers, Carpio's most serious challenger was ex-president Efraín Rios Montt. How could someone identified with the worst period of human rights violations have wide appeal in the population? Evangelicals—at that moment probably more than a fifth of the population—no doubt were happy to support one of their own. Rios Montt campaigned as an outsider, and indeed was shunned by even the right-wing political establishment. His style was populist: "Guatemala is not the police, the captain, the mayor, or the congressman—Guatemala is you." He continually made homey comparisons between the nation and the household. Eschewing economic proposals, Rios Montt reduced all issues to morality and to following the law. "Democracy isn't letting people do whatever they want. Democracy means fulfilling your duties."

David Stoll found that even in areas hardest hit by army violence, people recalled the predictable counterinsurgency under Rios Montt as an improvement over the chaotic slaughter of the Lucas period. He offered people "the chance to surrender without being killed." Stoll compares the situation to that of an evangelical preacher who in a personal testimony tells of the murders and rapes he has committed. This, says Stoll, is like "the double identity of the Guatemalan state. De facto, the army is the country's most destructive institution, responsible for the murder of tens of thousands of citizens. De jure, it maintains peace and stability." Rios Montt paradoxically held out the hope that "he could overpower the most flagrant abusers of authority."

Catholic church officials were clearly worried. Archbishop Penados called Rios Montt "terribly fanatical," and told a reporter, "He is a dictator in his thinking. He will deliver us into a religious confrontation." As he campaigned Rios Montt did not explicitly invoke his evangelical convictions; indeed he had no need to do so.

The wording of the 1984 Guatemalan constitution clearly seemed to bar from the presidency anyone who had become president through a coup. Rios Montt nevertheless challenged that interpretation and threatened to mobilize his supporters in the streets. When the electoral commission finally ruled on the case and it was clear that the military would stand by the ruling, less than three months remained in the campaign.

With Rios Montt out of the race, Jorge Serrano Elías, whom polls had put in fourth or fifth place, now surged forward, no doubt picking up whatever there was of an evangelical bloc. Serrano was by no means a stand-in for Rios Montt. Reared a Catholic, he had become a Baptist and then a pentecostal while studying in the United States. Politically, he had been a Christian Democrat when young, but turned more to the right in the late 1970s. He helped set up a right-wing think tank in 1982 and then served on the three-man Council of State under Rios Montt. After garnering only 15 percent in the first round of the 1985 election, he had formed his own political party and began to downplay his own religious convictions. In the intervening years he had participated in peace processes in Guatemala, and had been an official observer at elections in Panama and Nicaragua.

In the November election he and Carpio each picked up 25 percent of the vote and hence prepared for a runoff vote in January 1991. Both candidates favored free market policies, and both had solid ties with the army. In the final weeks of the campaign they accused each other of waging a dirty campaign and making use of religion. In a pastoral letter the Catholic bishops warned of the danger of a "religious war." They were "worried" that many votes might be cast for religious reasons rather than "in the search for the common good, justice, mutual respect, and brotherly love." In a statement to be read at Mass they urged, "Before casting your vote, verify in your conscience whether or not the candidate has all the qualities needed to be a good leader so that the new government will agree to negotiate with the rebel movement's Guatemalan National Revolutionary Unity (URNG), and thus guide the country toward brotherly reconciliation and peace."

Serrano's astonishing victory margin—one million votes to less than 450,000 for Carpio—forced Guatemalans to reexamine him. Jorge Skinner Klee, an upper-class member of congress, saw him as sophisticated and yet authoritarian and stubborn. A European diplomat on the other hand described him as "very thoughtful, very determined, very well-intentioned."

As he took the reins of government, Serrano faced the interlocked problems of economic deterioration, continuing human rights abuses, and a thirty-year guerrilla war. Without a working majority in the Guatemalan congress, he opted to reach out by appointing Mario Solórzano, one of the few moderate leftists in public life, as labor minister.

Labor assumed that Serrano's "neoliberal" economic philosophy did not bode well. Using the familiar language, the Serrano government announced that it was creating a forty-member "Social Pact Committee" chosen from government, the private sector, and labor. The UASP, however, said it would not participate unless the government halted its announced deregulation of prices on basic goods, guaranteed the right to organize, and committed itself to avoid massive layoffs and privatizations of state enterprises. The government also engaged in negotiations with the IMF, but promised to avoid an economic shock program.

Less than a month after his inauguration Serrano took the initiative of visiting the offices of the Mutual Support Group, and promised to create a commission to investigate the fate of the "disappeared" and also to assure government assistance for the education of one thousand children left homeless as a result of violence. Nineth de García, the head of GAM, welcomed the gesture but pointed out that Cerezo had made similar promises.

An incident during the election campaign put human rights on the agenda in what seemed to be a new way. On December 2, 1990, soldiers had opened fire on a group of Indians in the town of Santiago Atitlán, as they protested an attempted abduction of a merchant by the army; in the process they left thirteen Indians dead and at least twenty wounded. What made the Santiago massacre different was that army responsibility was undeniable. For the first time it became possible to state categorically that the army had committed a specific massacre.

The residents of Santiago formally petitioned the army to withdraw the troops that had been stationed there since 1980 and offered to set up their own volunteer patrols to handle local security matters. Almost a year after the massacre a military court sentenced a sergeant to sixteen years and a lieutenant to four years in prison. Some expressed the cautious hope that the military's impunity might be coming to an end.

Such a development was not so clear in a number of other notable cases, however. The U.S. government, which initially showed no zeal over the kidnapping and rape of Sister Diana Ortiz, was now pressing the government on the murder of Michael Devine, an American who ran a hotel in the Petén. Evidence indicated that the local military was responsible, perhaps because Devine had detected their involvement in drugs. U.S. military aid to Guatemala was suspended over the Devine killing.

In September 1990 Myrna Mack, an anthropologist, was stabbed to death as she left a research institute in Guatemala City. Her "crime" was her research on displaced people in Guatemala, and serving as liaison between victims of human rights violations and international monitoring organizations. Mack had also been a participant in a group of several dozen church-related researchers and activists throughout Central America who met annually to share their analyses. At their 1990 meeting as the group pondered the recent murder of their Jesuit colleague Ignacio Martín-Baró,

Mack wondered aloud which members of the group might be next.

A homicide detective who was prepared to testify on the involvement of security forces in her killing was shot down in broad daylight less than fifty yards from police headquarters by gunmen who used a pickup truck owned by a former police officer. Authorities denied that there was any political motivation or involvement by official forces. In April Dinora Pérez, who had returned from years of exile and started a moderate left party, was gunned down by two men on a motorcycle.

Church people once more came under fire. Moisés Cisneros, a Spanish lay brother, was stabbed to death in his Guatemala City office. He had been accused of guerrilla sympathies and received death threats for his work among the poor. Julio Quevedo, a chief aide to Bishop Julio Cabrera of Quiché, was murdered in July. A Catholic human rights official said that instead of murdering major leaders like Cabrera, "they will try to go after middle-level people and try to scare them away. That's why Quevedo was killed—as a warning to others and to make the bishop back down."

Most shocking was the fact that death squads were deliberately pursuing street children. The government forced the Guatemalan office of Covenant House to close the legal office it had set up to pursue the cases of murdered street children.

By the end of August 1991 by one estimate 548 people had died as a result of political violence, 114 had been kidnapped, and another 124 had been attacked, tortured, or threatened. The fact that Serrano did not dismiss or downplay human rights violations and indeed admitted the existence of a "culture of death" was a modest step forward.

CHAPTER 5

MAKING DISCIPLES

Evangelical Growth and What It Means

On Sunday mornings in Guatemala City in every poor neighborhood dozens of small evangelical chapels resound with singing, clapping, praying, and preaching. Bibles in hand, the evangelicals on their way to church are conspicuous on the buses. In this Catholic country, Protestants seem to have more people in church.

Elementary data on the churches bear out that intuitive impression. If an average of 50 people attended each of the 10,500 evangelical churches in Guatemala in 1987, there would be 525,000 at worship. In order to reach that figure, an average of 1,513 Catholics would have to attend each of the country's 347 parishes. While some urban parishes would surpass that figure, many would scarcely approach it in the total of their several Masses.

Catholic church authorities have no accurate idea of how many people come to Mass since systematic studies have not been carried out. The executive director of CONFREGUA estimated that about 3 percent of Guatemalans attend Mass on any given Sunday, that is, about 240,000 people in a population of 8 million. Similarly, a priest in Ciudad Sandino in the outskirts of Managua said that about 3.5 percent of his parish attended Sunday Mass.

Although the percentage of Protestants in Nicaragua and El Salvador is not as high as it is in Guatemala, it is likely that the number of worshipers rivals or surpasses that of Catholics in those countries as well. Certainly attendance at worship is not the only measure of how "Catholic" or "Protestant" a person may be. Nevertheless, these simple indicators raise the possibility suggested by David Stoll that the number of "real" Protestants may be on a par with that of "real" Catholics.

The concern of this book is the role of churches and church people in the midst of revolution and counterrevolution, and thus the focus is on those who see a connection between their faith and some form of political involvement. It would be a mistake, however, to ignore the rapidly growing evangelical churches, which in quantitative terms are far more successful than Catholic base communities or similar Protestant groups. Hence this chapter examines evangelical growth and its implications.

Estimates of the numbers and growth rates of Protestants are varied. Government censuses do not inquire about religion, and researchers by and large have not had the resources to carry out valid national-level surveys. Statistical information gathered by the Catholic church is limited to what must be sent to Rome: the number of clergy, the number of church institutions, and so forth. A 1987 CELAM publication made astonishingly low estimates of the Protestant proportion of the population: Nicaragua, 4.4 percent, El Salvador, 4.5 percent and Guatemala, 4.9 percent. At the more local level, however, the signs of evangelical growth are harder to deny. A lay Catholic activist in Estelí, Nicaragua, said that the number of Protestant churches has grown from three to fifty (a Baptist cited the number as forty). A sister pointed to the twenty-eight Protestant churches in Santa Cruz de Quiché as opposed to one Catholic priest (the bishop lives there as well).

If Catholic bishops insist on seeing their countries as Catholic, certain Protestants see themselves as a new emerging majority. At the one hundredth anniversary of the first Protestant church in Guatemala, the evangelist Luís Palau urged evangelicals to make theirs the first reformed country in Latin America. A professor at the Evangelical University in El Salvador confidently told me in 1990 that 30 percent of Salvadorans were evangelical, a figure he said secular poll takers supported. Dawn Ministries, a worldwide evangelistic enterprise headquartered in Pasadena, California, reported that at a 1987 conference Salvadoran evangelical pastors committed themselves to the goal of making their country one-half Protestant by 1996.

This concern for numbers reflects the U.S.-based church-growth movement, which uses social science and marketing research techniques to help churches be more effective in carrying out Jesus' words at the end of the Gospel of Matthew (28:19–20), "Go and make disciples of all nations," a text they refer to as the "Great Commission." In 1981 the International Institute for In-Depth Evangelization published a 440-page directory of churches and church agencies in Guatemala, listing 6,448 local Protestant congregations, complete with the street address of the church, the name of the pastor, and denominational connections. Each church surveyed gave the number of its adult (over age twelve) members.

The influence of evangelical churches extends beyond adult full members to encompass children and other members of a household, nonmembers who attend worship, and congregations in formation. Taking these and other factors into account, evangelical researchers concluded that in the case of Guatemala the "Protestant community" is four times as large as the number of formal members. Thus on the basis of the 334,453 adult members reported by the churches the directory's compilers assumed that the Protestant community in 1981 included 1,337,812 people or 18.4 percent of Guatemala. A Guatemalan church-growth agency concluded in 1987 that the evangelical community had grown to 31.6 percent of the whole population. Since statistics often take on a life of their own once they are in print, such statements soon went uncontested.

Such a methodology is problematic, however. The sources of membership data were the local churches. Presumably none of the pastors would offer a low count, and some might even provide inflated figures. Since evangelicals easily move from one church to another, the same individual or household might be counted in more than one congregation. Even though the multiple of four is the result of some research, it remains a hypothetical projection. In the case of Nicaragua, for instance, Abelino Martínez used a multiple of three to arrive at a Protestant community of 626,529 in 1986 (19.5 percent of the population).

Surveys of the general population should yield more accurate figures than projections based on declared church membership. A 1988 survey directed by Arely Hernández and Ignacio Martín-Baró of the UCA found that 16.4 percent of Salvadorans identified themselves as evangelical. The same survey found that 64.1 percent called themselves Catholics (30.6 percent nonpracticing), 4.8 percent belonged to "other religions" (primarily Mormons, Adventists, Jehovah's Witnesses), while a surprising (for Latin America) 14.7 percent claimed to have no religion. A Costa Rican Gallup affiliate, the Consultoria Interdisciplinaria en Desarrollo (Interdisciplinary Consultants on Development), in polls at the end of the 1980s found the following percentage of respondents who identified themselves as evangelicals: Guatemala, 26 percent; El Salvador, 17 percent; and Nicaragua, 14 percent.

Finally, David Stoll offers the following more conservative set of figures, which nevertheless indicates striking rates of growth.

Percentage of population			*Growth factor, 1960–85*
	1960	1985	
Guatemala	2.81%	18.9%	6.7 times
El Salvador	2.45%	12.8%	5.2 "
Nicaragua	2.26%	6.3%	2.8 "

One-Dimensional Explanations

Catholics during the 1980s were strongly tempted to attribute evangelical growth in Central America to deliberate policies of the local military and of the new religious right in the United States. The secular left, in both Latin America and the United States, spoke freely of the "evangelical penetration" and the "invasion of the sects," and publications by liberal mainline churches often reflected similar ideas or assumptions. To prove that the U.S. government was behind rapid evangelical expansion, Latin Americans ritually pointed to the 1969 "Rockefeller Report" (submitted to President Nixon by Nelson Rockefeller after a trip around the continent) and the 1980 Santa Fe Report, most of whose authors went on to work for the Reagan administration on Latin American policy.

A January 1989 pastoral letter of Archbishop Próspero Penados del Barrio on non-Catholic groups well exemplifies the attitude of many Catholics, even those who were progressive or radical in areas such as defense of human rights. Early in the letter Penados emphasizes the Reformation's connections with the ambitions of secular leaders, going so far as to affirm that Protestantism spread and was consolidated "more as a political weapon than as a religious concern." Likewise in the 1870s the anticlerical Liberal government of Justo Rufino Barrios invited Protestant churches into Guatemala to counter Catholicism, and their expansion was connected to growing U.S. dominance of the region. Penados invokes sixteenth- and nineteenth-century history to bolster his claim that Protestants today are benefiting from the secular power as they have in the past. Due in part to their connections with the United States and their image as "defenders of freedom and promoters of order and peace . . . Protestants, especially in times of crisis as has been painfully the case in Guatemala, are protected, while the Catholic church is persecuted and calumniated."

The fullness of Christianity is found only in the Catholic church, says Penados. He admits that Protestant advance is partly the result of the pastoral inadequacy of the Catholic church, and that conversion to Protestantism often helps people overcome vice and live better lives. Nevertheless, Protestantism is said to be responsible for "the breakup of the family unit, the loss of cultural identity, and perhaps what is most serious, the loss of the deep sense of community and the particularly humane sensitivity found in the Guatemalan people."

Latin American bishops and Pope John Paul II have frequently invoked this cultural identity argument. "Guatemala," says the archbishop, "has been forged as a people and as a nation under the sign of Catholicism. If we analyze our history we realize that Catholicism has been the only element that has been able to establish a certain kind of integration between the various races and social or economic groups." Likewise at the local level, Protestant individualism leads to the loss of the community sense; one's "brothers and sisters" are narrowed to one's own religious group. Here Penados notes that hundreds of Catholics have fallen "victims to the new ethic that Protestantism was spreading." He seems to have in mind the many cases in which people informed on others, who were then abducted and murdered. Finally, he strongly suggests that although their first attempt to take political power failed (with Rios Montt), Protestants "do not seem to have lost the hope that at some point this dream could become a reality."

This pastoral letter has been cited at some length because it summarizes the chief criticisms heard among Catholics and reflects a number of blind spots. Although Penados recognizes the historical and contemporary links between Protestantism and the civil power, he nowhere notes that Catholicism arrived as an integral component of the sixteenth-century subjugation of the native peoples, or that until very recent times most church leaders willingly played their assigned role in buttressing the existing order. In making his case for the Catholic character of Guatemala, he gives no hint that Catholicism might be "foreign" in its own way. Part of the success of pentecostalism may be that poor people feel more at home, more "Guatemalan," in local evangelical chapels in their neighborhoods than attending Mass celebrated by a non-Guatemalan at a more distant church.

The archbishop seems unaware of the prejudice and violence Protestants have experienced at the hands of Catholics. Their folklore includes tales of "martyrs" killed in the early decades of this century, and older members tell of being isolated after priests told parishioners to shun these "heretics," for example, by refusing to sell to them. While drawing attention to the use of religious division for political purposes, Penados ignores the fact that in the "dirty war" in Guatemala most of the people issuing the orders, adjusting the hoods, attaching the electrodes, and pulling the triggers were Catholics. In his onesided explanations and his lack of a critical perspective on Catholic history, he reflects the attitudes of many other Catholics toward what they persist in calling "sects."

Evangelicals themselves are likely to attribute their growth to the Holy Spirit and to resent efforts by nonevangelicals to explain it. When I wrote to a church-growth agency requesting elementary statistical information, a researcher at first refused, mentioning earlier experiences with nonevangelical researchers who "denied ... the supernatural world," and thus reduced him and his colleagues and their motivations "to the merely social, economic and political sphere." (Upon my further request he did supply some information.)

In practice, evangelicals readily talk about nonsupernatural reasons for their growth. Bartolomé Matamoros, the head of the Assemblies of God in Nicaragua, told me that the Sandinista years had been very rich for the church, and listed three "factors" that had led them to be more committed to the Lord: persecution, the war, and emigration from Nicaragua (which had led to further conversions). Being persecuted was a purification, similar to the experience of the Israelites in the desert. "Throughout history, the evangelical church has grown when persecuted." While many other pastors were involved in politics—a dig at Protestants who viewed the revolution itself as an opportunity that should be embraced in faith—"we were praying and fasting. The people want to hear about the Bible, not politics, so they came looking for our churches."

Individual converts to evangelical churches tend to emphasize differences between their new belief and practice and what they left behind. The Salesian priest and sociologist Luís Corral Prieto interviewed 270 Protestants who had formerly been Catholics. His respondents frequently mentioned their discovery of the Bible and of Christ as Savior, an awareness of personal sins, and commitment to Christ. When asked what had changed in their lives, many said "everything": They no longer smoked or drank, their marriage and family life was completely changed, and even their economic situation had changed for the better. Protestant converts responding to the UCA survey in El Salvador expressed a conviction that they had now found the truth.

An anthropologist studying the differences between active Catholics and evangelicals in an Indian town in Guatemala told me he was finding little difference in beliefs about God or Christ or other doctrinal points or even about politics. The sharpest cleavage was over liquor: Evangelicals renounce it entirely while Catholic church authorities preach against drunkenness but in practice look the other way and do little to help alcoholics overcome their addiction. For many men becoming evangelical is heavily identified with renouncing alcohol—and for their families it signifies the end of alcohol-related abuse.

Varieties of Evangelical Experience

In order to understand better the nature of this movement, let us observe some examples of the evangelical experience at the congregational level. The Iglesia Pentecostal Mi Redentor (My Redeemer Pentecostal Church) is situated near a busy intersection in the sprawl of Managua. The church building, set back some distance from the road on an uneven and unlandscaped piece of property, is an inelegant cement block structure, like many others in Nicaragua. Ditches in front of the present church indicate that foundations are to be laid to expand the building, although construction does not seem to be moving rapidly.

Inside the church a gauzy yellow parted curtain hanging from the ceiling and another one halfway back are almost the only decorations. The church could almost be a Catholic chapel built in recent years in poor barrios, except for the lectern standing where a Catholic altar would be situated and the numerous plaster casts with Bible passages hanging on the four rows of square wooden pillars.

It is 7 P.M. on Saturday night and people greet one another as they come drifting in. An electric guitarist and a drummer are warming up. "Glory to God," shouts a young man over a microphone in the front. He is perhaps in his early twenties, and wears a black jacket and bow tie. "Glory to God!" responds the crowd. "Let's give the Lord a hand!" he says, and everyone applauds. He asks for prayers and everyone prays out loud at once, as the guitarist and drummer sustain the mood. One of the first hymns, which goes on for several minutes, sounds like a Colombian *cumbia*, and I wonder if from a hundred yards away I might mistake this scene for a Saturday night dance.

A woman steps to the lectern and asks people to take out their bibles.

They read a long passage from Romans 8, alternating the verses. The next song is *"Así, así se alaba a Dios"* ("This is, this is, how we praise God"), and now the young man in the bow tie, who serves as a kind of emcee, jumps up and down, despite a disability in his leg that gives him a noticeable limp. Next, individual members of the congregation step forward to sing songs. One is like a Mexican *corrido* and others are like other Latin American popular music, including a plaintive ballad that goes:

> You gave me your love when no one wanted to love
> me
> And that is why I love you Christ,
> that is why I love you Lord,
> that is why I will love you.

Preaching this evening is a young woman — the pastor has been invited to another church. Her text is from Romans 12:2: "Do not conform yourselves to this age but be transformed by the renewal of your mind." She begins with the story of a country boy whose ambition was to go to school and become a neurosurgeon. Rather remote from Nicaraguan experience, I think, and indeed, the "country boy" goes to Boston and eventually realizes his ambition; perhaps she got the story from the Spanish edition of *Reader's Digest.* Her point is ostensibly about helping one's neighbor but it also seems to reflect the upward striving orientation of the pastor, who in an interview expressed his belief that "God is real, God exists, and if you are faithful to God, He will make you prosper." The young woman now says you must have a goal and go after it; fear of making mistakes should not hold one back from striving.

"Christian life is a dynamic, joyful life. . . . What we need are Christians who are courageous and determined." Young people should not worry — about whether they will find the right marriage partner, for example — but simply set off for God's kingdom and personal problems will work themselves out.

The pastor has already told me his own story and that of the church before the service. He accepted the Lord at the age of twenty, when he attended an evangelical service and suddenly understood the meaning of the cross. His conversion also cured him of problems in his lower spine, which otherwise would have required an operation; X-rays confirmed that he had been cured. Originally a member of the Assemblies of God, he and about fifteen other people were meeting in daily Bible study groups in their houses, when in late 1980 they were moved to organize a revival and healing campaign. Around eight hundred people declared for Christ in that campaign, but partly due to the group's inexperience, only a much smaller circle continued to attend their worship, which was held in his house. His own constancy and work with the church led to his becoming a pastor.

I try to get his view of the ten years of Sandinista government — we are talking in mid-1990 — saying that some Christians believed it was important to become involved with the revolution while others said it was Marxist and even called the Sandinistas "demonic." What does he think? "For us they're all human beings and they need God. We have to love and respect them all." Thank God, he and his church have never had problems with the government. "We have to pray for them because that is what the Lord commands."

Asked about who Christ is for him he says, "a person who is with us, who teaches us, and gives us faith so that we may grow and mature in the knowledge of the Bible — and faith in order to trust that he is going to give us what we need economically to live on." During the week he spends his time making pastoral visits and studying the Bible on his own. He does not read other books, even theology. He feels he has to teach people the "principles for them to prosper." None of the worshipers looks like they are prospering, except perhaps one individual who joins the emcee toward the end and who, in his tropical dress shirt, looks like he might run a business and own a pickup. At the end of the service he tells the congregants that there will be another service next Saturday at 7 P.M. — provided that the Lord has not come in the meantime.

Pentecostal preachers freely weave a variety of observations around biblical texts. For example, at the Church of God on Calle Martí in Guatemala City, one young man chooses the exhortation of the letter to Timothy (1 Tim. 4:16), *Ten cuidado de ti mismo* ("Take care of yourself"), which in the biblical text is part of a long series of exhortations on how Timothy should exercise leadership in the church community. In this preacher's hands, it becomes the linchpin for a half-hour or more of salutary observations: For example, students should not study so late that they fail to get enough sleep; believers should be careful not to listen to erotic lyrics of popular songs blaring at them on all sides. At the Church of the Complete Gospel in Coban, a man gives his testimony: Before his conversion he and his wife were at odds for four years, but now things have changed. You can enjoy an "eternal honeymoon," he assures them.

The Elim church in Guatemala City is what is sometimes called a "neo-pentecostal church," that is, one traceable to a new wave of pentecostalism in the 1960s. The church is such a well-known landmark that buses use "Elim" signs to indicate their route. From the outside it is a plain white structure, set back from the street, with ample parking spaces. Men and women in a kind of uniform stand ready to greet people at the entrance. Inside I estimate that there might be as many as ten thousand sitting on folding chairs and I am told that an overflow crowd is watching the service on closed circuit television in a basement. This is the largest worshiping congregation of any kind in Guatemala.

Again decoration is sparse — here it is ivy dangling from pots hung along the walls. On a very high stage are several ministers and a singing group with guitars, keyboard, and percussion. It looks like a Guatemalan version of the churches of U.S. televangelists, and the television camera and lights reinforce that impression. In the pentecostal manner, the service alternates between prayer, singing, and preaching. At various moments the people pray, most with eyes closed, some kneeling, some weeping; sometimes they sing spontaneous prayer, harmonizing as musicians supply background. At one point a woman begins praying in rhythmic nonsense syllables, which gradually evolve into paraphrases of Scripture; another woman takes up the prophecy and then another. Gentle, gradually crescendoing sounds from a guitar signal that this period of praying in tongues is coming to an end. Basing his sermon on a text from the prophet Micah, a preacher marvels at how God's plan unfolds according to the Scriptures. Several times he asks those who believe that Christ is coming again to raise their hands or to applaud. Despite the obvious absorption of the worshipers in the service, a continual stream of people arrives and steps out. Some take their children to buy them a soda or snack at the stands outside, where radios are tuned to the broadcast of the worship.

Mi Redentor, the Church of God, the Complete Gospel, and Elim are all pentecostal. Nonpentecostal churches seem quite sedate by comparison. The congregation of the First Church of the Central American Mission in Guatemala City dates back to the early years of the century. Its church, an A-frame structure that has a modern but recognizably churchy look, is located in a row of buildings near the downtown district. Here there is no guitar or drum, but rather a piano, violin, and trumpet. Classic Protestant hymns are the mainstay; at one point a male quartet sings a song about David and Goliath in a bouncy country idiom, and another which says if Satan knocks at your heart tell him to go away. Today the guest preacher, Emilio Nuñez, the best known theologian at the Central American Seminary, seems to be concerned that traditional churches like this one are being surpassed by the fast-growing pentecostals. He mentions large evangelistic campaigns including the 700 Club's "Project Light." He then recalls how this church can trace its origins to a missionary from Honduras who arrived in Guatemala City and preached 150 nights in a row. The point seems to be that they need not imitate the techniques of the pentecostals, but should return to the practice of their founders. As I look around, however, I find it hard to imagine the fifty well-mannered people present out street preaching with abandon.

The various forms of Protestant churches are largely the result of successive waves of missionaries. In the mid-nineteenth century the Moravian church was established on Nicaragua's Atlantic coast. A first wave came around the turn of the century and a second, pentecostal, wave came in the 1930s.

Obviously, in comparison to the Catholic church Protestants are extremely atomized. For example, the 1981 directory of Protestant churches in Guatemala lists 210 separate organizations. The list varies from the Assemblies of God, which with 674 churches and 35,909 members constitutes over one-tenth of all evangelicals, to dozens of churches made up of a single congregation. Evangelical churches grow through the formation of new congregations. When congregations divide over doctrinal or disciplinary disputes or struggles between personalities, the result may be new independent churches.

Evangelical churches are both rivals and associates in the same enterprise. Over against the larger society, whether seen as Catholic or as unchurched, evangelicals have much in common religiously and socially. However, in a given locale they are inevitably somewhat in competition with one another not only in outreach to unconverted people, but even for one another's members, as people often move from one evangelical church to another.

Both Catholics and secular critics who saw recent evangelical growth as an "invasion" seemed unaware that Protestants have a history of over a century in Central America. It is helpful to be reminded that the Baptist school has stood in Managua since 1917 and the Baptist hospital since 1930. During the first eighty years of their existence, however, the evangelical churches had very modest success. To what extent was the recent rapid expansion — from 2 or 3 percent of the population in 1960 to approximately 15 percent by the mid-1980s — the outgrowth of what had been developing slowly in previous decades, and to what extent did it reflect new developments?

Catholic "Push" and Evangelical "Pull"

One rather obvious reason for the effectiveness of evangelical churches in attracting Catholics is the scale of their communities. In 1987 there were 2,200 Protestant pastors in Nicaragua serving an estimated 203,000 evangelicals, and thus an average of one pastor for every 92 members. At the same time there were 14,755 Catholics in the average parish (187 parishes for 2,759,146 Catholics). The Catholic church of course also has sisters and brothers, many of whom are teachers. However, even totaling priests, diocesan and religious, with sisters and brothers, there is only one such representative of the church for every 3,190 Nicaraguans. It is quite impossible for most Nicaraguan Catholics to have a personal relationship with a priest or sister. By contrast an evangelical pastor whose whole congregation consists of a few dozen people, who often live within a few minutes' walk, inevitably knows his own congregation well.

Indeed, the Catholic church is not organized on congregational lines at all. Although today a parish may be called a "community," it is primarily an administrative unit: The priest or priests of the parish are in charge of all the Catholics within their boundaries, who for their part are expected to go to their parish church for their religious needs. When surveyed in El Salvador, 76.7 percent of evangelicals said they had been visited by their pastor whereas the rates for Catholics were 28.2 percent (practicing) and

16 percent (nonpracticing). Since the number of Catholics who attend Mass regularly is quite small, many Catholics encounter official church representatives primarily at the baptism of their own or other people's children or at a funeral. Except for the relative few who may be active members of a parish organization, most Catholics do not interact with others as members of a congregation. Even those who attend Mass may feel little connected to their fellow worshipers.

Lack of such contacts does not in itself make people merely "nominal" Catholics. People who do not attend Mass regularly may pray in their homes or even drop into the church to pray; they would be indignant if told they were not good Catholics. The point here is simply that official representatives of the Catholic church cannot have personal contact with the bulk of the Catholic population.

Not only are evangelical churches able to reach out to people; ongoing outreach is central to their understanding of what their faith demands. Of crucial importance are Jesus' final words in the Matthew's Gospel: "Go, therefore, and make disciples of all the nations. . . . And know that I am with you always, until the end of the world!" Fulfilling this Great Commission will hasten the coming of Christ. All church members are expected to be active missionaries. The frequently mentioned "work" of the church is largely its own expansion. Such a vision stands in sharp contrast to those, both Protestant and Catholic, who think that the churches should devote themselves to disinterested service of others (such contending visions are the subject of Chapter Seven).

Witnessing is thus integral to the life of the believer. Evangelicals are encouraged to communicate their faith with neighbors and family members; indeed some local churches are largely made up of extended family networks. Evangelicals find prisons and hospitals especially fruitful. A hospital visit may not lead to an immediate conversion, but the crisis of illness may present an opening to religious change. An ex-prisoner whose life is transformed is a powerful witness for further conversion. Congregations do outreach in what are called "missions" (congregations not fully independent) and "target areas," where congregations are still in formation. Thus the 4,527 Guatemalan churches in the 1981 directory claimed to be working in 1,735 missions and 1,959 target areas.

Evangelicals themselves were increasingly convinced that "The most effective evangelization methods seem to be close personal contact, in the family or one's work group, by a person who genuinely finds the Lord Jesus Christ," as a 1988 document by several umbrella evangelical organizations in Guatemala stated. Mass campaigns were said to be "less effective than expected, except when there are true miracles that everyone can verify and when the participating churches have been personally involved and engage in follow up." The report questions the value of mass campaigns. Many of those who step forward to "accept Christ" are not new converts; they may be evangelicals curious to see a famous preacher up close, or they may have fallen away and now seek momentary renewal of their hope for salvation. Hence the numbers of people who profess to accept Christ as their Savior should not be taken at face value. The resources and energies invested in such campaigns might be better spent in other types of evangelism.

A similar criticism could be leveled at the mass media, especially televangelism. Radio has probably been the most effective media tool. The first evangelical radio stations were established over thirty years ago, and today most Central Americans can tune in to more than one evangelical station to hear a mixture of preachers, religious music, and Bible verses. Those listening to the radio in the privacy of their homes — women, for example, while doing their endless washing by hand — are exposed to Protestant preaching and music without visibly attending church. By itself radio might win few converts, but it has been a gentle and nonthreatening way to present the evangelical message.

Changes in the Catholic church in recent decades — changes ironically intended to bring the church closer to the people — also help explain the rapid expansion of Protestantism. For years priests railed against the beliefs and practices of evangelicals and forbade Catholics to associate with them, even though their numbers were minuscule. Abruptly in the 1960s Catholicism made a dramatic turnaround on a number of seemingly irreformable points: The Latin Mass was dropped, Bible reading was encouraged, and ecumenism replaced religious intolerance. If "heretics" could turn into "separated brethren" overnight, perhaps they had not been in error after all.

Moreover, priests now suddenly seemed embarrassed by traditional Catholicism, which they found difficult to reconcile with biblical Christianity. In their concern for a more interior and committed Christianity, they ignored or perhaps disdained popular religious practices and beliefs. Churches full of saints' images now made them uncomfortable. In order to make the church building more "Christocentric" and aesthetically satisfying, a pastor might remove a number of saints' shrines. The new form of worship in the vernacular, however, might fail to satisfy the religious needs of those who had previously found solace praying before the saints. What priests perhaps saw as implementation of Vatican II or Medellin, the people might experience as a sudden and arbitrary changing of the rules. The church's representatives were attacking their traditional religious practices or were ignoring them, without replacing them with anything more satisfying. Such were the "perverse effects" of Vatican II in Latin America, as one researcher put it.

As different as a pentecostal service is from traditional Catholic devotions, one has a sense that it taps into popular religiosity — or better, taps into popular culture, including religiosity. Pentecostal services combine liveliness with moments of intense emotional prayer. Catchy rhythms and tunes make you tap your feet, clap your hands, and sway — indeed, a kind of dancing is part of the service in some churches. The musical language is often that of Latin American popular music, so close it sometimes seems plagiarized, although the lyrics tend to be rather unimaginative arrangements of Scripture verses, especially from the psalms. As church-growth writer J. Peter Wagner says, "It's fun to go to church."

Many evangelicals are quite convinced that God works directly in healing and other manifestations, such as prophecies. An Assemblies of God pastor in Nicaragua told me the story of a man who lived far up in the hills who one day dropped into an evangelical church. A woman spoke up, "That man who just came into church, has done something shameful with his stepdaughter and lives with her." Thus confronted, the man confessed his sin. Awe and fear over such events or their legends have helped the churches grow. The evangelical conviction that miracles and prophecies are still taking place as in early Christian times is plausibly closer to poor Central Americans, whose traditional religion sees God and the saints intervening in everyday life, than is a Catholic church which in practice is skeptical of miracles. Indeed the survey in El Salvador found that an astonishing 95 percent of both Catholics and evangelicals believed in miracles.

This same survey sheds light on the similarities and differences between Catholics and Protestants. Beliefs about God, sin, and the afterlife were rather similar. One striking difference was on the matter of hell. A rather surprising 31 percent of Catholics, both practicing and nonpracticing, said they saw hell as taking place on earth, and only 47 percent of practicing Catholics believed in a hell beyond the present life as opposed to a solid 75.4 percent of evangelicals.

Differences over behavior are sharper. For evangelicals the "rules" are clear—no extramarital sex, gambling, drinking, smoking, or dancing—and those rules are enforced by expulsion from the church in order to maintain the purity of witness. Such moral absolutism no doubt keeps some people away, but those who are converted regard their very change of life as a kind of miracle and an affirmation of God's active presence. Money saved from drinking, primarily by males, can go into meeting a family's needs; in some instances, a new work ethic may lead to noticeable material betterment. A woman convert who draws her partner into the church may get a responsible and faithful spouse; if the man does not convert the wife will at least find solace and support.

More sophisticated evangelicals realize that their rules are relative. An evangelical leader in Managua had seen European evangelicals smoking and enjoying their beer, and realized that the prohibitions are largely cultural. He nevertheless maintained that in Nicaragua such behavior is a sin, and invoked the biblical notion that the body is a temple of the Holy Spirit "even though people didn't smoke in biblical times." On the whole, the clarity of evangelical moral demands and their effectiveness in helping individuals and families overcome problems of drinking and abusive behavior contribute significantly to attracting converts.

Contrary to Archbishop Penados' depiction of evangelical churches as foreign and Catholicism as part of Guatemalan identity, in many ways the evangelical churches are more at home in the popular culture than official Catholicism. The pastors are from the village or barrio, and most have not had formal seminary training, which by its very nature absorbs Catholic priests into middle-class culture.

As indigenous as they might be, however, most of these churches can be traced back to U.S. missionaries and some still retain ties. Their theology comes from the United States and Europe and a casual perusal of evangelical bookstores shows that most devotional and theological works are translations from English.

Clifton Holland, a church-growth specialist, suggests that an identification with the United States and U.S. culture, however, may help explain current growth in Central America. He notes that the many missionaries who arrived in the 1950s and 1960s were "bright, young, attractive, and had money, automobiles, money to buy church buildings." Their Spanish might not have been very good but they obviously meant well. All this began to create a more favorable image of Protestants. This "preevangelization" was part of a larger overall process of changing attitudes.

Evangelical churches were seen as connected to the modernization of Central American countries. To become an evangelical was not to step out of society, as it might have once seemed, but rather to step into the most dynamic part of it. One sign is the growing numbers of evangelicals in the universities and in the professions, and the presence of evangelical universities in Central American countries. Relative lack of success in Mexico, where evangelicals numbered only 3 percent, might reflect longstanding Mexican resistance to the United States, Holland speculated.

In sum, the growth of evangelical, especially pentecostal, churches reflects many factors: the Catholic church's inability to reach the masses of baptized Catholics; the focus on continued outreach in evangelical churches; extensive use of personal contacts, family networks, and house visiting; mass evangelistic campaigns and televangelism; alienation from some recent trends in Catholicism; liveliness of pentecostal worship; apparent wonders such as healings, prophecy, and speaking in tongues; strict, clear moral codes enforced by church discipline; an ability to tap into popular culture; connections with the United States and "modernization." Hence it should be clear that one-dimensional explanations—particularly, funding from the United States—are quite unsatisfactory. Certainly during the "dirty wars" in Guatemala and El Salvador, joining an evangelical church offered some people a measure of protection from the army. However, these churches are growing in countries with little or no such repression (Costa Rica, Panama) and indeed throughout Latin America, Africa, and Asia. It is therefore important to take seriously their inherent popular appeal.

Existential Needs, Electronic Media

"It was the largest evangelistic project ever carried out in El Salvador, and reached the largest number of people ever with the gospel." Alejandro

Amaya, newly appointed executive director of Pat Robertson's 700 Club in El Salvador, was emphasizing how Project Light (*Proyecto Luz*) differed from the traditional evangelistic crusade built around a famous preacher and held in a tent or stadium. The centerpiece of this campaign was a series of three hour-long television programs to be shown on successive nights in Guatemala, El Salvador, and Nicaragua (Robertson himself apparently chose these countries).

The entire campaign, however, lasted from January to June 1990 (although events in Nicaragua, including the election, pushed the timetable back there). For weeks prior to the programs themselves, church workers were enlisted and trained, and the film *Jesus* was made available for showings in neighborhoods. Viewers touched by the programs were encouraged to pray, to accept Jesus as their Savior, and to dial a phone number if they wanted to speak with counselors.

As 700 Club officials explained, their programs were designed to touch the most basic questions facing all people, such as the future, suffering, and death, and to provide the scriptural answers to those questions. That approach was most obvious in the second program titled "Don't Ask Me, Ask God," which consisted of a series of skits, each dramatizing one of these central life questions.

That this program was originally prepared for a U.S. audience was obvious. One skit portrayed life in an Orwellian state — obviously scripted before the fall of communism. Spotting Michael J. Fox, a media-hip U.S. audience would think, "Oh yeah — 'Back to the Future' "; they might also smile at seeing Vincent Price host a takeoff on old mummy pictures. Another skit was about a man seeing his car break down, his house go up in flames, and his wife leave him, all in two or three minutes. For a U.S. audience the whimsical tone might suggest a subtext: These evangelicals aren't so humorless after all. In Central America, however, it all seemed rather bizarre, despite sporadic appearances by a Latin American man and woman grafted on as co-hosts. Another segment had a montage of murder, revolution, pornography, and drugs, with scriptural assurances that devils really exist. The last segment was structured to lead viewers to the news that Jesus Christ had died for them. A televangelist gently encouraged them to pray along with him "the most important prayer of your life," that is, to accept Jesus Christ as their Savior.

The final program consisted of three Latin American dramas. Each told of an individual sinking deeper into sin and despair: a man who kills his own child, a woman whose childhood experiences seem to doom her, and a young man who progresses from making bombs as a revolutionary to drug addiction. An encounter with Christ enabled each of them to reorganize his or her life. The actors' faces and the settings in Guatemala and Peru imparted at least a superficial verisimilitude.

These programs used personal and social ills to tap into anxiety but only in order that Christ — represented by Scripture texts — could emerge as the answer. Strikes, marches, demonstrations, and guerrilla violence were all fused as symbols of social unrest, but without any sense that they were rooted in economic and political structures or that they might represent people's efforts to assert their dignity. The function of the programs was to generate anxiety that could be relieved through conversion to Christ and a changed personal and family life.

In each country researchers spent a month conducting elaborate follow-up surveys, the results of which were printed in hefty volumes. The 700 Club staff people were quite convinced that this evangelization enterprise had produced dramatic results. Amaya told me that their viewer ratings were higher than the World Cup soccer championships, and that one hundred thousand people had been reached in El Salvador alone; a composite of several indicators (church membership, attendance at worship, baptisms) showed an overall increase of 17 percent in six months. In Guatemala I was assured the first program had touched 1,162,900 persons and that two million people had been converted, according to the follow-up survey.

Pastors were enthusiastic about the programs. Mi Redentor Church in Managua changed the time of its worship so people could see one of the programs rerun. Bartolomé Matamoros, the head of the Assemblies of God in Nicaragua, called Project Light a "blessing from God," and claimed that his church had done 70 percent of the organizing work. None of my conservative evangelical interviewees questioned the overall enterprise, although a seminary professor in Guatemala wondered whether follow-up was adequate.

Project Light encountered numerous problems in Nicaragua. During the transition period after their electoral defeat, Sandinista officials canceled the programs shortly before they were scheduled to be broadcast. The Chamorro government, like any monopolist, then demanded rather high prices. A minor scandal broke out when it was revealed that popcorn, candy bars, and other items accompanying the programs as part of Robertson's Operation Blessing, turned out to be spoiled. A 700 Club executive said that Amway had donated the food, probably as a tax writeoff, but a local former employee of the Christian Broadcasting Network (CBN) said they were not worth a fraction of the declared value and accused CBN of running a great business "where the poor of the world are just another factor on the spreadsheet, someplace to dump old food or defective toothbrushes."

U.S. televangelism had become a fixture on Central American television several years before Project Light. In 1985 a church-connected research and training center conducted a survey in four countries of the region in order to assess the impact of religious broadcasting. Since the survey was conducted among active churchgoers, Catholic and Protestant, it cannot be seen as representative of the whole population. Jimmy Swaggart had the highest program recognition level (73.2 percent). A similar high percentage regarded his programs as more useful than those of their own local church. The author of the report, Dennis Smith, noted that Swaggart's popularity was all the more remarkable in view of the fact that he often referred to political issues specific to the United States: He attacked perceived liberal trends in the federal government and court system and secular humanism in the schools, and urged support for the divinely approved policies of the state of Israel.

Smith suggested reasons for Swaggart's appeal. Most of those surveyed were poor, and their moralistic churches ruled out many ordinary entertainments such as movies, dancing, playing soccer, or having a drink — even watching television was suspect. "Swaggart, being both a rousing preacher and a master showman, lets a rather strait-laced audience feel good about feeling good." Furthermore, a U.S.-made television production offers an idealized preacher and worship service. The electricity does not go off in the middle of the sermon, people sing on key, and everything happens as planned. In their local churches the pastor, like members of the congregation, may have had only a few years of schooling and may even support himself with other work. They are well aware of his shortcomings and those of their fellow worshipers. Special credit was due to Swaggart's Spanish translator, a Costa Rican named Stanley Black, who could reproduce his inflection, gestures, and emotions.

Observing a Swaggart stadium campaign, an American church worker in El Salvador found himself recalling his boyhood in Arkansas, when he had sweltered in the summer heat in the local Baptist church where guest preachers impressed him with their self-assurance. Swaggart's organization had put $6 million into El Salvador, primarily into schools run by the Assemblies of God. An indication of his organization's efficiency was the fact that people arriving at the bus terminal in San Salvador from the interior found vehicles waiting to take them to the stadium.

At one point in his discourse, Swaggart told viewers, "You're sitting in a lonely hotel room, and there are needle tracks up and down your arms. You're on drugs . . ." or maybe alcohol. "Maybe you sit there watching me on television." You are hurting, your life is a wreck, you've ruined your family, you have considered suicide. "But through this TV screen, Jesus Christ is speaking to you." This set speech betrayed Swaggart's unfamiliarity with El Salvador: Few people have to spend lonely nights on the road, since well over half of the population lives within an hour of the spot where Swaggart was preaching.

Although upon arrival Swaggart had disavowed any political intent, that night he told his stadium audience he had prayed with their president and first lady. Pausing for the expected applause, he was obviously unaware that Duarte had lost credibility throughout El Salvador, and especially with the middle classes who were heavily represented in the stadium. Alluding to the civil war, which he attributed to hatred, he went on to say that sometimes people did not even know why they hated. "You want to steal and kill and destroy, to strike out at your government or your neighbor. This is the reason for all the terrorist activity in the world today. Hate. Love turned into hate. Until you love God you cannot love your fellow man. When a person has accepted Jesus Christ it's impossible for them to curse or hurt their fellow man."

Days after returning from this tour through Central America Swaggart was forced to confess that he had met regularly for voyeuristic sessions with a prostitute. Evangelical leaders who had once basked in his light now made public statements distancing themselves.

In a detailed study of Central American reactions to the Swaggart controversy, Alberto Piedra, a Costa Rican church historian, noted that for the first time evangelicals were looking critically at the televangelism in their midst. They were questioning whether canned television programs were really adequate, and were beginning to realize that the gospel cannot be proclaimed in universal terms, but must be "contextualized." Even though some Costa Rican evangelicals were beginning to perceive the differences between U.S. and Costa Rican values, Piedra nevertheless doubted they would act on this insight. The theological and social perspectives of his own church were not very different from those brought by U.S. televangelists. Thus he was skeptical of proposals to train local televangelists since in the end they would purvey the same kind of Christianity, with technically inferior programs that would therefore have less audience appeal.

Middle-Class Varieties

The Verbo church in Guatemala City occupies a corner a few blocks from the U.S. embassy, along the broad la Reforma avenue which runs from downtown toward wealthy residential districts. The functional church building, a large open space with a cement floor, which seems to suggest an evangelistic tent, was once a roller skating rink. Folding chairs are arranged in a wide arc. Behind the center stage in green letters against pale yellow, the color scheme of the whole building, are the words "For my house will be called a house of prayer" (Jesus' reference to Isaiah and Jeremiah as he drove the money changers from the temple). Large banners, bearing titles like "Lion of Judah" and "King of Kings," hang along the walls, along with smaller flags that worshipers may pick up and wave.

The service begins with an extended period of singing. Several of the songs have Israeli melodies; the words from the psalms are projected onto the back wall. "Dance before him, and shout, 'Victory is ours!' " Young women in long aprons holding tambourines move forward and flow with the rhythm as others clap and sway in their places. A slow hymn, "Rise Up, O Jehovah," has the feel of a U.S. folksong. Another slow song could be a round, "Father, I adore you, I surrender to you my life, How I love you! Son, I adore you, . . . Holy Spirit . . ." A period of generalized prayer follows as musicians improvise harmonies. Another ballad-like song goes "In your presence I find my delight; my heart fills up with joy, peace, and love; in your presence I see your greatness, I see you, Sovereign and King of my life." One of the songs is very reminiscent of the hit from the 1970s,

"Lágrimas" (English "Feelings"). Early in the service, the leader, in blue blazer and grey slacks, asks those who have a burden to raise their hands, and prays, "You are love and mercy; Thank you, Jesus!" At one point people come forward to microphones to give personal testimonies.

Most of the people look upper middle class—that is, they belong to the upper tenth of the population. There is one military officer in uniform. No one in Indian clothing is present. Visitors can hear a simultaneous translation into English over headphones at the back of the church.

The real strength of the Verbo church, I am told later, is in the house churches, each one made up of ten to twenty-five people. Eighty percent of those at Sunday worship are said to participate in one of the 160 house churches around the city. There they meet socially, have some coffee and rolls, and study the Bible. People know each other in a way they cannot at Sunday worship in church. Participants in the house churches are "discipled," that is, subjected to the discipline of living in accordance with Jesus Christ, and are reprimanded for lapses or failures.

The emphasis in the Verbo church is on "freedom of spirit": At worship people are free to pray, to weep, to say what they feel in their heart, to open themselves to God's Spirit. A church leader tells me of his own experience of being brought up a Catholic, and attending a Catholic school run by the Christian Brothers. He claims that at one point, although he was attending Mass regularly, saying the rosary, and so forth, he realized that he was doing things that offended God, and asked for God's help. He began to read the Bible and entrusted his life to God in prayer. One day he found a passage, "Cry out to me and I will answer you with great and difficult things of which you are not aware" (Jer. 33:3), which led him to understanding. "When a person is searching for God wholeheartedly, he or she will find God, and God will show what has to be done." This man attended another evangelical church before finding the Verbo church. He now acknowledges that today baptism in the Holy Spirit also occurs in the Catholic church that he has left.

When I note the upper middle-class composition of the congregation, and specifically the lack of Indians, he protests. "We have all kinds of people. We preach to a homosexual just as we do to an engineer, and to a prostitute as we do to a housewife. In his grace God may have allowed a certain kind of financially secure person to come here, but we have our work in Quetzaltenango and Coban and there you will see people in Indian clothing as you will in Chajul" (in the Ixil triangle, where a Verbo-organized aid foundation worked hand in glove with the military's counterinsurgency starting in 1982). "God has used this church to get to places not reached before. We don't just go one place; we go to preach the gospel to the world."

The Verbo church has congregations elsewhere in Guatemala and in San Salvador, and as far away as New Orleans and Miami, and Verbo missionaries have gone to Nicaragua, Brazil, Ecuador, and Mexico. However, it seems clear that the church reflects a tendency of evangelical churches to target the middle classes. David Stoll points out that church-growth specialists have justified such a strategy on the " 'homogeneous unit principle' — that persons prefer to become Christians together with members from their own social group." Since experience shows that upper-class conversions cease when the poor come into a church, specifically targeting the middle class is justified on the grounds of the apostle Paul's policy of being "all things to all men."

Elim, the very large church described earlier in this chapter, and the Fraternidad Cristiana, whose church stands on a major highway not far from the Elim church, resemble the Verbo church in worship style, and likewise encourage house churches. Parachurch organizations such as the Fraternidad de los Hombres Cristianos de Negocio (Full Gospel Businessmen's Association) are prominently featured in the society pages of Guatemalan papers. Evangelical churches often use major hotels for prayer breakfasts and even for Sunday worship. For example, in March 1989 the evangelist Luis Palau gave a luncheon address at the Hotel El Dorado. He began by expressing appreciation for the efforts of business executives, and showing how they become God's collaborators through their work. The event received a full page in the society section of *Prensa Libre*.

Although the overall pattern of worship in middle-class milieus is similar to that of other pentecostal churches, the theological accent is notably different. The devil does not seem to be nearly so active as he is elsewhere, and in general the atmosphere is more optimistic than it is in poorer churches. The world seems to be more a place of opportunity than of threats and dangers. This is sometimes called "prosperity theology," or a "name it and claim it" stance developed by U.S. evangelists such as Kenneth Copeland. A Protestant observer described certain features of middle-class neopentecostalism: "it tends to be urban, to have roots in the Catholic charismatic movement, and to be especially attractive to middle-class merchants and professionals. It . . . provides a model for upwardly mobile folks who are looking for a disciplined belief system to help them survive and to get out there and have God bless them in the extremely hostile economic environment, particularly of the city." Numerous Protestant executives, bankers, and government officials now attend the historic Presbyterian church in the heart of Guatemala City as well as the newer neopentecostal churches.

Social positions taken by the Catholic church have no doubt played a role in the advance of Protestantism in the upper classes and the military. They feel disappointed and even betrayed, not only by priests defending some form of liberation theology, but by church representatives like Archbishops Rivera and Penados, and the Guatemalan bishops' conference. Many members of the elite were introduced to evangelical churches through house churches, as was Rios Montt.

Further confirmation of class affinities of various forms of Protestantism comes from a detailed study of the process of conversion in the region of

Quetzaltenango by Timothy Evans. He found that there were no neopentecostal churches in the Indian mountain villages, and that few Indians joined neopentecostal churches in the city or in the coast area. Ladinos (non-Indians) tended to convert to nonpentecostal denominational type churches.

The appeal of evangelical churches to various classes derives not from any agreed upon master plan, but rather from a process in which a wide variety of churches seek and find niches in a broad religious market.

Meeting the Competition

On a Monday evening at a Catholic church in the lower middle-class and working-class area of Zone 7 in Guatemala City about 175 people have come together for the weekly session of charismatic prayer. A short mustached man perhaps in his fifties takes the microphone and with no introduction begins to pray "Oh, Lord Jesus," and invokes God's presence in the group. The chorus of adolescents with a guitar leads the group in a well-known handclapping hymn made up largely of the word *Alabaré* ("I will praise").

In between songs the leader exhorts the group. After considerable coaxing a high school age girl musters her courage and comes forward to give her testimony. She tells of her efforts to bring a friend to church over the objections of the girl's parents. The father was an alcoholic and the mother was, in some unspecified way, "worse," and refused permission. When her friend finally was able to come to church she was cured of a cancer, which doctors had been powerless to treat. Worshipers applaud the miraculous denouement, and the service continues.

In the center of Guatemala City the Catholic Charismatic Renewal's House of Prayer holds dozens of prayer services a week. At all hours of the day and night volunteers are praying, as registered by a clock-like sign on the wall. The movement has a twenty-four-hour hotline that people can call to request prayers for their needs. Charismatic groups function throughout the city and as many as 25,000 or 30,000 have gathered to pray at the army's stadium. There are several radio programs of Catholic charismatics in Guatemala City, and one station has religious programming all day on Sunday.

The Catholic Charismatic Renewal, as its adherents prefer to call it, began at the universities of Notre Dame and Duquesne in 1967, grew rapidly in the late 1960s, and spread around the world in the 1970s. Catholic charismatics are found throughout Central America, often with little or no encouragement from the local pastor. The movement spreads from group to group and priests and nuns provide spiritual leadership on a regional or national level. Only a few priests support the charismatic movement enthusiastically. Those who regard commitment to justice as crucial to faith may see it as alienating; even traditional priests and bishops are wary of its independence.

The Catholic Charismatic Renewal obviously resembles the pentecostals. However, its similarities to pentecostalism derive from its origins, not from local emulation. To what extent is it a response, conscious or unconscious, to evangelical competition? Can Catholics find within their own church what many seem to have been seeking and finding elsewhere?

Like evangelical house churches, the Catholic charismatic renewal seems to spread primarily through personal contacts and invitation. After initial participation people are invited to a seminar on "Life in the Spirit," which calls for a deep conversion, prompting them to ask for baptism in the Spirit. Participants are encouraged not only to learn about the Bible but to use it. Like evangelical converts members claim that their lives have been changed.

Another Catholic initiative that looks "evangelical" is Trigo ("Wheat"), a preaching ministry, which unlike the charismatic movement, is native to Guatemala. Salvador Gómez, its central figure, is Central America's first successful Catholic televangelist. Gómez, who had been a Catholic seminarian for a number of years, was participating in a charismatic group in a parish in Guatemala City, when his own preaching ability was discovered. He began to be invited to other parishes, and then started his own call-in radio show. By 1982 he was preaching every night, and eventually gave up a successful career selling office furniture to devote himself to full-time preaching.

His particular skill was not only in preaching but in systematically teaching others to preach, particularly through week-long intensive seminars. Trigo grew to the point where a full-time staff of several preachers was kept busy responding to requests from parishes and other groups. Gómez himself is frequently invited to go to El Salvador, Mexico, and Honduras, and as far away as Chile. His programs are broadcast regularly on the radio in Nicaragua.

Gómez has systematized his ideas on how to preach in a small book, which grounds its methodology in Scripture rather than psychology or secular fields of knowledge. Trigo preachers claim that in keeping with the example of Jesus, they use human experience as a basis for preaching, although violence and injustice do not seem to be part of that experience. Gómez defends his refusal to deal with political issues on the grounds that he seeks to respond to people's inquiries—and they do not ask about politics.

Operating with the assumption that Latin American Catholics are "baptized but not evangelized," some church workers have adopted a pastoral method from Europe called the Neocatechumenate. The name comes from the process of the ancient church in which prospective converts ("catechumens") spent years learning the Scriptures, doctrines, and ethical teachings of Christianity. The Neocatechumenate is in effect a heavily doctrinal and authoritarian seven-year program of scriptural formation. Its attraction to some Catholic priests perhaps lies in the fact that it supplies a complete and ready-made methodology for pastoral work.

In the early 1980s Salesian Father Luís Estrada felt he needed something to counteract the growth of evangelicals who already had nineteen chapels in his parish in Guatemala City. He considered the Neocatechumenate but was convinced it would be too slow. He had been one of the pioneers of the charismatic renewal, but now he was looking for something more systematic.

He heard of the work of Alfonso Navarro, a Mexican priest, who had been a charismatic but had gone on to develop an approach to parish renewal called by its acronym SINE (Integral System for Evangelization), which combines several of the features from the charismatic movement, cursillos, base communities, and other pastoral initiatives. Navarro believes that Catholic parishes, which are presently structured around worship, must be reorganized for evangelization.

After observing SINE in Mexico and sending some of his parishioners there for training, Estrada launched a campaign in one of the three main sections of his parish. One hundred and sixty people were enlisted for the campaign. Preparation included house-to-house visiting, talking to people about their needs, and identifying families willing to host meetings. The mission itself lasted five nights, each with its own topic (God loves you, You are a sinner . . . Accept Jesus as Savior). The similarities to evangelical campaigns are obvious.

Those who accept Christ in the SINE method are invited to form or join a regular community that meets each week in a home to participate in a two-and-a-half-hour meeting divided into five clearly marked segments: welcome, prayer, catechesis (systematic discussion of doctrine according to printed guidelines), sharing experiences, and praying for one another. Participants in these house meetings also gather in a larger group once a week for further instruction.

Over four years this parish held four such missions, and formed eighty small communities throughout the three neighborhoods. It also carried out ministries to adolescents, families, and the sick. Five lay people were working full-time on the parish staff, a situation practically unknown in Latin America. Father Estrada was quite convinced that SINE offered the means for reorienting Catholic parishes to do the job that had to be done and thereby to counter the Protestant advance.

In Ciudad Sandino, an outlying barrio of Managua, Jesuit priests were also using SINE. In the 1970s this parish had introduced the neocatechumenate, but the priests had decided they were reaching only the small elite that attended Mass. In order to pursue the large mass of nonchurchgoing Catholics, they had enlisted and trained 105 "missionaries." The crux of their pastoral method was to go house to house, "a bit like the evangelicals," admitted Father Valentín Martínez. The parish was divided into eleven zones, each of which had a community with its own pastoral council. (It is perhaps worth noting that these two parishes in Guatemala City and Managua were among the pioneers of base community pastoral work in the early 1970s.)

The Catholic charismatic renewal, Trigo, and SINE have a number of evangelical-like features in common. All emphasize the Bible, and their printed materials are often overflowing with biblical quotes and references. They see their primary role as evangelizing Catholics to the point where they accept Jesus as their personal Savior, and they propound a morality centered on the individual and the family. Yet their devotion to the Virgin Mary and respect for the pope mark them as distinctively and conservatively Roman Catholic. As we will see in Chapter Seven, they shun any effort to discover and act on the societal implications of the Christian faith.

Protestants Coming of Age

"My mother was born in an evangelical household. My grandfather was a pastor. But my mother moved and then my father abandoned us. We were the only evangelicals in a town of five thousand people. To go to worship we had to go to another town five kilometers away. Or my mother would invite pastors to our house for worship. I can still remember being called a 'heretic' during Holy Week. The priest said, 'Don't buy from or sell to these heretics!' I was six years old at the time. When he led processions, he had the people surround the house, chanting so the devil would leave. We had to have a new roof put on because of all the damage done by rock throwing."

Obviously, growing up an evangelical in a rural town in El Salvador in the 1950s was not easy. Bethuel Henríquez went out of his way to tell me these details to indicate how far Protestants have come. Now there are seven evangelical chapels in his hometown. He works as a spiritual counselor at the Universidad Evangélica.

This chapter has examined the rapid evangelical growth in Central America during the past three decades. Obviously many factors are at work: the liveliness of evangelical worship, the simplicity of the evangelical message and its moral code, the fact that evangelical communities exist at the level of the barrio or village, opportunities for participation and leadership, disappointment over the Catholic church's way of dealing with popular religiosity or sometimes with public stands taken by the hierarchy—and violence against committed Catholics in some instances, especially in the early 1980s.

Just how to understand the reasons for growth will occupy scholars and church people for some time to come. David Stoll has drawn attention to the fact of evangelical growth and pointed out how academics and the left have ignored it while paying considerable attention to liberation theology and related pastoral work. Will some Latin American countries become predominantly Protestant in the coming years as evangelical church-growth specialists predict? Or are their figures somewhat inflated and has the period of rapid growth already begun to level out?

Whatever future growth trends might be, the religious situation has already undergone a qualitative change. No longer a tiny minority in a society that is culturally Catholic, Protestants are "coming of age" or are in the process of coming of age. As recently as two or three decades ago, to become a Protestant was in some sense to opt out of the dominant culture. In withdrawing from the universal public religion, Catholicism, and entering what was sociologically a sect, one became less Guatemalan, Salvadoran, or Nicaraguan.

That is no longer the case. When being an evangelical can help catapult a candidate into the presidency, the evangelical movement is inevitably becoming public.

CHAPTER 6

ACOMPAÑAMIENTO

Standing by the People

"The first thing I want to impress on you is that in our desire to be faithful to the gospel we had to come close to the people, to get to know the people better in order to communicate God's love," said Lutheran Bishop Medardo Gómez in his methodical, almost plodding style. What I wanted from the interview was information on how the various churches had become involved in humanitarian aid for refugees and war victims in El Salvador, but he was resisting my questions about organizational nuts and bolts in order to make sure I grasped the starting point for this activity.

"Along the way we encountered this person who was abused, beaten, pleading for help. At first we continued on our way, but eventually the cry was so loud we had to come over. And when we came closer we found we couldn't get away—we were trapped, so to speak. The needs were so pressing that out of our Christian commitment we had to do something to change the situation of that person crying for help. The church began to understand that person's cry."

We were sitting in his office at Resurrection Church in San Salvador in July 1990. Gómez had been forced to go into hiding and then fled the country during the November 1989 FMLN offensive. For some time now at least one foreigner was always at Gomez's side, to deter attempts to kill or abduct him. Some months previously a bomb had been set off near this office and might have killed neighbors had not a tree absorbed much of the shrapnel.

While growing up in the eastern city of San Miguel, Gómez had wanted to be a priest but circumstances had prevented him from entering the seminary. When he joined the Lutheran church in 1964, he seems to have had his sights set on the ministry, and soon he was sent to the seminary in Mexico. Returning to Central America he first worked for several years in Zacapa, Guatemala (where he was threatened by a death squad).

Upon his return to his country in 1972 he began work at Resurrection

Lutheran Church in the capital, which had declined to the point where there were only a few active members left. Indeed there were only four other Lutheran congregations in the entire country. Gómez devoted himself to traditional evangelism and the church grew. In the late 1970s contact with Archbishop Romero, whom he had known as a child in catechism class in San Miguel, left a deep imprint on Gómez. The growth of the Lutheran church during the 1980s was closely related to its involvement in humanitarian aid, development, and defense of human rights. Some people gravitated to the church because of the forthright stand of Gómez himself, who seemed to be carrying on the tradition of Archbishop Romero in defending the legitimacy of popular organizations more than Archbishop Rivera, who had positioned himself as a potential mediator in the conflict.

According to Pastor Eliseo Rodríguez, in 1990 there were thirty Lutheran churches, twelve communities on their way to being churches, and perhaps another ten that had not yet made such a decision. About two hundred fifty people were staffing church programs, primarily in humanitarian relief. Each Monday morning many of them gathered for a worship service at Resurrection Church. The day I was there, about one hundred were in attendance. Instead of a sermon, staff members were taking turns reading a document issued recently by an international meeting of Lutherans held in Brazil. Although on one level the cadences of a homogenized ecclesiastical language seemed very distant from the war and misery of El Salvador, the overriding sense was that, contrary to the accusations of their local critics, the activities of these Lutherans were in line with the commitments and spirit of their worldwide church.

Salvadoran elites and their U.S. government sponsors might be surprised to see the photo poster of the tearing down of the Berlin Wall on the wall near my pew: After all, for them the destruction of the wall only deepened their conviction that they were on the winning side and that the left, whom Gómez and the Lutherans were reputed to support, was an anachronism. Yet these Lutherans obviously saw in the wall a symbol of hope for their own struggle with, and on behalf of, the poor of El Salvador.

Some Catholics thought the Lutherans were stealing from their flocks. Eliseo Rodríguez, who himself had switched from the Baptist church, said people often came to the church because they did not want to put up with ambiguity. The Lutherans encouraged Catholics to stay with their parishes and Protestants to go to existing local churches, but some people still chose to join the church.

When I asked him about accusations of onesidedness, Gómez said, "We've worked with those who have suffered the government's repression, mainly women, old people, and children. That has led some who don't understand the Christian spirit to assume that we are doing it because we are part of the subversive movement. Unfortunately, it is the neediest who have sought us out, because the other half, more or less, has some kind of aid, whether from the government or USAID. Since these people have come from the communities where the guerrillas were very active, the armed forces, following their own logic, don't believe that our inspiration for helping them is the gospel." Here he made a reference to Jesus in the synagogue quoting Isaiah, "He has sent me to bring glad tidings to the poor, to proclaim liberty to captives . . ." It is God's plan that the poor be evangelized.

"Seeing these churches work this way, many people with social concerns came seeking us out. They've had an image of an oppressive God, but when they hear of another, they come to us. It wasn't faith that drew them, but when they came and saw that our commitment has its origins in the altar, in our experience of practical prayer, many people have found faith here." He cited the example of a nonbelieving Spaniard, who was changed when he saw the spirituality of the refugees and is now a church leader. "Some people came with the idea of taking advantage of things here, but to their own surprise many have changed their lives."

What is specifically Lutheran about this? I wondered. Gómez pointed to the Reformation doctrine of the "priesthood of all believers," understanding it to mean that each Christian is to give witness, sharing in the community, and developing his or her leadership. He saw the growth of the church not only in quantitative but in spiritual terms. The cost had been great: One pastor, David Hernández, who had introduced Gómez to the Lutheran church, was murdered in 1984, one hundred Lutheran families had been forced to leave El Salvador, and others had "disappeared."

Reading from the same Bible, Bishop Gómez and his church drew rather different conclusions from those of the evangelicals and Catholics discussed in the previous chapter. It would be simplistic, however, to regard one side as "political" and the other as "religious."

This chapter examines a number of other examples of pastoral work based on ideals of solidarity and liberation similar to those articulated by Gómez.

Accompanying the People

When Bishop Gerardi and the priests and sisters made their decision to withdraw from the diocese of Quiché, they saw it both as a measure dictated by necessity and as a prophetic gesture to call world attention to the ferocity of repressive violence in Guatemala. After the killing of Archbishop Romero and the murder of approximately fifteen priests in Guatemala and El Salvador, an ambush attempt on a bishop in a rural diocese was scarcely noticed by the international media. Not all church people in Guatemala agreed with the decision. A priest later commented that it was a misnomer for the priests from Quiché who opened offices in Mexico and Nicaragua to call their organization the "Guatemalan Church in Exile": A portion of the clergy was in exile; the church as people remained.

A sister in Huehuetenango said that observing the situation of Quiché taught the lesson that it was "extremely important for the whole church that its official representatives remain present." Having started a process, they could not run away when things became difficult. For the people the message had to be that the "church is present and loves you in your suffering as much as in your efforts to better yourselves." Nevertheless, she refrained from judging those who felt they had to leave the country after receiving direct threats. When his bishop called him home, a North American priest in Guatemala refused to go. "The way I understood the priesthood was that if there's repression against the people you can't just pack your bags and leave them."

Church workers who remained during the heaviest repression often experienced a frustrating impotence. In the countryside priests found that it was too dangerous to go visiting people, let alone undertake ambitious educational programs. They could only make themselves available at the church office.

On one occasion the army brought to a medical center a guerrilla combatant who had thrown himself off a cliff and fractured his skull in an effort to commit suicide to avoid being captured and interrogated. They wanted a church worker to bring him back to consciousness so they could torture and question him. When she refused they pulled out the life support tubes and took him away. The other people on the staff restrained her from chasing after the troops on behalf of their prisoner. Such an action, they believed, would only get them all killed.

The term most often used for this option to stand by the people was *acompañamiento* (accompaniment or accompanying). This usage apparently derives from Archbishop Romero who in his final pastoral letter (August 1979) stated that one of the church's roles was to "accompany the people." Elsewhere he offered a more specific definition: "By 'pastoral work of accompanying' or 'of following' I understand the personal evangelization of those Christian individuals or groups who have taken on a concrete political option," in response to the demand of their conscience.

Romero had in mind the situation of a priest or sister working with people who had become collaborators with, or members of, left mass organizations. Normally priests or sisters should not themselves join such organizations nor should they withdraw from the community; rather they should maintain a pastoral relationship with the people. Romero emphasized that what he had in mind was "not a politicized pastoral activity, but a pastoral activity that has to give gospel-based guidance to Christian consciences in a politicized environment." It was important to respect the diversity of options people might make and not pressure them either to join particular organizations or to quit them.

Some Salvadorans might be scandalized by that possibility—although they would not be shocked by bishops who have breakfast with the president or defense minister. The logic of Romero's position was that just as church figures had not shunned those who wielded established political power, some church workers could relate to those who were struggling to change the political and economic system itself.

During the 1980s *acompañamiento* took on the more general sense of standing by the people. Catholic priests and sisters regularly used the term as a one-word encapsulization of their pastoral approach. In Guatemala and El Salvador they devoted much of their energy to humanitarian aid. When asked how he understood his ministry to a highly politicized barrio in San Salvador, a foreign priest said he came to accompany, and self-deprecatingly quoted Milton, "They also serve who only stand and wait." Such accompaniment might translate into helping a parishioner get out of jail, or helping someone obtain the basic identification papers without which it was dangerous to even be on the street, or attending a base community meeting, or celebrating Sunday Mass. The pastor at one parish in Guatemala in 1989 spent the better part of a month aiding the brother of an abducted and murdered leader of the Coca-Cola labor union prepare to leave the country.

Often enough "accompaniment" was literal. In mid-1988 I witnessed the last-minute arrangements for helping a family leave El Salvador after its members had been jailed several times and had received numerous death threats. Two foreign lay volunteers would be traveling on the same bus. The time of greatest danger would be early in the morning as they were heading toward the Honduran border and might be stopped by troops arbitrarily searching the bus and asking people for their papers. If the people were arrested or abducted, these church workers were to immediately alert others in San Salvador, who could bring pressure to bear on the government. The air of holy conspiracy in this planning was heightened by the flickering shadows of candlelight due to a power outage, probably as a result of guerrilla sabotage.

In Guerrilla Territory

"Rolando," a Salvadoran priest, described how he had come to live with people in FMLN-held territory in Chalatenango. He was first threatened in 1977, when some of the people joined the militant organization FECCAS and local military authorities accused him of being an organizer. In 1980 troops came into his parish north of San Salvador to round people up. In consultation with parishioners, he decided not to sleep at the parish house anymore. One of the staunch members of the parish and his family were shot at night and dumped into a latrine ditch. In July 1981 Treasury Police came to a woman's house, told her to lie down, and shot her, her baby, and five other children. A fellow priest agreed to take the parish but death threats forced him out.

Meanwhile, Rolando had gone to Honduras where he worked with refugees for a half-year until he was expelled by Honduran authorities. He could certainly continue to work outside El Salvador, but "I recalled that when we began to work with the communities we always said that the Christian must follow through with his or her faith, as Jesus had followed through"—and as the murdered catechists and priests had done. It would be inconsistent to be involved in consciousness-raising and leadership formation, but then hold back when the moment for deeper commitment arrived. "I saw that if I had helped people in their process I had to continue to accompany them."

This priest's option was to go to the guerrilla-held zones of Guazapa and Chalatenango. Assured that Rolando and a fellow priest would not have to bear arms, Archbishop Rivera accepted their decision on the grounds that civilians in guerrilla-controlled areas had a right to pastoral ministry.

Periodic military sweeps of the area forced the people to go out on a *guinda*, their word for prolonged periods of flight. One Good Friday a community near the Guazapa volcano learned that troops were on their way. After burying clothes and grinding stones and other items they would not be able to carry, the people gathered a few belongings, such as a sheet of plastic for the rain, a little food, a toothbrush, and set out. For the next week this group of two thousand people was on the move by night and seeking to hide by day. When under air attack they sought shelter as best they could under trees and behind large rocks.

Rolando described the anguish of watching a six-month-old baby cry with each shell or bomb and how other people feared that the infant's cry would lead to their being detected. The mother could not quiet the baby by offering her breast since it was not hungry but frightened. In El Salvador there are many stories of babies being suffocated to death when mothers stifled their cries to avoid detection by troops.

This particular moment passed and the group kept moving until nightfall when once more they came under fire. This time they had to escape by tumbling down a hill. Returning later they found that four adults had been killed and a child injured, but not being able to risk detection by using a flashlight, they had to leave without identifying the bodies. Throughout the week there were further encounters with the military. A bomb dropped by an A-37 killed an eight-year-old girl and wounded her parents. As the week went on they became increasingly hungry. At one point someone offered the priest uncooked rice, since they could not build a fire, but it felt like gravel in his mouth and he could not eat it. One woman had to continue walking only two hours after giving birth. On the final day two children became separated from their family and were never seen again. In the same camp one mother anguished over her lost children while another joyfully cradled her newborn. An old woman told Rolando that they were like God's people wandering in the desert and awaiting the promised land. She would not live to see it, but she had the satisfaction of knowing that they were all on their way to liberation.

Assured that the army had withdrawn from the area, the people returned to their village where they found their houses destroyed, their clothes burned, their water buckets smashed. They could not walk around freely until "experts"—presumably from the FMLN—had deactivated mines. They then had a celebration to give thanks to God. The army had come and gone and they were still alive; it was a kind of victory.

A woman told Rolando that the fact that he had come to stay with them gave them more hope. Later, while he was saying Mass at the ruins of a house where only the walls were standing, a bomb fell so close he could feel the rush of hot air. Recalling the woman's words he told himself he should not tremble any more than the people whom he sought to comfort.

This priest's understanding of accompaniment included some participation in organizing responsibilities, not in the sense of taking care of specific tasks, but rather in providing guidance and encouragement. For example, when one group was unwilling to dig antiaircraft ditches at the school because they did not have children there, he argued that defending life was a duty for everyone.

A foreign layman described his own experience with people in the eastern part of Chalatenango for a year and a half beginning in mid-1983. About thirty villages in this area, with a population of three thousand to five thousand people, had been liberated from the army and were in the process of establishing their own local government structures. One indication of the influence of prior church work was the fact that the presidents of five of the seven local governments were, or had been, catechists. Accompaniment meant to go with people in their "moment of Calvary," their suffering, living day-to-day life in extreme poverty and insecurity from bombing and army sweeps. Pastoral work itself was limited to Bible study groups, discussions, and celebrations of some events, such as funerals. A six-month program to teach some leaders literacy skills so that they could in turn teach others to read was initiated, but army attacks and bombings prevented the program from moving forward. More important than specific accomplishments was the very act of being with the people, of not abandoning them, even when it seemed that the official church had largely done so.

Matilde, a Salvadoran sister, also saw her three years in FMLN territory in San Vicente as "accompaniment." Growing up in a peasant family, she learned to read from her mother, a catechist, before she was able to go to school at the age of nine. When she was nineteen she entered the Oblates of the Sacred Heart, but gradually became disenchanted when she felt constricted in her desire to serve the poor. In December 1970 she and two other women formed what was simply called the "small community" and did pastoral work in Zacamil and elsewhere. At one point she served as Archbishop Romero's secretary. Left without work after his murder, and facing increasing repression in San Salvador, in late 1980 she decided to go to San Vicente (just as her colleague Silvia Arriola went to Santa Ana and Father Rogelio Ponceele went to Morazán).

For three years she also lived with the people sharing their *guindas*, where she observed children die of malnutrition. In March 1982 the army slaughtered 156 civilians near Apastepeque, Canton Laguna Ciega. She then experienced a crisis of faith "because I'd always believed in the God of the poor and oppressed," but it was those poor who were dying. "Where is God, I asked. The poor are always near the door of death, sunk in poverty and misery and when they struggle, they die in wars."

She was close to two more massacres in August 1982. People from Tecoluca, where Father David Rodríguez was serving, were attacked with grenades. "People were literally blown to pieces. I found pieces of flesh in the trees, in the bushes." With the children's cries engraved in her memory she continued, but two days later, she and three other people who had gone up a hill to reconnoiter, witnessed the killing of 179 people below. The man beside her saw his pregnant wife, children, and mother killed, fourteen people in all. Years later she looked back at this moment as a crisis of faith that had been transformative.

Three other women in El Salvador, "Juanita" and "Tonita," both sisters, and "Elizabeth," a lay woman, also regarded their work as "accompaniment." "The Church refuses to accept the oppression of the poor," explained Juanita, "and even though we have few resources to give to the poor, we can offer ourselves. And so we must be with the poor, in their communities and sharing their dangers with them." When the armed forces invaded their parish during the November 1989 rebel offensive, they stayed in the parish. Juanita worked with the youth group, whose activities included dances, picnics, and the like, but also prayer and discussions of values. Young people were active in catechetics and the liturgy, and even in small-scale ecology projects such as planting bushes and a garden. The group was independent of political organizations, even though some of its members were politically active.

Sister Tonita was in charge of pastoral work in the parish, which had no full-time priest. Much of her activity was devoted to refugees, and specifically to helping them overcome the dependence fostered by traditional structures and even by church-administered aid, which can be paternalistic. A small credit union and a carpentry shop were among the means used to develop independence.

While living as a refugee for three years at the archdiocesan seminary, Elizabeth had learned health care skills and she later trained others in a clinic staff at the same parish. As part of a general philosophy of self-reliance, she emphasized preventive measures and the rediscovery of traditional medicinal plants, some of which were grown by the youth group. For her community work she came under close surveillance by the Guardia.

Laura López had five children when she responded to an interior call to go to Guazapa. She also said that the basis of her pastoral work was accompaniment, to give people life and show them what faith is. Under pressure from army attacks, the number of communities with which she worked dropped from twelve to six. Religious celebrations took place under trees since the churches had all been destroyed. Since they had been left without priests, she said, "We ourselves are the priests. . . . What little we know, we teach others, with a lot of love." One year she led the way of the cross on Good Friday and other Holy Week ceremonies. Nuns sent her teaching materials, and together with Father Rutilio Sánchez she worked with fifty lay volunteers. For the stations of the cross, they made posters with the names of people who had died. "As Christians we remember them, and we keep repeating that Christ continues to die in El Salvador." After her husband was killed by a land mine in 1981, she felt lonely and experienced misunderstanding. Some could not understand why this woman who was neither a priest nor a sister nor a guerrilla had gone to the hills. Two of her brothers were said to be members of death squads who had sworn to kill her. Laura López went from village to village leading religious services and recording the effects of military violence against civilians. She frequently carried her notebooks and tapes to human rights monitors in San Salvador. Sometimes the sounds of bombs falling and machine guns rattling could be heard on her taped interviews and reports. Her final recording was made in a bomb shelter. "We are trying to defend our lives, although we can no longer defend our huts or belongings. It looks like the army intends to launch an invasion of this area. God doesn't want it to be that way. They want to terrorize us, but we will not be swayed. We will be victorious in the justice of our cause!"

Laura López's thirteen-year-old daughter lived to describe what happened afterwards. López and her daughter left the bomb shelter to make room for others. They then met up with a group of thirty-five people, all suffering from hunger and thirst. At 3 P.M. on April 24, 1985, as the group was fleeing from the military, Laura López was hit in the back but kept running until she was hit in the leg. She handed her knapsack to her daughter and told her to run. That knapsack was her "office," containing her bible, papers, and records. Three days later the survivors of the attack found Laura López's body with her skull caved in and indications that she had been tied up for further torture.

Laura López was a catechist, said theologian Pablo Richard, whose course she had attended in San Salvador two months before, "but in a certain sense she was also 'priest' and 'bishop' in an area entrusted to her," and an example of how women were participating in the church. In her effort to keep running even after being struck by the first bullet and then in handing on her knapsack to her daughter, Richard saw a symbol of the power of the church in Guazapa and El Salvador.

Looking back on his experience, Father Miguel Ventura discerned three phases of his work in the FMLN-held territories of Morazán. In the early 1980s he and Rogelio Ponceele assumed that an insurrectionary victory was imminent and saw their pastoral work as helping build the revolutionary organization. Many lay pastoral co-workers went directly into political organizing with the FMLN.

By 1983, said Ventura, "we understood that there was not going to be an immediate insurrection and the conflict would be prolonged. Our vision matured." Now they saw their mission as building base communities "in order to restore a sense of community in the liberated areas so that the people could find ways to meet their basic needs for education, health care, water, and so forth." Such work was intended to strengthen the people in order to defeat the military, the oligarchy, and U.S. intervention, and hence entailed providing a base of support for the FMLN. Nevertheless, the church had to remain independent within the revolutionary process. The revolutionary organization should not tell the church what its pastoral role should be; pastoral work, however, should be developed in dialogue with the leadership of the revolutionary organization.

Ventura said he learned another lesson after 1985, as non-FMLN popular organizations reemerged and became increasingly important actors, namely "that it isn't just the FMLN combatants who make the revolution, but rather all the people."

Pastoral Resurgence

Despite the official pullout and continued repression, some Catholic church personnel in Guatemala continued to maintain ties with Quiché. Except for a relatively brief period, one priest continued to live in Chichicastenango even during the worst years. Priests from the nearby diocese of Sololá sometimes came to say Mass. In 1983 a bishop was appointed; soon two priests, both Indian, were ordained; and in 1984 a group of sisters returned. By 1986, according to official statistics, there were seven priests and twelve sisters in the diocese, and other church workers continued to arrive.

In Guatemala and El Salvador church workers sought to rebuild from the ruins left by the "dirty wars" of the early 1980s. The March 1983 visit of Pope John Paul II helped to restore morale. Slowly, church people moved away from concentration on sheer survival to taking modest initiatives — largely binding up wounds and helping people cope. In Quiché and other rural areas they were involved in relief work, although they sought to move toward development projects so that the people would not become dependent. A sister described her pastoral work as being attentive to what people were asking for, whether it be Bible study groups, leadership training, development projects, or training to become health promoters.

Asked whether they were working with people who had previously been active in church programs a sister said, "Yes, those who are still alive." Elsewhere, however, a priest said that those formerly active were "either dead, gone away, or in another church." One sister said that in her area of Quiché there was not a single family that had not lost members, but that the people nevertheless had an astonishing ability to forgive.

In one area where four or five thousand people had been killed in the early 1980s, sometimes in large massacres, church workers found people surprisingly willing to talk about the violence; *la violencia* was a common reference point in their conversation. People were ready to participate in church meetings, even those with a consciousness-raising content. They even spoke of their own dignity and would remark, "They treated us worse than dogs," referring to how the army acted toward those it suspected of guerrilla ties. However, as soon as the discussion moved toward any sort of organization, they would resist: "Oh, this is like the meetings they used to have at night" (referring apparently to a period when peasant organizers were at work in the area). Even representatives of the Christian Democrats encountered such resistance.

With help from the parish one small community began a successful irrigation project that improved their yields so dramatically that the families no longer had to sign up for migratory labor crews at harvesttime in order to survive. Although Guatemalan Indians are normally keen to innovate when they can see economic results, in this instance none of the neighboring communities showed interest in undertaking their own irrigation projects. Instead of emulation the project aroused envy and even accusations from other villages, just as the army had provoked envy and recriminations between villages during the worst phase of violence. A social scientist concluded that here the army had been successful in its strategy of breaking up social organization based on ethnic ties. He suggested that it might be necessary to engage in projects that would require no commitment, and to work in the most open and public way possible, even with government agencies, in order to begin to overcome the resistance to any form of common endeavor.

The Indians' seemingly passive way of coping with repression and violence inspired a foreign sister in another rural area of Guatemala. "I was one of those people who said we must always speak the truth, that it is better to be killed than to kill. But there came a moment when too many had been killed; there were too many martyrs. . . . We had to go under water," she said, including herself with the Indians, "and submit to unthinkable terrible cruelty and repression, and submit without saying a word. It was important that each of us survive for the survival of the race. That didn't mean we condoned what was going on; it meant taking a longer view, saying there is hope, but not for now." Deep within themselves people were saying to the military, "I know very well what you're doing, but I will be true to myself." It was not easy for her to adopt such a stance, which ran counter to her own culture.

In the aftermath of years of repression, pastoral renewal proceeded by very modest steps. For instance, one group of sisters went to live in a small barrio in Guatemala City; they spent their first four months there visiting house to house. In this community some families had built permanent houses, but most lived in crowded wooden shacks on streets frequently filled with mud during the rainy season. The sisters then had house meetings, beginning with discussions of the people's issues and experiences, and then bringing in the Scriptures—"reading the Word in context," as a sister put it. By the end of their first year fifty people were attending the house meetings.

The sisters saw their role as developing critical consciousness, but the people seemed to be more interested in religion in the traditional sense. When the sisters were absent for a few weeks the group continued to meet but began to act like other religious groups in the neighborhood. They built a lectern and one of their number functioned like a preacher—perhaps imitating Salvador Gómez. This was the reverse of the participatory and egalitarian model that the sisters had in mind.

Trying to proceed carefully, the sisters used official church documents, such as the letters of the bishops, and their own house meetings were presented in the framework of the archdiocese's plans for parish renewal. During their first Lent they held a stations of the cross with participants in traditional dress, representing Jesus and others as seen in religious paintings. In their third year they began to insert references to contemporary Guatemala at about every third station. Once when a sister noticed three military observers present she had to drop the prepared script and improvise the stations on the spot. On another occasion this same sister spotted army or police observers present and realized that she could not alert the young people who had prepared incisive contemporary commentaries because they were scattered throughout the crowd; her only recourse was to use the prayers to tone down the confrontational side of the meditations.

In the process of articulating their needs, the group began to discuss building a parish facility. Although the sisters proposed a single building for various purposes including worship, the priest wanted a more traditional church. Since a European agency was willing to provide funds, the project became a chapel with adjacent community buildings. People from the community provided much of the labor and raised a small portion of the money. After the buildings were finished people's enthusiasm waned and a number of parish leaders dropped out for various reasons. By the late 1980s a sister admitted that the pastoral work seemed to have reached an impasse. The small group of people with whom she had been working had indeed progressed from their originally more traditional religious concerns to a critical consciousness of events within their barrio and in Guatemala as a whole. However, she was concerned that their day-to-day struggle put limits on their commitment, and feared that the city government might draw away some of the leaders she had trained.

A lay woman who had worked with these sisters doubted that they were really willing to accept strong lay leaders. Whatever they might say about empowering people, the sisters wanted docile leaders. When some of the original leaders were showing independence, the sisters set about training a new group of leaders. This authoritarian streak had led to the failure of several projects, such as a mother and infant feeding program, she believed. Whatever the merits of this criticism, pastoral work in an urban setting like Guatemala City is considerably more complex and often more frustrating than work in rural villages where relatively few outside forces compete with pastoral programs.

Elsewhere in Guatemala City at about the same time two priests had begun to work in a newly formed parish made up of three barrios. They made no attempt to form basic Christian communities, however, because simply calling a group a "Christian base community" could make it a target for repression. Moreover, after years of trauma people had a need to be "reintegrated," both personally and in their family life. These priests opted to work with several dozen leaders, meeting with them one night a week on the parish premises.

Parish activists, when asked about their social ministry, did not describe anything radical, but rather activities like taking up a collection for a woman who had been left a widow when her husband, a security guard, was killed on the job. Like evangelicals, they visited their neighbors, but their motive was not to proselytize but simply to serve their needs. The priests regarded their own work as "consciousness-raising," and hence as innovative while the people saw the present as a continuation of their earlier efforts, and particularly getting the church built. The people's interpretation of church activity is often less radical and more "religious" than that of priests and sisters.

A pastoral team working in Mezquital at the southern end of Guatemala City offered yet another example of the new wave of pastoral efforts in the 1980s. Mezquital is situated at the south end of the plateau on which Guatemala City is located, on a large irregular tract of land that slopes gradually downward from the upper middle-class area of Monte Maria to the edges of cliffs that drop into the deep ravines that border the capital plateau. Land invasions were first triggered when the government housing agency began a project for middle-class families. A first invasion attempt was stopped by force, but the second in May 1983 held firm. As a result of this and subsequent invasions, by 1984–85 sixty thousand or more were living in the area, most in makeshift houses that leaned up against one another, some of them dangerously perched along cliff edges. Because of its size, Mezquital could not be ignored politically, and it received far more attention than dozens of other smaller invasion neighborhoods around the city. A number of international agencies were eager to provide aid of various sorts.

After initial pastoral efforts, a number of Catholic church people in 1987 coalesced into a parish team made up of Father Luís Rama, a Franciscan, sisters from three congregations and several nationalities, a Guatemalan diocesan priest, a Canadian lay volunteer, and several young Franciscan students. Father Rama's small house and office, built out of the same rough cut planks most of the people used for their houses, gradually expanded into offices and further rooms and a chapel for the Franciscan community. Although a European agency would have been willing to build a cement block church and many Protestant chapels were being built that way, the team decided not to construct a more permanent church until the people of Mezquital had solid homes. The rather unusual (for Catholics) name chosen for the parish, *Dios-con-nosotros* ("God with Us") was a way of affirming God's presence in a barrio that many outsiders viewed with contempt or fear.

The pastoral plan drawn up in 1989 described the team's objectives as evangelization, organization, and formation. In practice, the emphasis was on Bible reflection groups along with other types of activities such as catechesis. When asked about their method of evangelization, Father Rama said, "It's the traditional method: Observe, judge, act." The notion is to get people to see their situation, not turn away from it.

Despite the presence of a large team, results were modest. About four hundred people were participating in one of the several formation programs and an estimated 1,200 people attended Sunday Mass in the parish (not even 2 percent of the population of Mezquital). Interestingly, with no real encouragement on the part of the team, over two hundred people were involved in the Catholic charismatic movement.

Housing was a major focus of the parish team and lay leaders. A government pilot project proposed settling people on lots of six by ten meters. Since a house alone would occupy almost all that space, the people organized a campaign around the slogan, "Six by ten, no; six by twelve, yes." They argued that existing legislation mandated lots no smaller than six by twelve. Moreover, the additional space, approximately 120 square feet, would provide room for a small backyard in which children could play, clothes could dry, gardens could be planted—and overcrowding could be ameliorated just a little. Educational materials on the issue prepared in the parish were written in accessible language and could serve to inform people about what was happening and help them deal with officials in a sophisticated way. Taking advantage of its connections, the parish team also appealed for international solidarity, citing provisions of the Guatemalan constitution and various international human rights documents.

For this and other activities the parish was branded conflictive by the military. In one instance, as the troops were about to carry a young man off in a truck, two of the priests sat down in the roadway, until other people, mainly women, gathered and with spontaneous nonviolent action stopped the truck. Parish team members regarded their work as helping the people press their just social demands but not as contributing to any political movement.

Elsewhere in Guatemala City, a priest described his own evolution from the early 1980s when he had been close to the guerrilla struggle. Gradually becoming disillusioned with internal divisions among the guerrillas and their inability to protect people in rural areas from the army's onslaught of abduction and killing, he and others came to the painful realization that they would have to begin anew. He returned to slow, patient, pastoral efforts to build up small Christian communities in which lay people would take major responsibility. The aim, however, was not for communities to be closed in on themselves but rather to influence and enrich the life of the whole community, "like leaven in dough." Learning the harsh lesson from the overly rapid politicization that had occurred earlier, he intended to go slowly "so people know what they're getting into. For people to work to change this country, they first have to get involved in their community." People in the parish had organized delegations to press their demands with municipal and national authorities. He was very concerned that it be the people who decide when and how to act, and not a left organization managing matters behind the scenes.

A priest in Guatemala said the new life arising in the church after years of repression was like tender weak "sprouts" just breaking out of the seed that would take a long time to grow. In El Salvador much pastoral work had been dismantled when pastoral agents had fled the country, gone underground, or escaped to the hills. Few new pastoral initiatives were taken in the early 1980s. By mid-decade, however, work was being renewed in some places and new initiatives were being undertaken.

One problem was the gap between people with different experiences or expectations. A team of priests arriving to work in one parish in San Salvador decided that to be identified with the existing base community, which was seen as radical, would alienate them from many others. They decided to have one priest work with the existing group while the others engaged in new outreach.

In another parish swelling with migrants from the countryside and people displaced by the earthquake, the pastoral team found that their parishioners ranged from FMLN sympathizers to ARENA supporters. Their pastoral work was largely that of helping people organize to meet community needs, for example, by training teachers and health promoters. In another parish a Salvadoran priest who was continually threatened and whom death squads came seeking three times, nevertheless managed to serve about ten base communities, and initiate development projects—carpentry and tailor shops and a bakery. For people active in the popular organizations, the base communities offered an opportunity for reflection and support. This priest believed he could have a pastoral influence on the mass organizations by working with base communities.

Nicaragua—Still Struggling for Liberation

During the 1970s Cuban theologians had argued that they did not need a liberation theology, since the essential structural changes were already underway in their country. Early in the Nicaraguan revolution, some church people similarly suggested that instead of, or at least alongside, the exodus paradigm they might take inspiration from the biblical books of Nehemiah and Ezra, which describe the rebuilding of Jerusalem after captivity in Babylon. Such optimistic hopes were soon forgotten; everyday pastoral work was closer to that of likeminded people in neighboring countries than one might expect, especially in the late 1980s.

In the area of El Viejo, west of Chinandega along the Pacific coast, a team of Catholic sisters who sympathized with the revolution found their work to be uphill. One sister admitted that there were many communities "where we have to use strictly religious language without referring to liberation." As we talked in mid-1989, one of the four women waiting in the next room to see the sister was opposed to the Sandinistas, who had "executed" her brother, a Guardsman under Somoza. Although there had been no contra attacks in this area, local young people had been killed while doing military service elsewhere.

The sisters encouraged the people to reflect that their God is a God of life, who is therefore pleased by whatever enhances life, even something as mundane as a campaign to eliminate malaria. In addition to promoting Bible study groups in twenty-three communities, they had initiated a number of development projects to aid people's economic survival: a women's bread-baking project, a sewing collective, the cultivation and use of soybeans, cooperatives for pig raising and selling basic grains at cost, and a preschool and day care center for working mothers. In appearance and day-to-day operation, little would distinguish these projects in revolutionary Nicaragua from similar projects in counterrevolutionary Guatemala or El Salvador. As often happens, they were working independently from their very traditional pastor, even though they lived in the shadow of the church tower.

One shift of emphasis was clear: Before Somoza's fall their effort had been to develop a consciousness of the oppression by the dictatorship and of the need for structural change; now the emphasis was on giving people a sense that "if they do not transform history, nobody will."

The conflictive parish of Waslala in the middle of the country included about sixty thousand people spread throughout sixty communities in addition to the town. Parish work was divided into five areas: evangelization, adult education, agricultural production, health care, and sewing (to enable women to make their own clothes). Such a division reflected perhaps a combination of needs expressed by the people and the abilities and inclinations of the parish team of two priests, four Brazilian sisters, and a Brazilian lay worker. While they were using what was in effect a base community method, they called them Catholic Action Committees, since well-defined base communities would further expose the people to contra violence. A team member described the mission of the parish as helping people "empower themselves, to take control of their lives and not to feel in a religious sense that God decides there will be a war and that they had to wait for the next life."

In each region of the parish the five-part structure was replicated so that the pastoral team would work primarily with the individuals responsible for evangelization, adult education, and so forth. The pastor, Father Enrique Blandón, and the rest of the team would spend two to three months circuit riding in order to visit each community twice a year. At other periods the leaders of local committees could consult with the team when they came to Waslala for marketing or other business. The people had built a small facility in Waslala for retreats and courses.

This parish worked in coordination with government programs. Some of the health and education materials came from government ministries and some parish programs were carrying out activities that under normal conditions would be the responsibility of the government (a vaccination campaign, for example), but which contra violence had made impossible. Both Blandón and his fellow priest, Ubaldo Gervasone, had been captured by the contras. Gervasone was also ordered to leave Nicaragua by his bishop in Bergamo, Italy, and by Bishop Schlaefer of Bluefields, Nicaragua. Attributing these orders to the displeasure of the papal nuncio over his denunciation of contra atrocities, Gervasone argued that his first loyalty was to the people and hence he opted to remain in the parish without celebrating the Mass or other sacraments.

Throughout Nicaragua, those committed to a liberating kind of pastoral work found themselves spending their energies legitimizing their option rather than taking new initiatives. They realized their constant preoccupation with the bishops was unhealthy—they were suffering from the disease of "Obanditis." Meeting on retreat in 1983 a group of church workers decided to form a coordination network, the CNP (National Pastoral Center), which served as a vehicle for sharing of experiences, and to organize occasional events in which communities from different parts of Nicaragua could come together.

Besides promoting contact among pastoral agents CNP people worked among those not reached through normal pastoral channels. Because representatives of the official church had repeatedly refused to celebrate funeral Masses for fallen Sandinista combatants, the CNP opted to work pastorally "accompanying" these relatives. At a Mass in Matagalpa in 1989 as the peace process was gathering momentum, I watched the priest lead a dialogue on reconciliation with the contras.

Defending the Victims: Human Rights Monitoring and Humanitarian Aid

Most of the examples of "accompaniment" thus far have been those of individual sisters, priests, or pastors working alongside the persecuted at the village or barrio level or even on the run in the mountains. Some of the most noteworthy instances of the kind of "Samaritan" behavior suggested by Bishop Gómez, however, are more institutional, particularly in the defense of human rights and in aiding refugees fleeing the war.

Much of this activity can be traced to initiatives by Archbishop Romero. "When we struggle for human rights, for freedom, for dignity," he said in December 1977, "when we feel that it is a ministry of the church to concern itself for those who are hungry, for those who have no schools, for those who are deprived, we are not straying from God's promise. . . . The church knows it is saving the world when it undertakes to speak also of such things." He was of course defending himself from an accusation that he and other church representatives were departing from their true, "spiritual" mission. Shortly afterward he spoke of the church's difficult mission: "to uproot sins from history, to uproot sins from the political order, to uproot sins from the economy, to uproot sins wherever they are."

He was convinced that the church must be concerned not only with individual conduct but with social implications, consequences, and structures. He denounced many specific incidents of abductions, murders, bombings, and arbitrary arrests; he analyzed and critiqued not only specific events but larger trends in El Salvador; the first refugees of the war camped out in the large yard behind the seminary and archdiocesan offices; and he insistently pleaded with right and left to pull back from the headlong rush toward war.

A specific conflict—the Holy Week 1978 clash between peasants of the progovernment paramilitary network ORDEN and of the militant FECCAS, which on the local level often had strong church ties—launched the Catholic church in El Salvador into human rights monitoring. When government sources and the media blamed FECCAS, an ad hoc investigation ordered by Archbishop Romero found that the violence—including the murder of a catechist, Tránsito Vásquez, whose head had been left impaled on a stick—had been started by ORDEN. Although FECCAS members had fought back at some point, the primary violence was inflicted by ORDEN and security forces. At least six were killed, sixty-eight were missing, fourteen were wounded, many were arrested, and refugees had fled to the seminary grounds in San Salvador.

From this point onward, the archdiocese continued to monitor human rights violations and issue occasional reports. A church-based agency, Socorro Jurídico, which had been formed at the Jesuit high school to provide legal aid to families whose members had been arrested or "disappeared," functioned as the official human rights agency of the archdiocese for several years. The secular Human Rights Commission of El Salvador, established around the same time, maintained informal ties with the church.

In the late 1970s it was by no means clear that the Catholic church should sponsor human rights monitoring activity. Although the Latin American bishops at Medellín (1968) had committed themselves to "defend, according to the gospel mandate, the rights of the poor and oppressed," the only episcopacy that had done so systematically was that of Chile, which set up a Vicariate of Solidarity in the aftermath of the 1973 military coup. The bishops of Argentina turned a blind eye to the "dirty war" of abduction, torture, and murder by the military beginning in 1976. The Brazilian bishops, the most forthright on the side of the poor in Latin America, did not establish human rights monitoring agencies as such.

By 1979 Socorro Jurídico was keeping a tally of human rights violations, based on the first-person testimonies it was gathering. In 1982 Archbishop Rivera severed Socorro Jurídico from the archdiocese and announced the formation of a new agency, Tutela Legal, which for the sake of greater evenhandedness, reported and denounced guerrilla actions as well as those of the government. In charge was María Julia Hernández, a woman with a strong church background, who was tenacious and enjoyed Rivera's confidence. High military officials regularly denounced Tutela, and U.S. embassy staff periodically questioned its accuracy or fairness. The international human rights community had a high regard for Tutela, and its files were a major resource for agencies such as Americas Watch and Amnesty International. As they went about their work, Hernández and her growing staff were aware that about a half-dozen members of the Salvadoran Human Rights Commission's members were murdered (notably Marianela Garcia, captured and killed in March 1983 near Suchitoto as she was seeking evidence on possible use of lethal chemicals by the Salvadoran military, and Herbert Anaya, gunned down in 1987).

The core of Tutela's activity was to transcribe the testimony of victims or eyewitnesses of abduction, murder, torture, and attacks on civilian populations, onto legal forms and to present the material in the Salvadoran legal system as appropriate. The agency also helped people make habeas corpus presentations for abducted relatives, even though they had little practical effect.

Meanwhile, the Salvadoran Human Rights Commission and Socorro continued to gather their own information and issue their own reports. In 1985 Segundo Montes began IDHUCA (Human Rights Institute of the UCA) to study not individual cases but the longer-range trends and underlying issues in human rights. In the early 1980s the government opened its own human rights commission, one of whose members was Monsignor Freddy Delgado, a priest whose conspiratorial view of the involvement of priests with the guerrillas was similar to that of the military. This agency's purpose was to defuse international human rights criticism by documenting guerrilla abuses. At no time did it confront the military.

Human rights monitoring evolved through the decade in accordance with changing circumstances. During the early 1980s, the period of the most intense "dirty war," human rights became something of a numbers game as the U.S. Congress required that President Reagan issue a certification of "improvement" in human rights as a condition for continuing military aid. A perverse logic made it possible to call the murder of thousands of civilians an "improvement" if the number of victims continued to decline from the 1980–81 levels of over ten thousand each year.

Until the mid-1980s it was extremely difficult to monitor events in the countryside since much of the territory was under the control of the FMLN or was disputed. The army was held little accountable for its shelling and bombing of civilians and people fled on forced marches. Tutela Legal and other organizations argued that these actions were in violation of the Geneva Conventions, which define the rights of civilians in a state of war as a matter of international law. Over time, the military was forced to acknowledge the existence of civilians and their rights. When Archbishop Rivera visited Guazapa to help negotiate the release of President Duarte's daughter, and in subsequent pastoral visits, he witnessed the destruction being wreaked on civilian communities. The ability to monitor human rights violations in the countryside after 1985 was due to a change in the conflict as the FMLN, in response to the armed forces' greater use of air power and more aggressive small patrols, ceased trying to hold large areas of the countryside and moved back into San Salvador and other areas.

In Guatemala the level of violence was such that it was impossible to openly monitor human rights violations during the worst phase of the "dirty war." Cardinal Casariego's stranglehold over the episcopal conference impeded any independent initiative from the Catholic church. Consequently, the bishops were limited to an occasional expression of concern in general terms.

Outside the country, the Guatemalan Human Rights Commission issued reports with the names of victims and the circumstances of their murder or disappearance. In the early 1980s the church-related Justice and Peace Commission quietly gathered information in Guatemala and sent it out of the country to be published internationally in the organization's reports. Church people, particularly sisters, were key contacts between the victims of violence and researchers for Americas Watch, which issued reports more or less annually.

The way to more open human rights activism was opened by GAM, which initially had help from some church people. Further space was opened by the Quiché-based CERJ movement, which opposed forced participation in civil patrols and the widows' organization CONAVIGUA, formed in September 1988. The work of each of these was related to human rights but no organization was formed to monitor human rights on a national level.

Soon after taking office, Archbishop Penados expressed interest in opening a church-based human rights agency. An early effort in 1984 foundered, and renewed efforts in 1986–87 also bore no fruit, partly because lawyers were convinced that death squads would kill any human rights monitors. Finally in January 1990 the Office of Human Rights and Social Services of the Archdiocese of Guatemala opened in the archdiocesan offices in the colonial complex facing the main plaza. In a deliberately low-key beginning, the new agency's objectives included offering courses in human rights to church workers and others and documenting some violations of human rights.

Although Cardinal Obando and the Nicaraguan bishops frequently criticized the Sandinista government on human rights grounds, they did not sponsor systematic monitoring of human rights violations, aside from a brief period in 1985 when the archdiocese of Managua established a Justice and Peace Commission. Perhaps the bishops saw no need for a specific church human rights agency since the Permanent Commission for Human Rights continued to function.

A more substantial question is to what extent the Nicaraguan bishops were truly defending human rights and to what extent they were utilizing the undeniable human rights violations of the Sandinistas for political purposes. The human rights most often violated in Nicaragua were political rights, such as the rights to expression and assembly. A principled monitoring of human rights would have put the right to life in first place. The number of civilians killed by the Sandinistas during their decade in power could be counted in the dozens. The Sandinistas sometimes covered up such cases, but they also sometimes brought to justice those responsible. In that regard they stand in sharp contrast to the regimes of Guatemala and El Salvador, whose victims were counted in the tens of thousands and where no officers, and virtually no enlisted men, were brought to trial. Moreover, the civilian victims of the contras—who repeatedly extolled Obando and invoked God—could also be numbered in the thousands. That inconvenient fact probably explains why the Nicaraguan bishops made no major efforts at systematic human rights monitoring.

Church-sponsored humanitarian aid could also trace its origins to Archbishop Romero. Although military actions forced some Salvadorans to flee their homes and lands in 1977 and 1978, it was military sweeps accompanying the March 1980 land reform that prompted the establishment of permanent refugee camps, as hundreds of people camped in the large backyard of the seminary. When the United States expressed interest in offering aid, church officials refused it on the grounds that the United States was heavily supporting the government whose troops were making people refugees. As military activity escalated and guerrilla war broke out the numbers of displaced people increased to the point where the churches were operating twenty-three refugee camps. Most were kept under military surveillance, and troops sporadically entered or shot into the camps so the refugees themselves were confined there. Thousands also fled to Honduras. Not all were fleeing the army. Some refugees, especially evangelicals, said they were fleeing the guerrillas or simply violence in general. Umbrella organizations of evangelical churches were set up to aid these people, generally with funds supplied by USAID.

During the early 1980s the Guatemalan and Salvadoran armies regarded humanitarian aid to civilians in remote rural areas as subversive. Indeed, in Guatemala it was impossible to administer aid independently. Some church people in exile, especially in Mexico City, sought aid for people struggling to survive under the conditions of the "dirty war." The Salvadoran military and some U.S. officials accused church agencies and particular individuals of being linked to the guerrillas. In El Salvador, the Catholic church ran the largest aid activities, primarily through its Social Secretariat. Funding was from church agencies in Europe and North America. It also continued to administer some food aid from the United States, at levels that had existed since the outbreak of war.

As Bishop Gómez explained, these churches did not operate according to a master plan, but responded to particular requests, often in communities in which their congregations were established or had members. They did not, however, link aid to proselytizing, nor did they give preferential treatment to their own members. In this respect, they differed from the conservative churches, which saw humanitarian programs as ancillary to evangelism.

Efforts to aid the victims of war became themselves conflictive in the highly charged atmosphere of Central America. "I would walk across the street to avoid talking with you if you received U.S. money and worked with the military," said a former official of a Catholic aid agency in El Salvador, "and people in other agencies would do the same to avoid talking with me." He described the work of his agency as "independent" humanitarian aid as opposed to the "political" humanitarian aid that was a part of counterinsurgency. His adversaries would reverse the adjectives, accusing church-related agencies of sheltering guerrilla sympathizers.

As the war changed in El Salvador the nature of humanitarian aid also changed. The year 1985 was pivotal as the FMLN, in response to increased air attacks, ceased to hold particular territories, and spread small units and organizers throughout El Salvador. In the meantime, some families had been moving back into the areas they had fled. Initially the refugee camps were a welcome haven from the danger the people had fled but as time went on there was a danger that people would become permanently dependent. Thus, when conditions made it possible, church agencies emphatically supported repopulation and repatriation efforts. The displaced themselves took initiatives from the formation of CRIPDES in 1984 to the return to Tenancingo in 1986 and then to El Barillo, San Jose las Flores, and other areas so that the refugee centers rapidly closed.

Refugees from the camps in Honduras then returned, beginning with the first large movement of over four thousand people from Mesa Grande in 1987. The army constantly harassed such people, refusing them travel permits, halting their vehicles to search them, and sometimes holding up their shipments of food supplies until they rotted. The presence of international observers was at least a restraining factor.

Church agencies also encouraged the resurgence of popular organizing, especially in the wake of the 1986 earthquake. A church aid worker noted that the earthquake focused attention on the "invisible population" that made up over half of San Salvador. He said that their message to people soliciting help was, "You have to get organized since we can't deal with you on an individual basis. Form some kind of group, like a block committee. If you need training, even to read and write, we'll provide resources." The organizing did not lead to many houses being built since few resources arrived, but the organizing spilled over into other areas. Groups began making other demands on the government and forming larger coalitions. The FMLN also intensified its urban work starting around the time of the earthquake. Thus, it is fair to say that the general philosophy of church agencies and the FMLN in favor of popular organization coincided more with each other than with the military and the government whose concern was population control.

When the FMLN launched its November 1989 offensive, the military ransacked church humanitarian agency offices, arrested employees, and removed files. Although the military's simplistic accusations that these agencies aided the guerrillas were untrue, politics inevitably influenced humanitarian aid. Left popular organizations that might have ties to guerrilla groups would understandably view church agencies as possible sources of funding. Given the presence of the left throughout El Salvador, it was impossible to assure that no food or other aid would ever end up in guerrilla hands. Those working in church agencies had to screen project proposals to make sure that they were not "phantom projects" designed to funnel resources to the guerrillas. To put it another way, the very act of working in relief and development thrust church agencies into highly politicized situations in which complete neutrality was generally impossible. Rivalries within the left often frustrated church workers.

The largest church-related humanitarian and development programs in Central America were those of CEPAD in Nicaragua, whose annual budget ranged between $2 and $3 million. CEPAD expanded its programs enormously during the 1980s and successfully attracted funds from Europe and North America, not so much because donor agencies wanted to help a left government, but because the overall atmosphere in Nicaragua favored grassroots development: A dollar or a deutsche mark bought more development in Nicaragua than it would elsewhere. CEPAD could draw on years of experience and a network of local churches and pastors especially on the Atlantic coast, where Protestants were a majority. During the 1980s several CEPAD workers were murdered by the contras, some were abducted, and clinics and other installations were destroyed.

CEPAD's capabilities were demonstrated when Hurricane Joan hit the Atlantic coast on October 20, 1988. Few lives were lost but whole villages and towns were flattened and crops were destroyed. Even before the storm hit, CEPAD designated some existing food for emergency relief. Within days a CEPAD appeal to the World Council of Churches had brought over a half-million dollars. Because of its local networks of pastors CEPAD became the major agency in the relief and rebuilding efforts on the Atlantic coast. CEPAD continued to play a major role in the development of the Atlantic coast area since the priorities of the UNO government lay elsewhere and unlike the Sandinistas it could not draw on cadres of idealistic young people willing to go to remote areas.

A Word of Truth in the Midst of Lies

Archbishop Romero was murdered the day after he directed his emphatic "Thou shalt not kill!" directly at the military. People came to his Sunday Mass and tuned in to it on the radio because they heard from him something that they could not hear elsewhere. He insisted that his sermons were "not political." "Of course they deal with politics; they deal with the situation of the people, but in order to shed light on them and state what it is that God wants and what God does not want." Preaching in 1979 after the recent murder of Father Octavio Ortiz, he said, "Trying to preach without mentioning the ongoing history in which one is preaching is not to preach the gospel." Not only was it legitimate to connect the Scriptures to important current events—it was inherent in good preaching.

The church continued to be a source of alternative perspectives on matters of life and death as Archbishop Rivera, despite his own more measured and middle-of-the-road perspective, denounced human rights violations. This activity was grounded in the Scriptures. I recall observing Monsignor Ricardo Urioste on a July morning in mid-1990 celebrate Mass in place of Rivera. Surrounded in the pulpit by several television camera crews and their lights, he made observations about Isaiah's description of God's word being like the rain and snow that make the earth fruitful (Isa. 55:10ff.). In contrast to the multiplicity of words around us, especially on radio and television, "God is word." He contrasted God's truth to the "realm of lies" around us, ranging from marital infidelity to public discourse. One indication of what he might have in mind was President Cristiani's recent— and blatantly untrue—assertion that weapons and uniforms had been found at the UCA during the army raid shortly before the killing of the Jesuits.

Indeed that murder highlighted this kind of church activity. "They were assassinated because they sought truth and spoke the truth—because their truth favored the poor," said Father Tojeira, their superior, shortly after the crime. It is perhaps well to pause over the claim that these university professors devoted themselves to "speaking the truth" and then paid the consequences. In the United States universities are ideally regarded as sites where teachers and students explore ideas and their consequences in the most open way possible. The very tolerance for a diversity of approaches and opinions—and accordingly of "truths"—makes the notion of "speaking the truth on behalf of the poor" sound rather quaint if not suspect. Furthermore, the ideal of the "community of scholars" is in practice often overshadowed by the fact that the students expect to be prepared for a lucrative career, teachers are interested primarily in research and academic advancement, administrators are managing a large and complex enterprise, and alumni and other funders may have their own expectations. Moreover, in a country like El Salvador, where over half the population does not finish elementary school and only a small percentage completes high school, the very fact of enrolling in the university marks an individual as part of an elite.

Hence it was by no means a foregone conclusion that the UCA should become a major center of criticism and of the formulation of alternatives for El Salvador; it was rather the outcome of a deliberate process. At its founding in 1966 the UCA was envisioned largely as an alternative to the National University, which the Salvadoran elites viewed as overly politicized and academically inadequate. By the late 1960s, however, a group of Jesuits, headed by Ignacio Ellacuría, was raising fundamental questions about their mission as Jesuits and about the UCA. In an address in 1982 Ellacuría retraced that questioning. A university is about culture and knowledge, and the use of intellect, he said, but also about society. A university "must transform and enlighten the society in which it lives." In a general sense this means working so that freedom will prevail over repression, justice over injustice, and love over hatred. A university should strive for those aims, however, with the means proper to universities: "We as an intellectual community must analyze causes; use imagination and creativity together to discover remedies; communicate to our constituencies a consciousness that inspires the freedom of self-determination; educate professionals with a conscience, who will be the immediate instruments of such a transformation; and continually hone an educational institution that is academically excellent and ethically oriented." As liberation theology has emphasized, an option for the poor is essential to Christian life. "Reason must open its eyes to the fact of suffering." For a Christian university to follow this route does not mean simply allowing the poor access to the university, and it does not mean abdicating academic excellence—which is required for addressing complex social problems. However, the university "should be present intellectually where it is needed: to provide science for those who have no science; to provide skills for the unskilled; to be a voice for those who have no voice; to give intellectual support for those who do not possess the academic qualifications to promote and legitimate their rights."

In short, Ellacuría and his colleagues held that a Catholic university in their setting should not simply turn out annual crops of young professional people nor provide a base for professors to do research on what they find intriguing or rewarding. The mark of a Catholic university, observed Ellacuría's fellow theologian and colleague Jon Sobrino, is not even attending the religious needs of students, or providing theology classes. Rather the university is a place for influencing society, with a clear ethical criterion. When in the mid-1980s the UCA created an ongoing forum in which major issues facing the country could be debated and called it the "chair of the national situation" it was asserting that whatever their particular discipline, all students should be majoring, as it were, in El Salvador itself (and its wider context) in order to make their contribution toward change, and that university-based research should operate with a similar criterion.

The UCA's embodiment of these ideals was primarily the work of a core of Jesuits and lay people: It was not the activity of the entire faculty, let alone the students, most of whom were attracted to the UCA by its academic quality. One of the first evidences of the shift taking place was a book published in the early 1970s studying the events surrounding the 1972 electoral fraud and frustrated military coup (*Ano Político 1972*). Written within the disciplines of political science and sociology, in Salvadoran terms the book nevertheless had a quality of investigative journalism, since it sought to reveal something of the normally closed world of the military. Around that time the journal *ECA*, which for decades had been a vehicle for the Jesuits themselves, generally on theological, philosophical, literary, or historical topics, had moved more toward a critical study of the problems of the country. In the early 1970s such problems might include the reality of population pressure, however inconvenient that might be in the light of the official Catholic position on contraception; in the late 1980s it might mean seeking to persuade the left that state-directed socialism like that of Cuba or Nicaragua would not be viable in El Salvador.

In 1975–76 the UCA threw itself into the controversy generated by the government's proposal of a land reform. Most organized groups opposed it—the landholders and business organizations because its modest plan to buy out large properties in two provinces and resell them to 12,000 peasant families represented a limit on private property; and the left, because the scheme was intended to blunt rising peasant militancy. Acknowledging the plan's shortcomings, Ellacuría and the UCA team opted to support it on the grounds that it could be improved and accelerated. Presciently, the UCA board said that population growth and the injustice of social structures were leading to increasing tensions; even if it were possible to keep things as they stood, the result would be "bloody convulsions, that would harm everyone." Among left organizations, only the Salvadoran Communist Party supported the land reform. A book-length issue of *ECA* in 1976 focused on land tenure and land reform issues and contained articles by Rubén Zamora and Guillermo Ungo, then both UCA professors. Ellacuría's own contribution was a polemic with ANEP—although it is unlikely that many ANEP members would read an essay on Hegel, the church fathers, the scholastics, and Catholic social doctrine entitled "The Historicization of Property as Principle of De-Ideologization."

Even as this issue of *ECA* was in preparation, a bomb was set off in the magazine's offices, the second of many. Lamenting that ideas were answered with bombs, the editorialists said their answer was this issue of the magazine, "dedicated with love to the explosive problem of agrarian reform. ... Our vocation is essentially Christian and we want to continue to use Christian methods in our activity. Let others use their methods, and may God forgive those who know not what they do." A few months later, when the government caved in to pressure from the oligarchy, Ellacuría wrote a scathing editorial ridiculing the military for capitulating ("Yes sir, Capital!"). The response was another bomb.

The UCA was close to the civilians in the government following the 1979 coup. Two of the three civilians on the junta set up as a result of the October 1979 coup were UCA rector Román Mayorga and professor Guillermo Ungo. When they and the other civilians resigned and went into opposition, the UCA team followed and served rather like a brain trust for the FDR, which emerged in April 1980. The March–April issue of *ECA* was largely devoted to articles analyzing various aspects of a "popular government." An editorial in the June issue welcomed the unification of the "revolutionary sector" (the guerrilla organizations), but also frankly criticized as a "grave . . . error" the fact that the "democratic sectors," such as political parties and professional organizations, had been subordinated to the mass organizations. Although the UCA team undoubtedly believed they were acting on their original commitment to make a university contribution to help resolve the Salvadoran crisis, the military regarded the UCA and its publications as part and parcel of the overall subversive enterprise.

By 1981 Ellacuría himself was critical of the FMLN and *ECA* was calling for dialogue and negotiations and continued to do so throughout the decade. In view of the relative impasse between the U.S.-backed armed forces and the FMLN, Ellacuría argued that a "third force" had to be involved in the solution. This force was made up of the organized groups in society representing those not committed to either side, such as cooperatives, professional associations, educational institutions, and so forth. The 1988 National Debate convoked by Archbishop Rivera was such a forum.

Contrary to the accusations of their adversaries, Ellacuría and the UCA team maintained their independence. The documentation section of *ECA* regularly printed statements from business groups and right-wing political parties, and most of those who made presentations at the UCA forums in the mid-1980s were also representatives of such groups. *ECA* editorials frequently criticized the left, as in the 1987 article "The Question of the Masses," which focused on the FMLN's tendency to involve the mass organizations in its national strategies at the expense of their local and more immediate struggles. Drawing attention to this problem risked reinforcing the simplistic view of the Salvadoran military and U.S. embassy that the popular organizations were nothing but FMLN fronts. Ellacuría evidently believed that the issue was important enough to warrant that risk. Even before the dramatic collapse of East European communism in 1989, he was pointing to the implications of the changing world situation for the Salvadoran revolutionaries. Ellacuría's willingness to disagree with the FMLN, while maintaining a posture of respect, was one of his most important contributions to El Salvador, according to Rubén Zamora.

In temperament and style Ignacio Martín-Baró and Segundo Montes, the other major writers among the murdered Jesuits, were rather different from Ellacuría. They enjoyed their weekend pastoral work with the poor, in contrast to Ellacuría, who confined himself largely to the university and occasional contacts with influential elites, on both the left and within the power structure. In this regard, he stood in the Jesuit tradition, as Zamora pointed out. Martín-Baró was a social psychologist who had received a doctorate from the University of Chicago. Although many researchers would not even attempt to do research under conditions of war like El Salvador's, Martín-Baró studied the psychological effects of war and violence. In addition to research, he counseled individuals, and served as a much respected mentor to other psychologists who worked with victims. He wrote two textbooks on psychology, and edited a journal of psychology.

Martín-Baró also made important contributions to public opinion polling in El Salvador and Central America. Much polling in Central America had been focused on the middle class, who constitute the most attractive body of consumers and who can be reached by telephone. Convinced that valid polling of the whole population could be a kind of mirror for society and help "de-ideologize" issues, from modest beginnings in the early 1980s, Martín-Baró and his colleagues constantly improved their techniques and widened their scope. Between August 1986 and September 1989 they carried out twenty-three national polls on issues ranging from Central American peace processes, to Salvadoran politics, to religion (the study cited several times in this book). Their polls most accurately forecast the results of the 1988 and 1989 elections in El Salvador. As the Salvadoran media opened somewhat in the later 1980s Martín-Baró became a familiar face on television talk shows, as he shared the results of the team's polling.

After the murders, a fellow Jesuit observed that Segundo Montes was the one who "best knew El Salvador up close." His Ph.D. thesis was on *compadrazgo* (the strong relationship between father and godfather acquired at baptism) in El Salvador, and he did further research in areas of land tenure, social class, refugees, and human rights. Juan Ramón Moreno, Amando López, and Joaquín Lopez y Lopez were not intellectuals in the same sense as Ellacuría, Martín-Baró, and Montes.

For two decades their aim was to serve El Salvador as intellectuals and academics. Within the limitations of a tiny Third World country at war, they sought to be methodical and even rigorous, without making a fetish out of methodology. Far from being propagandists, they were not afraid of results that might displease the left, such as Martín-Baró's surveys, which, even making allowance for the climate of violence and fear, showed only a small proportion of the population supporting the FMLN. Relevance was not their only criterion: Ellacuría continued to edit and comment on the works of Xavier Zubiri, his mentor in philosophy, and wrote on seemingly abstruse philosophical topics at the height of the dirty war. What would make their endeavors Christian, as they understood it, was not aiding the institutional church or offering religious guidance to their students, but striving for justice on behalf of the poor and supporting the efforts of the poor and thereby helping advance God's purposes in the world.

Refugees who returned to Meanguera, Morazán, in eastern El Salvador from the refugee camp at Colomoncagua, Honduras, in 1989 renamed the area Ciudad Segundo Montes. People there recalled that Montes had visited them in Colomoncagua in 1982 and again in April 1989 and that he had told them that he saw them as the hope for peace and for the future and that he hoped to live one day with them in Meanguera.

In July 1990 the hamlet of Guancorita, Chalatenango, was renamed Comunidad Ignacio Ellacuría. After an outdoor Mass concelebrated with about ten priests and hundreds of people in attendance, everyone ate a lunch of chicken soup and hefty tortillas, and watched dances, skits, and puppet shows performed by UCA students and the local community. A peasant who would probably not be able to read a paragraph of Ellacuría's prose, sang a clever traditional-style ballad celebrating him. Here and there FMLN guerrillas mixed with the crowd. This community also perhaps gave a hint of the possibilities of a new El Salvador, for which the UCA community had been striving.

In Guatemala the Jesuit-run Universidad Rafael Landivar, which had been founded a few years earlier than the UCA, did not play a similar critical role. The difference may be less in the intentions of the Jesuits than in the ruthlessness of repression in Guatemala. Massive repression began in El Salvador in the late 1970s, after the UCA had already embarked on its course. In Guatemala death squads operated continuously from the mid-1960s onwards.

Where was the critical word in Nicaragua—and whose truth was to be spoken to which power? The Nicaraguan bishops, dominated by Cardinal Obando, believed the power they had to confront was that of the Sandinista state, and they in effect shrugged off U.S. intervention, sometimes by referring to Soviet-bloc intervention. Was this comparable to denouncing death squads in El Salvador and Guatemala? Again, judgment on where prophecy lies depends largely on the power that must be confronted.

Nicaraguan Christians who in 1979 opted for "critical support" of the revolution believed they remained faithful to that commitment. Read closely, the 1981 letter of "Christians for the Revolution," made up largely of middle-class Catholics in leadership roles in the revolution, has a number of criticisms of the FMLN for its handling of the Atlantic coast, expanding bureaucracy, authoritarian attitudes and practices, and so forth. In one of their letters in the mid-1980s the Jesuits listed a similar catalogue of criticisms of the Sandinistas. Such criticism had little public impact, however: Their main effect was probably to remind revolutionary believers that they must remain "critical."

The UCA in Managua sought to play a critical role. Jesuit and other social scientists helped temper the doctrinaire Marxism of some Sandinistas. From the first few months of the revolution, UCA-conducted surveys of how local communities and the Nicaraguan population as a whole viewed things often ran counter to a priori revolutionary theory. In private conversations UCA people criticized the Sandinistas for orienting their development strategy toward grand and costly development projects, rather than encouraging the many existing small enterprises. The UCA magazine *Encuentro* published the first detailed critical study of the Atlantic coast region in Nicaragua, and criticized Sandinista policy. The UCA also criticized government maladministration, and the dollar shop where foreigners and government people with access to hard currency could buy foreign goods, while most Nicaraguans were reeling from an economy careening out of control.

César Jerez, the UCA rector, admitted that it was a continual struggle to decide whether to make their criticisms public or private, but he rejected the comparison with El Salvador. "Here the situation is different; the line with which we agreed, an option for the poor, was victorious. So we took a posture of critical support; some say it's more support than critical and others say we're more critical than supportive." Their basic posture was not one of criticism, however, as was that of the UCA in El Salvador; in Nicaragua they believed that the revolution should be criticized and corrected, but not confronted in its entirety. Jerez cited an instance when they had decided not to publish a study of human rights violations by the Sandinistas because it would be used by the contras and the United States. Submitting the material privately, they stressed that those guilty of human rights violations should be jailed. Over the course of the Sandinista decade, UCA criticism became increasingly open, especially about the impact of economic policies on the poor.

In Nicaragua Protestants sympathetic to the revolution acted generally like the Catholics, making their criticisms from within a posture of overall support. CEPAD in particular often mediated between the Sandinista government and conservative local churches that sometimes ran afoul of the authorities. On the Atlantic coast the Moravian church, which was the majority church and like the Catholic church encompassed pro- and anti-Sandinistas, also tended to play a mediating role. Even those Moravians who supported the revolution did not idealize Sandinista behavior.

By hindsight it may seem that church people supportive of the revolution should have been more forthright with their criticism. The dilemma — acknowledged by Jerez — was how to do so in a condition of war when the U.S. government with all its means would utilize any negative information in its efforts to overthrow the revolution itself. In any case, those who supported or legitimized U.S. aggression have the least authority to criticize the options people took in Nicaragua.

This chapter has largely consisted of sketches of church people in Central America who see their work as "accompaniment." The term, which connotes journeying alongside people rather than in front of them, is rather modest. Indeed, "accompaniment" describes the position of those who come from outside a community: priests, sisters, and some pastors, such as Medardo Gómez, or middle-class lay people who voluntarily cast their lot with the poor. The poor themselves would not normally speak of their own struggle in terms of "accompaniment." Nevertheless, this deeply spiritual experience has left its mark on a generation in the churches.

CHAPTER 7

CONTENDING VISIONS

Central America, as previous chapters make clear, was something of a religious bazaar: Evangelicals were sniffing at the chance to become the religious majority; Catholic charismatics were emulating Protestant pentecostals; some Catholic priests and sisters felt called to serve in guerrilla-held territory; televangelists periodically swept through the region, addressing stadium crowds and praying with presidents; church music ranged from the revolutionary *Misa Campesina* of Nicaragua or the *Misa Salvadoreña*, to Reformation hymns, to Israeli music, to ballads and salsa. If Bishop Medardo Gómez insisted that the church must devote itself to serving the victims of war and repression and reordering the priorities of society to serve the poor, a Catholic evangelist like Salvador Gómez could assert that people are hungry for religion, not politics.

Pondering these often clashing understandings of Christian faith, I asked Kenneth Mahler, bishop of the Evangelical Lutheran church in the region, what the story of the church is. "It's two stories," he said. "The church is divided between those involved in radical change and those who are resisting — for different reasons. Among those involved you find the development of a theological rationale" (liberation theology). This new development "plunks Christians in the middle of history again." He meant that the founding events of Christianity as recorded in Scripture were public and did not take place only in people's souls.

Consequently, faith is tied to historical actions; people "don't live in another world — of 'faith' or of 'salvation' — but live in a history that is contextualized." Talking about "history" like this sounds a little strange in English, he admitted, and "would require several words, 'power,' 'politics,' and so forth."

Faith entails striving to achieve "a more equitable, more human society. Everything is linked to that, entry into history."

Although he had begun by speaking of "two stories," he had been talking about only one side, so I asked him to put himself in the shoes of those opposed. What would they say is happening? They are "defending Christian truth from an alien ideology that threatens to destroy that truth." Here in

Nicaragua, where Cardinal Obando regarded Sandinista Marxism as a threat to the faith, that seemed clear, but was that also true among evangelical Protestants? "Yes, but it is not so conscious." Confronted by movements for change, the evangelicals' tendency "is to withdraw, to 'follow Christ,' to say, 'We don't get involved in politics,' which is 'worldly.' They would not actively oppose, say, a latrine digging project, but they would not support it either, and sometimes that resistance moved into opposition. The Sandinistas are demonic; you cannot apply Romans 13 [which urges acceptance of state authority] to them."

When pressed about his simple two-part typology, he admitted that those who wanted to maintain a middle ground were probably a majority. These divisions cut across denominations, although those involved in working out a new theology in the light of this experience tended to come from the historical churches. People from pentecostal and faith churches got involved not in theology but in action. Some pentecostal pastors, for example, were Sandinistas, and many others were willing to cooperate in practical matters.

We were sitting in their house in a comfortable middle-class section of Managua in mid-1989. After working as Lutheran missionaries in Panama for more than twenty years, Ken and Rhoda Mahler had settled in Nicaragua in the early 1980s. Bishop Mahler was something of a mentor to a number of leaders of the Lutheran church, which had had an impact beyond its small numbers.

He pointed to a key difference in the way Protestants and Catholics become involved in history. "Because the Catholic church can involve an entire community, being involved in history and power happens automatically. Protestants almost never work with entire communities, but rather with people gathering from different places, so penetration into collective life is much less. When repression begins as it did in Aguilares [El Salvador] in 1977, it's easy to say 'This doesn't concern us.' " Nevertheless, repression sometimes hits a humanitarian nerve, and contact with the suffering of others prompts change.

Mahler illustrated the point with a story he had heard in El Salvador some years before. Twenty or thirty evangelicals showed up bleeding and starving and in flight from their hamlet after an attack by the armed forces. As the local community prayed, someone mentioned Acts 4, which describes how members of the first Christian community in Jerusalem put their goods in common, and so they decided to share their stocks of corn, rice, and beans, confident that the Lord would provide. When their food reserves were running low, knowing that other pastors got some food aid through the church, the pastor went to San Salvador in search of supplies. To his surprise, he was expelled from his denomination for involvement with the left and was forced to become an independent pastor. Mahler said that this story was not unique, and that a number of pastors and congregations had been led by their faith to provide help to those in need. "They listen to the people they are helping, and a process of conversion — of the congregation — begins." In practice, such an understanding of the faith brought these congregations close to Catholic base communities. As a result of such evolution in Guatemala, Mahler estimated that from thirty-five to fifty Guatemalan pastors had been martyred.

It should be kept in mind that the numbers of church people Mahler speaks of as "entering history" are not large. We have already noted that Philip Williams estimates that no more than 40 percent of the Nicaraguan Catholic clergy were sympathetic to the revolution, and only 20 percent actively so.

Even those numbers did not translate into congregations. Active members of base communities in Nicaragua taken all together would not reach one percent of the population (30,000 people). Many Nicaraguan Catholics who were not members of base communities saw some connection between the aims of the revolution and their faith, and expressed that conviction by participating in events such as the "Gospel Insurrection" (1985) and the Way of the Cross (1986) with Miguel D'Escoto. However significant they might be from a qualitative standpoint, such people remained a minute fraction of the population.

Prorevolutionary Christians often stated, "The Nicaraguan people are Christian and Sandinista." In other words, the vast majority of the people were both Christians (even if they rarely attended either Catholic or Protestant worship) and were in favor of the revolution (even if they were not actively involved in Sandinista organizations). Such a position could end up reifying "the people." Convinced that the revolution was not only for the people, but was being carried out by the people, the Sandinistas and their supporters might overlook the signs that the empirical "people" were less and less resembling their construct of "the people." The survey of El Salvador already cited produced a number of sobering findings for those who assumed that most people were revolutionary. Even though almost 70 percent believed that Salvadoran society is (either very or somewhat) unjust, only a minority believed the church should take an active role in society. Thus only 38.2 percent believed the church should be involved in social conflicts (56 percent opposed such involvement). Significantly almost half of practicing Catholics (48 percent) agreed, whereas only 23.2 percent of evangelicals did so. Only a minority of 42.8 percent agreed with the proposition that the church should favor (*preferir*) the poor. Asked about what role the church should assume, almost half gave spiritual answers ("pray," 24.8 percent, and "bring the message of salvation," 20.6 percent) while smaller but significant percentages favored a social role (serve as mediators, 19.5 percent; help the needy, 8.9 percent; do consciousness-raising, 8.4 percent). Nevertheless, as a whole Salvadorans rated favorably the actions of the Catholic church and specifically of Archbishop Rivera and Bishop Rosa Chávez. On the other hand, only 22.1 percent favored canonization of Archbishop Romero; 40.7 percent were opposed and 37.2

percent were not sure. (That only 6.6 percent of evangelicals supported the idea is not surprising since they vehemently oppose traditional Catholic veneration of saints.)

Asked whether a Christian could support the guerrillas, a solid 73 percent answered negatively. The reasons given for this judgment were that killing is against God's law (40.2 percent) or that the guerrillas are evil, destructive, or atheists (36.8 percent), or that the church's mission is to preach the Word and not be involved in politics (9.1 percent). Among the minority willing to admit the possibility of Christians supporting the guerrillas, the widest variation was between practicing Catholics (32.6 percent) and evangelicals (12.7 percent). The respondents' levels of education and social class revealed important variations on this question: 46.8 percent of those with more than a high school education thought that Christians might possibly support the guerrillas. A surprising 37.2 percent of those in the upper middle and upper classes accepted that possibility, as opposed to only 19.2 percent of urban marginal people and 23.8 percent of rural people (in each of the latter two categories, over 17 percent were not certain of the answer). Reasons given for such an acceptance were that the guerrillas are human beings like others (36.66 percent), God has given us the ability to make up our own minds (27.2 percent), and the guerrillas are struggling for a more just system (16.6 percent).

Thus, a majority of Salvadorans held conservative positions with regard to the role of the church and Christians in society. In other words, the standard positions of the evangelical churches and the conservative majority of Catholics were closer to the majority opinion than that of revolutionary or socially active Christians. Those who have willingly accepted being "plunked down into history," in Mahler's words, reflect only a minority— albeit a significant minority—in society. Similar surveys in Guatemala and Nicaragua would no doubt produce comparable results. This is but one more reminder that the liberation vision, which has been central to much of this book, is not a majority position in Central America.

Liberation Vision—Central American Kairos

Theologians have made much of the peculiar nuance of the Greek word *kairos*, which can be translated as "time," but not in the ordinary English notion of a chronological sequence of moments (for which Greek uses *chronos*) but rather of a special time, a period of grace, a moment pregnant with possibility—for believers, a moment when God is acting or is about to act. In early 1988 a group of church people in Central America issued a document titled, "Kairos Central America: A Challenge to the Churches of the World," which offered a vision of their sense of God's action.

It was modeled after the "Kairos Document" (1985) issued by representatives of Christian churches in South Africa, which offered a sharp analysis of the evil of apartheid and of stances of the churches, a critique of the kinds of theology underlying such stances (often implicitly), and a call to the churches to be faithful to the gospel despite the cost. The authors declared that apartheid was a confessional issue, one on which the churches must by their nature take a stand. They were consciously likening the moment to that of the 1930s when a small prophetic minority of theologians and church leaders declared that Nazism was a confessional issue.

"Kairos Central America" was an attempt to read the significance of Central America at a particular moment: after years of the contra war, when the Reagan administration had been weakened by the Iran-contra revelations and was constrained by the political realities of an election year. The Central America Peace Plan had gathered momentum, at least in Nicaragua, but the United States was successfully resisting the efforts of the region's governments to have the contras disbanded. In the first section the document situates the region's wars in its history and in the context of U.S. intervention, much as numerous other collective documents have done. In the churches, "the most important new feature . . . is the participation by sizable Christian groups in . . . people's movements and in the people's armed forces."

The central part of the document, "Seeing This Historic Hour in Central America from a Perspective of Faith," was a theological reading of this situation. A central category in liberation theology is that of God's kingdom or realm, which might be described as the working out of God's will to bring about communion among all humans and all creation: "We cannot but feel the Lord's saving footsteps present when we arrive at more human living conditions, when peace and life come out to meet us, when we take a step—however small—toward full liberation." God's Kingdom is both ultimate utopia and a call for transformation of whatever is impeding God's will.

The first sign of this kingdom is that the people are becoming "subjects of history." They are less of a mass and more of a people—indeed they are becoming "people of God." Like the Servant of Yahweh in Isaiah (chaps. 42–53), they have been chosen by God "to actively redeem the world by their fruitful sufferings, and establish justice among the nations." The Kairos authors were saying that poor people involved in the Nicaraguan revolution or in popular movements in El Salvador and Guatemala were the agents of God's purposes today. "Together with Mary of Nazareth," they said, "we also proclaim the greatness of God, because God sees the humiliation of the poor, pulls down the mighty from their thrones and fights at our side to deliver us from the hand of our enemies" (cf. Luke 1). In the struggles of the poor "there is something of the divine" and the fact that the poor become subjects of history is good news or gospel.

Today, as in the time of Jesus, the powerful seek to prevent God's realm from arriving; thus "the Empire and its accomplices" unleash persecution, the cross, and death against the poor. The poor have discovered that "the God of Western Christian Society was not the God of Jesus, but rather an idol of the Empire," and they are rising up against that idol by appealing to "the God who is truly Christian, the God whom Jesus rediscovered as unmistakably the God of the poor and of Life." Hence, "the war in Central America is a religious and theological war, a struggle between gods situated on both sides of the conflict."

In their observations on "signs of the anti-Realm" this Kairos document, like its South African predecessor, criticized various kinds of theology and pastoral practice that legitimize oppression. The authors no doubt had in mind stances like that of bishops and other church figures who justified contra aid or who might collaborate with the Salvadoran or Guatemalan governments. Their critique of "fundamentalist apocalyptic theology" that claims that "all human work in history is the devil's work until Christ comes" was aimed at those Protestant churches whose belief in the imminent coming of Christ, if taken seriously, would undermine any efforts to build a more human society. They went on to mention a "series of theologies" that considered themselves above politics, which in fact "represent a false and evasive spiritualism that alienates people," and is used by the enemies of the poor.

Having criticized their fellow believers they went on to speak of "sin in the people's movements." Examples of such sins were betrayals, rivalries, and infighting that override the people's interests, and other vices such as demagoguery, militarism, bureaucratism, abuses, discrimination, and so forth. Since many of the writers had seen the Sandinistas, the guerrillas, and the popular movements up close, the terms stood for numerous personal experiences. They offered a similar catalogue of sin on the part of committed Christians—"personal inconsistencies, weariness and faintheartedness, community conflicts, attitudes contrary to the gospel, ambition for power or desire to rule, intolerance and suspicion, lack of generosity in our pardoning, cowardliness in the face of the radical demands placed on us by the defense of the rights of the poor." Their conservative adversaries would hardly be mollified, however, since they were not criticizing themselves or others for excesses on behalf of the revolution, but rather for failure to do their utmost for the cause of the poor.

Affirming their commitment to democracy, they denounced its manipulation, especially when formal democracy is a facade used to hide the reality of repression. After centuries of legitimizing institutionalized violence, the churches now tend to uncritically condemn all violence, thereby equating the struggle of the poor and systematic oppression by the powerful.

Even worse, churches give the oligarchies and militaries a good conscience. It is "especially scandalous" that the churches, which are normally so ready to condemn violence "no matter where it comes from," have not done so in the case of Nicaragua. The authors questioned the frequent calls to reconciliation, stating that the conflict is between "justice and injustice, between good and evil, between life and death"; hence reconciliation and peace must be the outcome of justice. What would make reconciliation possible would be "the people's capacity for pardon as an act of dignity and humanity toward the enemy, once the causes that brought about the injustice and conflict have disappeared."

They reiterated their conviction that they were living in a kairos, "a chance for grace, a decisive hour, an especially tense time within . . . salvation history." They felt that the conflict was reaching a climax. "This is the moment. The hour is decisive. It is the passing of God throughout history, through Central America. Abel's blood cries out to heaven. Lazarus's shout demands immediate attention." The writers exhorted themselves and their churches to deepen their option for the poor in order to continue to nourish the hopes of the people, while being nourished by them, and to be radical in serving God's realm rather than the churches' own concerns.

Part III of "Central American Kairos" urged continued collaboration between churches, and went on to make a number of recommendations with regard to U.S. policy toward Nicaragua, Panama, and other countries of the region; strongly endorsed the Esquipulas peace process underway; urged further progress in demilitarization under UN auspices; and called for solidarity among other churches. They singled out U.S. peace activist Brian Willson, who had lost his legs during a protest on a military base when he was run over by a train carrying ammunition bound for Central America.

"Kairos Central America" has been described here at some length because its authors, Catholic and Protestant, from several countries, were striving to discern God's action in the experience of Central American Christians and to issue a prophetic cry in their name. Even at that time, however, I must confess that I did not share the enthusiasm for the document in some church circles. Somehow the tone struck me as wrong, and the document itself did not give me deeper insight. For all the concern for the poor, the document does not seem to reflect their voice. Like the left as a whole, the authors implicitly assumed that the bulk of the poor—who were not organized, even in Nicaragua—were represented by the active militant minority. A truly prophetic document would have questioned the verities of the left in a more forceful way, perhaps as Ignacio Ellacuría was doing in El Salvador.

Sidestepping the Question

Conservatives, Catholic and Protestant, have produced no equivalent "Kairos"-type document. When I sought to find such a view articulated, I repeatedly encountered resistance or seeming incomprehension.

Toward the end of an interview at Guatemala's main El Verbo church, for example, when I began to ask about the church's stand on social issues, Leonel Soberanis, a lay church representative, told me the church holds that there are "three spheres of government: family, church, and state."

Just as the state should not intervene in the family or the church, the church should not interfere with the state. When I pointed out that the Catholic bishops had written their letter, "The Cry for Land," precisely to carry out an essential part of their evangelizing mission, he said, "The church has taught me to be a good chemical engineer by honoring God in my profession." As the manager of a food processing plant, he could honor God by acting in accordance with God's principles, as taught by the church. When I replied that personal honesty did not affect land tenure, he went back to the three spheres of government. I tested him: "So if you're a Catholic landholder, your church at least raises the issue of land tenure; if you're a member of the Verbo church, it is not even mentioned."

"I go back to what I was saying," he responded. "If the church teaches us to fear God, my activity, no matter what it is, will be correct. The crucial thing is human beings; if people don't fear God, they don't have wisdom."

Stubbornly, I kept pressing my point. "The most serious research indicates that between 1978 and 1985, from 50,000 to 75,000 people were killed in Guatemala, primarily civilians killed by official troops. Some churches took a stand and some did not. I find it too easy to dismiss this all by saying there are three spheres of government. Do you understand what I'm trying to say?"

"I understand," he replied, "but now we're getting away from what you said you wanted to talk about, the story of El Verbo church. We're getting into areas I don't know about. All I know is there are three spheres of government and we must respect each one. I think your question is political so I can't answer. If you ask me about praising God or preaching the gospel, I can answer better. Talking about the three spheres of government is not washing our hands but respecting the other spheres of government."

"Frankly," I went on, "as a Christian I think the churches must find a contemporary way of saying, 'Thou shalt not kill!' ... What you've said just leaves the responsibility in the hands of others. Aren't you in danger of being one of the 450 false prophets of Baal?" (over whom Elijah triumphed when he was vindicated by fire from heaven—1 Kings 18). Again he had a ready answer: "False prophets are those who deny the divinity of Christ and so forth. The Bible says, 'Thou shalt not kill,' to all of us, just as it says, 'Thou shalt not commit adultery ... steal,' and so forth."

As a final step in the verbal escalation, I mentioned the fact that the churches largely failed to stand up to Nazism, while tranquilly upholding their creeds and doctrines. Granting all the differences between the two cases, I feared the churches in these countries might fail in a similar way. Untroubled, he repeated that if people feared God, many problems would be resolved. Their obligation as a church was to preach the gospel; they were doing so and they could see lives changed and families healed.

My aim in recounting this exchange in such detail is not the content so much as the reflex thought patterns of this Verbo representative. Despite his assertion, I believe he did not really understand the questions—at least as I understood them. It strikes me that the theology of El Verbo church, rather than being a way of dealing with the issues, was a way of evading them, a kind of mental astrodome protecting its members from actually confronting such questions.

The serenity of the Verbo representative was that of a person who did not seem to have experienced official violence up close. By contrast, when I asked a conservative seminary professor about violence, he said, "Innocent people died, and many of them were Christians. Violence was indiscriminate and you didn't know who was who. In some places small churches were closed and others lost members, as people were forced to emigrate. Churches were burned. But overall, we didn't see a large falling off, because those who emigrated strengthened churches elsewhere. Churches that were economically and spiritually powerful could take care of widows and orphans."

We were sitting in his office in the seminary complex of the Central American church. Situated on Avenida Bolivar, a thoroughfare noisy with buses and lined with small shops, the seminary had graduated hundreds of pastors, and was a bulwark of the evangelical establishment. When I raised the question of the church taking public stands on crucial issues, he answered that unlike the Catholic church, evangelical churches are very heterogeneous and no one wants to take responsibility for the evangelical church as a whole. Existing parachurch agencies often represent only personal opinions. He did not agree with my Nazi analogy, but when pressed on the practice of torture and murder, he said that the church has taken a stand on sin as social evil, but does not directly tell the army or the government that such and such a practice or policy is not right. The church's message has been that the Bible says that evil is terrible and that we are witnessing the results.

At this point, he began to warm up. "What does the Bible say about the things we're witnessing? Rumors of war, plagues, men loving themselves — that is what the Bible tells us about. It's eschatological." The crisis is not just in Guatemala but worldwide, although particular countries apparently experience it at different times. The church's task is not to denounce either the army or the guerrillas, but to affirm justice; otherwise, "we become enemies and not peacemakers," and the church loses its mission. The implication was that if the church were to denounce things too forthrightly it might alienate the very individuals whom it is sent to evangelize. The army and the guerrillas are equally bad; neither respects human rights. No one gives the right to wage war, but punishment will come in due time: " 'Vengeance is mine,' says the Lord."

The Verbo leader and seminary professor differed somewhat in their perspectives. With its doctrine of the "three spheres of governance" the neopentecostal Verbo church neatly brackets off the activities of those who hold the reins of government, even when they use violence against the people. Perhaps because the nonpentecostal but doctrinally conservative

Central American church was closer to the situation of those suffering repression, the seminary professor acknowledged the evil and suffering, but it quickly became part of the background to the church's activities rather than the result of actions for which some human beings are responsible. In neither case did Christian faith seem to call for anything beyond individual conversion.

Very much the same thing can be observed among Catholics who have a similar understanding of their faith. Interviewing one of the young preachers at Trigo, the ministry started by Salvador Gómez, I noted that the movement arose at a time of violence, and asked if he knew how many Indian villages had been destroyed. When he answered, "I sincerely don't know," I provided some information from Guatemalan government sources, such as the army's estimate that 440 Indian villages were destroyed, and asked if Trigo had any light to shed on this violence. After first denying that Trigo had arisen during the time of intense repression, he said, "Our response is God's; everything you see is violence. People have expelled God from their hearts. The answer is: new person, new society. Peace in a nation begins in the heart of each citizen, so we try to change the person: a transformed person will transform society."

"But aren't you familiar with official church documents of the Latin American bishops stating that the church is called both to announce and denounce?" I asked.

"That's the role of the prophet," he replied. "But we don't want to fall into the error of just denouncing, like always telling a child what he or she can't do." To my mention of a Guatemalan bishops' statement that denounces murder and torture—without waiting for conversion—he responded, "We believe all extremes are bad." The public statements of the Guatemalan bishops were evidently an example of the kind of "extreme" to be avoided. Asked whether Archbishop Romero was an extreme, he hesitated and then acknowledged that Romero was a man of God, but said he could not remember what Romero had said, and would have to analyze his messages. "To be purely social or purely spiritualist is extreme. We need balance. People must be transformed, not only to put aside vice but to serve their brothers and sisters."

Since Trigo claims to make use of local events in its preaching, I brought up the abduction of a GAM member that had taken place just a few days previously. "We do use events as raw material but we don't judge them," he responded. "God is not on the side of death or injustice, but we cannot get involved in any of these movements." A few weeks earlier the Guatemalan bishops had made a statement pointing to the country's serious problems, and had said that the problem was not simply one of intentions, but was structural. I expressed my concern that a movement like Trigo could fail to have a sufficiently critical vision; I was asking, in effect, why this assertively Catholic group seemed unwilling to incorporate into its preaching the repeatedly expressed concerns of their bishops. His ready answer was that they are not a movement but a ministry. "We're happy the bishops have said this—they are the pastors. We're not pastors but preachers." The teaching authority of the church and the work of the laity go together, but they are distinct.

Charismatic Catholics have similar instinctive reactions. When I asked the woman in charge of the House of Prayer in downtown Guatemala City about how Catholic charismatics saw the many church statements on social questions her first words were, "I can't say anything. I think the Renewal operates more in the realm of the spiritual." She paused as though I had asked her something she had never thought about. When I insisted, she said that charismatics were aware of what was happening. Referring to the strike of teachers and public employees (who had been camped in the plaza facing the National Palace for weeks) she said the only thing they could do was to pray.

When I brought up the bishops' letter on land to Father Luís Estrada, he immediately leaped to the notion that what had to be avoided was confrontation, since many people had been victims in the past. Another priest distinguished charismatics from participants in base communities. "The [charismatic] renewal is not like these Christian base communities who move toward violence; it's just the opposite." In each of these conversations, simply mentioning the bishops' letter on land or Christian base communities triggered associations with violence. "We do speak about people being a temple of the Holy Spirit," said Father Estrada, "and that we should see our brother or sister as a child of God—but not for political or organizational reasons, but rather out of a gospel sense."

However, in their 1976 letter "United in Hope" the Guatemalan bishops did draw social consequences from the Scriptures. Invoking the basic biblical images about human beings (image of God, called in Christ to share in God's life) as the basis for human dignity, they immediately declared that people should have equal rights and opportunities for their own development. They went on to say that therefore "the most humble of all Guatemalans, the most exploited and outcast, the sickest and most unschooled, is worth more than all the wealth of Guatemala, and his or her life is sacred and untouchable."

Thus one set of church people sees a clear distinction between the gospel text and any kind of militant organizing, which is immediately likened to violence; the other set, representing not left-wing splinter groups but important sectors of the hierarchy, asserts that these same scriptural motifs are the foundation for a kind of pastoral work aimed at people's empowerment.

Facing Social and Political Responsibility

"Let everyone obey the authorities that are over him, for there is no authority except from God, and all authority that exists is established by God." To evangelicals who believe that God speaks from the text of their particular translation, those words from the beginning of Romans 13 are unequivocal. The apostle Paul goes on to assert that those who oppose existing political authority are rebelling against God's ordinance and will "draw down condemnation upon themselves." Only those who are doing evil have reason to be afraid of rulers. One need only do what is right, "for the ruler is God's servant to work for your good."

As God's servant, the ruler carries his sword "to afflict [God's] avenging wrath upon the wrongdoer." Believers are to obey, not simply in order to avoid punishment but as a matter of conscience. Likewise, Titus 3:1 says, "Remind people to be loyally subject to the government and its officials, to obey the laws." Such words are the source of the evangelical acquiescence to existing power structures, as reflected in the Verbo church's "three spheres of power."

Liberal Christians do not believe they are less respectful when they insist that Scripture must be interpreted historically. Such an approach would first situate texts such as Romans 13 in their original context, that of a small and weak new religious movement in the first century Greco-Roman world. The first generations of Christians could not see the social implications of their faith (for example, they did not condemn slavery as an institution), nor could they even conceive that one of their own might some day be "ruler." Passages such as those quoted above must be seen in relation to what is central in the biblical message, and then interpreted for today, not ignoring the lessons that the churches have learned in dealing with state power over almost twenty centuries.

Events such as the Rios Montt presidency were forcing at least some conservative Christians to rethink their fundamentalist principles. In October 1983, two months after the Mejía Víctores coup, a group of about thirty-five evangelical church leaders in Guatemala met to consider both the need for reflection on politics and faith and for practical steps in this area. Further meetings in January and February 1984 led to the formation of a National Commission on the Social Responsibility of the Evangelical Church in Guatemala, whose purpose was to stimulate church leadership to reflect on this matter.

Long accustomed to assuming that all social questions should be dealt with at the individual level, these evangelicals were now speaking of social concerns, and sustaining their assertions with theological considerations and scriptural citations. They said, for example, that the church's concern should be "integral," meaning that God's concern extends to the material and social as well as to the spiritual aspect of God's children; that the evangelical church should be motivated socially and politically by God's word rather than by outside pressure groups; and that the church's social responsibility extends to all of society—although the family of faith should come first. From Episcopalians, Lutherans, or Methodists such ideas would have been unremarkable; the novel element was that those taking part in this new group were primarily traditional evangelicals. The commission may not have had much impact on local congregations, but it was a sign that rethinking was slowly taking place.

Such reflection on social responsibility had precedents in a number of international meetings of evangelicals, especially the meeting at Lausanne, Switzerland (1974), regarded by evangelicals as a landmark conference. A key paragraph from the Lausanne Covenant reads: "Although reconciliation with man [sic] is not reconciliation with God, nor is social action evangelism, nor is political liberation salvation, nevertheless, we affirm that evangelism and socio-political involvement are part of our Christian duty. ... The salvation we claim should be transforming us in the totality of our personal and social responsibilities."

Hence as they articulated their own position in Guatemala in early 1984, the evangelical group could draw on a developing body of evangelical doctrine on the social responsibility of believers and churches. In the Dominican Republic the previous year delegates had condemned repression, in the form of "disappearance," torture, and death, and rejected machismo, affirmed women's equality, and specifically committed themselves to the defense of human rights, and especially to "struggle against the physical, social, and cultural extermination to which [indigenous populations] are subject." The Guatemalan evangelicals listed public issues of a less controversial nature: "Freedom of worship, free expression of ideas, pornography, indiscriminate cutting of trees, industrial pollution."

In August 1988 a group of evangelical theologians from around Latin America were invited to Medellín, Colombia, for a consultation on liberation theology. A keynote speaker was Emilio Nuñez of the Central American Seminary in Guatemala. The aim of the meeting was to prepare a statement that could "orient the evangelical churches of Latin America as they confront liberation theology and strive for full obedience to the gospel." Although their purpose was to analyze liberation theology, they found themselves talking more and more about what the evangelical church itself was doing or not doing. Rather boldly they stated, "The recognition that most of us have not raised our voice against social injustice even though evangelicals have been in Latin America for a century, moves us to repentance, for our silence has been culpable, even when one of the causes of that silence is the fact that we were given a message whose strongest emphasis is individualistic, dualistic, too future-oriented, and too pessimistic about social problems." After expressing their respect for the work of liberation theologians, the authors of the document listed a number of theological reservations about its biblical exegesis, its emphasis on social, as opposed to personal notions of sin, and so forth. Many of their objections are similar to those the Vatican raised about Catholic liberation theologians. However, that critique constitutes about a fifth of the document: The rest is largely a critique of evangelical theology and pastoral practice, and a call to new commitments. Few of the observations are very directly political, and most are appeals to greater fidelity to biblical faith. Nevertheless, it is striking that in tone and spirit it has some affinity with the 1968 Medellín meeting of Catholic bishops. Far from distancing evangelical theologians and leaders from Catholics who take inspiration from liberation theology, it calls evangelicals to extend their own tradition in a similar direction. The 1988 "Medellín Statement" may not become a magna carta for Latin American Protestants, but it demonstrates that the kinds of issues raised by liberation theologians can arise even in staunchly evangelical circles.

In practice, however, evangelicals continued to have a restricted sense of what their political responsibility might be. Interviewed in early 1990, Edmundo Madrid, the director of the Evangelical Alliance, the main umbrella organization of Protestant churches, said that some people ask what the evangelical churches do about skyrocketing living costs, and responded, "We don't organize demonstrations, which don't go anywhere. Nor do we carry out peasant marches from Quiché to Guatemala City, since that just wastes energy. Bringing in peasants or burning buses doesn't bring living costs down." This off-the-cuff remark is perhaps more revealing than a carefully thought out statement. Where some might see important affirmations of human dignity by the poor, Madrid sees wasted effort or violence. He is implying that good Protestants would not take part in a demonstration. Madrid insisted that their weapon was prayer. "We pray every day for the president, his ministers, and the congressional deputies, not that they become evangelicals, but that God give them wisdom."

The issue of politics could surface in a more concrete manner when evangelicals accepted major government posts or ran for office. Thus the group of evangelical leaders who met in Guatemala in 1984 called for support and prayer for "those who have a political vocation" and urged that evangelical candidates for the Guatemalan assembly should strive to give Christian witness and be prepared to suffer for their principles. Toward the end of the document, unrealistically imagining that Guatemala would be almost half evangelical by 1990, they asked, "What kind of leaders will we have? If we should again have the opportunity for a government led by evangelicals, will it have support and well-trained leaders?"

That possibility of an evangelical candidate was ever present in the minds of evangelical leaders, as well as among politicians and pundits wondering about a potential evangelical electoral bloc. In his 1985 open letter to the evangelical community, Jorge Serrano said that God had put in his heart the conviction that he should run for office. Unfortunately, because Christians had remained aloof from politics, the field had been left open for "foolish and corrupt men" to take power. That situation had changed and now there was a new awareness of responsibility and service. Serrano both affirmed his evangelical identity—he had accepted Christ as his Lord and personal Savior—and his respect for the Catholic church and for freedom of worship. Under a monarchy, Christians would have to be subject to the king in accordance with the Scriptures, but in a republic they are to be subject to the law. This was perhaps his way of dealing with Romans 13.

More important, "if we Christians can do something for our nation, *we must do it.*"

On the other hand, Edmundo Madrid said that the Evangelical Alliance had urged churches not to be involved with any political position, because that could "cast a shadow over the church." He also said it was a "fallacy" to think evangelicals voted as a bloc.

Convergences

Church leaders often saw things in sharply etched terms: the crisis in Central America was a "kairos" calling for believers to take a stand—or was the church simply to save individuals without any concern for society?

From the standpoint of individual believers the contrast might not be nearly so sharp. In mid-1989 as I was driving out of Nebaj, an Ixil man perhaps in his sixties asked for a ride. He wanted to pray at a particular image in the church in Cotzal. As we rode along in the jeep I discovered that he was a charismatic Catholic. Treading carefully, I mentioned that I had been to Nebaj ten years before, and knew the priest at that time (who was now identified with the Guatemalan Church in Exile). This man spoke warmly of that priest. Viewed conceptually, these three versions of Catholicism—popular, charismatic, and revolutionary—seem mutually exclusive. Had he moved from a liberating embodiment of Christian faith to a spiritualistic alienating religion?

Or, was this simply one more example of the way Indians have dealt with outsiders since the conquest? Without pretending to be able to peer into his heart, I would hold that his own inner biography is not to be understood simply in terms of tactical adaptation and is more coherent than it might seem. His underlying religious understanding of life, family, community, and cosmos transcended particular expressions, whether in Catholic Action, the charismatic renewal, or his visit to the shrine.

Researchers Luis Samandú and Oscar Rolando Sierra suggested to me that pentecostals are more in touch with people's deeper beliefs and feelings than the rational constructions of liberating pastoral work, which offers an interpretive framework and develops people's analytical ability. "When you get down into people's consciousness, down in the basement"—how they conceive of their world and their relationship to God—"you find the God of the pentecostals." In a meeting with some lay leaders, Sierra once wrote on the chalkboard a statement to the effect that it is God who gives human beings good or bad health, and asked whose idea it was. "The sects," they answered, meaning evangelicals. In the pedagogical context they knew that attributing health and illness to God was the "wrong" answer. "One of you said it," he replied; he had heard the statement in a casual conversation during a break. His point was that deep down in people's consciousness lies a sense that human beings are caught in a struggle between good and evil over which they have little control by themselves, and hence they must seek God's intervention. Such a vision runs counter to the liberating pedagogy that highlights a God-given human power and responsibility, which is the theological grounding for struggles for change. On a rational level, say Samandú and Sierra, people grasp that notion and are committed to that effort. Nevertheless, at a deeper level, people have another sense, and pentecostals and other religious groups are able to tap into that deeper level, they suggest.

A young woman who was involved in a base community went to a charismatic mass, witnessed speaking in tongues, and responded to the invitation to step forward for healing. She had an ecstatic experience and felt herself healed. Later she told a progressive priest that she had felt at ease and asked whether she had experienced God. He told her he thought it was 90 percent psychological, but admitted to me that the "charismatic movement gets to psychological factors that we in the liberation line don't reach." Among the positive aspects of the charismatic renewal he mentioned were participation, personal renewal, and a festive sense of life. Liberation-oriented pastoral work was deficient in prayer; participants pray in connection with their efforts to work for change, but such prayer lacks the intensity found in these other church movements.

Likewise, a Guatemalan sister whose own work was in a liberation line acknowledged the positive values in the evangelicals she observed in the barrio where she worked, which she estimated to be now half evangelical. "Their pastoral work is more personal. They are very zealous and energetic. When someone gets sick they go to see them. One of ours can get sick and no one notices. They also give people a chance to participate. They play guitars; our masses sound like philosophical discussions in the air. I'm impressed by how they get people going. They present Christ directly. While we accentuate secondary things, like the sacraments, they focus on the person of Christ."

Although this chapter began with the notion that there are two rather distinct trajectories of the churches in Central America—two "stories"—I have also tried to note points of contact or convergence. Neither believers nor the churches are static. Ana Langerak, who was working at the Costa Rican Office of CELEP (Latin American Evangelical Center for Pastoral Studies), an ecumenical agency in Costa Rica that provides training for Protestant and evangelical church people in Central America, observed that growing numbers of evangelical church leaders are tiring of the theologies they were taught and are looking for help in deepening their reading of Scripture. One of the keys, she says, is a basic confidence in a new approach. As they become more engaged with reality, they have to feel that their new direction is grounded in Scripture: that it is not God's will that there be oppression or that children die of malnutrition, but that God desires the fullest development of all people. Pastors then come to see their work as "accompaniment, . . . a willingness to start where the people are and go just a bit further, a little ahead, but always with an impatient patience that doesn't skip steps, but respects the processes that people have to go through."

Years of experience have taught that progress will be made only if the people themselves are the active agents.

One example of what Langerak is talking about was COPEN (Committee of Evangelical Pastors of Nicaragua), which was set up in 1984. As Denis Romero, a pentecostal pastor in Matagalpa, explained to me, a group of pastors in that northern area of Nicaragua recognized the need for an organization that would link pastoral formation to development. Their agency was working in three areas: workshops and training for pastors and their wives, development and educational projects, and communication with other religious organizations in Nicaragua. I observed a simple example at the Saturday classes for pastors being held at a local public school building. Most pentecostal pastors have not finished primary school and some are even illiterate. Even if it takes them years to finish primary and then secondary school, their study will lead some to raise critical questions about their role as pastors and their understanding of the Scriptures from which they preach.

Since the late 1970s COPEN pastors had sought a more contextualized way of understanding the Scriptures. In this effort they had received help from agencies giving continuing education to ministers. Romero and others were adapting certain features of liberal Protestantism without ceasing to be pentecostals. The development projects he enumerated, such as a bakery and sewing classes, were like typical spinoffs from base communities — with the intriguing wrinkle of programs especially devoted to pastors' wives.

Several programs throughout Central America are providing formation for pastors along the lines suggested by Ana Langerak. CELEP runs courses and workshops. The Seminario Biblico in San Jose, which is academically the best Protestant seminary in the region (although too liberal in the eyes of the conservative majority), also organizes seminars, edits publications, and offers in-service training. CIEETS (Interchurch Center for Theological Study) operates a number of programs with a similar approach within Nicaragua. One interesting CIEETS undertaking was to encourage each of Nicaragua's dozens of evangelical churches to research and write its own history. Since most of these churches have been founded in recent decades this endeavor would entail interviewing older members in order to reconstruct the story of their origins and growth. In addition to the inherent value in simply compiling the information, the congregations themselves should come to a realization of their historicity and their kinship with other religious bodies in the country. Thus the project would modestly contribute to a more critical understanding of their faith and more openness to other churches.

In a similar spirit, in Guatemala several denominations and church organizations (Brotherhood of Mayan Presbyteries, Methodists, Church of God, Mennonites, Nazarenes) in 1987 came together to form CIEDEG

(Conference of Evangelical Churches of Guatemala). Since it represented only several hundred of the more than ten thousand evangelical congregations, by no means could CIEDEG claim to represent evangelical churches as a whole, but it was not insignificant. Its programs included development, education, and pastoral training.

After a decade of war, events were pressing those Christians who had signed the Kairos document to raise some questions about their own theological and pastoral options. Likewise, those who started from a naively literal reading of the bible were finding that they might have to take the world more seriously in order to understand their own message.

CHAPTER 8

SHRINKING REVOLUTION, STUBBORN HOPE

In the introduction I mentioned my 1980 "vision" that someday an Indian woman would be prominent in a revolutionary government in Guatemala in order to invoke a particular moment that seemed pregnant with possibilities for a new kind of society. This book has been about what happened to that dream, and how church people were involved in the struggles as they have evolved since then.

Until the end of the 1980s Central America occupied center stage as a geopolitical hotspot and was a source of inspiration to others. On a 1985 visit the Brazilian theologian Leonardo Boff said that Nicaragua was proving "that revolutionary change is possible," and foreshadowed "all our utopias, all our hopes," for a new kind of society and a new kind of church.

Over time those who had hoped to forge an entirely new kind of society found themselves struggling for far more modest goals. The Sandinista revolution was reduced to an appeal for faith—help us hold off the contras, deter a U.S. invasion, maintain legitimacy in Nicaragua and internationally, and eventually it will be possible to return to our development agenda. After the electoral defeat, Sandinista leaders spoke of defending the gains of the revolution, but the Nicaraguan economy was in shambles. Revolutionaries in El Salvador acknowledged that socialism was not on the agenda—at least not the kind of socialism that they had imagined—and accepted a future in which they would be but one political force contending with others in the framework of the periodic elections that they had once scorned as bourgeois democracy. The Guatemalan guerrillas had similar aspirations, but less bargaining power.

What has been gained after so much struggle, pain, anguish, and death? For me the question is not an idle one. I knew or met many of the fallen mentioned in these pages: Bill Woods, Archbishop Oscar Romero, Conrado de la Cruz, Walter Voordeckers, Enríque Alvarez Córdova, Stan Rother, Fernando Hoyos, Marianela Garcia, Ignacio Ellacuría, Ignacio Martín-Baró, Segundo Montes, Amando López, Myrna Mack. I could have included the names of others, lesser-known or unknown friends and associates in Guatemala: "Wiwi" (Mario Mujía), who had worked with Maryknoll-sponsored development projects and then as a labor organizer, machine gunned in 1978; Nehemías Cumes and Anastasio Sotz, Cacquichel leaders in Comalapa, Guatemala, who had staffed a development project with which I was associated, and who were abducted and "disappeared" in 1980; Kai Utah Clouds, an American pacifist who lived and worked with Indians in San Jose Poaquil, who was abducted and tortured to death in 1980; César Vera, a CUC organizer who was abducted and whose parents and father-in-law were also abducted and "disappeared" in 1980. What remains of the ideal for which they—and tens of thousands of others— died?

Bonds across Borders

Many people in the United States and Europe also shared in the dream of Central Americans for a more just and humane society. Central America now matters to many in the United States because through the rise of a Central America movement we have become partners with Central Americans in a number of ways. Hence it seems appropriate at this point to reflect on this relationship.

A major strength of the Central America movement was that it was rooted in personal experience, that is, in the living testimony of Central Americans and of people from the United States who had lived in the region. For example, when the crisis was recognized in the late 1970s, WOLA (Washington Office on Latin America), which had been set up by church people in the wake of the 1973 military coup in Chile, had been placing Latin American human rights on the agenda in Washington.

Very early—in 1979 and 1980—a number of missionaries, particularly of Maryknoll, were important witnesses to the brutality of the Nicaraguan, Salvadoran, and Guatemalan regimes, under which their congregations had lived since the 1950s and 1960s. They and other church people had spent years working at the village or barrio level, and knew the history of Central American countries at a time when the number of academic specialists on the region could be counted on one hand. They had experienced the brutality of military rule and now shared the hope for a new order of justice and equitable development.

In late 1979 and 1980, corresponding roughly to the last year and a half of the Carter administration, the incipient Central America movement was made up of religious activists, secular leftists, and academic specialists on Latin America. Speaking tours by Central Americans or U.S. citizens with firsthand experience in the region put a human face on the crisis. For example, the Salvadoran FDR made a tour of the United States in mid-1980. One of the participants was Enríque Alvarez, the dairyman brutally murdered at the Jesuit high school along with five other leaders in November 1980.

The constellation of events in late 1980 and early 1981 — Ronald Reagan's election, the murder of the FDR leaders, the rape/murder of the U.S. church women, the murder of two U.S. labor advisors in El Salvador, the FMLN offensive, and U.S. reactions — all brought a new sense of urgency. By spring 1981 the Reagan administration's rhetoric was prompting fears of "regionalization": A U.S. intervention in, say, El Salvador, would tend to spread, as the Vietnam war had become an Indochina war.

The representative bodies of the Catholic church and virtually all mainstream Protestant denominations issued statements during this period, sometimes in congressional testimony, generally making similar points. In November 1981, for example, the U.S. Catholic bishops issued a statement on Central America, questioning whether the conflicts in Central America were correctly seen in an East-West framework. Basing their analysis on contact with the churches in Central America, they insisted that U.S. policy should be rooted in "an understanding of these internal realities and the way in which our policies and practices affect them." Citing Archbishops Romero and Rivera, they said "we are convinced that outside military assistance from any source to any party is not a useful contribution, but simply intensifies the cycle of violence." They also supported Rivera's appeals for peace and called for a moratorium on deportation of Salvadorans. Acknowledging the concerns of their Nicaraguan fellow bishops over human rights, they nevertheless urged that Nicaragua not be isolated, but instead be aided in its efforts at reconstruction. Virtually all mainline Protestant denominations took similar positions, questioning the thrust of Reagan administration policy.

Critics argued that ideological leftists, who did not represent the bulk of the people in the pews, had taken over church bureaucracies. In 1979 such dismay had led neoconservatives such as Richard John Neuhaus and Michael Novak to establish the Institute for Religion and Democracy (IRD). During the 1980s the IRD devoted more attention to Central America than to any other region. Church agencies took public stands on Central America, however, not because of an a priori position, but because their leaders had been dealing with development and human rights issues for years, had visited their counterparts in Third World countries, and maintained contact with them.

From the outset the "Central America movement" was a sprawling series of initiatives with no more than ad hoc coordination; its driving force was a fear that the region could become "another Vietnam." At the 1980 founding meeting of CISPES (Committee in Solidarity with the People of El Salvador) in Washington, D.C., a Salvadoran speaker noted that "a U.S. invasion in El Salvador could give rise to a large anti-war movement," but he went on to say, "We're asking you to stop it before it happens."

Developments in Central America and the effects of U.S. policy continued to prompt initiatives that then grew into movements and organizations, as can be seen from the following partial chronology, which emphasizes the role of faith-based solidarity.

CHRONOLOGY OF CENTRAL AMERICA SOLIDARITY

1970s	Rise of concern for human rights, especially through WOLA
1976–78	Hearings in U.S. Congress on human rights violations in Nicaragua and El Salvador
1979	Spring—establishment of Network in Solidarity with the People of Nicaragua
	July 19—fall of Somoza regime
	November—meeting of Nicaragua network in Detroit
1980	March 24—murder of Archbishop Romero; some church leaders attend funeral; shock and outrage when funeral is attacked
	Speaking tours by Central Americans
	Establishment of CISPES
	Murder of FDR leaders (November) and church women (December)
1981	January—murder of U.S. labor representatives; FMLN offensive; Ronald Reagan inaugurated president, determines to draw the line in El Salvador
	Spring—foundation of NISGUA (Network in Solidarity with the People of Guatemala)
	Establishment of Interreligious Task Force on Central America (New York-based, primarily Protestant) Religious Task Force on Central America (Washington-based, primarily Catholic)
	Reagan secretly approves $19.5 million for contras
1982	Southside Presbyterian church (Tucson) and University Lutheran Chapel (Berkeley) declare sanctuary for Central American refugees. Soon they are joined by dozens and then hundreds of church congregations, Quaker meetings, and synagogues.
	"Born-again" Efraín Rios Montt becomes president of Guatemala in coup, obtains support from conservative church organizations.

U.S. sponsorship of contra war becomes major public issue

1983   Pope John Paul II visits Central America, clashes with Sandinista supporters, supports bishops against "popular church."

Witness for Peace established with large vigil on July 4 in Jalapa, Nicaragua. Delegations organized by state begin to arrive every two or three weeks.

October — U.S. troops invade Grenada, overthrow government.

November — peacemakers' retreat leads to formation of Pledge of Resistance; tens of thousands of people pledge themselves to engage in nonviolent actions. Jim Wallis (*Sojourners* magazine): "if Reagan invades Nicaragua, he's going to have to put thousands of U.S. Christians in jail around the country."

1984   Kissinger Commission Report provides "bipartisan" justification for U.S. policy.

New York Times reports that United States has bases and installations for direct military involvement in Central America; CIA mines ports in Nicaragua; CIA-prepared contra manual advises "neutralization" (= murder) of pro-Sandinista civilians.

Trial of Sanctuary workers Stacey Merkt and Jack Elder

1985   Sanctuary trial in Tucson; eight of twelve defendants sentenced (in 1986)

World Court hears Nicaragua's case and rules against the United States and later orders restitution for mining of ports and contra war; Reagan administration has previously refused to accept judgment of World Court.

December — Quijote Center announces its intention of matching $27 million in contra aid with an equal amount of humanitarian aid to the victims; six hundred local organizations take part and meet that aim by mid-1986.

1986   Congress debates and at midyear passes $100 million in contra aid.

Crash of Eugene Hasenfus reveals CIA involvement in contra aid; Iran-contra scandal produces disarray in administration and makes further U.S. escalation in region unlikely.

1987	Pacifist Brian Willson run over by munitions train while protesting in California, loses his legs.
	Central America Peace Plan (Esquipulas II)
	Benjamin Linder killed by contras near Matagalpa
	First return of refugees to El Salvador; U.S. volunteers accompany them to border
1988	August—contras attack boat, killing two Nicaraguans and wounding Lucius Walker of IFCO (Intercommunity Foundation for Community Organization); IFCO counterattacks by organizing "Pastors for Peace," a caravan of twenty trucks with $350,000 in humanitarian aid.
1989	George Bush inaugurated president.
	Fall of communism in Eastern Europe precipitates end of Cold War and a new context for Central America.
	November—FMLN offensive; murder of Jesuits; intense persecution of church people; arrest and expulsion of pacifist Jennifer Casolo under accusation of hiding weapons

The 1985 *Directory of Central America Organizations* compiled by the Central America Resource Center (Austin) listed 850 organizations, ranging from national networks such as those already mentioned, to their local chapters, to many local groups and coalitions. All states had at least two such organizations, and California had 175. Many of the organizations were working directly with religious congregations.

Writing in July 1983, Gary MacEoin contrasted the Central America movement with the earlier anti-Vietnam war movement, whose natural constituency had been young people facing the draft. In the Central America movement the "main focus of opposition" was neither the "traditional liberal lobby" nor the "marginal leftist parties" but groups within the Catholic and Protestant churches. He found this to be a "historic change, especially for the Catholic Church which until recently had unquestioningly endorsed every U.S. foreign policy."

Much of the strength of the movement came from face-to-face encounters with Central Americans. Hundreds of thousands of refugees fleeing from the "dirty wars" in El Salvador and Guatemala came to the few centers where they had relatives and contacts: Los Angeles, Washington, D.C., San Francisco, New York, Long Island, Chicago, Houston, Miami. Chance encounters with some of them led to the Sanctuary Movement. Another chance encounter led to the formation of Witness for Peace, and over time hundreds and then thousands of Americans went to Nicaragua under its auspices. The Institute for Global Education and other organizations also took thousands of Americans on tours in which they met with development workers, small farmers, women's groups, church congregations, and political groups. Many people went to Nicaragua to participate in coffee picking brigades. Some were working in development projects or as health workers. State-wide campaigns organized by IFCO took Central Americans and Americans who had lived in Central America to classrooms and even to Rotary and Kiwanis meetings. By 1986 IFCO campaigns in seven states had organized 3,315 face-to-face events in 505 communities involving 114,786 people, according to the organization's tally sheets. Much of the organizational infrastructure for IFCO campaigns was supplied by churches. Coalitions periodically organized large-scale demonstrations in Washington and elsewhere, especially until 1983, but these were not the mainstay of the movement. Its strength lay rather in the hundreds of groups across the United States, which, for example, regularly held vigils outside the local federal building.

The specter of "another Vietnam," which had driven the movement from the outset, became all the more compelling after the U.S. invasion of Grenada, and as it became clear that in its new military installations in Honduras and elsewhere the United States had laid the basis for direct military action. The movement could point to polls repeatedly showing that two-thirds of the U.S. public disapproved of the Reagan administration's policy in Central America, particularly insofar as it seemed to be leading to deeper U.S. involvement. However, by invoking the specter of Marxism and claiming to be defending democracy the administration was able to send relatively vast sums of aid, largely military, to the region's governments and to fund the contra army. Opponents of the policy—and their allies in Congress—could only restrain the policy by imposing some conditions, such as the Boland amendment prohibiting covert aid to the contras. When the region's presidents signed the Central America Peace Plan in August 1987, solidarity groups worked against Reagan and Bush efforts to sabotage it.

Throughout the decade most solidarity was directed at Nicaragua. Far more Americans had been there and the levels of repression in El Salvador and Guatemala made solidarity with groups in those countries more difficult. However, the resurgence of popular organizations and new church pastoral activity were followed by new initiatives of solidarity. CRISPAZ (Christians for Peace) set up an office in El Salvador and quietly began to host visiting groups. Repopulation and repatriation efforts in 1986 and 1987 brought volunteers to share in the "accompaniment" of people newly returned to their lands. Numerous local organizations established sister-city and sometimes sister-church relationships with groups in El Salvador. Until the end of the 1980s such relationships were virtually impossible in Guatemala. One of the few such initiatives was Peace Brigades International (PBI), whose activity was to accompany members of the Mutual Support Group and others nonviolently in order to provide a measure of protection from abduction. The stabbing of three PBI volunteers in late 1989 seemed to be intended to send a message. Nevertheless, delegations from Witness for Peace and other organizations began to visit Guatemala as well.

New initiatives in people-to-people humanitarian aid were undertaken to offset in some small measure the wreckage left by U.S. policies. As the sense of urgency characteristic of the Reagan era faded—and especially after the 1990 electoral defeat of the Sandinistas—solidarity networks and organizations were hit by financial crisis. Writing in *The Nation* in November 1990, Alexander Cockburn noted that direct mail appeals and support from progressive foundations were falling off drastically. Funding for the Nicaragua Network, for example, was down 40 percent. Tecnica, which had sent more than $5 million in aid and had been sending three hundred people a year to provide technical aid for development projects, was forced to close.

Without the thousands of activists in hundreds of organizations throughout the United States who organized demonstrations, lobbied their representatives, and communicated through the media, the Reagan administration would probably have sent U.S. troops to intervene in Nicaragua or El Salvador with unforeseeable consequences. That was scant consolation, however, since the U.S. aim of halting revolution was ultimately attained through other means.

The struggles recounted in this book and the fate of the peoples of Central America are irreversibly intertwined with the United States. Certainly the relationship is asymmetrical: U.S. policy wreaked havoc in the region for a decade, and in the 1990s actions by the U.S. government (pressing for prosecution of the Jesuit murder case, holding up aid, free trade agreements) continue to be decisive for Central Americans, whereas Central American actors have little impact in the United States, especially after the demise of the (always absurd) "threat" of Marxism.

The Central America movement was fueled by more than altruism. During a delegation to Honduras and Nicaragua in 1987, I remember noting that half the participants were not first-time visitors. They were returning, primarily, it seemed, to "recharge their batteries," as one woman put it. They found inspiration in the example of a tiny poor country like Nicaragua whose government even in the midst of a war was attempting to make meeting the basic needs of the poor its paramount concern. Their own government was meanwhile hastening to dismantle as much as it could of its own safety net and presiding over policies that made the rich richer and the poor more desperate.

The experience of solidarity with Central America has led to other initiatives. Witness for Peace and the Center for Global Education have continued to organize tours to the Middle East and elsewhere. In early 1991 Ed Griffin-Nolan, who had spent years documenting contra attacks in Nicaragua, was sent to Iraq to document the effects of U.S. bombing on the civilian population for Witness for Peace. Indeed, the 1991 Gulf War emphasized how the emerging international order was both a break from and in continuity with the Cold War that had justified U.S. policies. Even though the "Evil Empire" was no more, the Iraqi regime—with which the United States had long collaborated—was demonized; the United States and its allies used overwhelming technological superiority to destroy what was a Third World army exposed on the desert; and civilians paid the highest price during the attack and in the disease and chaos that followed.

A Radical "No"—"They Can't Cut the Spring"

Not only is there no qualitatively new kind of society being built; in the post-Cold War world, the very possibility of a different kind of society is ignored or dismissed.

In 1991 representatives from a number of private Central American development agencies gathered in Washington, D.C., at the invitation of WOLA in order to discuss the impact of geopolitical and economic changes on their work. I watched a State Department official state with utter aplomb, "We know what works: markets and electoral democracy." His implication was that the problem of development has been solved: If Central Americans failed to fit into the "new world order," the fault would be theirs alone.

Central American countries were becoming "normal" Latin American countries once more. The whole continent had suffered a "lost decade" during the 1980s in which the so-called debt crisis was one element in an overall economic crisis. Prices for exports vis-à-vis manufactured imports declined; import substitution industrialization had reached its limits. Country after country accepted the major policy changes dictated by international lending agencies as a condition for new loans: Privatize state enterprises, free the market by lifting price controls, cut government payroll and social spending (but not the military), increase exports so as to earn foreign exchange. Such measures were intended to enable governments to pay at least their debt service and thus avert a potential collapse of the international financial system. They were also, so it was argued, a bitter medicine that had to be taken in order to prepare these countries for economic recovery. It was hardly surprising that the poor bore the burden; as unemployment increased, even government schools charged fees and became prohibitively expensive, and public health services were cut back. The cholera epidemic in Peru and elsewhere was simply one indication of how the "neoliberal" economic policies were aggravating the crisis.

Military governments one by one ceded to a tide of "democratization"—which might more accurately have been called "civilianization." Governments were once more in the hands of elected civilians, undoubtedly as a result of pressure from organized society, but also because the military found it convenient to let civilians deal with seemingly intractable economic dilemmas. The postmilitary governments could do little to improve the lot of the poor, and the power of business elites remained largely intact. In Brazil, for example, landholders could have farmworker agitators murdered with impunity; runaway inflation hardly mattered to the very wealthy since they had holdings in dollars and could speculate on currency markets.

By 1993 the U.S. business press was running upbeat stories about Latin America, the region in the world whose stock exchanges recorded the greatest growth. According to *Forbes*, between 1991 and 1992 the number of Latin American billionaires jumped from eight to twenty-one. Around the continent leadership was said to be passing to a new generation of people in their thirties, most of whom hold degrees in economics from prestigious U.S. universities and who know their counterparts around the continent. They have abandoned the statism of their elders and are enthusiastic advocates of market liberalization. All such press accounts ritually noted that the good economic news has not benefited the poor majority. Societies were being further polarized into a few winners and a majority of losers.

Becoming "normal" Latin American countries again did not mean that Central America was returning to the pre-1979 situation. The North American Free Trade Agreement between the United States, Canada, and Mexico was being seen and promoted as a step toward fashioning a single market reaching from Alaska to Patagonia. For Latin America such a development would entail an economic shift as momentous as the one that took place in the 1930s when the larger countries consciously adopted policies aimed at developing their own industries (import substitution).

Latin American left parties and intellectuals were at a loss in the new situation and did not have clear alternatives to propose. The Chilean left, for example, did not propose changing the export orientation established by the Pinochet regime, but simply sought to shift government priorities more toward social spending in order to ameliorate poverty directly.

Even as it remained doubtful whether left parties had a clear alternative, they were advancing in the new framework of electoral politics. In 1988 the coalition around the candidacy of Cuahtemoc Cárdenas in Mexico seriously challenged the PRI's (Institutional Revolutionary Party) longstanding one-party rule. In Brazil the following year the Workers Party (PT) candidate Lula (Luís Inácio da Silva) came within four percentage points of winning the presidency. After President Collor's impeachment on grounds of corruption in 1992, Lula was the most popular politician in the country. The PT and other left parties and candidates were the electoral outgrowth of a multiplicity of emerging grassroots movements (labor, neighborhoods, women, indigenous, ecology). What they would — or would be permitted to — accomplish if elected was by no means clear.

In mid-1992 a group of theologians and social scientists met in Spain to consider the new situation of the Catholic church in Latin America. The Chilean political scientist Miguel Antonio Garretón summarized: "We have moved — with a great deal of hardship and suffering — from guerrilla struggle, revolution, ways to socialism, civil war in some more tragic instances, and military dictatorships with state terrorism, to the struggle to rebuild institutional frameworks, thus making it possible to enter or reenter the democratic political game." The best symbol of what was happening was Nicaragua, "which went from being the last of the revolutions to one of the last transitions to democracy . . . [through] . . . elections." Two decades of experience had shown that growth or development by themselves did not bring greater equality, democracy, or social integration; those political models that attempted redistribution through revolution had likewise failed. The new situation of Latin America in the 1990s demanded squaring the circle, "effecting a kind of social change entailing redistribution of power and wealth, but doing it by democratic methods, that is, by formulas that do not eliminate conflict, but that come from an institutional framework and certain basic consensual agreements." Overcoming the categories of the past would entail a "multidimensional view of society" and realizing that "the most utopian goals can always be partially attained." Garretón's relatively sanguine view reflected the situation in Chile, which had successfully pursued an economic strategy based on identifying niches for its products in world trade, although many Chileans did not share in the new growth.

José Comblin described the period from the meeting of the bishops at Puebla (1979) to the present as one of "ambiguity, uneasiness, and uncertainty." The new democracies that had replaced military dictatorships had led to the anguishing impression that "all paths are blocked off." He listed features of the early 1990s: "a peculiar kind of democracy, the triumph of neoliberalism, the rise of charismatic presidents, the new attitude of large urban masses, the demobilization of social movements, a youth that is depoliticized, the seemingly immense power of television." Base communities had arisen among rural small farmers and factory workers. However, small farmers are rapidly disappearing, as youth leave the land for the cities, and deindustrialization is leaving workers in a weaker position. In such a context talk of liberation sounds like empty rhetoric that does not lead to action.

Xabier Gorostiaga, a Jesuit economist who worked in Nicaragua throughout the 1980s, noted that the twenty years that had passed since a similar meeting at El Escorial seemed like a century. Indeed that might be the case "since we are now in the twenty-first century, and the historic, geo-political, and geo-economic axes are qualitatively different from those we experienced twenty years ago." The "dematerializing" of production as a result of the technological revolution means that the South's raw materials and cheap labor are worth even less. The gap between North and South is widening. A supranational global elite, organized around the Group of Seven wealthy nations and international agencies, manages the international economy. Their control is reinforced by ideology and cultural mechanisms. "Big Mac democracy is also producing a Big Mac Christianity and a Big Mac culture."

Countries that raised hopes for something new, like Nicaragua and El Salvador in the 1980s, had to be not only destroyed but discredited. The "geo-culture of despair and the theology of inevitability" must now be spread everywhere to serve the "new restructuring promoted by the global power elite." With the end of the Cold War it is no longer necessary to stigmatize an "evil empire," but countries of the South and those who share with them "an alternative horizon of hope for the twenty-first century" have to be demonized as the "evil slum."

Despite the "lost decade" of the 1980s—which in Nicaragua meant losing three or four decades—these years brought some positive results, especially the emergence of the impoverished masses as actors. Here Gorostiaga had a more hopeful reading than Comblin. Because these actors are diverse, with a multiplicity of interests, they cannot be simply led by a single vanguard group. Leninism broke down in Latin America before the crisis in Eastern Europe. The failure of neoliberal economic policies and the crisis of a number of the new democracies might open the way to alternatives on the left.

The upshot was that Latin Americans had to elaborate their own agenda. They must demand that international institutions, like the World Bank, and likewise technology and knowledge, be democratized. Rather than wholesale integration into free trade schemes, which are unfair since the wealthy countries practice the protectionism that they profess to oppose, Latin America and the South should be incorporated into the world economy "selectively and in accordance with the phasing and demands of their own chosen course."

Nevertheless, Gorostiaga admitted that Latin America did not have a clear-cut alternative. He invoked the cry of the sixteenth-century Dominican friar Antonio de Montesinos protesting the conquest of the Indians: "By what authority, by what justice?" He then quoted Pablo Neruda (who was himself referring to the Mayan text, the Popul Vuh): "They can cut all the flowers but they can't cut the spring." On another occasion he told a Peruvian interviewer that the great temptation is despair and that "the empire wants to manipulate hope. 'There's no solution but mine, so be pragmatic,' it's telling us. I think that the answer to this imperial pragmatism has to be a bold pragmatism, that is, pragmatism with utopia."

Indeed, while formerly radical Latin American social scientists were becoming "realists," theologians were among those protesting most vigorously the direction being taken in the post-Cold War world. In the course of a theological essay prompted by the publication of the United Nations Truth Commission in El Salvador, Jon Sobrino noted that the very notion of "utopia" had lost respectability, especially in the First World, but that it is "essential for us." The very existence of hope in El Salvador is crucially important. "Perhaps they now want to make it disappear" or make it no longer so central, "that is, they want to replace it with moderate optimism which at best would come as the result of working together, tolerance, forgetting, pragmatism, realism." Such things are important but without hope they lose their meaning. Sobrino was speaking about hope in a theological key "because today it seems that only in theology is there room for observations of this sort, whereas elsewhere they are regarded with reserve and suspicion, if not with contempt."

Ignacio Ellacuría had anticipated some of these concerns in his final public address, given in Spain in November 1989. He argued that the current "tidal wave of ideology" — he was speaking days before the Berlin Wall became rubble — had to be unmasked. Reiterating convictions that he had developed elsewhere, he stated that the present capitalist civilization is failing on several grounds: The gap between rich and poor is increasing on all levels; exploitation and oppression are becoming harsher, although more sophisticated; present patterns are leading to ecological breakdown.

The crucial flaw in the present order is the fact that it "cannot be universalized": There are simply not enough material resources on the planet to allow all of humankind to consume at the level of the wealthy 25 percent of the world population. The life style of the wealthy minority is "motivated by fear and insecurity, by inner emptiness, by the need to dominate so as not to be dominated, by the urge to exhibit what one has since one cannot communicate what one is." Far from indicating how to "overcome poverty, let alone injustice," the developed world "is the sign of what should not be and of what should not be done."

The underdeveloped world is enduring the most aggravated forms of what is wrong with capitalism, symbolized by repeated efforts by industrialized countries to dispose of their toxic wastes in poor countries. Only a new order that can be universalized is acceptable. Such a new civilization will not be based on capital accumulation — whether by individuals, corporations, or nation-states — or on the possession of wealth, but rather on the satisfaction of basic needs through human labor in solidarity.

This vision is more compelling in what it condemns — the present order, which excludes a majority of human beings — than in what it proposes. Ellacuría acknowledged the failings of existing socialist regimes and even noted that "liberation theology has on occasions been naive and tolerant towards the theory and practice of Marxism because of a certain inferiority complex vis-à-vis the commitment of the revolutionaries." As signs of where this new order might be coming from Ellacuría pointed to the poor in refugee camps, displaced people, and people in marginal communities who despite everything were seeking to "begin anew."

In mid-1993 Pablo Richard, a Chilean theologian who had lived in Central America from the late 1970s, spoke in much the same vein. Few people were noting, he argued, that the failure of "development capitalism" in the South was as significant as the failure of "historic socialisms" in the East. With the fall of socialism, capitalism no longer needs to claim to be generating development; the result is "savage capitalism" (a term borrowed from Pope John Paul II), which "leaves many people on the outside looking in" and destroys nature as well.

In the current crisis of hope in which the market is absolutized, liberation theology must rebuild hope. Although its very belief in a God of life makes it utopian, today "more than ever it must be utopian, within the context of the new international order, which radically destroys all utopias."

Richard said that Latin American theology must "move beyond prophecy." The biblical prophets issued their warnings within an "organized world" that included the monarchy, the city, the temple, law, and tribes. However, after the destruction of this world in Samaria and Jerusalem in the sixth century B.C., there arose an apocalyptic literature to encourage hope and resistance to the empire. Richard suggested that while not ceasing to be prophetic, liberation theology was moving toward a more apocalyptic function.

Such sweeping observations presenting matters in such polar opposites leave me somewhat frustrated; it is hard to know what to do with them. Nevertheless, I find them to be an essential tonic for the present moment when the message seems to be so strongly: "This is all there is and all there can be." On the basis of faith more than on social science, these theologians are refusing to sing in unison and are insisting that it must be possible to organize society in such a way that all human beings are assured of a minimally decent human life.

The Grace of Resistance

Even before the events of 1989 and 1990 church people in Central America were realizing that such a world will not come about primarily as the result of the seizure of state power. Some of its features can be seen in the myriad of modest steps people are taking to become organized, work for their own survival, and defend their rights. I will close with a few examples of such hope in action.

Let us consider first the release of the report of the United Nations Truth Commission in El Salvador, as interpreted theologically by Jon Sobrino. The peace agreement signed at the end of 1991 stipulated that a Truth Commission to be made up of respected and impartial non-Salvadorans was to investigate some of the most notorious cases of human rights violations. On April 30, 1993, the commission published its findings on thirty-two such cases, including the murders of Archbishop Romero, the UCA Jesuits, the Sumpul and Mozote massacres, and some acts by the FMLN.

Acknowledging some of the report's limitations—for example, it does not mention the oligarchy that was certainly behind the death squads—Sobrino calls the report "a genuine victory of the truth over lying." It is a "good news for the poor," a "grace, insofar as it is gift, unexpected, miraculous." The Truth Commission did not come out of a vacuum, but is itself the outgrowth of a tradition of those who courageously told the truth. "To speak the truth . . . is an important way of expressing love for the people." Indeed, the Salvadoran people themselves have forged that truth.

Unfortunately, Sobrino notes, not only was the report attacked and ignored, but it was undermined by an amnesty proposed by President Cristiani and rapidly approved by the Salvadoran assembly, on the grounds that the country needed to "forgive and forget." The issue, Sobrino counters, is not to forget the past but to break with it, and an overhasty amnesty does not serve that end. From a Christian standpoint, moreover, forgiveness comes only after the sin has been confessed. While the FMLN had indeed admitted its wrongdoing and asked forgiveness, there had been no such admission on the government side.

The upshot is that people "wonder whether things are not going to go on as always, since the winners are the same as ever; whether such enormous suffering has been worthwhile, since the military are doing as they please; whether there is any solution for the country, since the powerful continue to make laws to make the rich richer while ignoring the poor."

His final reflections are on hope, which he describes as strength for journeying toward utopia. The report and especially its recommendations (for example, that those guilty of the worst violations be discharged) point toward that utopia. Ordinary poor people, the crucified people, those who suffer the evils of the present, are the bearers of that utopia. Yet all are called to make such hope a reality, even the military. Thus, "those who have power should put it at the service of those who have hope, and those who have hope should guide society in the right direction."

Some might dismiss Sobrino's observations as theological prestidigitation, a word-game to distract from the reality of an entrenched oligarchy and an unrepentant military. I believe—and hope—that he is pointing to a real advance, one that seemed impossible a few years previously, and is pointing ahead to where the struggle must continue.

The continuing struggle of Communities of Population in Resistance (CPRs) in Guatemala offers another example of the laborious forging of a different kind of society. In the early 1980s, as thousands of Guatemalans left their villages and fled to Mexico and beyond, some remained within Guatemala, living on the run from the army. Throughout the 1980s they managed to survive and formed communities in three areas: north of the Ixil triangle, in the Ixcán lowlands, and in the Petén near the river that constitutes the border with Mexico. In so doing they became a powerful symbol of resistance. The army portrayed them as URNG supporters or as captives forced to supply food or provide a human shield, and repeatedly directed campaigns against them, especially the "end of the year campaign" in 1987 into early 1988. Over the years sisters and priests visited and lived with them, sometimes helping them obtain resources. Bishop Julio Cabrera and some other bishops defended their rights and maintained contact with them.

Living under continual threat of military attack and cut off from normal commerce and government services, these communities of necessity have become highly organized. They established schools taught by community members despite the lack of basic supplies such as pencils. Their health clinics combined traditional and Western medicine. They farmed both individual and communal plots but army harassment prevented them from selling their surplus. The communities were run by a committee structure at local and regional levels. Sentries and roving patrols were always on duty, ready to detect signs of army incursions. Communities were prepared to evacuate at a moment's notice, carrying only the most basic items, rather like the *guindas* in El Salvador.

In September 1990 the communities of the Ixil triangle made a public statement demanding that their rights as civilians be respected in Guatemala; those in the Ixcán and the Peten made similar public statements in January and October 1991. They asked that military activity in their area be suspended and army posts withdrawn; that they be allowed to travel within Guatemala and to receive visitors; that the civil patrols and other army measures be suspended; and that CPR members illegally captured by the army be released.

Church organizations, particularly the bishops' conference, CONFRE-GUA, and CIEDEG joined with popular (UASP) development and human rights organizations to form what was called the Multi-Partite Commission to support the CPRs. The government's human rights ombudsman, Ramiro de León Carpio, visited the CPRs in 1991 and also spoke in their defense. However, the CPRs rejected his proposal for reincorporation into Guatemalan life because they saw it as too close to counterinsurgency.

On February 15, 1993, four hundred people departed from Guatemala City to make a public visit to the CPRs, half to the Ixil highlands and half to the Ixcán. Participating were Catholic church figures including bishops, Protestant pastors, representatives of labor and popular organizations, journalists, and visitors from fourteen countries. At a mass in Quiché Bishop Cabrera told the delegation, "Wash your feet, because the land where you are going is holy land, watered with the blood of countless martyrs. You are going to meet crucified Christs from the Communities of Population in Resistance, to see them with your own eyes, to hear them and to touch them. You are going to help them come down from the cross and offer your solidarity to them. Pay attention to them; they have much to teach us. They have been formed in the school of suffering." Cabrera went at the head of the delegation.

Passing through Nebaj they continued to Chajul, where they found the electricity cut off to stir up resentment against the CPRs among the townspeople. Despite threats from the leaders of the civil defense patrols, local people welcomed the delegation. They continued to the army-occupied town of Chel—now in effect a concentration camp holding civilians captured from the CPRs by the army—where civil patrollers fired machine guns hoping to intimidate them. The following day they continued toward the area of Caba, where they then spent three days with the people of the CPRs. By publicly deepening CPR ties through international solidarity, this visit helped make the Guatemalan military realize that the costs of extreme repression would increase.

For more than a decade Guatemalan Jesuit anthropologist Ricardo Falla worked pastorally with Guatemalan Indians who had fled to Mexico and with the CPRs inside the country. In all his anthropological work he sought to put his research at the service of the people. In October 1992 (coinciding with the five-hundredth-year anniversary of the conquest) the national university published his book, *Massacres de la Selva*, which painstakingly documents the army's scorched earth campaigns in the Ixcán, especially in the early 1980s. The very fact that it was published in Guatemala was an unprecedented step, forcing open the space of the permissible since the unwritten rules of the game forbid accusing the army of violence. The army absurdly claimed that it had been written by Rolando Morán, the commander-in-chief of the EGP.

In January 1993 President Serrano presented documents allegedly found by the army at an EGP camp that linked the EGP with the refugees and CPRs and accused Falla of being a "Comandante Marcos." In response, Falla said that indeed the people called him "Marcos," but that in late November the army had seized his writings when it attacked the CPRs using the same kinds of scorched earth tactics he documented in his book. Among the items taken were a cache of his documents (including marriage and baptism records); he insisted that they be returned. His Jesuit superiors and the Guatemalan bishops assured that Falla's pastoral work was known and approved.

In reflecting on his pastoral work, Falla invoked the term "accompaniment," which he said means following Jesus, whom "today we do not see . . . in the flesh even though He is risen. We only see Him in our brothers and sisters, who are everyone, but especially the persecuted and the poorest. . . . Therefore . . . we have to follow our persecuted brothers and sisters to the limits of our strength, both physically and spiritually. This is the root of accompaniment by the Church which does pastoral work among people in resistance."

Such work means staying with the people, who are surrounded by military posts and cannot go to market. It means being isolated with the people and "experiencing the constant threat of attack that the people experience every day." One has to be ever ready to react to the buzz of helicopters, and, for example, take drying clothes out of the sun. Those in accompaniment must endure attacks and periods of living on the run.

Accompaniment is not limited to a silent presence, but entails providing the Word of God, "leading the people to green pastures, providing them with spiritual nourishment. The center is Jesus Christ, his life, death, and resurrection." Falla said that in women's classes he and the catechists ask whether any present have had to give birth while on the run. Someone always tells her own story; the group can then identify with Mary, who fled with Joseph when Herod ordered that male infants be killed.

Falla regarded his documentation of the massacres in Ixcán as "good news": The good news, he said, is that despite the massacres "we are alive."

He further saw the communities of the CPRs as analogous to the early Christian communities, since life was "egalitarian and very communal." Food stocks were shared according to need; basic supplies of corn were distributed according to family size, although individual households cooked for themselves. Resistance, said Falla, was a gift of God and a struggle for life. The people had succeeded in overcoming their suffering through their heroic faith. He said he was content if his "pastoral work has been able to help nourish this faith."

Finally, consider events in Guatemala in May and June 1993. President Jorge Serrano, whose evangelical image had eroded considerably two and a half years into his term, suspended the Guatemalan congress and judicial system in a "self-coup." Appealing to public disgust over the corruption and inefficiency of the Guatemalan congress, and claiming that his move was necessary to halt corruption and drug traffic, he apparently hoped to emulate President Alberto Fujimori of Peru, who had capitalized on popular sentiment in a similar maneuver in 1991. However, he may have been acting preemptively so as not to suffer the fate of President Fernando Collor of Brazil, who had been impeached in 1992, and President Carlos Andrés Pérez of Venezuela, who was indicted for corruption and forced to step down.

The army supported Serrano's move—to what extent officers were behind the coup was disputed—but miscalculated the degree of opposition it would arouse. Virtually all sectors of society protested: politicians, the media (now being censored), business, Catholic and Protestant church people, and the popular sectors.

In the thick of the confrontation was Rigoberta Menchú, who in 1992 had won the Nobel Peace Prize, much to the chagrin of the military and Serrano. She was the daughter of the catechist Vicente Menchú, who was burned alive in the 1980 Spanish embassy massacre. The army had burned her brother to death in 1979 and raped and killed her mother in 1980. She herself had been a catechist and then a CUC organizer until she left Guatemala. By 1982 she was part of the civilian opposition in exile and spent each fall in New York as part of a five-person group lobbying United Nations delegations to put Guatemalan human rights violations on the organization's agenda. Over the years she became a politically sophisticated spokesperson, while retaining the strength of her ties to Guatemala's Indians and poor. People around the world came to know her through her autobiography, which had been translated into several languages.

When international opposition to the self-coup, including that of the Clinton administration in Washington, indicated that Guatemala would be isolated, Serrano had little choice but to resign. In the process of deciding the next step, the military and business sectors ignored the popular organizations, and Menchú and other leaders stomped out of negotiations. The attempt to replace Serrano with Gustavo Espina, his vice-president who had supported Serrano's self-coup, led to further popular resistance and potential international isolation.

On June 4 the Guatemalan bishops' conference articulated the feelings of many Guatemalans when they spoke of the still unresolved "institutional crisis," which revealed a "serious imbalance in the powers guiding the country." They went on to mention the "disproportionate power of the army," which thus decides the fate of the country on its own. Yet they discerned some positive features of the moment, such as the reaction of some agencies of the government and some individuals. Ramiro de Leon Carpio, the human rights ombudsman, to whom they alluded, had made a bold rooftop escape, and was serving as a symbol of resistance.

The bishops said that in such a critical and complex moment it would be a serious mistake to continue with the longstanding practice of "arranging everything at the top, on the basis of political deals, or ties of personal loyalty, or under the table arrangements." The "cry of the people" should be heeded. "It is truly regrettable that the popular, labor, and student organizations were left out of the negotiations seeking a just and worthy way out of the present situation." Those who guide the country should be the first to obey its laws and constitution; hence those who have flagrantly broken or helped break the constitutional order, violated the country's laws, and led the nation to a chaotic and despairing situation should be absolutely prohibited from leading the country." This stand by the bishops was in line with the sentiment of most Guatemalans.

The army thus found itself in a ticklish situation: Forces within Guatemala and outside, including the U.S. government, did not regard the hasty installation of the vice-president as a return to democracy. The Guatemalan congress met to consider whom to elect as president. Ramiro de León, the human rights ombudsman who had escaped from house arrest, was now elected president. De León was not a human rights activist but a politician who had been chosen for the ombudsman post by the Cerezo government, to some extent to blunt human rights criticism. He had grown in the process, however, and enjoyed the respect of those struggling for human rights, including Rigoberta Menchú. This turn of events was not a revolution. The murder of his cousin, newspaper owner and former presidential candidate Jorge Carpio, three weeks later sent a clear message. Nevertheless, a human rights advocate was now president and the once all-powerful military was being constrained by an Indian woman.

NOTES

Introduction

Murder of Jesuits: Instituto de Estudios Centroamericanos and El Rescate, *The Jesuit Assassinations: The Writings of Ellacuría, Martín-Baró and Segundo Montes, with a Chronology of the Investigation*; for further references, see notes to Chapter Three.

1. Wager of Faith

For this whole chapter: Phillip Berryman, *The Religious Roots of Rebellion: Christians in Central American Revolutions*; Urioste: interview, San Salvador, July 1990.

A Church Both Strong and Weak: syncretism: Leonardo Boff, *Church: Charism and Power*, all of Chapter Eight; Santo Domingo story: interview with Donald Mendoza in Leon, Nicaragua, August 1989; post-independence weakening of the Catholic church: although the Assembly of God arrived in El Salvador in 1912, its expansion came later.

Crisis Rooted in History: among the numerous works, a selection: Ralph Lee Woodward, Jr., *Central America: A Nation Divided*, James Dunkerley, *Power in the Isthmus: A Political History of Modern Central America*, Morris J. Blachman, William M. LeGrande, and Kenneth Sharpe, *Confronting Revolution: Security through Diplomacy in Central America*, Robert G. Williams, *Export Agriculture and the Crisis in Central America*, John A. Booth and Thomas W. Walker, *Understanding Central America*.

Pastoral Work as Liberation: Juanita: author's visit to Ciudad Segundo Montes, July 1990; Gutiérrez speech in Hennelly, *Liberation Theology: A Documentary History,* pp. 62-76; pastoral team in Izabal: author's visits in late 1970s, and "La Iglesia de los pobres en las parroquias de Morales y Bananera, Quiriguá y los Amates (Izabal)" (typescript, 39 pp.); Operation Uspantán: interview, Guatemala City, August 1990; for a published account of El Salvador, Pedro Henríquez, *El Salvador: Iglesia Profética y Cambio Social*.

Cycles of Struggle: in greater detail in Berryman, *Religious Roots* with sources.

2. Nicaragua: Vicissitudes of Revolution

D'Escoto and Cuadra: interviews, July 1990; early period of revolution: author's visits to Nicaragua, starting in 1967; Berryman, *Religious Roots;* bishops' July letter and responses: *Noticias Aliadas*, September 6, 1979, and September 20, 1979, reprinted in

CRIE (Centro Regional de Información Ecuménica), nos. 76–77 (July 1981): 5; November letter of bishops: Carta Pastoral del Episcopado Nicaraguense ("Christian Commitment for a New Nicaragua"), in Alfred T. Hennelly, ed., *Liberation Theology*, pp. 282–91; Protestant pastors' RIPEN statement: *La Prensa*, October 6, 1979; "72-Hour Document": " 'The 72-Hour Document': The Sandinista Blueprint for Constructing Communism in Nicaragua—A Translation" (Washington, D.C.: Coordinator of Public Diplomacy for Latin America and the Caribbean, 1986); September conference: proceedings in IHCA (Instituto Historico Centroamericano), *Fe Cristiana y Revolucion Sandinista en Nicaragua*; Casalis sermon: interview at CEPAD, July 1990; second thoughts on slogans: "The Catholic Church in Nicaragua and the Revolution: A Chronology," *Envío*, no. 30 (December 1983): 5b–6b.

First Clashes: The 1980–81 period is covered in greater detail in Berryman, *Religious Roots*, pp. 237–67; "Christians for the Revolution" document: "Los cristianos interpelan a la Revolución" (pamphlet, Managua, 1981); Borge at rally: author's observation, February 1981; Giaconda and Humberto Belli: *La Prensa*, September 17 and 18, 1980; Betto and Cardenal: *La Prensa*, August 4, 1980; 6,500 items: *Envío*, no. 30 (December 1983): 13b; FSLN statement: "Comunicado oficial de la Dirección Nacional del FSLN sobre la Religión," *Barricada*, October 7, 1980 (translation in Hennelly, *Liberation Theology*, pp. 318–22); bishops' response in *CRIE*, no. 61 (November 11, 1980); Cuapa and "sweating Virgin": *Envío*, no. 30 (December 1983): 11b, 13b–14b; see also Edward Sheehan, *Agony in the Garden: A Stranger in Central America*; Enders visit: Roy Gutmau, *Banana Diplomacy*, pp. 66-73.

Contra Complications: Christopher Dickey, *With the Contras*, Holly Sklar, *Washington's War on Nicaragua*, Roy Gutman, *Banana Diplomacy*; Atlantic coast conflicts: Philippe Bourgois, "Ethnic Minorities," in Walker, ed., *Nicaragua: The First Five Years*; Justiniano Liebl, "Viejo silencio de Obispos fue roto 'repentinamente' " *El Nuevo Diario*, February 22, 1982; Margaret Wilde, "The Church as Advocate in Eastern Nicaragua," *The Christian Century*, January 6–13, 1982, and "Church Crisis Mounts in Eastern Nicaragua," *Christian Century*, April 28, 1983; John Paul II letter: reprinted in Hennelly, ed., *Liberation Theology*, pp. 329–34; August 1982 conflicts: author's observations and Nicaraguan dailies; San Francisco del Norte: Witness for Peace, "Bitter Witness," pp. 24–34; Barredas: "Bitter Witness," pp. 40–51, and Teófilo Cabestrero, *Dieron la Vida por Su Pueblo*.

John Paul II Confronted (or Insulted?): Margaret Wilde, *Christian Century*, March 23–30, 1983; addresses: Juan Pablo II, *Mensajes a Centro America*; International Observers, "Open Letter Regarding the Papal Mass," in Hennelly, ed., *Liberation Theology*, pp. 335–37; *Envío*, no. 30 (December 1983): 16b–17b; *CRIE*, no. 120 (March 1983), reprints many newspaper accounts of the event, survey: IHCA Chronology (1984), p. 9b note; Philip J. Williams, "The Catholic Church in the Nicaraguan Revolution: Differing Responses and New Challenges," in Mainwaring and Wilde, eds., *The Progressive Church in Latin America*, pp. 68ff; statistics on p. 78.

Responses to War: Ortega figures and Pantasma: Witness for Peace, "Bitter Witness," pp. 54, 66–100; Reagan speech: *New York Times*, April 28, 1983; Obando quote: *El Nuevo Diario*, May 18, 1983, reprinted in *CRIE*, no. 126 (June 14, 1983); draft law: decree in *Barricada Internacional*, August 22, 1983, and response of bishops' conference, *El Nuevo Diario*, September 1, 1983, both reprinted in *CRIE*, no. 132 (September 6, 1983); response of lay group: *Amanecer*, no. 20; October 9; procession, Baptist Convention statement, conflicts in parishes: *Amanecer*, no. 21, in *CRIE*, no. 138 (November 22, 1983); non-Catholics and conscientious objection: interviews, 1989, 1990.

"Reconciliation" Call Widens Gap: bishops' letter: *CRIE*, no. 150 (May 22, 1984) (translation in Hennelly, ed., *Liberation Theology*, pp. 375–80); ministry of interior note: *Envío*, no. 38 (August 1984): 6c; Dominicans and Jesuits: *CRIE*, no. 152 (June 19, 1984); Peña case: *Proceso* (Mexico City), July 16, 1984, in *CRIE*, no. 154 (July 17, 1984); ten priests close to Obando: interview, Managua, July 1990; Humberto Belli: *Breaking Faith*, pp. 226–27; election process: LASA (Latin American Studies Association), *The Electoral Process in Nicaragua: Domestic and International Influences* (Austin, Tex.: LASA, 1984), summary in Walker, ed., *Nicaragua;* nuncio statement: *Envío*, no. 50 (August 1985).

Managua and Rome: Fernando Cardenal, "A Letter to My Friends," in Hennelly, ed., *Liberation Theology*, pp. 341–47; summary of situation of priests in government: "Two Models of Church: Chronology of the Catholic Church in Nicaragua–August '84– July '85," *Envío*, no. 50 (August 1985): 6b–9b; Obando made cardinal: *Envío*, no. 50 (August 1985) and no. 58 (April 1986); d'Escoto fast: *CRIE*, nos. 174–176 (August 6–September 17, 1985) and Pedro Casaldáliga, *Prophets in Combat*; events in later 1985: IHCA, "Church-State Relations: A Chronology–Part I," *Envío*, no. 77 (November 1987): 29ff.; march from Jalapa: ibid., pp. 33–37; Penny Lernoux, "Polarization, Confusion Ravage Nicaragua," *National Catholic Reporter*, May 16, 1986; Obando op-ed, *Washington Post*, May 12, 1986, cited in IHCA, "Church-State Relations . . . I," *Envío*, no. 77 (November 1987): 38; Vega statement: ibid., p. 39; killing the soul: IHCA: "Two Models of Church," *Envío* no. 50 (August 1985) 3b–4b; events around passage of $100 million in contra aid: IHCA, "Church-State Relations . . . I," *Envío*, no. 77 (November 1987): 38–42; new nuncio: author's meeting with nuncio, August 1987, and "Church-State Relations: A Chronology–Part II," *Envío*, no. 78 (December 1987): 32–39; *Newsweek* story, Virgin of Cuapa, Vega radio broadcast, Zavaleta killing: IHCA, "Chronology . . . II" *Envío*, no. 78 (December 1987): 40, 43–44.

Winding Path toward Peace: López Vigil: interview, August 1989; role of churches in reconcilation process: *CEPAD Newsletter*, nos. 38–41 (August–November 1987); figures on church workers on committees: *Envío*, no. 78 (December 1987): 48; Blandón and Tiffer: *CEPAD Newsletter*, no. 42 (December 1987); Avila: *CEPAD Report*, no. 41; negotiations and Sapoa: William Goodfellow and Jim Morrell, "From Contadora to Sapoá and Beyond," in Walker, *Revolution and Counterrevolution in Nicaragua;* "The 'Plan Melton': A Chronology of Relevant Events" (photocopy); discussion of Obando and money: Irene Selser, *Cardenal Obando*, esp. Appendixes nine and ten; hyperinflation: Joseph Ricciardi, "Economic Policy," in Walker, *Revolution and Counterrevolution in Nicaragua;* 1990 election: Jerez: interview, Philadelphia, March 1990; *Envío*, no. 104 (March–April 1990): 3–14 30–42; "Whose Side Was God On?" *CEPAD Report* (January–February 1990); Joseph E. Mulligan, *The Nicaraguan Church and the Revolution*, p. x.; López Vigil comment: interview, July 1990.

Looking Back, Looking Forward: Jerez: interviews, Philadelphia, March 1990, and Managua, August 1990; Carrión criticism: series by Sergio de Castro, "Revisión a Fondo en FSLN," four-part interview with Comandante Luis Carrión, in *Barricada*, June 20–29, 1990; 1988 poll: *Envío*, no. 89 (December 1988); Obando at inauguration: interviews, Managua, 1990; La Paz Centro and new language: observation, July 1990; "Rubén": Mulligan, *The Nicaraguan Church and the Revolution*, p. 290; cathedral project: "New Cathedral Provokes Criticism, Church-State Relations Come under Fire," *CEPAD Report* (May–June 1990); Catholics in Chamorro government: Noel Irías, "Ciudad de Dios," *Crítica*, no. 1 (June 1990), Russell Bellant, "God's CEOs," and accompanying articles, in *National Catholic Reporter*, November 18, 1988, tracing in great detail Sword of the Spirit and the activities of Humberto Belli in the United

States in the 1980s; interview with Humberto Belli, July 1990; Mulligan, *Nicaraguan Church and the Revolution*, pp. 274ff.

3. El Salvador: God's Patience Exhausted

October 1979–March 1980: author's visits to El Salvador during the period; Berryman, *Religious Roots*, pp. 140–52; Raymond Bonner, *Weakness and Deceit*; Romero forewarned of coup: *Oscar Arnulfo Romero, Su Diario*; pp. 297, 298; January 22 demonstration: Francisco Andres Escobar, "En la linea de la muerte (La Manifestacion del 22 de enero de 1980)," *ECA*, nos. 375–376 (January–February 1980): 21–35; Mario Zamora killing: UN Truth Commission Report, "From Insanity to Hope," pp. 69–70; Romero sermons and letter to Carter: Cardenal, Martín-Baró, Sobrino, eds., *La Voz de los Sin Voz: La Palabra Viva de Monseñor Oscar Arnulfo Romero*; final sermon: ibid., pp. 269–92; murder: James R. Brockman, *Romero, A Life*, Appendix ("Romero's Killers"), pp. 249–55, and UN Truth Commission, "From Insanity to Madness," pp. 62–65; post-Romero period: *ECA*, nos. 377–378 (March–April 1980), esp. editorial "En Busca de Un Nuevo Proyecto Nacional"; Sumpul River massacre: UN Truth Commission Report, pp. 59–61; "Vicki" narrative: David Blanshard, *Kingdoms without Justice, a Church of Hope: Salvadoran Militarization and the Christian Response*, pp. 122–25; violence against church workers and institutions: Socorro Jurídico, *El Salvador: Del genocidio de la junta militar a la esperanza de la lucha insurreccional*, pp. 21–29, esp. list of incidents on pp. 22–25; church people making options: interview, San Salvador, July 1990; Ponceele: María López Vigil, *Muerte y Vida en Morazán: Testimonio de un Sacerdote* (his name is often spelled "Ponselle"; I here follow López Vigil, who spells it "Ponceele"); U.S. church women: Donna Whitson Brett and Edward T. Brett, *Murdered in Central America: The Stories of Eleven U.S. Missionaries*, pp. 189–320; Ana Carrigan, *Salvador Witness: The Life and Calling of Jean Donovan*; Sobrino, *Spirituality of Liberation: Toward Political Holiness* (Maryknoll, N.Y.: Orbis, 1988), pp. 153–56; Rivera on offensive: *El Día* (Mexico City), January 18, 1981, reprinted in *CRIE*, no. 65 (March 30, 1981); Silvia Arriola: interview with Salvadoran organizer, Philadelphia, Spring 1989; Rivera's efforts at mediation: Bonner, *Weakness and Deceit*, pp. 230–31, 285; human rights statistics: Centro Universitario de Documentación e Información (CUDI), "La violación de los derechos humanos en El Salvador," in *ECA*, nos. 403–404 (May–June 1982): 543–56, charts on pp. 545 and 548; Mozote: UN Truth Commission Report, pp. 55–59; Blanshard, "A Myth in the Making: Colonel Domingo Monterrosa and the Mozote Massacre," in *Kingdoms without Justice*, pp. 47–54, and Bonner, *Weakness and Deceit*, pp. 337ff., also pp. 112–13; Mexican-French declaration: text in *El Día* (Mexico), August 29, 1981; Rivera statements: *Uno Más Uno* (Mexico), September 7, 1981; bishops' conference, *El Día* (Mexico), September 6, 1981, along with numerous other reactions in *CRIE*, no. 81 (September 8, 1981); Rivera denunciations: *Carta a las Iglesias*, no. 6, October 11–20, 1981, reprinted in *CRIE*, no. 85 (November 10, 1981).

War Becomes Routine: Woerner plan: Gutman, *Banana Diplomacy*, pp. 61–62; ARENA origins: investigative reporters Craig Pyes (*Albuquerque Journal*) and Laurie Beckland (*Los Angeles Times*), jointly written series on the death squads running December 18–23, 1983, in both papers; bishops on elections: *Carta a las Iglesias* (January 16–31, 1982), reprinted in *CRIE*, no. 93 (March 2, 1982); vote count: "Las elecciones y la unidad nacional: diez tesis criticas," *ECA*, no. 402 (April 1982) 233–58, esp. pp. 240–43, 253; situation of church: Iván D. Paredes, "Evolución de la Iglesia salvadoreña

24 de marzo 80/28 marzo 82," *ECA*, no. 403–404 (May–June 1982): 439–52, estimates of clergy decline, p. 446. It should be noted that *Annuarium Statisticum Ecclesiae* shows a significant but less dramatic decline of the total number of priests from 399 (1978) to 347 (1981), that is, about one-eighth of the priests in El Salvador, thirty-six of them being diocesan priests. The largest concentration was in the archdiocese of San Salvador. Letters from Rutilio Sanchez: Scott Wright et al., *El Salvador: A Spring Whose Waters Never Run Dry*, pp. 62–65; Sister "Rosa," interview in *Brecha* (Mexico), nos. 9–10, 1982, reprinted in *CRIE*, no. 117 (February 22, 1983): 8–13; Aparicio accusations: *Excelsior* (Mexico), reprinted in *CRIE*, no. 109 (October 19, 1982); Boulang's reply, in *CRIE*, no. 111 (November 16, 1982): 5; bishops' letter: *Uno Más Uno* (Mexico), July 19, 1982; pope's reply: *L'Osservatore Romano* (extracts), August 8, 1982–both reprinted in *CRIE*, no. 105 (August 17, 1982); FMLN-FDR proposal: *ECA*, no. 409 (November 1982): 1049–50; pope's visit: author's interviews, 1989, 1990, news accounts gathered in *CRIE*, no. 120 (March 1983), entire issue of *ECA*, nos. 413–414 (March–April 1983), texts of speeches, Juan Pablo II, *Mensajes a Centro América*; Bishop Rosa Chavez's remarks: *Uno Más Uno*, March 9, 1983 in *CRIE*, no. 120 (March 1983); Rivera defending humanitarian work: August 14, 1983, *CRIE*, no. 132 (September 6, 1983), 7; National Plan for Security and Development: Chris Hedges, "Salvadoran 'Pacification' Falters," *Latin America Press* (Lima), January 26, 1984; baptism on the run: "El bautismo de Sonia," *Carta a las Iglesias*, no. 42 (April 1983), María López Vigil, *Primero Dios: Siete Años de Esperanza – Relatos de "Carta a las Iglesias,"* pp. 64–66; layman: interview, 1990.

President – and Nation – Prisoners of War? UCA analysis: "El Salvador 1984," entire issue of *NACLA Report on the Americas*, vol. 18, no. 2 (March–April 1984); Rosa Chavez on FMLN-FDR proposal: *Uno Más Uno*, February 10, 1984, in *CRIE*, no. 143 (February 14, 1984); bishops on election: "Salvador Bishops: Elections Don't Make Democracy," *Latinamerica Press*, May 17, 1984; 1984 military aid: chart, "Military Assistance to Central America: FY 1983–85"; Zacamil anniversary: *Carta a las Iglesias*, in *CRIE*, no. 145 (March 13, 1984); Romero anniversary: *Excelsior* (Mexico), March 25, 1984, in *CRIE*, no. 146 (March 27, 1984), also interviews, San Salvador; workers' march: *Uno Más Uno*, May 2, 1984, in *CRIE*, no. 149 (May 8, 1984); labor resurgence: Horacio Castellanos Moya, "El Salvador: New Union, Political Activism Emerging," *Latinamerica Press*, December 6, 1984; see also Kenneth E. Sharpe, "El Salvador," in *Latin America and Caribbean Contemporary Record*, no. 5 (1985–86) B287; origins of CRIPDES: interview with CRIPDES organizer, San Salvador, July 1990; La Palma: interview with Rubén Zamora, San Salvador, July 1990; Carlos Fazio, "La inexistencia de una tregua, indicio del fracaso de las previsiones de Duarte," *Proceso* (Mexico), October 22, 1984, in *CRIE*, no. 161 (October 23, 1984): 10–11; Monterrosa crash: Blanshard, "A Myth in the Making," in *Kingdoms without Justice*; Rivera on Zona Rosa: *El Día* (Mexico) June 29, 1985, in *CRIE* no. 174 (August 6, 1985); 1985 election: Sharpe, "El Salvador"; bishops' 1985 letter and FMLN response: *ECA*, nos. 443–444 (September–October 1985): 743–50; kidnapping of Duarte's daughter: Tomás R. Campos, "Lectura política de los secuestros," *ECA*, nos. 443–444 (September–October 1985): 684–700; Rivera pastoral visit: "Visita de Mons. Rivera a Chalatenango y Guazapa," *ECA*, nos. 443–444 (September–October 1985): 701–4, and *Letter to the Churches*, no. 108 (January 16–31, 1986): 5–9, esp. text of Rivera's homily in the church at San Jose Las Flores, January 7, 1986; UCA team analysis: entire issue of *NACLA Report on the Americas*, vol. 20, no. 1 (January–March 1986).

Opening Space for Reconciliation: interviews, 1989, 1990, in United States and San Salvador; Guazapa: testimonies in *Letter to the Churches*, nos. 108–110 (January–February 1986); Tenancingo: Beatrice Edwards, "The Repopulation of Rural El Salvador," paper prepared for LASA meeting, 1989 (Miami); Rivera speech at LASA meeting in Miami, 1989 (no title, photocopy, pp. 7–8); situation of returnees: Peter Shiras, "El Salvador: The New Face of War," *Commonweal*, May 8, 1987; peace efforts in 1986: "Cronología del proceso de dialogo entre el gobierno salvadoreño y el FDR-FMLN," *ECA*, nos. 454–455 (August–September 1986): 767–88 (the entire issue is on dialogue for peace; see articles by Archbishop Rivera recounting his efforts, pp. 670–74; and major article by Ellacuría, "Análisis etico-político del proceso de diálogo en El Salvador," pp. 727–51); earthquake: reports from El Salvador, esp. documentation called "Chronology: El Salvador, October 13–18, 1986," bulletins from Secretaría de Comunicación Social of the archdiocese, Catholic Relief Services, "Situation Report on El Salvador Earthquake" (October 20, 1986), and *Carta a las Iglesias*, no. 125 (October 1–15, 1986); U.S. aid exceeding Salvadoran government's own revenues: Sen. Mark O. Hatfield (R-Oreg.), Rep. Jim Leach (R-Iowa), and Rep. George Miller (D-Calif.), "Bankrolling Failure: United States Policy in El Salvador and the Urgent Need for Reform – A Report to the Arms Control and Foreign Policy Caucus" (Washington, D.C.; November 1987), p. 5; aid from remittances: Segundo Montes, "The Salvadoran Crisis and the Consequences of a Massive Repatriation of Refugees in the U.S." (translation by Congressional Research Service, the Library of Congress, February 25, 1987); Duarte letter to Reagan: *New York Times*, April 16, 1987; "War Tax": Chris Norton, "El Salvador: Tax Issue Shatters Uneasy Truce between Government, Oligarchy," and "U.S.-backed Center-right Coalition on Rocky Ground," both in *Latinamerica Press*, February 17, 1987; FMLN documents: "Fase preparatoria de la contraofensiva estratégica" (November 1986), "Apreciación estratégica" (n.d.), and other documents provided by U.S. embassy and Salvadoran military to journalists in mid-1988; see also Janet Shenk, "Can the Guerrillas Win?" *Mother Jones*, April 1988; study week: *Carta a las Iglesias*, no. 149; Ellacuría critique: "third force" argument appears in "Análisis ético-político del proceso de diálogo en El Salvador," *ECA*, nos. 454–455 (August–September 1986), esp. pp. 746ff.; "La cuestión de las masas": *ECA*, no. 464 (July 1987); peace plan and meeting at nunciature: interviews, 1990; *Carta a las Iglesias*, no. 149 (October 1–15, 1987): 10–11; Anaya killing: Chris Norton, "Amnesty Pardons Death Squads Accused of Massacring Thousands of Salvadorans," *Latinamerica Press*, November 19, 1987; return from Honduras: *Carta a las Iglesias*, no. 149 (October 1–15, 1987): 12 and account by Mary Ann Corley, who accompanied refugees from the camp to the border.

ARENA Triumphs – and Faces Reality: Phillip Berryman, "El Salvador," in James Malloy and Eduardo Gamarra, eds., *Latin America and Caribbean Contemporary Record* 1987–88; officers' report: Lt.-Col. A. J. Bacevich et al., "American Military Policy in Small Wars: The Case of El Salvador" (John F. Kennedy School of Government, Harvard University, March 1988); corruption in Duarte government: Hatfield, Leach, Miller, "Bankrolling Failure," pp. 5ff.; March 1988 election: *Central America Report* (Guatemala) (March–June 1988), and *ECA*, nos. 473–74 (March–April 1988); account of the growth and formalization of women's organizing: Renny Golden, *The Hour of the Poor, The Hour of Women*, pp. 106–15; Corr speech to the American Chamber of Commerce in San Salvador, July 14, 1988 (unclassified embassy cable); human rights violations: Kenneth Freed, "Salvador Killings Up Sharply Rights Group Says," *Los Angeles Times*, October 2, 1988, in *Newspak*, vol. 3, no. 17 (September 26–October 9, 1988); National Debate: *Debate Nacional, 1988, Documento Final* (photocopy); Phillip

Berryman, "El Salvador's National Debate," *Christianity and Crisis*, no. 18 (November 12, 1988); subsequent march: *Carta a las Iglesias*, no. 175 (November 1–15, 1988): 4; Duarte cancer: Douglas Farah, "Problems Persist as Duarte Era Comes to End," *Washington Post*, June 27, 1988, in *Newspak*, vol. 3, no. 10 (June 20–July 3, 1988); d'Aubuisson at campaign rally: interview with priest, San Salvador, July 1990; FMLN proposal: Marta Harnecker, "La propuesta del FMLN: un desafío a la estrategia contrainsurgente—entrevista a Joaquín Villalobos (25 de febrero de 1989)," *ECA*, no. 485 (March 1989): 211–28; text of FMLN proposal: *Newspak* vol. 3, no. 26 (January 30–February 12, 1989); Tovar march: *Carta a las Iglesias*, no. 181 (February 1–14, 1989): 5; upsurge of political violence in 1989: account based on a number of unsigned reports on human rights from within El Salvador; also Marjorie Miller, "Salvador Society Polarized, Confused by Wave of Slayings," *Los Angeles Times*, September 15, 1989; Eugene Palumbo: interview with Maria Julia Hernández, *National Catholic Reporter*, September 29, 1989; Merino accusations and Rivera's support for David Sanchez: interview with priest in San Salvador, 1990; and CAR 28 April 1989, vol. xvi, no. 16, p. 124; Ellacuría position: Ignacio Ellacuría, "Una nueva fase en el proceso salvadoreño," *ECA*, no. 485 (March 1989): 167–98; events leading to November offensive: El Rescate (Los Angeles), *El Salvador Chronology*, vol. 4, nos. 10–12 (October, November, December 1989); offensive: interviews, July 1990; reports prepared by church groups in San Salvador in November–December 1989; El Rescate, *Chronology* (November 1989); killing of Jesuits: sources cited in the introduction; extensive coverage in *National Catholic Reporter*, November 24, 1989, December 1, 1989, December 8, 1989, December 29, 1989; reporting in dailies, gathered in *Newspak*, vol. 4, no. 20 (November 6–19, 1989,) and (November 20–December 3, 1989).

Moving toward Peace: FMLN reactions to Nicaraguan election: Chris Norton, "Salvadoran Hopes Fade," *Christian Science Monitor*, March 8, 1990, in *Newspak* vol. 5, no. 2, (February 26–March 11, 1990); "Salvadoran Factions Feel Growing Heat to Bring Halt to War," *Christian Science Monitor*, May 4, 1990, in *Newspak* vol. 5, no. 6 (April 23–May 6, 1990); "squeezing a bag of water": Phil Bronstein, "U.S. Officials Reverse View on Salvadoran Army," *San Francisco Examiner*, May 6, 1990, in *Newspak* vol. 5, no. 7, (May 7–20, 1990); Jesuit case: Whitfield, *Paying the Price*, Lawyers' Committee for Human Rights, "Update on Investigation of the Murder of Six Jesuit Priests in El Salvador" (October 2, 1990) and "Jesuit Murder Case Update, August 1991"; UN Truth Commission, "From Insanity to Hope," pp. 20–25, quote from p. 21; threats: Katherine Ellison, "Salvadoran Clerics Keep Low Profile," *Austin American-Statesman*, February 11, 1990, in *Newspak*, vol. 4, no. 26, no. 104 (January 29–February 11, 1990); Corral de Piedra: "Six Said to Die in Salvador Air Force Raid," *New York Times*, February 12, 1990, and "Salvador Army Did Attack Refugees, Says a Colonel," *Excelsior*, February 18, 1990, both in *Newspak* vol. 5, no. 1 (February 12–25, 1990); Romero canonization: Blanshard, *Kingdoms without Justice*, pp. 103–10; aid vote cut: Lindsey Gruson, "Salvador Arms Aid: Will Congress's Tactic Work," *New York Times*, October 22, 1990, in *Newspak* vol. 5, no. 6 (October 8–21, 1990); November 1990 offensive: Lindsey Gruson, "Missiles Give Salvador Rebels a New Advantage," *New York Times*, December 10, 1990, in *Newspak* vol. 5, no. 22 (December 3–16, 1990); Tom Gibb, "Inside the El Salvador Armed Forces," *San Francisco Chronicle*, December 31, 1990, and Joyce Hackel, "U.S. Deaths Shift Advantage to Salvadoran Military," *Christian Science Monitor*, January 14, 1991, both in *Newspak* vol. 5, no. 24 (December 31–January 13, 1991); Doyle McManus and Ronald Ostrow, "U.S. Targets Salvador Rebel Chief for Prosecution," *Los Angeles Times*, January 15, 1991, in *Newspak* vol. 5, no. 25; El Zapote: Thomas Long, "Salvadoran Army Accused in Massacre,"

Miami Herald, February 4, 1991, in *Newspak* vol. 5, no. 26, and Thomas Long, "Church Challenges Government's Probe of Peasant Massacre," *Miami Herald*, February 10, 1991, in *Newspak*, vol. 6, no. 1; FMLN rethinking: "Internal Debate Rages within FMLN," *Excelsior* (Mexico), June 18, 1991, in *Newspak* vol. 6, no. 10 (June 17–30, 1991); UN team: Lee Hockstader, "U.N. to Monitor Rights in Salvadoran Civil War," *Washington Post*, July 17, 1991, in *Newspak*, vol. 6, no. 12 (July 15–28, 1991); Jesuit murder trial: author's viewing of entire trial on video, Court TV, New York, October 1991; Lawyers' Committee for Human Rights, "The 'Jesuit Case,' The Jury Trial" (*La Vista Pública*), September 1991, along with many updates and other documentation over the two years from the murder to the trial; Instituto de Derechos Humanos de la UCA (IDHUCA), "La vista pública en retrospectiva," *ECA, nos.* 517–518 (November–December 1991): 1025–31; Jose Maria Tojeira, "El Caso de los Jesuitas dos años despues," conference at UCA in same issue of *ECA*; see also reactions in *Carta a las Iglesias*, no. 244 (October 16–31, 1991) no. 245 (November 1–15, 1991), and no. 246 (November 16–30, 1991); end of war: *Central America Report*, January 17, 1992; Lee Hockstader, "Guerrillas Celebrate Openly in Capital," *Washington Post*, January 17, 1992.

4. Guatemala: Persecuted but Not Defeated

Events from 1979 through early 1982 treated in greater detail in Berryman, *Religious Roots*, with sources; Spanish embassy massacre: author interviewed four of the peasants, including Vicente Menchú, shortly before the occupation, was present at Justice and Peace Mass, helped prepare initial reports on the massacre, observed funeral march; interviews, 1989–90; see also *Noticias de Guatemala*, no. 35 (February 4, 1980).

"They Will Kill Us All!": CUC strike: *Noticias de Guatemala*, no. 38 (March 4, 1980): 1; Tiquisate: *Noticias de Guatemala*, no. 44 (June 16, 1980): 15; union leader abductions: *Noticias de Guatemala*, no. 45 (June 30, 1980); Santiago Atitlán: *News from Guatemala* (Toronto), vol. 2, no. 11 (December 1980): 7–8; catechist: Bernice Kita, *What Prize Awaits Us: Letters from Guatemala*, pp. 117, 120; Uspantán: IGE (Iglesia de Guatemala en Exilio), *The Church of Guatemala: Lessons of History*, p. 23; de la Cruz and Voordeckers: *Church . . . Lessons*; Villanueva and Gerardi ambush attempt: "Genocide in El Quiché: A Testimonial of the Persecuted Church," *Popular History*, no. 1, Guatemala Information Center, pp. 8–10; sister: interview, Guatemala City, 1989; Gerardi in Rome, Lucas at rally: interview with Gerardi in *Ecclesia* (August 1980), translation in IGE, *Church . . . Lessons*; pope's letter: Kurt Greenhalgh and Mark Gruenke, FSC, eds., *The Church Martyred: Guatemala*, p. 23; Guatemalan Church in exile, "alternatives": Bolletin No. 1, August 1980, issued in San Jose, Costa Rica; sister and priest: interviews, Guatemala, 1989, 1990; EGP statement on Christians: *CRIE*, no. 56 (September 1, 1980); CONFREGUA statement: translation of text *The Church Martyred: Guatemala*, p. 35; Alonso: documents by Justicia y Paz and IGE; EGP promises: interview with church worker from Huehuetenango, 1989; sister: Nueva Catarina: interview, 1989; safe houses: Mario Payeras, *Trueno en la Ciudad* gives a revealing look at a guerrilla organization during this period; development organizations: "Foreigners Threatened," *National Catholic Reporter*, July 3, 1981; McKenna: interview with church worker in Guatemala City, August 1990; Leger and Martínez, Maruzzo: Berryman, *Religious Roots*, p. 212; Rother: Brett and Brett, *Murdered in Central America*, pp. 89–118; Pellecer: "Declaraciones del P. Luis Pellecer" (transcript of statement and question period) and URNG statement (mimeo); priest interviewed in

Guatemala, August 1990; Sister Victoria de la Roca: *El Gráfico* (Guatemala), January 9, 1982, *Prensa Libre*, January 7, 1982, and other material in *CRIE*, no. 90 (January 30, 1982), and author's conversation in Matagalpa, Nicaragua, in August 1987; James Miller: Brett and Brett, *Murdered in Central America*, Chapter Six; note that the killing of conservative Mennonite missionary John David Troyer took place the night of September 13–14, 1981. Troyer's relatives and colleagues said that the killers identified themselves as guerrillas, but the Bretts conclude that the identity cannot be determined with certainty: *Murdered in Central America*, Chapter five.

"Born-Again" Ruler: situation in Huehuetenango: interview with church worker, 1989; URNG manifesto: "Proclama unitaria de las organizaciones revolucionarias EGP, FAR, ORPA, y PGT, al pueblo de Guatemala"; election, coup, and Rios Montt: George Black, "Guatemala – The War Is Not Over," *NACLA Report on the Americas*, vol. 17, no. 2 (March–April 1983): 14ff.; Joseph Anfuso and David Sczepanski, *Efrain Rios Montt: Siervo o Dictador?: La Verdadera Historia del Controversial Presidente de Guatemala*, quote, p. 20; bishops: IGE, *The Church of Guatemala*, p. 34; Casariego quote: *El Gráfico* (Guatemala), April 1, 1982, in *CRIE*, no. 96 (April 12, 1982); IGE statement: "Reflexiones en Torno a la Visita de la Conferencia Episcopal a la junta militar," IGE bulletin no. 12, April 1982, in *CRIE*, no. 98 (May 11, 1982); initial Rios Montt period: Jean-Marie Simon, *Guatemala: Eternal Spring, Eternal Tyranny*, pp. 109ff., Chapin quote on p. 110; massacres, 1982, Robert M. Carmack, *Harvest of Violence*, pp. xv–xvi; two exhaustive studies: Ricardo Falla, "Masacre de la finca San Francisco, Huehuetenango," (photocopy) and *Masacres de la Selva: Ixcán Guatemala (1975–1982)*; numbers of people in resistance: Ricardo Falla, "El hambre y otras privaciones inducidas por el ejército de Guatemala sobre la población civil," published by IGE, September 1983, p. 7; evangelical role: David Stoll, "Evangelicals, Guerrillas, and the Army: The Ixil Triangle under Ríos Montt," in Carmack, *Harvest of Violence*, quote p. 107; pastor Nicolas and pastor in Salquil: ibid., pp. 104–9; growth figures in Cotzal and Salquil Grande: Stoll, *Is Latin America Turning Protestant?* p. 202; Evangelical Confraternity: newsletter, *En Comunión* (Guatemala) beginning with no. 1, June–July 1982; Rios Montt in presidency: Simon, *Guatemala*, p. 109; Kill Legally, p. 111; code of conduct, pp. 122, 126; bishops' May 28 statement: "Massacre of Peasants," in Edward Cleary, ed., *Path from Puebla: Significant Documents of the Latin American Bishops since 1979*, pp. 207–9; Boldenow, Dekker: report and open letter to Rios Montt from Andrew Kuyvenhoven, *Banner* (denominational magazine), October 28 and November 15, 1982; sisters working with displaced people: interviews, Guatemala, 1989, 1990; Protestant hundredth anniversary: interviews, 1989, *Christianity Today*, "Mass Palau Rally Caps Guatemala Centennial Year," and "Luis Palau: Evangelist to Three Worlds," *Christianity Today*, May 20, 1983; pope's visit: overwhelmingly Catholic nation, "Comunicado de la Conferencia Episcopal de Guatemala," (Dec. 22, 1982), *CRIE*, no. 115 (Jan. 25, 1983) pp. 7–8; letter from Protestants and press accounts in *CRIE*, no. 120 (March 1983): 44–53; interviews, 1989; text of address: John Paul II, *Mensajes a Centroamerica*, quote on p. 97; see also account "Guatemala: Un escala muy difícil," *ECA*, nos. 413–414 (March–April 1983): 314–18.

Rejecting the "Peace of the Graveyard": sister: interview, 1989; the official source used for statistics is Vatican Secretariat of State, *Annuarium Statisticum Ecclesiae*, 140, 168; the notion of a drop from 700 to 450 that appeared in an internal CELAM document sounds very impressionistic, but was probably given from a bishop to the visiting team; I heard the same figure from a sister (interview, 1990). Bishops and religious superiors reporting to Rome may have seen the absences as temporary and not fully reflective of the true number of people who had fled. It may be noted that at least according to the official figures there was no drop in the number of sisters: they increased every year from 1978 (787) to 1983 (890) and afterwards; "Confirmed in Faith": text in *Prensa Libre,* July 6 and 8, 1983; Mejía Víctores accusation, *Uno Más Uno,* June 9, 1983, in *CRIE,* no. 126 (June 14, 1983); commentary of Pellecer, *El Día,* June 16 and 20, 1983, both reprinted in *CRIE,* no. 127 (June 28, 1983); Casariego death: *Church . . . Lessons,* p. 41; Penados interview: *Esquila Misional* (Mexico), August 1983, reprinted in *CRIE,* no. 130 (August 9, 1983); August coup: Simon, *Guatemala;* Protestant churches: Americas Watch, *Guatemala: A Nation of Prisoners,* p. 31; Rios Montt's attitude toward democracy: "El General Efraín Rios Montt opina sobre el movimiento del 23 de marzo, sobre su gobierno y enjuicia a la cúpula del ejército del General Lucas (Entrevista con Roberto Cruz S. hecha el 15 de abril de 1985)" (typescript); interpretation of reasons for coup: observers in Guatemala, August 1989; Alfredo García, visit to Rome, Mejia Victores remark, and Ramírez Monasterio: *Church . . . Lessons,* pp. 4–5; interview with unnamed bishop: Americas Watch, *Guatemala,* p. 30; Peace Commission: IGE, *Church . . . Lessons,* p. 45; "To Build Peace": "Para construir la paz," *El Gráfico,* June 9, 1984, in *CRIE,* no. 153 (July 3, 1984) (translation in Cleary, ed., *Path from Puebla,* pp. 137–51); CONFREGUA: proceedings in III Congreso de Religiosos de Guatemala Sobre la Doctrina Social de la Iglesia Aplicada a Guatemala (Guatemala 12, 13 y 14 de abril de 1984); GAM: interviews, Guatemala, April 1985, and July 1989; Penados on "peace of graveyards": *El Día* (Mexico), June 5, 1984, in *CRIE,* no. 152 (June 19, 1984); cf. Simon, *Guatemala,* pp. 159–61, 192–97 and *passim;* "triple murder": IGE, *Church . . . Lessons,* p. 40; Coca-Cola: "We Will Neither Go Nor Be Driven Out: A Special Report by the IUF Trade Union Delegation on the Occupation of the Coca-Cola Bottling Plant in Guatemala"; also Henry Frundt, *Refreshing Pauses: Coca-Cola and Human Rights in Guatemala;* Americas Watch report: quote from introduction, pp. iv–v; 1985 Americas Watch report; title soccer stadium in Mazatenango: FBIS, January 11, 1985, in "On the Road to Democracy? A Chronology of Human Rights and U.S.-Guatemalan Relations — January 1978–April 1985" (Washington, D.C.: Central American Historical Institute, 1985); anthropologists' report: Chris Krueger and Kjell Enge, "Security and Development Conditions in the Guatemalan Highlands," (Washington, D.C.: Washington Office on Latin America, August 1985); September 1985 disturbances: Simon: *Guatemala,* pp. 197, 200; bishops' letter: "La verdad os hará libres," in *CRIE,* no. 179 (November 14, 1985); Serrano Elias: "Carta abierta al pueblo evangelico," *La Palabra,* October 13, 1985.

Civilian Government, Army Rule: Simon, *Guatemala,* p. 246; Inforpress Centroamericana, *Guatemala 1986: The Year of Promises*; Giron: interviews: with Giron (1988) and aide (1989) in Tiquisate, Guatemala; Giron tells his own story in great detail in J. C. Cambranes, *Agrarismo en Guatemala,* pp. 37–190; Episcopado Guatemalteco, "El Clamor por la Tierra"; interview with Bishop Juan Gerardi, August 1989; Quezada and oligarchs: interviews 1989, 1990 Guatemala; see also Colectivo de Analisis de Iglesias en Centroamerica, art. "Guatemala: Iglesia y Sociedad," pp. 5ff. esp. pp. 24–34, in *La Iglesia en Centroamerica* (Mexico: Centro de Estudios Ecumenicos, 1989).

Groping Steps toward Peace: labor unification: art. "Guatemala" in Inforpress Centroamericana, *Centro America 1988: Análisis económicos y políticos sobre la región,* esp. pp. 102–6, and *Central America Report* (Guatemala) March 6, 1987, March 11, 1988, and March 18, 1988; URNG: press conference with guerrilla leader Rodrigo Arias ("Gaspar Ilom"), San Jose, Costa Rica, March 29, 1988, reprinted in *Ceri-Gua* (Mexico), vol. 2 (March–April 1988) (issue carries interview with Pablo Monsanto and Rolando

Moran); officers' speech to chamber of commerce: "Twenty-Seven Years of Struggle for Freedom," in Inforpress Centroamericana, *Centro America 1988*, pp. 114–18; failed coups: Brook Larmer, "Guatemalan Right Pushes to Reagan Political Footing," *Christian Science Monitor*, May 19, 1988, in *Newspak* vol. 3, no. 7 (May 9–22, 1988), "El golpe que no fue," *Crónica* (Guatemala), August 18, 1988, and "Loyal Troops Foil Coup Attempt in Guatemala," *Los Angeles Times*, May 10, 1989, in *Newspak* vol. 4, no. 7 (May 8–21, 1989); El Aguacate: Haroldo Shetemul, "Guatemalan Government Rejects Accusations of Murdering Peasants," *Excelsior*, November 30, 1988, in *Newspak* vol. 3, no. 22 (December 5–18, 1988); dossier of reprints from Guatemalan press; peace process: interviews, Guatemala City, 1989, 1990; documents from Permanent Assembly of Christian Groups; Diana Ortiz: "Testimony of Sister Diana Ortiz" in lawsuit against Hector Gramajo in U.S. District Court District of Massachusetts; "U.S. Nun Says Abductors in Guatemala Tortured Her," *Miami Herald*, November 7, 1989, in *Newspak* vol. 4, no. 20 (November 6–19, 1989), and Nancy Nusser, "American Nun Tortured as Violence Increases in Guatemala," *Austin-American Statesman*, March 25, 1990, in *Newspak* vol. 5, no. 3 (March 12–25, 1990); Oquelí and Flores: UN Truth Commission, "From Insanity to Hope," pp. 46–48; Americas Watch, "Messengers of Death," *Newspak* vol. 5, no. 2 Feb. 26–March 11, 1990); "U.S. Recalls Envoy to Protest Guatemala Killings," *Miami Herald*, March 6, 1990, in *Newspak*, vol. 5, no. 2 (February 26–March 11, 1990); U.S. disenchantment with Cerezo, turn to military: Kenneth Freed, "U.S. Is Taking a New Tack in Guatemala," *Los Angeles Times*, May 7, 1990, in *Newspak* vol. 5, no. 7 (May 7–20, 1990), and "U.S. Halts Guatemala Health Aid," *San Francisco Chronicle*, March 21, 1990, in *Newspak* (March 26–April 8, 1990); Wilson Ring, "Guatemalan Guerrillas Take Fight Close to Cities," *Washington Post*, April 14, 1990, in *Newspak* vol. 5, no. 5 (April 9–22, 1990); Oslo: "Guatemala, Guerrillas Agree on Talks to End War," *Miami Herald*, March 31, 1990, in *Newspak* vol. 5, no. 4 (March 26–April 8, 1990); *Central America Report*, April 6, 1990; "Guatemalan Rebels, Parties Reach Agreement," *Austin American-Statesman*, June 2, 1990, in *Newspak* vol. 5, no. 8 (May 21–June 3, 1990) and *Central America Report*, June 1, 1990; Reece Erlich, "Guatemalan Civilians Talk Peace, Nudge Reluctant Military," *Christian Science Monitor*, September 26, 1990, in *Newspak* vol. 5, no. 17 (September 24–October 7, 1990), and David Clark Scott, "Guatemala Peace Talks Stalled without Army Role," *Christian Science Monitor*, October 29, 1990, in *Newspak* vol. 5, no. 19 (October 22, November 4, 1990).

Evangelical President: disenchantment with Cerezo government: author's interviews and observations, 1989 and 1990; Lindsey Gruson, "Voting Isn't Helping in Guatemala," *New York Times*, June 3, 1990, in *Newspak* vol. 5, no. 8 (May 12–June 3, 1990); Gruson, "Guatemala's President Stars in Political and Personal Drama," *New York Times*, June 24, 1990, and "Political Violence on the Rise Again in Guatemala, Tarnishing Civilian Rule," *New York Times*, June 28, 1990, both in *Newspak* vol. 5, no. 10 (June 18–July 1, 1990); Rios Montt: David Stoll, "Why They Like Rios Montt"; Penados on Rios Montt: Lindsey Gruson, "Churches Clash in Guatemala," *New York Times*, October 17, 1990, in *Newspak* vol. 5, no. 18 (October 8–21, 1990); bishops' statement: Haroldo Shetemul, "Catholic Church Warns against Religious Electoral War in Guatemala," *Excelsior*, December 3, 1990, in *Newspak* vol. 5, no. 22 (December 3–16, 1990); Serrano Elias: Christopher Marquis, "New Guatemalan President Faces Formidable Challenge," *Miami Herald*, January 15, 1991, in *Newspak* vol. 5, no. 25 (January 14–27, 1991), and Haroldo Shetemul, "Serrano Calls on Workers, Business, and Cooperatives to Negotiate a Social Pact," *Excelsior*, March 3, 1991, in *Newspak* vol. 6, no. 2 (February 25–March 10, 1990); Haroldo Shetemul, "Serrano Promises to Aid

GAM for Families of the Disappeared," *Excelsior*, February 15, 1991, in *Newspak* vol. 6, no. 1 (February 11–24, 1991); Santiago massacre: Joyce Hackel, "Guatemala Army Killings Raise National Debate," *Christian Science Monitor*, December 11, 1990, and Lucy Hood, "Guatemala Apologizes for Killings," *Washington Post*, December 8, 1990, both in *Newspak* vol. 5, no. 22 (December 3–16, 1990); Myrna Mack: biography supplied by AVANSCO (Guatemala), "Myrna Elizabeth Mack Chang (40) Guatemalan Anthropologist, Murdered on September 11th 1990," along with extensive press clippings; Mack remark to Central American colleagues in *Envío*, no. 117 (April 1991); Haroldo Shetemul, "National Blackout in Guatemala; Police Chief Assassinated," *Excelsior*, August 6, 1991, in *Newspak* vol. 6, no. 13 (July 29–August 11, 1991); Christopher Marquis, "Crime Mounts Even as Guatemala Seeks End to Guerrilla War," *Miami Herald*, August 23, 1991, in *Newspak* vol. 6, no. 15 (August 26–September 8, 1991); "Perpetual Violence," *Central America Report*, vol. 18, no. 26 (July 12, 1991); Kenneth Freed, "Cracking a 'Culture of Death,' " *Los Angeles Times*, September 19, 1991, in *Newspak* (September 9–22, 1991).

5. Making Disciples: Evangelical Growth and What It Means

10,500 evangelical churches: SERPAL et al., "Retrato de Guatemala," p. 2; Catholic parishes: CELAM, *Hacia un Mapa Pastoral de América Latina*, p. 154; 3 percent estimate: interview with Isidro Perez, S.J., executive director of CONFREGUA, July 1989; Ciudad Sandino: interview with priest, July 1990; "real" Protestants and Catholics: Stoll, *Is Latin America Turning Protestant?* p. 6; low estimates of evangelicals: CELAM, *Hacia un Mapa*, pp. 208, 138, 153; "Luis Palau: Evangelist to Three Worlds," *Christianity Today*, May 20, 1983; professor: Bethuel Henríquez, Universidad Evangélica, July 1990; Rodolfo Rodriguez and Gilberto Provedor, Estelí, July 1989, and sister in Santa Cruz, August 1989; DAWN Ministries, *Amanecer* (publication of DAWN Ministries, Pasadena, Calif.), vol. 1, no. 1 (January 1990); estimate of "Protestant community" in Guatemala: Proyecto Centroamericano de Estudios Socio-Religiosos (PROCADES), *Directorio de Igleisas Organizaciones y Ministerios del Movimiento Protestante: Guatemala* (December 1981), p. 61; 1987 estimate in SERPAL et al.: "Retrato de Guatemala," 8; Nicaragua: Abelino Martínez, *Las Sectas en Nicaragua: Oferta y Demanda de Salvación*, p. 61; El Salvador: Instituto Universitario de Opinion Pública (IUDOP), "La Religión para los Salvadoreños (Una encuesta de opinion pública," pp. 4–5; Gallup affiliate: figures supplied in letter to author (1990) from Juan Kessler, church researcher in San Jose, Costa Rica; Stoll, *Is Latin America Turning Protestant?* Appendix Three, p. 337.

One-Dimensional Explanations: Penados letter: Próspero Penados del Barrio, "La Iglesia Católica en Guatemala: Signo de Verdad y Esperanza" (Guatemala, January 6, 1989), quotes on pp. 9, 14, 16, 17, 18, 19; church growth worker: correspondence, 1990; Assemblies of God: interview with Bartolomé Matamoros, Managua, July 1990; Luís Corral Prieto, "Las Iglesias Evangélicas en Guatemala" *Estudios Teológicos* no. 13, January–June 1980; anthropologist: David Stoll, Nebaj, 1989.

Varieties of Evangelical Experience: observations and interview at Mi Redentor Church, Managua, 1990; Guatemala City, August 1989; Elim church, Guatemala City, August 1990; PIECA (Primera Iglesia Evangelica Centroamericana), August 1990; for similar observations of neopentecostal churches in Guatemala, see Susan D. Rose and Steve Brouwer, "Guatemalan Upper Classes Join the Evangelicals," revision of paper presented at American Sociological Association, and Association for the Sociology of

Religion Meetings, Atlanta, August 1988; history of Protestantism in Central America: Nelson, *Protestantism in Central America*; discussion of typologies: Heinrich Schäfer, "Una Tipología del Protestantismo en Centroamerica," *Pasos* (San Jose), no. 24 (July–August 1989); Baptist hospital and school: Albino Meléndez, *Los Evangélicos en Nicaragua: Aproximación Evangelística* (Managua: CEPAD, 1987), p. 18.

Catholic "Push" and Evangelical "Pull": numbers of pastors and evangelicals in Nicaragua: *CEPAD Newsletter*, July 1987; number of evangelicals: Stoll, *Is Latin America Turning Protestant?* p. 335; number of Catholic parishes: CELAM, *Hacia un Mapa*, . . . p. 209; survey in El Salvador: Instituto Universitario de Opinión Pública (IUDOP), "La Religion para los Salvadoreños," p. 9. The percentage of Catholics who claim to have been visited by their priest should not be taken at face value. In the same study Catholics obviously overstate the frequency of their Mass attendance. If the 33.5 percent of practicing Catholics attend Mass 4.9 times a month as they claim, every priest in El Salvador would be saying Mass for six thousand people a week, a figure far from the reality; just as they exaggerate frequency of Mass attendance, actual contact with pastors may be less. Target areas (*"campos blancos"*): *Directorio*, p. 61; effective methods: SEPAL et al., "Retrato de Guatemala," p. 11; "perverse effects" of Vatican II: expression of Federico Coppens, researcher in Nicaragua, July 1989; "fun to go to church": J. Peter Wagner, *Spiritual Power and Church Growth*; prophecy story: Bartolomé Matamoros, interview, Managua, 1990; belief in miracles and afterlife in El Salvador: IUDOP, "La Religion para los Salvadoreños," pp. 19–22; relativity of rules: interview, Managua, 1990; identification with the United States: interview with Clifton Holland, San Jose, Costa Rica, August 1989.

Existential Needs, Electronic Media: Alejandro Amaya, interview, San Salvador, July 1990; also 700 Club staff in Guatemala City, August 1990; Project Light in Nicaragua: *CEPAD Report* (March–April 1990); televangelism in Central America: Dennis A. Smith, "The Impact of Religious Programming in the Electronic Media on the Active Christian Population in Central America," pp. 67–84; Swaggart in El Salvador: Patrick Lacefield, "Swaggart Swings Through El Salvador," *Commonweal*, May 8, 1987; Alberto Piedra, "Estudio de una ruptura en un protestantismo latinoamericana" (typescript).

Middle-Class Varieties: El Verbo church: observations and interview, August 1990; homogeneous unit principle: Stoll, *Is Latin America Turning Protestant?* p. 127; Palau luncheon address: *Prensa Libre* (Guatemala), March 10, 1989; neopentecostalism and middle class: church worker, Guatemala, July 1989; disenchantment of upper classes with Catholic church in El Salvador and Guatemala is heard frequently from many sources, including an analyst in the U.S. embassy in San Salvador, July 1990; Evans study: Timothy Edward Evans, *Religious Conversion in Quetzaltenango, Guatemala* (dissertation submitted to the University of Pittsburgh, 1990).

Meeting the Competition: observations and interview in Parroquia San Jose Obrero, Guatemala City, August 1990, and Casa de Oración, August 1989; and Father René Estrada, interview, 1990; Trigo, interview, August 1989; cf. Salvador Gómez and José H. Prado Flores, *Formación de Predicadores*; charismatics and Trigo: communication with Bruce Calder; the Neocatechumenate is frequently mentioned but it is very difficult to document; SINE: Father Luis Estrada, interview, August 1990; interview with Father Valentín Martínez, S.J., Ciudad Sandino, July 1990.

Protestants Coming of Age: Bethuel Henríquez, interview, Universidad Evangélica, San Salvador, July 1990.

6. Acompañamiento: Standing by the People

Bishop Medardo Gómez: interview, July 1990; interviews with other Lutheran church workers, 1989, 1990; Medardo Ernesto Gómez, *Fire against Fire: Christian Ministry Face-to-Face with Persecution*; interview, Eliseo Rodríguez, July 1990.

Accompanying the People: interviews with church workers, 1989, 1990, in Guatemala, El Salvador, and the United States; Oscar Romero, *La Voz de los Sin Voz*, pp. 168–69.

In Guerrilla Territory: "Rolando" and lay worker, interviews, El Salvador, 1990; Matilde: Rennie Golden, *Hour of the Poor, Hour of Women*; Juanita, Tonia, Elizabeth: Blan-, shard, "Pastoral Practice as Rebellion: The Humanization of Social Life in El Salvador," in *Kingdoms without Justice*, pp. 78–92, esp. 86–90; Laura Lopez: Golden, *Hour of the Poor, Hour of Women*, and mimeographed material on Laura Lopez; Ventura: Miguel Ventura, "El Salvador: The Church of the Poor and the Revolution."

Pastoral Resurgence: visit to several parishes in Quiché in 1989; interview with social scientist in Guatemala, 1990; pastoral work in Guatemala City: field work and interviews, July–August 1989 and 1990; Mezquital: interview, August 1990, and parish printed materials; interviews, San Salvador, 1990.

Nicaragua — Still Struggling for Liberation: interviews with sister in El Viejo; interview in Managua with members of Waslala pastoral team, July 1989; interview with Arnaldo Zenteno, S.J., CNP, July 1989; Estelí: interviews, August 1989, and Guillermo Meléndez, "Nicaragua: Estelí Bishop Pulls Back on Revolutionary Christian Experiment," *Latinamerica Press*, September 17, 1987.

Defending the Victims: Romero quotes: Romero, *Violence of Love*, 28, 35; FECCAS-ORDEN clash: Berryman, *Religious Roots*, p. 131; Medellin: par. 22; Tutela Legal: author's observations and interviews with Maria Julia Hernández throughout the 1980s; humanitarian aid: author's observations; interviews with director of church aid agency, 1990; CEPAD: interviews and *CEPAD Report*.

A Word of Truth in the Midst of Lies: Romero: Romero, *La Voz de los Sin Voz*, pp. 304–5; Urioste Mass: author's observation, July 1990; Tojeira quote in Sobrino, et al. (eds.), *Companions of Jesus*, p. xxvi; profiles in *Noticias SJ Provincia Centroamericana*, no. 159 (Extraodinario), (San Salvador), December 1989; Ignacio Ellacuría, S.J., "The Task of a Christian University," in Sobrino et al., *Companions of Jesus: The Jesuit Martyrs of El Salvador*; Jon Sobrino, "The University's Christian Inspiration," in ibid.; land reform: *ECA*, nos. 335–336 (September–October 1976), and no. 337 (November 1976); Ellacuría's work: Phillip Berryman, "Ignacio Ellacuría: An Appreciation," *America*, July 7, 1990; *Revista de Psicología de El Salvador* (January–March 1990) is completely devoted to Martín-Baró and reprints eight of his articles; William Bollinger, "Taking the Pulse of Social Justice in Central America: The Public Opinion Research of Ignacio Martín-Baró," paper prepared at the meeting of LASA, Miami, December 4–6, 1989; visits to Ciudad Segundo Montes and Comunidad Ignacio Ellacuría, July 1990.

7. Contending Visions

Mahler interview: Managua, August 1989; Philip Williams, "The Catholic Church in the Nicaraguan Revolution," p. 64; UCA survey, IUDOP, "La Religión para los Salvadoreños," pp. 22–33.

Liberation Vision—Central American Kairos: "Kairos Centroamericano," in *Amanecer*, no. 55 (March–April 1988).

Sidestepping the Question: Verbo: interview with church spokespersons Soberanis and Baldizón, El Verbo church, Guatemala City, August 1990; seminary professor at SETECA, August 1990; interview at Trigo, August 1989; interview at Casa de Oración, August 1989; Guatemalan bishops' letter: Episcopado Guatemalteco, "Unidos en la Esperanza."

Facing Social and Political Responsibility: "III Encuentro sobre la responsabilidad social de la iglesia evangélica de Guatemala" (photocopy); "Acta de la Estructuración de la Comisión Nacional Sobre la Responsabilidad Social de la Iglesia Evangélica en Guatemala" (minutes), February 8, 1984; "La Tarea Politica de los Evangelicos: Ideas para una nueva Guatemala"; Lausanne Covenant: Klaus Bochmuehl, *Evangelicals and Social Ethics*; Declaración de Jarabacoa: Los cristianos y la acción política, "Declaración de Medellín" (n.d., probably 1988); Madrid: *Crónica*, February 2, 1990; Serrano letter published in *La Palabra*, October 13, 1985.

Convergences: Samandú and Sierra: interview, San Jose, Costa Rica, August 1989; story of charismatic Mass: interview with priest in Guatemala City, 1989: interviews, Guatemala City, July–August 1989; Ana Langerak, interview at CELEP, August 1989; Denis Romero and COPEN, interview, Matagalpa, August 1989; CELEP, CIEETS, CIEDEG: interviews in Guatemala, Nicaragua, Costa Rica, 1989 and 1990.

8. Shrinking Revolution, Stubborn Hope

Boff quote: from sermon in Nicaragua, "We Have a Lot to Learn from the Nicaraguan Church," (mimeo).

Bonds across Borders: bishops' statement: "U.S. Bishops' Statement on Central America," *Origins* (Washington, D.C.) Nov. 19, 1981; "stop war before it happens": author present at founding CISPES conference in Washington, D.C., September 1980; MacEoin comment: Gary MacEoin: "U.S. Central American Policy: Churches Lead Protest," *Latinamerica Press*, vol. 15, no. 26 (July 14, 1983); IFCO campaigns: IFCO reports; crisis of solidarity networks: Alexander Cockburn column, *The Nation*, Nov. 19, 1990, pp. 586-87.

A Radical "No": 1991 meeting in Washington, D.C.; billionaires: Joel Millman, "The Americas," *Forbes*, July 20, 1992, p. 150; Latin American left: Carr, Ellner, *The Latin American Left from the Fall of Allende to Perestroika*; meeting at El Escorial: Manuel Antonio Garretón M., "Transformaciones socio-políticas en América Latina (1972–1992)," in José Comblin, José I. González Faus, and Jon Sobrino, eds., *Cambio Social y Pensamiento Cristiano en América Latina*, quotes on pp. 17, 27; José Comblin, "La Iglesia latinoamericana desde Puebla a Santo Domingo," in ibid., quotes on pp. 29, 38; and Xabier Gorostiaga, "La mediación de las ciencias sociales y los cambios internacionales," ibid., quotes on pp. 123, 125, 130; also interview in *Punto Crítico* (Lima), November 1991, p. 23; Sobrino article: Jon Sobrino, "Reflexiones sobre el informe de la Comisión de la verdad," in *ECA*, nos. 534–535 (April–May 1993): 389–408; Ellacuría speech in Spain: "The Challenge of the Poor Majority," in Hassett and Lacey, eds., *Towards a Society That Serves Its People*, pp. 171–76; see also "Utopia and Prophecy in Latin America," in ibid., esp. pp. 56ff.; Richard: Pablo Richard: "Liberation Theology: Theology of the South," *Envío*, vol. 12, no. 143 (June 1993): pp. 28–40.

The Grace of Resistance: Sobrino, "Reflexiones teológicas sobre el informe de la Comisión de la verdad"; CPRs and Falla: Fernando Bermúdez, "This Ground is Holy Ground" vol. 3, no. 3 (Summer 1993), pp. 3ff., Cabrera quote on p. 3; Ricardo Falla, "The Dark Night of Resistance," pp. 8ff. in *Challenge,* Washington, D.C., vol. 3, no. 3, (Summer 1993); see also EPICA "Out of the Shadows"; Serrano self-coup and aftermath: dossier of documents from Guatemala, including bishops' statement, and news accounts.

BIBLIOGRAPHY

BOOKS

Americas Watch. *Little Hope: Human Rights in Guatemala—January 1984 to January 1985.* New York: Americas Watch, 1985.

Americas Watch. *Guatemala: A Nation of Prisoners.* New York: Americas Watch, 1984.

Anfuso, Joseph, and David Sczepanski. *Efrain Rios Montt: Siervo o Dictador?: La Verdadera Historia del Controversial Presidente de Guatemala.* Guatemala: Gospel Outreach, 1984. (Translation of *He Gives, He Takes Away: The True Story of Guatemala's Controversial Former President Efraín Rios Montt.* Eureka, Calif., Radiance Publications, 1983.)

Annis, Sheldon. *God and Production in a Guatemalan Town.* Austin: University of Texas Press, 1987.

Arzobispado de San Salvador. *Mons. Oscar Arnulfo Romero, Arzobispo y Mártir: Su Muerte y Reacciones.* San Salvador: Arzobispado de San Salvador, 1982.

AVANSCO (Asociación para el Avance de las Ciencias Sociales en Guatemala). *La Política de Desarrollo del Estado Guatemalteco 1986–1987,* Cuadernos de Investigación, no. 2. Guatemala: AVANSCO, 1988.

Barron, Bruce. *The Health and Wealth Gospel: What's Going on Today in a Movement That has Shaped the Faith of Millions?* Downers Grove, Ill.: InterVarsity Press, 1987.

Barry, Tom. *Guatemala: The Politics of Counterinsurgency.* Albuquerque: Inter-Hemispheric Education Resource Center, 1986.

Belli, Humberto. *Breaking Faith: The Sandinista Revolution and Its Impact on Freedom and Christian Faith in Nicaragua.* Westchester, Ill.: Crossway Books, 1985.

Bermúdez, Fernando. *Death and Resurrection in Guatemala.* Maryknoll, N.Y.: Orbis, 1986.

Berrigan, Daniel. *Steadfastness of the Saints: A Journal of Peace and War in Central and North America.* Maryknoll, N.Y.: Orbis, 1985.

Berryman, Phillip. *The Religious Roots of Rebellion: Christians in Central American Revolutions.* Maryknoll, N.Y.: Orbis, 1984.

Blachman, Morris, J., William M. LeGrande, and Kenneth E. Sharpe. *Confronting Revolution: Security Through Diplomacy in Central America.* New York: Pantheon Books, 1986.

Bochmuehl, Klaus. *Evangelicals and Social Ethics: a Commentary on Article 5 of the Lausanne Covenant.* Downers Grove, Illinois: InterVarsity Press, 1979.

Boff, Leonardo. *Church: Charism and Power—Liberation Theology and The Institutional Church.* New York: Crossroad, 1985.

Bonner, Raymond. *Weakness and Deceit: U.S. Policy and El Salvador.* New York: Times Books, 1984.

Booth, John A., and Thomas Walker. *Understanding Central America.* Boulder: Westview Press, 1989.

Brett, Donna Whitson, and Edward T. Brett. *Murdered in Central America: The Stories of Eleven U.S. Missionaries.* Maryknoll, N.Y.: Orbis, 1988.

Brockman, James R., S.J. *Romero, A Life.* Maryknoll, N.Y.: Orbis, 1989. (Revised version of *The Word Remains: A Life of Oscar Romero* [Maryknoll, N.Y.: Orbis, 1982]).

Brown, Cynthia, ed. *With Friends Like These: The Americas Watch Report on Human Rights and U.S. Policy in Latin America.* New York: Pantheon Books, 1985.

Cabestrero, Teófilo. *Revolutionaries for the Gospel: Testimonies of Fifteen Christians in the Nicaraguan Government.* Maryknoll, N.Y.: Orbis, 1986.

Cabestrero, Teófilo. *Dieron la Vida por Su Pueblo: Felipe y Mary Barreda.* Managua: Asociacion de Comunicacion Popular, 1984.

CAICA (Colectivo de Análisis de Iglesias en Centroamérica). *La Iglesia en Guatemala, El Salvador y Honduras: Análisis del Año 1986.* Mexico: Centro de Estudios Ecuménicos, 1987.

CAICA. *La Iglesia en Centroamérica: Guatemala, El Salvador, y Honduras — Información y Análisis.* México: Centro de Estudios Ecuménicos, 1988.

CAICA. *La Iglesia en Centroamérica: Guatemala, El Salvador, Honduras, y Nicaragua — Información y Análisis.* México: Centro de Estudios Ecuménicos, 1989.

CAICA. *La Iglesia en Centroamérica: Guatemala, El Salvador, Honduras, y Nicaragua — Información y Análisis.* México: Centro de Estudios Ecuménicos, 1990.

Calder, Bruce Johnson. *Crecimiento y Cambio de la Iglesia Catolica Guatemalteca — 1944 – 1966.* Guatemala: Editorial Jose de Pineda Ibarra, 1970.

Cambranes, J. C. *Agrarismo en Guatemala.* Guatemala: Serviprensa Centroamericana, 1986.

Cardenal, Rodolfo. *Historia de una Esperanza: Vida de Rutilio Grande.* San Salvador: UCA Editores, 1985.

Cardenal, Rodolfo, ed. *Historia General de la Iglesia en América Latina: VI — América Central.* Salamanca: Sígueme, 1985.

Carmack, Robert M., ed. *Harvest of Violence: The Maya Indians and the Guatemalan Crisis.* Norman and London: University of Oklahoma Press, 1988.

Carr, Barry and Steve Ellner, eds. *The Latin American Left: From the Fall of Allende to Perestroika.* Boulder: Westview Press, 1993.

Carrigan, Ana. *Salvador Witness: The Life and Calling of Jean Donovan.* New York: Simon and Schuster, 1984.

Casaldáliga, Pedro. *Prophets in Combat: The Nicaragua Journal of Bishop Pedro Casaldáliga.* Oak Park, IL: Meyer Stone Books, 1986.

CAV-IHCA (Centro Antonio Valdivieso — Instituto Histórico Centroamericano). *Apuntes para una Teología Nicaragüense: Encuentro de Teología — 8–14 de septiembre de 1980 — Managua, Nicaragua.* San José: DEI, 1981.

CELAM (Consejo Episcopal Latinoamericano). *Hacia un Mapa Pastoral de América Latina.* Bogota: SIDEAT Sección de Información, Documentación, Estadística y Asistencia Técnica, 1987.

Central America Resource Center. *Directory of Central America Organizations.* Austin: Central America Resource Center, 1985.

Cleary, Edward, OP. *Path from Puebla: Significant Documents of the Latin American Bishops since 1979.* Washington, D.C.: Secretariat, Bishops' Committee for the Church in Latin America — National Conference of Catholic Bishops, 1989.

Comblin, González Faus, José I. José, and Jon Sobrino. *Cambio Social y Pensamiento Cristiano en América Latina.* Madrid: Editorial Trotta, 1993.

Crittenden, Ann. *Sanctuary: A Story of American Conscience and the Laws in Collision.* New York: Weidenfeld and Nicholson, 1988.

Cruz, Arturo, Jr. *Memoirs of a Counterrevolutionary.* New York: Doubleday, 1989.

Dickey, Christopher. *With the Contras.* New York: Simon and Schuster, 1985.

Dilling, Yvonne (with Ingrid Rogers). *In Search of Refuge*. Scottdale, Pa.: Herald Press, 1984.

Dunkerley, James. *Power in the Isthmus: A Political History of Modern Central America*. London: Verso, 1988.

Ezcurra, Ana María. *Agresión Ideológica contra la Revolución Sandinista*. México: Nuevomar, 1983.

Falla, Ricardo. *Quiché Rebelde: Estudio de un Movimiento de Conversión Religiosa, Rebelde a las Creencias Tradicionales, en San Antonio Ilotenango Quiché (1948–1970)*. Guatemala: Editorial Universitaria de Guatemala, 1980.

Falla, Ricardo. *Masacres de la Selva: Ixcán Guatemala (1975–1982)*. Guatemala: Editorial Universitaria, 1992.

Frundt, Henry J. *Refreshing Pauses: Coca-Cola and Human Rights in Guatemala*. New York: Praeger, 1987.

Girardi, Giulio. *Faith and Revolution in Nicaragua: Convergence and Contradictions*. Maryknoll, N.Y.: Orbis, 1989.

Girardi, Giulio, et al., eds. *Nicaragua Trinchera Teologica*. Salamanca: Loguez Ediciones, 1987.

Girardi, Giulio, et al. *Pueblo Revolucionario, Pueblo de Dios: Aspectos del Cristianismo Popular en Nicaragua*. Centro Ecuménico Antonio Valdivieso, 1989.

Golden, Renny. *Hour of the Poor, Hour of Women*. New York: Crossroad, 1991.

Golden, Renny, and Michael McConnell. *Sanctuary: The New Underground Railroad*. Maryknoll, N.Y.: Orbis, 1986.

Gómez, Medardo Ernesto. *Fire against Fire: Christian Ministry Face-to-Face with Persecution*. Minneapolis: Augsburg, 1990.

Gómez, Salvador, and José H. Prado. Flores. *Formación de Predicadores*. Mexico: Publicaciones Kerygma, n.d.

Greenhalgh, Kurt, and Mark Gruenke, FSC, eds. *The Church Martyred: Guatemala*. Minneapolis: Guatemala Solidarity Committee of Minnesota, 1981.

Griffin-Nolan, Ed. *Witness for Peace: A Story of Resistance*. Louisville: Westminster/John Knox Press, 1991.

Gutman, Roy. *Banana Diplomacy: The Making of American Policy in Nicaragua—1981–1987*. New York: Simon and Schuster, 1988.

Haslam, David. *Faith in Struggle: The Protestant Churches in Nicaragua and Their Response to the Revolution*. London: Epworth Press, 1987.

Hassett, John, and Hugh Lacey, eds. *Towards a Society That Serves Its People: The Intellectual Contribution of El Salvador's Murdered Jesuits*. Washington, D.C.: Georgetown University Press, 1991.

Hennelly, Alfred T., ed. *Liberation Theology: A Documentary History*. Maryknoll, N.Y.: Orbis, 1990.

Henríquez, Pedro. *El Salvador: Iglesia Profética y Cambio Social*. San José: DEI, 1988.

Hodges, Donald C. *Intellectual Foundations of the Nicaraguan Revolution*. Austin: University of Texas Press, 1986.

Hussey, Pamela. *Free from Fear: Women in El Salvador's Church*. London: Catholic Institute for International Relations [CIIR], 1989.

IGE (Guatemalan Church in Exile). *The Church of Guatemala: Lessons of History*. Managua: IGE, 1987.

IGE. *Guatemala: Security, Development, and Democracy*. N.p., 1989.

IHCA (Instituto Historico Centroamericano), ed. *Fe Cristiana y Revolucion Sandinista en Nicaragua*. Managua: IHCA, 1979.

IHCA, ed. *Evangelio en la Revolucion*. Managua: IHCA, n.d. (prob. 1979).

Inforpress Centroamericana. *Centro América 1988: Análisis Económicos y Políticos sobre la Región*. Guatemala: Inforpress Centroamericana, 1988.

Instituto de Estudios Centroamericanos and El Rescate. *The Jesuit Assassinations: The Writings of Ellacuría, Martín-Baró and Segundo Montes, with a Chronology of the Investigation*. Kansas City: Sheed and Ward, 1990.

Juan Pablo II. *Mensajes a Centro América (2–9 de marzo de 1983)*. Guatemala: Instituto Teológico Salesiano, 1983.

Kirk, John M. *Politics and the Catholic Church in Nicaragua*. Gainesville: University Press of Florida, 1992.

Kita, Bernice. *What Prize Awaits Us: Letters from Guatemala*. Maryknoll, N.Y.: Orbis, 1988.

Lernoux, Penny. *People of God: The Struggle for World Catholicism*. New York: Viking, 1989.

Levine, Daniel H., ed. *Religion and Political Conflict in Latin America*. Chapel Hill: University of North Carolina Press, 1986.

López Vigil, María. *Don Lito of El Salvador*. Maryknoll, N.Y.: Orbis, 1990.

López Vigil, María. *Muerte y Vida en Morazán: Testimonio de un Sacerdote*. San Salvador: UCA Editores, 1987.

López Vigil, María. *Primero Dios: Siete Años de Esperanza — Relatos de "Carta a las Iglesias."* San Salvador: UCA Editores, 1988.

Mainwaring, Scott, and Alexander, Wilde, eds. *The Progressive Church in Latin America*. Notre Dame, Ind.: University of Notre Dame Press, 1989.

Martin, David. *Tongues of Fire: The Explosion of Protestantism in Latin America*. Oxford: Basil Blackwell, 1990.

Martínez, Abelino. *Las Sectas en Nicaragua: Oferta y Demanda de Salvación*. San José: DEI, 1989.

Meléndez, Guillermo. *Iglesia Cristianismo y Religión en América Central: Resumen Bibliográrico (1960–1988)*. San José: DEI, 1988.

Menchú, Rigoberta. *Me Llamo Rigoberta Menchú y así me Nació la Conciencia*, ed. Elizabeth Burgos. Mexico: Siglo XXI Editores, 1985 (English translation: *I, Rigoberta Menchú: An Indian Woman in Guatemala* [London: Verso, 1983]).

Müller-Monning, Tobías Martín (ed.) et al. *Protestantismo y Conflicto Social en Centroamérica*. San Salvador: Universidad Luterana Salvadoreña, 1989.

Mulligan, Joseph E., S.J. *The Nicaraguan Church and the Revolution*. Kansas City: Sheed and Ward, 1991.

Nelson, Wilton M. *Protestantism in Central America*. Grand Rapids: William B. Eerdmans Publishing Company, 1984.

Payne, Douglas W. *The Democratic Mask: The Consolidation of the Sandinista Revolution*. New York: Freedom House, 1985.

Pochet, Rosa María, and Abelino Martínez. *Nicaragua — Iglesia: Manipulación o Profecía?* San José: DEI, 1987.

PROCADES (Proyecto Centroamericano de Estudios Socio-Religiosos). *Directorio de Iglesias, Organizaciones y Ministerios del Movimiento Protestante: Guatemala*. Guatemala: IINDEF (Instituto Internacional de Evangelización a Fondo) and SEPAL (Servicio Evangelizador para América Latina), 1981.

Quebedeaux, Richard. *The New Charismatics II*. San Francisco: Harper and Row, 1983.

Richard, Pablo, and Guillermo Meléndez, eds. *La Iglesia de los Pobres en América Central: Un Análisis Socio-Político y Teológico de la Iglesia Centroamericana (1960–1982)*. San José: DEI, 1982.

Romero, Oscar Arnulfo. *The Violence of Love: The Pastoral Wisdom of Archbishop Oscar Romero*, ed. James R. Brockman, S.J. San Francisco: Harper and Row, 1988.

Romero, Oscar Arnulfo. *Su Diario — Desde el 31 de Marzo de 1978 hasta jueves 20 de marzo de 1980*. San Salvador: Imprenta Criterio, 1990.

Romero, Oscar Arnulfo. *La Voz de los Sin Voz: La Palabra Viva de Monseñor Oscar Arnulfo Romero*, ed. R. Cardenal et al. San Salvador: UCA Editores, 1980.

Samandú, Luís, Hans Siebers, and Oscar Sierra. *Guatemala: Retos de la Iglesia Católica en una Sociedad en Crisis*. San José, Costa Rica: DEI (Departmento Ecuménico de Publicaciones), 1990.

Schäfer, Heinrich. *Church Identity Between Repression and Liberation: The Presbyterian Church in Guatemala*. Geneva: World Alliance of Reformed Churches.

Selser, Irene. *Cardenal Obando*. México: Centro de Estudios Ecuménicos, 1989.

Sheehan, Edward R. F. *Agony in the Garden: A Stranger in Central America*. Boston: Houghton Mifflin Company, 1989.

Simon, Jean-Marie. *Guatemala: Eternal Spring, Eternal Tyranny*. New York: W. W. Norton and Company, 1987.

Sklar, Holly. *Washington's War on Nicaragua*. Boston: South End Press, 1988.

Sobrino, Jon. *Archbishop Romero: Memories and Reflections*. Maryknoll, N.Y.: Orbis, 1990.

Sobrino, Jon, et al. *Companions of Jesus: The Jesuit Martyrs of El Salvador*. Maryknoll, N.Y.: Orbis, 1990.

Spykman, Gordon, et al. *Let My People Live: Faith and Struggle in Central America*. Grand Rapids, Mich.: William B. Eerdmans Publishing Company, 1988.

Stoll, David. *Is Latin America Turning Protestant? The Politics of Evangelical Growth*. Berkeley: University of California Press, 1990.

Stoll, David. *Between Two Armies: In the Ixil Towns of Guatemala*. New York: Columbia University Press, 1993.

Synan, Vinson. *In the Latter Days: The Outpouring of the Holy Spirit in the Twentieth Century*. Ann Arbor: Servant Books, 1984.

Tomsho, Robert. *The American Sanctuary Movement*. Austin: Texas Monthly Press, 1987.

UCA Editores. *La Fe de un Pueblo: Historia de una Comunidad Cristiana en El Salvador (1970–1980)*. San Salvador: UCA Editores, 1983.

UCA Editores. *Rutilio Grande: Mártir de la Evangelización Rural en El Salvador*. San Salvador: UCA Editores, 1978.

Vatican Secretariat of State. *Annuarium Statisticum Ecclesiae*. Vatican City: Secretaria Status, 1981.

Vigil, Jose Maria, ed. *Nicaragua y los Teólogos*. Mexico: Siglo XXI, 1987.

Wagner, J. Peter. *Spiritual Power and Church Growth*. London: Hodder and Stoughton, 1986.

Walker, Thomas W., ed. *Nicaragua: The First Five Years*. New York: Praeger, 1985.

Williams, Robert G. *Export Agriculture and the Crisis in Central America*. Chapel Hill: University of North Carolina Press, 1986.

Woodward, Ralph Lee, Jr. *Central America: A Nation Divided*. New York: Oxford University Press, 1976.

Wright, Scott, et al., eds. *El Salvador: A Spring Whose Waters Never Run Dry*. Washington, D.C.: EPICA, 1990.

ARTICLES, REPORTS, DISSERTATIONS, MANUSCRIPTS

Aburto, Nora, et al. "Kairos Centroamericano." *Amanecer*, no. 55 (March–April 1988).

American Friends Service Committee. "Struggle over Autonomy: A Report on the Atlantic Coast of Nicaragua." American Friends Service Committee – International Division, 1987.

Americas Watch. "Nightmare Revisited: 1987–88 – Tenth Supplement to the Report on Human Rights in El Salvador." New York: Americas Watch, 1988.

Amnesty International. "El Salvador: 'Death Squads'—A Government Strategy." London: Amnesty International Publications, 1988.

Antonio Valdivieso Ecumenical Center. "A Christian Analysis of the Expulsion of Bishop Vega." (photocopy of typescript).

Arms Control and Foreign Policy Caucus. "Bankrolling Failure: United States Policy in El Salvador and the Urgent Need for Reform," a Report to the Arms Control and Foreign Policy Caucus by Sen. Mark O. Hatfield (R-OR), Rep. Jim Leech (R-IO), and Rep. George Miller (D-CA), Washington, D. C., November 1987.

Bacevich, Lieutenant Colonel A.J., et al. "American Military Policy in Small Wars: The Case of El Salvador." John F. Kennedy School of Government, Harvard University, March 1980.

Bastian, Jean-Pierre. "Religión popular protestante y comportamiento político en América Central: clientela religiosa y estado patrón en Guatemala y Nicaragua." *Cristianismo y Sociedad*, no. 88 (1986).

Bastian, Jean-Pierre. "Para una aproximación teórica del fenómeno religioso protestante en América Central." *Cristianismo y Sociedad*, no. 85 (1985).

Bellant, Russell. "God's CEOs." *City Paper* (Philadelphia), April 27–May 4, 1990, no. 298.

Berryman, Phillip. "Ignacio Ellacuría: An Appreciation." *America*, vol. 163, no. 1 (June 30–July 7, 1990): 12–15.

Berryman, Phillip. "El Salvador." In James Malloy and Eduardo Gamarra, eds., *Latin America and Caribbean Contemporary Record*, vol. 7 (1987-88): B 241–258.

Blanshard, David. *Kingdom Without Justice, a Church of Hope: Salvadoran Militarization and the Christian Response* (Manuscript).

Burnett, Virginia G. "Jerusalem under Siege: Protestantism in Rural Guatemala—1960–1987." Paper no. 89–15, of Texas Papers on Latin America.

Castro, Sergio de. "Revisión a Fondo en FSLN." (interview with Comandante Luis Carrión), *Barricada* (four part interview, June 20ff. 1990).

Central American Historical Institute, "On the Road to Democracy? A Chronology of Human Rights and U.S.-Guatemalan Relations—January 1978–April 1985." Washington, D.C.: Central American Historical Institute, 1985.

Colby, Benjamin. "Playing the Religious Card in Guatemala." University of California, Irvine, February 15, 1983.

Comblin, José. "La Iglesia Latinoamericana desde Puebla a Santo Domingo." In Comblin et al., eds., *Cambio Social y Pensamiento Cristiano en América Latina*.

Conferencia Episcopal de Guatemalteca. "Carta Pastoral para las Elecciones 1985."

Conferencia Episcopal Guatemalteca. "Plan Global de la Conferencia Episcopal Guatemalteca para 1988–1992." Guatemala: Conferencia Episcopal, 1988.

CONFREGUA. *III Congreso Nacional de Religiosos: Fe Cristiana y Compromiso Social.* Guatemala: CONFREGUA, 1984.

Debate Nacional. "Debate Nacional 1988, Documento Final." San Salvador, September 1988.

Edwards, Beatrice. "The Repopulation of Rural El Salvador." Paper presented at LASA (Latin American Studies Association) meeting, 1989.

EPICA (Ecumenical Program on Central America and the Caribbean)/CHRLA (Center for Human Rights Legal Action). "Out of the Shadows: The Communities of Population in Resistance in Guatemala." Washington, D.C., 1993.

Episcopado Guatemalteco. "El Clamor por la Tierra: Carta Pastoral Colectiva del Episcopado Guatemalteco." Guatemala, 1988.

Episcopado Guatemalteco. "Unidos en la Esperanza." In UCA Editores, *Los Obispos Latinoamericanos entre Medellín y Puebla: Documentos Episcopales 1968–1978.* San Salvador: UCA Editores, 1978.

Falla, Ricardo. "El hambre y otras privaciones inducidas por el ejército de Guatemala sobre la población civil." Managua: IGE, 1983.

Garcia, Jose. "El Salvador." In James Malloy and Eduardo Gamarra, eds., *Latin America and Caribbean Contemporary Record*, 1986–87. New York: Holmes and Meier, 1989, B 279–95.

Garretón M., Manuel Antonio. "Transformaciones socio-políticas en América Latina (1972–1992)." In José Comblin et al., eds., *Pensamiento Cristiano y Cambio Social en América Latina*.

Goodfellow, William, and James Morrell. "From Contadora to Sapoá and Beyond." In Thomas W. Walker, *Revolution and Counterrevolution in Nicaragua*, Boulder: Westview Press, 1991.

Gorostiaga, Xabier. "La mediación de las ciencias sociales y los cambios internacionales." In José Comblin et al., eds., *Pensamiento Cristiano y Cambio Social en América Latina*.

Griffin-Nolan, Ed., ed., "Civilian Victims of the U.S. Contra War – February–July 1987." Washington, D.C.: Witness for Peace, 1987.

Hernández Pico, Juan. "El pueblo nicaragüense educó a los educadores." *Amanecer* (Managua), no. 66 (March–April 1990): 18–33.

IGE (Iglesia Guatemalteca en el Exilio). "The Church of Guatemala: Lessons of History," no. 1, May 1987.

IGE. "Compendio: 1980–1982." Managua: IGE, 1984.

IHCA. "Church-State Relations: A Chronology – Part II." *Envío*, vol. 6, no. 78 (December 1987).

International Union of Food and Allied Workers Associations. "We Will Neither Go Nor Be Driven Out." Special Report by the IUF Trade Union Delegation on the Occupation of the Coca-Cola Bottling Plant in Guatemala." Washington, D.C.: IUF, n.d.

Irías, Noel. "Ciudad de Dios." *Crítica*, no. 1 (June 1990).

IUDOP Instituto Universitario de Opinión Pública. "La Religión para los Salvadoreños (Una encuesta de opinión pública)." San Salvador: Universidad Centroamericana José Simeón Cañas, 1988.

Kinsler, F. Ross. "Red de Educacion Teológica Diversificada (RED)." *Vida y Pensamiento* (San José, Costa Rica), vol. 8, no. 2, 1988.

Krueger, Chris, and Kjell Enge. "Security and Development Conditions in the Guatemalan Highlands." Washington, D.C.: Washington Office on Latin America, 1985.

Lacefield, Patrick. "Swaggart Swings Through El Salvador." *Commonweal*, May 8, 1987.

Lara Figueroa, Celso A. "Notas bibliográfiocas sobre cultura y religiosidad popular en Guatemala." *Estudios Sociales Centroamericanos*, no. 51 (September–December 1989): 145–150.

LASA (Latin American Studies Association) Task Force on Human Rights and Academic Freedom. "Peace and Autonomy on the Atlantic Coast of Nicaragua."

Lawyers' Committee for International Human Rights. "Justice Denied: A Report on Twelve Unresolved Human Rights Cases in El Salvador – March 1985." New York: Lawyers' Committee for International Human Rights, 1985.

Lawyers' Committee for International Human Rights. "Update on Investigation of the Murder of Six Jesuit Priests in El Salvador."

Lawyers' Committee for International Human Rights. "Nicaragua: Revolutionary Justice – A Report on Human Rights and the Judicial System." New York: Lawyers' Commiteee for International Human Rights, 1985.

Nieto, Trinidad Jesús. "Seeds of a Liberating Church." *Challenge: Faith and Action in Central America*, vol. 1, no. 2 (March 1990).

O'Brien, Conor Cruise. "God and Man in Nicaragua." *The Atlantic Monthly*, August 1986, pp. 50–72.

Pellecer, Luis. "Declaraciones del P. Luis E. Pellecer." (transcript).

Penados del Barrio, Próspero. "La Iglesia Católica en Guatemala: Signo de Verdad y Esperenza." Guatemala, 1989.

Piedra, Arturo. "Estudio de una ruptura en un protestantismo latinoamericana (Entrelones de la caída de Jimmy Swaggart)." (MS).

Resource Center. "Evangelicals Target Latin America." *Resource Center Bulletin* (Albuquerque), no. 15 (Winter 1988).

Ricciardi, Joseph. "Economic Policy." In Thomas W. Walker, ed., *Revolution and Counterrevolution in Nicaragua.* Boulder: Westview, 1991.

Richard, Pablo. "La iglesia de los Pobres en la década de los noventa." *Pasos,* no. 28 (March–April 1990).

Richard, Pablo. "Liberation Theology: Theology of the South." *Envío,* no. 143 (June 1993).

Richard, Pablo. "Salvadoran Church Accompanying Its People in Journey toward Liberation." *Latinamerica Press,* April 25, 1985.

Rieke, Tom. "Word of God and Nicaragua." Printout of article in *Ann Arbor Observer.*

Rivera Damas, Arturo. Untitled speech on Catholic church work in the Salvadoran conflict, given at LASA meeting, Miami, December 1989.

Rose, Susan D., and Steve Brouwer. "The Export of Fundamentalist Americanism to Guatemala." (paper).

Samandú, Luis. "Estudios de lo religioso-popular en Guatemala, Nicaragua y Costa Rica." *Estudios Sociales Centroamericanos,* no. 51 (September–December 1989): 151–55.

Samandú, Luis. "El universo religioso popular en Centroamérica." *Estudios Sociales Centroamericanos,* no. 51 (September–December 1989): 81–96.

Sharpe, Kenneth. "El Salvador." In James M. Malloy and Eduardo A. Gamarra, eds., *Latin America and Caribbean Contemporary Record.* New York and London: Holmes and Meier, 1988, B 275–98.

Shiras, Peter. "El Salvador: The New Face of War." *Commonweal,* May 8, 1987.

Smith, Dennis A. "Coming of Age: A Reflection on Pentecostals, Politics and Popular Religion in Guatemala." (paper).

Smith, Dennis A. "The Impact of Religious Programming in the Electronic Media on the Active Christian Population in Central America." *Latin American Pastoral Issues* (San Jose, Costa Rica: CELEP [Latin American Evangelical Center for Pastoral Studies]), no. 1 (July 1988).

Sobrino, Jon. "Reflexiones teológicas sobre el informe de la Comisión de la verdad." *ECA,* nos. 534–535 (April–May 1993): 389–408.

Socurro Jurídico. "Del genocidio de la junta military a la espereanza de la lucha insurrectional." San Salvador: Socorro Jurídico, 1981.

Stoll, David. "Guatemala: Why They Like Rios Montt." *NACLA Report on the Americas,* vol. 24, no. 4, pp. 4–7.

Swedish, Margaret, and Lee Miller. "Like Grains of Wheat." Washington, D.C.: Religious Task Force on Central America, 1989.

Tutela Legal. "Informe Mensual," March 1988.

United Nations Truth Commission for El Salvador. "From Insanity to Hope: The 12-Year War in El Salvador," translation by FBIS (Foreign Broadcast Information Service) (April 30, 1993).

U.S. Committee for Refugees. "Aiding the Desplazados of El Salvador: The Complexity of Humanitarian Assistance." Washington, D.C.: U.S. Committee for Refugees, 1984.

Vega, Pablo Antonio. "La Iglesia en Nicaragua: Urgida por los cambios." Ponencia en Washington, Marzo de 1986.

Ventura, Miguel. "El Salvador: The Church of the Poor and the Revolution." *Challenge: Faith and Action in Central America*, vol. 1, no. 2, March 1990.

Wisdom, Alan. "Churches in the Crossfire: A Report on Religious Liberty in El Salvador." Washington, D.C.: Institute on Religion and Democracy, 1990.

Witness for Peace. "Bitter Witness: Nicaraguans and the 'Covert' War, A Chronology and Several Narratives." Santa Cruz, Calif.: Witness for Peace Documentation Project, 1984.

INDEX